THE LIFE AND TIMES

OF

HENRY LORD BROUGHAM,

WRITTEN BY HIMSELF.

IN THREE VOLUMES.

VOL. I.

NEW YORK:
HARPER & BROTHERS, PUBLISHERS,
FRANKLIN SQUARE.
1871.

CONTENTS OF VOL. I.

CHAPTER I.

EARLY LIFE.

CHAPTER II.

EARLY LIFE—*continued.*

CHAPTER III.

VISIT TO DENMARK AND SCANDINAVIA.

A 2

TO THE READER.

The following instructions were given by Lord Brougham to me, as his executor:

"Before the Autobiography can be published, you must see that it is arranged chronologically.

"If (writing from memory) I have made mistakes in dates, or in proper names, let such be corrected; but the *Narrative* is to be printed *AS I HAVE WRITTEN IT.*

"I alone am answerable for all its statements, faults, and omissions. I will have no Editor employed to alter, or rewrite, what I desire shall be published as *EXCLUSIVELY MY OWN.*

"Brougham, *November*, 1867."

In publishing Lord Brougham's Autobiography, the above explicit directions have been scrupulously obeyed.

BROUGHAM & VAUX.

Brougham, *January*, 1871.

THE LIFE AND TIMES

OF

HENRY, LORD BROUGHAM.

CHAPTER I.

EARLY LIFE.

My Birth and Childhood.—Precocity, as told by my Mother.—Parentage and Ancestry.—Why my Father settled in Edinburgh.—His Marriage there.—My Mother's Highland Ancestry, through the Struan Robertsons.—Death of my Paternal Grandfather.—Savage Festivities at his Funeral.—Anecdotes told me by my Father's Mother.—Character of my Maternal Grandmother.—The High School of Edinburgh.—Dr. Adam the Rector.—Gilbert Stuart.—My Progress at School.—My School-fellows.—Family Reminiscences.—Robertson the Historian and his Father.—The Adams.—John Clerk, of Eldin.—His Naval Tactics.—Lord Buchan and his Brothers Tom and Harry Erskine.

I HAD frequently been asked by persons whose opinion I value to write a life of myself, with some account of the many great public events of my time. In undertaking this task, I can not but regret that I did not some years ago begin to put down many details which I now may find it difficult to recall, with that accuracy which a narrative professing to be in many respects historical, essentially requires, and to note down many circumstances relating to myself and others which I may now find it impossible to remember. My present object is to relate, as far as my memory will serve, some circumstances of my early life, which may form a sort of introduction to my autobiography, and to my account of matters of higher importance.

I found among my mother's papers, at Brougham, the fragment of a notice respecting me she had begun to write a good many years ago. I am tempted to give it exactly in her own words, because it accurately represents her own impressions; and so little was she given to laudation or exaggeration, that what she has recorded of my early years may be received as perfectly impartial. I only regret the briefness of her notes:

"NOTES ABOUT HENRY.

"Brougham, Oct., 1826.

"In putting down what may hereafter be read with some interest, I feel how unequal I am to the task. His years of infancy and youth passed without my contemplating that he would fill so high a place among men as he now does, or I should have kept memorandums that would have preserved in my memory many circumstances that would have thrown light upon his early life, and shown how soon his great mental powers showed themselves. From a very tender age he excelled all his contemporaries. Nothing to him was a labor—no task prescribed that was not performed long before the time expected. His grandmother, a very clever woman, was an enthusiastic admirer of all intellectual acquirements, and used to compare him to the Admirable Crichton, from his excelling in every thing he undertook. From mere infancy he showed a marked attention to every thing he *saw*, and this before he could speak. Afterwards, to every thing he *heard*, and he had a memory the most retentive. He spoke distinctly, several words, when he was eight months and two weeks old; and this aptitude to learn continued progressive. When barely seven years old, he was sent to the High School in Edinburgh, his father preferring that school to Eton or Westminster. He went to school before the 19th of September, 1785, having been born on that day in the year 1778, at No. 21, north side of St. Andrew's Square. He went through all the classes with credit, and came away dux of the fifth or rector's class, taught at that time by Dr. Adam.

"The examination was in August, 1791, at which time he had not reached the age of thirteen—an age unusually early, considering, too, that he had been only one year, instead of two, the usual number, in the rector's class.

"As, then, when he left it, he had not completed his thirteenth year, he was considered too young to be sent to college; and therefore we left Edinburgh and went to Brougham, taking with us the three eldest boys, and Mr., afterwards Dr., Mitchell, as their tutor. We did not return to Edinburgh till the winter of 1792; and Henry was then entered at the class which is called the Humanity class. Next year he attended the Greek class, taught by Professor Dalzell. In addition to these classical studies he attended the classes of natural philosophy and chemistry, and of mathematics under Professor Playfair, a great and good man, who bore ample testimony to the large amount of knowledge Henry had acquired when he was only sixteen. When he was about this age, he wrote a very able paper on 'The Refraction of Light,' which gained the prize adjudged to that subject by a German university. By some mistake, he never got the prize, but he did get the honor. At a very early age he showed considerable talent for speaking in public: really, in infancy, I may say, he showed this tendency; for he used to get up a make-believe court of justice for the trial of a supposed prisoner—he himself acting as counsel, prosecuting the prisoner, examining the witnesses, summing up the case, and ending by passing sentence. Before he was seventeen, he became a member of the Speculative Society, a debating club which met weekly from six to ten in the evening, or even later. There he distinguished himself both for close reasoning and even for speaking that almost amounted to eloquence. But he was most distinguished for close argument and extreme quickness and readiness in reply—sometimes seasoned with perhaps a little too much sarcasm. I have said we took a tutor to Brougham, but really he was more wanted for my two other sons, because Henry always did his work by himself, scorning assistance, and never applying for help when he could possibly avoid it."

Among the earliest of my own recollections is the account my father's mother gave me of the circumstance which led to her son's marriage with my mother.

My grandmother was born in Queen Anne's reign, so that I have conversed with a person who was alive a hundred and eighty years ago, and who *might* have heard her relative, Ann Brougham, who lived to the age of a hundred and six, speak of events that happened in Queen Elizabeth's time! This is only conjecture; but it is, at all events, a certain fact that I, now writing in the latter half of the nineteenth century, have heard my grandmother, being, at the time I refer to, about ninety years of age, relate all the circumstances of the execution of Charles I., as they had been told her by an eye-witness who stood opposite to Whitehall and saw the king come out upon the scaffold. I think the story was told to her about the year 1720, and she talked of her informant as having been quite old enough at the time of the execution to have carried away a clear and accurate recollection of all the details. Her own memory was most perfect; nor did the event appear to her to be so very remote, for she herself perfectly remembered the attempt of the Pretender in 1715—not that she ever called him by *that* name, for she was rather a Jacobite, but yet a very High-Church Protestant, continually fighting with her neighbor Mr. Howard, of Corby, a most strict Papist, about transubstantiation, which she called by a very expressive term, when she referred to one of their angry discussions, which Mr. Howard ended by exclaiming, "It's no good your denying it, Madam Brougham, for I myself have crunched the bones!"—meaning when he took the sacramental wafer.

She had a strong feeling for Charles II., and entertained a high regard for her husband's cousin, Father John Hudleston, who attended Charles in his last moments.

But to return to my father's marriage. My grandmother told me that he left Eton before the accession of George III., and for some years travelled on the Continent; his brother John, then captain of the school, going to Cambridge, as he was intended for the Church.

On my father's return to Westmorland, he fell in love with his cousin, Mary Whelpdale, the last of a perfectly pure Saxon race. Her father's estate, to which she was sole heiress, was close to Brougham, so that the alliance was all that could be wished. Every thing was in readiness for the nuptials—the wedding-coach bought, and all the paraphernalia prepared.

The very day before the wedding Mary Whelpdale died. My father, struck down by the shock, lost for a time the use of his reason. He was again sent abroad, but on his return to Westmorland found the scene of his calamity unendurable.

A very intimate friend of my grandfather, Lord Buchan, lived sometimes at Dryburgh Abbey, in Scotland, and sometimes in Edinburgh. To him my father was consigned, in the hopes that, introduced by him to the best Edinburgh society, he might find occupation and distraction enough to dissipate his grief.*

Accordingly to Edinburgh he went, and there, among other distinguished personages, made the acquaintance of Dr. Robertson, at whose house he met his eldest sister, then a widow, and her only child Eleanor. This acquaintance ended in a marriage, and then my father and his bride moved to St. Andrew's Square, to the house in which Lord and Lady Buchan lived, and there I was born on the 19th September, 1778.†

It has often struck me that what seemed to my father an irretrievable calamity may have been the means of saving me from obscurity. If Mary Whelpdale had been my mother, she would no doubt have materially enriched the Saxon blood I derived from my father; but I should have remained in the state of respectable mediocrity which seems to have characterized my many ancestors, none of whom, so far as I have been able to discover, were ever remarkable for any thing. Many, no doubt, were fighters, but even in that career of doubtful usefulness were rather prudent than daring. Thus Udardus, who had the custody of Appleby Castle, instead of keeping it for his employer, Henry II., allowed William the Lion of Scotland to take it, and appears even to have gone over to the enemy. This, indeed, is incontestably proved by the Pipe Roll, 22 Henry II., an official copy of which, stamped with the seal of the Public Record Office, is now before me, and is in these words: "Itẽ de Placitis eorundem in Westmarieland. Vdardus de Broham redd. comp. de q^or^ t^a^ xx. m. quia fuit cũ inimicis Reg." After he had paid his fine, as appears by a record of a subsequent date, he turned crusader; but instead of fighting and dying for the Holy Sepulchre, he returned to Brougham, and there died quietly in his bed.

His son and successor, Gilbert de Broham, paid fifty marks to King John, "ut remaneat, ne transfretet, termin' ad passag̃,

* Lord Buchan; see Appendix I. † Dr. Robertson; see Appendix II.

Dñi Reg̃.," as appears in the Oblata Roll of the second year of the reign of King John, preserved in the Tower of London; so, instead of going to fight with the king's army in Normandy, he paid this fine, that he might be allowed to stay at home. He afterwards got into hot water with King John, who mulcted him of half of the diminished estate he had inherited from Udard, and gave it to his creature Veteripont, from whom it passed to the Cliffords, and from them to the Tuftons. Nor do I find we improved in intellect even after an infusion of very pure Norman blood, which came into our veins from Harold, Lord of Vaux, in Normandy.

I think, then, I am fairly entitled to argue that I, at least, owe much to the Celtic blood which my mother brought from the clans of Struan and Kinloch-Moidart.*

I heard also from my grandmother a remarkable story about her husband's funeral. He died at Brougham in December, 1782. Neither my father, nor his brother John, were then in Westmorland. Charles, Duke of Norfolk (father of the Duke who went by the name of the "Jockey of Norfolk," after his ancestor of Bosworth), was then living at Greystoke, in Cumberland, and being a most intimate friend of the family, attended the funeral as representing the chief mourner. In that character his place was at the head of the table at the funeral feast, where he was supported by all the gentlemen of the county. After the dinner the Duke rose and addressed the guests as follows: "Friends and neighbors, before I give you the toast of the day, the memory of the deceased, I ask you to drink to the health of the family physician, Dr. Harrison, the founder of the feast!"

Many toasts followed. The guests drank long and deeply. The funeral then proceeded on its way to the parish church of Brougham, called Nine Churches, a corruption of St. Ninian, to whom it is dedicated, a distance of three miles, the road winding along the steep banks of the river Eamont. Arrived at the church, the hearse was met by the rector, but the coffin had disappeared! The shock was enough to sober the merry mourners. On searching back, the coffin was discovered in the river, into which it had fallen, pitched down

---

* See Appendix II.

the steep bank, at a place where probably the hearse, driven by the drunken coachman, had lurched against a rock. The oak outer coffin was broken to pieces, but the lead remained intact at the bottom of the river, too heavy to be carried down by the stream. The shock and the scandal produced by all this had the effect not only of sobering every body, but of putting an end to such disgraceful orgies in the county for the future. The accuracy of my grandmother's story was strongly confirmed by an event which happened many years afterwards. In October, 1846, the wall of our vault in the chancel of Nine Churches had given way: on the vault being opened to make the necessary repairs, I myself saw the lead coffin of my grandfather, battered and bulged from its tumble down the rocky bank of the river.

My grandmother well remembered the events of 1745, for she was then past the middle age of life, and the mother of several children, my father having been born in June, 1742. She used to talk of the stirring events of that time, the battle of Clifton Moor, the burial of a number of "Willie's dragoons" (the Duke of Cumberland) in a ditch by the river Lowther, close to Brougham, and the executions at Carlisle. But these were comparatively recent events, and had little interest even for me, compared to her account of the execution of Charles.

I have alluded to the intimacy that existed between my grandfather's family and the Howards of Norfolk. Among many letters now at Brougham from different members of that family, but on subjects too private for publication, I give, as a specimen of the style and habits of the time, the following, *verbatim et literatim:*

"Norfolk House, March 9 [1778].

"The Duchess of Norfolk presents her compliments to the two Miss Broughams. She has taken the liberty to send 30 yds. of silk, with triming, for a night gown & pettycoat for each, which I hope they will do me the favour to accept of.

"The Duchess desires her compliments to Mrs. Brougham.

"To the two Miss Broughams."

So much for my paternal grandmother; but I should be most ungrateful if I said nothing of my other grandmother,

Dr. Robertson's sister, for to her I owe all my success in life. From my earliest infancy till I left college, with the exception of the time we passed at Brougham with my tutor, Mr. Mitchell, I was her companion. Remarkable for beauty, but far more for a masculine intellect and clear understanding, she instilled into me from my cradle the strongest desire for information, and the first principles of that persevering energy in the pursuit of every kind of knowledge which, more than any natural talents I may possess, has enabled me to stick to, and to accomplish, how far successfully it is not for me to say, every task I ever undertook.

I was sent when very young to a day-school in George Street, Edinburgh, kept by a Mr. Stalker, a sort of infant-school, in which girls as well as boys were the pupils. Before I went there my father had taught me to read; but my grandmother, from day to day, worked with me at my lessons, so that when I was only seven years old I had outgrown Mr. Stalker's academy, and was sent to Luke Fraser's class at the High School. All the time I was there, my grandmother was my daily help and instructress: under her careful tuition I not only won and kept a good place in my class, but, with a perseverance that almost amounted to obstinacy, I on one occasion made Fraser confess he had been wrong and I right, in some disputed bit of Latinity for which he had the day before punished me. My victory gained me immense credit with all my school-fellows, and I was called "the boy that had licked the master." I am bound to say Mr. Fraser bore no malice, and when I left him to go into the rector's (Dr. Adam's) class, we parted the best of friends.

I remained in the class of Luke Fraser, according to the course of that seminary, for four years, from September, 1785, when I was seven years old, to October, 1789, when I entered the class of the rector, Dr. Adam, under whom I was two years nominally, but really only the second of these two, having been kept at home by illness almost the whole of the first year.* During some months of that year, before I fell

* An account of Luke Fraser will be found in Steven's "History of the High School of Edinburgh," p. 92. Dr. Alexander Adam, the rector, of whom so much interesting matter follows, is sufficiently eminent to be commemorated in the usual works of biographical reference.

ill, I had a private tutor, Mr., afterwards Dr., Mitchell, an excellent scholar, who afterwards went to India as a medical man, and died in the service of the Rajah of Travancore, whose chief physician he became. I had, however, the great benefit, before my illness, of attending Dr. Adam's class, and hearing daily his comments upon the classics which we read, interspersed with his general remarks upon political subjects and allusions to the great events then engrossing the attention of the world, for the French Revolution had broken out three months before his course began. He was a zealous friend of liberty, and in those times and in that place was termed a democrat. Yet with all the violence of party and the influence of the predominant powers—the Dundases—no exception was taken to his dwelling on those topics in illustration of, and in connection with, the books he taught. Of course, three or four years later, when party violence was at its height, but when the crimes of the French mob had alienated many admirers of the Revolution, he carefully abstained from such subjects, though he still continued of that class which clung to the Revolution more or less, in spite of its crimes. His great learning, his able and useful works, and his irreproachable character, as well as his untiring diligence and exemplary patience in the discharge of his duties, commanded the respect of all, and endeared him to those who had the inestimable benefit of his instruction. He had the faculty of exciting both an ardent love of the subjects he taught and a spirit of inquiry into all that related to them. Stirred by his precepts and example, I spent the months during which I was kept from school by indisposition in reading and trying my hand at composition. The progress I made during this illness clearly proved to me two things: first, the importance of allowing boys sufficient time for reading, instead of devoting the whole day, as at school, to Latin and Greek exercises; next, the great benefit of having a teacher who would dwell upon subjects connected with the lessons he taught, but beyond those lessons, thus exciting the desire of useful knowledge in his pupils.

Dr. Adam had been violently assailed for his excellent grammar by Gilbert Stuart, who had also attacked Dr. Robertson's "History of Scotland," in various reviews both in London and in one which he established in Edinburgh. Stuart was in both instances, and, indeed, in all his writings, entirely influenced by his violent temper and his self-interest. The historian was attacked because he was supposed to have, as principal, defeated his attempts to obtain a professorship; the grammarian was attacked because his work had superseded one by Stuart's cousin, Ruddiman. Stuart was a man of extraordinary talent and learning, displayed in many works, one of which, published before he was of age, obtained for him the degree of doctor of laws. But his profligate life and want of all principle brought him into contempt; and his works, some of which have great merit, have sunk into oblivion, in consequence of the spite and the unfairness that runs through them, and deprives them of all trustworthiness.*

I returned to school, my health being re-established. The work did not at all oppress me, and I left it at the head of the class and of the school—what is there called *dux.* This was in some respects accidental. I was at the head of the class with Keay (afterwards high at the Scotch bar), and acknowledged him my superior—possibly from his having attended the whole of the former year.† I never disputed the place with him; but on his leaving Edinburgh, before the breaking up and the examination, I succeeded to the headship. Horner, a year after, belonged to that class, but it was his first year under the rector. Next year he also left it at the head. Murray (afterwards Lord Murray) had been of his year, but left the school for Westminster. I had always, except during the illness I have referred to, the blessing of robust health, only interrupted, when a child, by putrid fever, which produced an extraordinary effect in destroying my memory almost entirely; for I had just learned to read, taught by my father, and I had in those ten days lost all knowledge even of the letters. I very soon recovered it, and in a few weeks was sent, as I have already said, to Stalker's day-school.

It is a great mistake, into which Lord Cockburn and others have fallen, the fancying that I at all distinguished myself at the High School—a mistake caused by persons reflecting

* Gilbert Stuart; see Appendix III

† See Appendix IV.

backward from one period to another. The only instance I have the least recollection of, was when the Principal of the University (Robertson) visited the school at one of the examinations yearly held before the vacation: he said to Mr. Fraser that I ought to have been at the head of his class. But the answer was, "No; Reddie is in his right place:" and so he was. My great kinsman was deceived, not by his partiality, but by my having a better voice and delivery: the manner prevailed over the matter—as I dare to say it has often done since, on greater occasions and with a far less critical audience. Reddie was afterwards in a very high station at the Scotch bar—one of the most learned and sound lawyers of his day. He distinguished himself especially in the great questions connected with maritime rights and international law, and enjoyed the friendship and patronage of Hope, afterwards lord-president; nor did any thing prevent him from rising to the top of the profession, and to the head of the bench, but his modest, retiring, and unambitious nature, which led him to accept an office at Glasgow of great importance and of judicial functions, though humble compared with what, by the consent of all, he was so well entitled to.

It was an inestimable advantage to my studies at all times that they were directed by my great kinsman the principal, after the first impulses they had received from my grandmother, his eldest and favorite sister, and who had lived with him, having the care of his family, for many years before the marriage of either. As a matter of course, he was consulted by my father in all that regarded the education of his children. And he used to visit us at Brougham, where I well remember accompanying him upon his walks in the woods, where he would occasionally repeat aloud Greek or Latin verses. We had to deplore his irreparable loss in 1793; but I recollect going to his villa in the neighborhood of Edinburgh, where he resided several months before his death, to tell him of an important debate in the General Assembly, in which his son, afterwards Lord Robertson, the judge, had greatly distinguished himself. My youngest brother, although born some years after the principal's death, was named after him, and the surname, as well as the Christian, ought certainly to have been given; but a little Cumberland family pride prevented this, as we supposed. He always recommended translation, as tending to form the style by giving an accurate knowledge of the force of expression, and obliging us to mark and estimate the shades of difference between words in phrases in the two languages, and to find, by selecting the terms or turning the idiom, the expression required for a given meaning; whereas when composing originally, the idea may be varied, in order to suit the diction that most easily presents itself, of which the influence produced by rhymes, and moulding the sense as well as suggesting it, affords a striking and familiar example.

He had much exercised himself, therefore, in translation, and even intended to publish one of Antoninus's Meditations, done while at college. The appearance of a translation at Glasgow prevented this publication, but the manuscript remains, and is in my possession; and the version is very ably and learnedly executed. With this strong opinion in favor of translation, which was also that of his son, Lord Robertson, both of them prescribed it to me, and among other things made me translate all the History of Florus. The following letter to Lord Robertson shows an extremely imperfect taste, and a considerable misconception of the task prescribed, possibly arising from the ambition of the writer:

"Brougham, January 15, 1792.

"DEAR SIR,—You would no doubt be surprised that I did not write to you by Mr. Mitchell, who was in Edinburgh. I was prevented doing this by reason of not having finished the task you were so kind as prescribe to me before I left town—a task which was so very delightful that nothing could have hindered me performing it, had not Mr. M. begged I would desist until I should make some improvement in my writing, which had been spoiled by beginning too soon to *scrawl* versions. I was in this manner prevented from making use of your kindness for three or four months.

"You will perhaps remember that you allowed me to translate either Livy or Florus. I pitched upon the latter—not that his style appeared to me any way superior to that of the other; but as I had read, partly at Edinburgh and partly here, almost the whole of the first five books of Livy (a copy of which was the only part of his works I had), it naturally occurred that there would be less field for exertion in translating an author with whose works I was acquainted than in trying one whose works were quite new to me. Besides, I was confirmed in my choice when I recollected that *you* seemed to give the preference to Florus. That author, though concise and nervous, is not the less elegant and instructive. Full of vigor, and just, in his descriptions, relating the conquests of Rome in that rapid manner, as it were, in which they were acquired. As he writes in a very peculiar stile, so I thought that by a literal translation his elegance would be lost. I have endeavored, therefore, by taking a little freedom, to transfuse his beauties into the English language, without impairing the sense. How far I have succeeded I must leave you to judge. This I can with truth affirm, that throughout the whole of the translation I am indebted to the assistance of no one, and I hope you will excuse its many defects and inaccuracies, particularly the badness of the writing. I am sorry, dear sir, that I can give you no news, as affairs in the country commonly wear a very uniform aspect. As for my studies, I have read about four books of Virgil's Æneid, beginning at the VI.; one of Livy; have got through above three parts of Adam's Roman Antiquities; and am employed in the Greek verbs. When business is over I amuse myself with reading, skaiting (*sic*), or walking. If you can find leisure to write me a few lines, I shall think myself particularly honored by it. As I fear I have already tried your patience, wishing many happy new years to yourself and Mrs. R., the college family—Russells and Brydons—in which I am joined by all this family, I beg leave to subscribe myself, dear sir, yours with the greatest respect and esteem, HENRY BROUGHAM."

Before I refer to my kinsman's answer, I may interpose a letter which the kindness of a member of the Kinloch-Moidart family has permitted me to use; and I give it merely as showing the local impressions made on me at the early age of thirteen.

"Brougham, July 14, 1792.

"MY DEAR COUSIN,—As my mother, ever since the receipt of your kind letter, has been in a great bustle with company, I, at her request, take advantage of a cover which is going to your friend Mr. Bell, from a gentleman who dines here to-day with a most abominably formal company; but if you expect much entertainment from my pen you will be disappointed, for nothing is more true than that the stillness of a country life furnishes few occurrences worthy of a place in black and white.

"To go back to April: James and I spent a very agreeable week at Skirwith Abbey, the seat of a neighboring gentleman. The house, which is modern, is a handsome building, somewhat like the Physicians' Hall, though without pillars: it is vastly naked, being placed in the midst of a moor, or common, with little or no wood of any size about it, and the garden above half a mile from the house. Mr. Yates's agreeable family consists of two grown-up daughters (the youngest of whom, with her mother, is now in Edinburgh consulting Mr. Bell), and three sons, the eldest about 16, the youngest 9.

"About the end of June, Mr. Mitchell, James, and I made an excursion to the Lakes, about twenty-five miles from this, and staid there a day or two. The lake at Keswick is certainly a most grand, romantic, and agreeable sight. A fine sheet of water expanded in the bottom of a most beautiful valley, surrounded by mountains of wood, and interspersed with woody islands (one of which is faced with a *mock* fortification, and is the residence of a country squire). The lake begins with a fine cascade and terminates in a beautiful river. The whole of this enchanting scene, lighted up by a most beautiful morning, presented to persons like us, unaccustomed to such sights, a picture of beauty and sublimity not to be easily forgotten. At one end is the celebrated vale of Borrowdale, at the other the neat town of Keswick, where we saw a very fine museum filled with great curiosities, both ancient and modern, but scarcely to be compared with Weir's in Edinburgh, though of a more universal nature. Besides the lakes, I have been much about since spring began, and as I ride a great deal, I have seen every one of the country seats hereabouts.

"I think the conduct of your wise baillies during the late riots proves them to be idiots and monsters that ought to be expunged from the face of the creation. I ought to make 1792 apologies to your sister for not answering her very kind letter, which I received by Mr. Mitchell. Read this to her, with my love, in which the rest of this family join, not forgetting my dear Peter.

"Tell your good mother that Mrs. Syme looks upon her letters, and those of my aunt Nelly (to whom, and all other friends, remember me), as her greatest consolation, and that she expects a letter from them soon. We were all sorry for B. Russell's death; indeed, except John, I think she was by much the best of that family.

"Expecting your answer by a parcel which is coming here from Mrs. Hope this week, I remain your most affectionate cousin,

H. P. Brougham."

To go back, then, to my holiday task, the translation of Florus. I consider that my learned kinsman was much more lenient in his judgment on the work than his illustrious father would have been, whom we never thought of troubling with it. The following is his answer to my letter of January:

"April 21, 1792.

"Dear Henry,—I should make an apology for having delayed so long to answer your letter. The truth is that I received it during the hurry of the winter session, when I could not command time; and since the commencement of the vacation I was prevented for some time by indisposition, and afterwards it took me some leisure times to read your work with that attention which I wished to bestow upon it.

"I have now perused it with very great pleasure, and compared a very great part of it, sentence by sentence, with the original, and I am happy that I can, with perfect sincerity, say that, high as my expectations from you were, they have been greatly exceeded. Instead of confining yourself everywhere to a literal translation, you have often given a turn to the expression which shows that you entered fully into the ideas of your author, and your translation discovers a knowledge both of the Latin and of the English far above what could have been expected. I will not say how much your translation has pleased me in another point of view, as affording a proof of industry and application, which, when joined with your abilities, can not fail to insure your success in any line of life which you may follow. I think you should persevere in translating: it is one of the best exercises, and improves your knowledge both of Latin and English.

"My father and mother, Mrs. Russell, Betsy and Elie, are at Lennell. John and Mary are with us. Mrs. Hope and all our friends here are well. Mrs. Robertson desires to join me in best compliments to your papa, mamma, and grandmamma, and all the children. I am, dear Henry, your affectionate cousin, WM. ROBERTSON.

"No. 67 Princes Street, April 21, 1792."

Notwithstanding any vices in my translation, I certainly had acquired no habit of inaccurate version, no contempt of strict closeness, or such faults must have been cured by subsequent experience and reflection, as well as the incorrect taste disclosed in the letter; for whatever I have since attempted in prose, and still more the only efforts in verse, which the entire want of poetical faculty has confined to translation, have nothing to distinguish them but the rigorous closeness, the whole poetical merit clearly belonging to the original. Of this an example may be given in the commotion among my Eton friends caused by my quoting from Horace in the House of Commons, when repelling some most absurd slander of the grossest description. Instead of the Latin—

"Falsus honor juvat et mendax infamia terret
Quem nisi mendosum et medicandum?"*

I gave—

False honor charms, and lying slander scares,
Whom but the false and faulty?

Next day, in Westminster Hall, I was mobbed by Eton friends at the bar, Jonathan Raine at their head, calling on me to say by what right I had used words which they could not find either in Francis or elsewhere, and requiring me to declare where I had found them, but I would only answer, "Nowhere."

No doubt the merit of extreme closeness depends much on

---

* Hor. Ep., I., xvi.

the frame of the original, and it may be given sometimes word for word without becoming actual prose, as—

"Vive vale. Si quid novisti rectius istis,
Candidus imperti; si non, his utere mecum."*

Live long, farewell: if better rules you see,
Candid impart; if not, use these with me:

which, literal as it is, can not be reckoned more prosaic than the Latin.

I have often heard the great historian preach, and, though very young at the time, was struck with the excellence and the usefulness of his discourses. His notions of practical moderation, and the wish to avoid the fanaticism of the High-Church party (what with us would be called the Low-Church, or Evangelical), led him generally to prefer moral to theological or Gospel subjects. Yet he mingled also three themes essential to the duties of a Christian pastor. He loved to dwell on the goodness of the Deity, as shown forth not only in the monuments of creation, but the work of love in the redemption of mankind. He delighted to expatiate on the fate of man in a future state of being, and to contrast the darkness of the views which the wisest of the heathens had with the perfect light of the new dispensation. He oftentimes would expound the Scriptures, taking, as is the usage of the Kirk, a portion of some chapter for the subject of what is called *lecture*, as contradistinguished from *sermon:* and in these discourses the richness of his learning, the remarkable clearness of his explanation, the felicity of his illustration, shone forth, as well as the cogency and elegance of his practical application to our duties in life, the end and aim of all his teaching. Such was he as a preacher.

But one sermon I can never forget.† The occasion was

---

* Hor. Ep., I., vi.

† "Cannes, November, 1866.

.... "After what Elwin said about the notices of Robertson, Black, and others, having been already printed in the 'Lives of Men of Letters, Philosophers,' etc., I have been doing my utmost to answer his objection, by an attempt to rewrite them, but I have entirely failed. I find I can not do this without utterly destroying any merit the original composition may possess. Hence, these notices *must* remain as I have placed them in the 'Autobiog-

the celebration (5th November, 1788) of the centenary of the Revolution; and his sister, considering that to have heard such a man discourse on such a subject was a thing to be remembered by any one through life ever after, took me (although only ten years old) to hear him. It was of singular and striking interest, from the extreme earnestness, the youthful fervor, with which it was delivered. But it touched in some passages upon a revolution which he expected and saw approaching, if not begun, as well as upon the one which was long past, and almost faded from the memory in the more absorbing interest of present affairs. I well remember his referring to the events then passing on the Continent as the forerunners of far greater ones which he saw casting their shadows before. He certainly had no apprehensions of mischief, but he was full of hope for the future, and his exultation was boundless in contemplating the deliverance of "so many millions of so great a nation from the fetters of arbitrary government." His sister and I often afterwards reflected on this extraordinary discourse with wonder, and I feel quite certain of some such expressions as these having been used, and of his foretelling that our neighbors would one day have to celebrate such an event as had now called us together. We dined with him the same day on leaving the church, for it was the afternoon service that he had performed. His eldest son, afterwards Lord Robertson, was of the company; and when the Principal expressed his satisfaction at having had his presence at church (a thing by no means of weekly occurrence), the answer was: "Aye, sir, if you'll always give us such sermons, you may make it worth

---

raphy.' But you may, if you think it necessary, state where I have taken them from: it is no plagiary to steal from one's self, and I would rather state the fact, than print the notices with inverted commas. They are much too long for notes at the foot of pages; besides, *all* foot-notes must, if possible, be avoided. In the MS. of the other volumes, there are notices, and characters, of men at the bar and public men: I dare say some of these will be found to have been already printed. Hence, let the best mode of dealing with all these be well considered. You can not do better than consult Forster; but bear in mind that they must not be omitted, and that I can not undertake to rewrite them. Yours, H. B.

"To William Brougham, Esq.,
"Brougham, Penrith, Angleterre."

our while." "Ah!" answered he, "you would like it, as the boys say," referring to a vulgar taunt. I have again and again asked my learned kinsman to show me the sermon, which he admitted he possessed among his father's papers, fairly written out. His answer was that he wished to avoid giving it publicity, because, in the violence of the times, the author would be set down for a Jacobin, how innocent soever he was at the date of its being preached. Those times have happily long since passed away; and the sermon having been found among the judge's papers, after a long and fruitless search, I am now possessed of it, written in his own hand, and can see the places where he added passages on the inspiration of the moment, particularly that above cited, my recollection of which is distinct, and is confirmed both by the conversation upon it I have often had with his sister, and by the judge's apprehensions, who was of the strong alarmist party.

It is fit that some mention should be made of Dr. Robertson's family, and of his private life as connected with these memoirs. His father, a Robertson of Struan, was settled for some years as minister of the Scotch Church in London Wall; and I recollect when the affairs of that establishment came before me in the Court of Chancery, and one of the counsel connected with Scotland was beginning to explain its nature, I told him that my great-grandfather, the historian's father, had been its pastor, so that I might be excused for taking an unusual interest in its concerns, reminding him of the Scotch saying that blood is thicker than water. He returned to Scotland in 1718, and was settled at Borthwick, in the county of Edinburgh, having married Miss Pitcairn, of Dreghorn; and it was always remembered in the family that Sir Richard Steele, with whom he had become acquainted in London, showed his respect for him by being present at the marriage. The historian was born at Borthwick, 19th September, 1721.

I have been curious to ascertain the kind of genius which distinguished his father, besides his talent for drawing, of which I possess a specimen showing some skill. It is a miniature in Indian-ink of James Earl, of Seafield, one of the forfeited lords, to whom he was distantly related. The family were also said to be descended from John Knox. The historian professed himself quite unacquainted with the reasons of this rumor which connected him with "the rustic apostle," whose character and conduct he has described so faithfully and strikingly.

By the kindness of a kinsman I have had the great satisfaction of receiving a copy of the only sermon which he ever published, as well as of two or three hymns, translations and paraphrases from the Greek of the New Testament. The sermon is able, judicious, correctly composed both for accuracy of diction and severity of taste, and contains passages of great beauty and effect. It resembles what in England would be called an Ordination Sermon or Charge, having been delivered at the opening of the Metropolitan Synod in May, 1737, and is a full description of the duties of ministers, the title of it being that "they should please God rather than men." His poetry is elegant and classical: one of his pieces is a beautiful paraphrase of the 14th chapter of St. John to the tenth verse:

"1. Let not your hearts with anxious thoughts
Be troubled or dismayed;
But trust in Providence divine,
And trust my gracious aid.

"2. I to my Father's house return;
There numerous mansions stand,
And glory manifold abounds
Through all the happy land.

"3. I go your entrance to secure,
And your abode prepare;
Regions unknown are safe to you,
When I, your Friend, am there.

"4. Thence shall I come, when ages close,
To take you home with me;
There we shall meet to part no more,
And still together be.

"5. I am the Way, the Truth, the Life:
No son of human race,
But such as I conduct and guide,
Shall see my Father's face."

When I went to Glasgow, in 1860, to preside at the Social Science Congress, and when, as usual on these occasions, I attended divine service in the Cathedral Church, I recollect being much struck with the accident of this hymn being sung, when, very certainly, I alone of all the congregation knew who was the author, for the hymn-book gives it without any name.*

Both sermon and poetry plainly show good taste, as well as strong but sober reason, came to the great historian by descent as well as by study; but that his father held opinions more strict on some subjects than the relaxed rigor of Presbyterian rule prescribed, half a century later, is proved by his requiring his son's promise never to enter a play-house. This was stated by him in reference to his father when debating the question of John Home's having written the play of "Douglas." It is needless to add that, however much he differed with his father on this subject, he strictly adhered through life to the promise thus given; insomuch that when Garrick and Henderson at different times visited him, they entertained and interested him by exhibiting to him in private specimens of the art in which both so eminently excelled.† The traditional character in his family of the venerable person whom I have mentioned was any thing rather than sour or stern, how severe and unbending soever may have been his moral feelings. For the sweetness of his placid temper, and the cheerfulness of his kindly disposition, I have heard him spoken of in terms of the warmest enthusiasm by such of his children as were old enough at the time of his decease to recollect him distinctly. The idea of again meeting him in another state was ever present to my grandmother's mind (who was his eldest daughter), and especially when stricken with any illness. It was with her a common source of argument for a future state—as proved by the light of nature, and in her pious mind a confirmation of the truth of Christianity—that, believing in the divine goodness, she could not conceive the extinction of so much angelical purity as adorned her parent, and so fine an understanding as he possessed. Their mother was a woman of great ability and force of character; but, like many of that caste, women especially, she was more stern and more severe than amiable, and this

* See Appendix V.

† See Appendix VI.

contrast, unfavorable to the one, redounded to the augmented love of the other. It can not be doubted that the son's character derived a strong tincture from both parents; but while he, like his father, was mild and gentle in his temper and of an engaging demeanor, his firmness and decision—nay, his inclination towards the Stoical system of morals, and even to a certain degree of stoical feeling, too—was derived from his mother.

The death of these two excellent persons was singularly melancholy, and served to impress on the minds of their family a mournful recollection of their virtues. Mr. Robertson had been removed to the Old Greyfriars' Church of Edinburgh in 1773; and ten years afterwards, both he and his wife, seized with putrid fever, died within a few days of each other, leaving eight children—six daughters and two sons—of whom William was the elder. William had been educated first at the school of Dalkeith, under a very able teacher of the name of Leslie, a gentleman at that time of the greatest eminence in his profession. On his father's removal to Edinburgh, he was taken thither and placed at the University, though only twelve years old.

The age of twelve was only a year or two less than usual at the Scotch universities. My contemporaries and myself were barely fourteen when we entered, attending the mathematical as well as the Latin and Greek classes, and next year that of natural philosophy.

His diligence in study was unremitting, and he pursued his education at the different classes for eight years with indefatigable zeal. He had laid down for himself a strict plan of reading; and of the notes which he took there remain a number of books, beginning when he was only fourteen, all bearing the sentence as a motto, which so characterized his love of learning, indicating that he delighted in it abstractedly, and for its own sake, without regarding the uses to which it might be turned—"Vita sine litteris, mors."

When the London University (now called University College) was founded in 1825, I had a good deal of correspondence with Lord Robertson, who strongly recommended taking as our motto this inscription in his father's note-books. I give what is above stated as his gloss upon the motto or text advisedly.

His whole life was spent in study. I well remember his constant habit of quitting the drawing-room, both after dinner and again after tea, and remaining shut up in his library. The period of time when I saw this was after the "History of America" had been published, and before Major Rennell's map and memoir appeared, which, he tells us, first suggested the "Disquisition on Ancient India." Consequently, for above ten years he was in the course of constant study, engaged in extending his information, examining and revolving the facts of history, contemplating ethical and theological truths, amusing his fancy with the strains of Greek and Roman poetry, or warming it at the fire of ancient eloquence so congenial to his mind, at once argumentative and rhetorical; and all this study produced not one written line, though thus unremittedly carried on. The same may be said of the ten years he passed in constant study from 1743, the beginning of his residence in a small parish, of very little clerical duty, to 1752, when we know from his letter to Lord Hailes he began his first work. But, indeed, the composition of his three great works, spread over a period of nearly thirty years, clearly evinces that during this long time his studies must have been much more subservient to his own gratification than to the preparation of his writings, which never could have required one-half that number of years for their completion.

In 1741, according to the constitution of the Scotch Church, he was licensed by the Presbytery of Edinburgh to preach, orders being only conferred upon a presentation to a living or kirk. Two years after, he was appointed minister of Gladsmuir, a country parish in East Lothian; and this event happened fortunately on the eve of the irreparable loss sustained by the family in the death of both their parents, which left his brother and his sisters wholly without provision.

He immediately took the care of them upon himself, and would form no connection by marriage until he had seen them placed in situations of independence. He thus remained single for eight years, during which his eldest and favorite sister superintended his household. In her sound judgment he always had the greatest confidence; for he knew that to great beauty she added a calm and a firm temper, inherited from their mother, but with greater meekness of disposition. An instance of her fortitude and presence of mind was sometimes mentioned by him, though never alluded to by her: a swarm of bees having settled on her head and shoulders while sitting in the garden, she remained motionless until they took wing, thus saving her life, which was in imminent jeopardy. She was married in 1750; and, the year after, he married his cousin Miss Nesbitt. She, after a long attachment, married Mr. Syme, minister of Alloa, where her daughter was born. He was a sound divine and a learned man, much esteemed by the principal, with whom he coincided on the great question of lay patronage which then agitated the Church, as it has in our day, having caused the great schism dividing the Establishment into two. He had under his care as pupils the sons of Mr. Abercromby, the chief person in the neighborhood, Sir Ralph and his brother Sir Robert.

If such as has been described was the principal's estimate of his sister, it is needless to say that her affection for him, and the veneration in which she held him all her life, and his memory when gone, knew no bounds. I recollect while very young, when he came to Brougham, being much struck with her manner of addressing him. It was always "sir," not brother; and he called her "Mally" (Molly); but this, I afterwards observed, did not betoken any distance, or want of perfect and cordial familiarity. His other sisters addressed him in the same manner, but in this case there was not by any means the same familiarity. She was indeed, as her brother always said, a very remarkable person, and this was apparent from his regard for her opinion and advice, as well as from the discussions on various subjects which I have heard between them. I well remember her great admiration of Lord Chatham, and that she did not quite agree with him in his estimate of the son, who stood a good deal higher in his opinion than in hers, not because of his being at all a Pittite, but probably from his friendship with the Dundases (the two presidents), father and son.* He was, as he told Walpole many years before Chatham's death, a moderate Whig, a

* 1. Robert Dundas of Arniston, born 1685, Lord President of the Court of Session 1748, died 1753; 2. Robert, his son, born 1713, Lord President 1760, died 1767.—*Brunton and Haig's History of the Senators of the College of Justice*, 507, 523.

Whig of 1688; to which Walpole says he made an answer that no one ever believed he ventured with such a person. His sister was avowedly a Whig in the mere party sense of the term. But as an *orator*, Chatham was the model she used to place before my eyes; and her dreams were, when she heard of my attempts, that her preaching had not been in vain. It was a subject on which she often came with her daughter (my mother), of whom she had a very high and most just opinion, as had the principal. But I greatly doubt if she herself, had she survived to 1830, would have exercised the self-control and self-denial which the daughter showed, in opposing, by her remonstrances and earnest advice, my being chancellor.

Some of my grandmother's nearest relatives were persons of eminence, to which they had raised themselves; and both from this and from her brother's great position, gained, like theirs, by his own exertions, she constantly impressed on my mind the duty of following such examples; but always required that distinction should be sought by just means; and above all, she used to inculcate the duty of benevolence, and to dwell upon its reward in the pleasure beneficence produced. An ardent love of liberty and hatred of oppression seemed part of her nature. A horror of war and delight in peace could with difficulty be overcome by any circumstances that could be urged to create an exception. The words "Peace is my dearest delight" were ever in her mouth. She felt an affection for the *Quakers* on this account; and when any one had any thing to say against them, her answer always was, "Well, but it is the only sect that never persecute;" and on the Independents being cited against her, she would say, "But Oliver Cromwell was an Independent, not a Quaker, and if he did not resist toleration, he made war." If it was hard to find an exception to peace and tolerance, no exception would she ever suffer to the necessity of strict economy, public and private. The necessity of economy must only yield to claims of humanity, irresistible in their nature and wholly undisputed. For next to a sense of strict justice, humanity was a constant topic.

Many an argument have I heard between her brother and her on some capital conviction, when she leaned towards mercy, and against that kind of punishment. Her view was perfectly sound, that the smallest punishment which was sufficient to prevent a repetition of the offense was all we had a right to inflict, and that punishing with death tended to counteract one of the objects of all punishment, by turning the feelings in the party's favor through the aversion felt to the punishment. The principal would say that her reasoning was owing to her feelings of misplaced pity for the offender. And this was the case latterly, when her mind had no longer its original strength, and the discussion was renewed with her daughter and the rest of us. We then saw that she was arguing from her feelings. But in former times these were the impressions on all subjects she has left, and they were inherited by her daughter. It used to be a joke among us that she had not inherited her mother's beauty; and we afterwards found that the extraordinary likeness to Dante of her profile and her bust, so much admired by Chantry, made some amends for the defect.

Of the relations who have been alluded to, the Adams and the Clerks were the most remarkable, as they were all first cousins of the principal and his sister. The Adams were famous as architects, breaking through the old and plain, but bad style, and introducing, with some variations, the Greek and Italian. They were patronized by Lord Bute and Lord Mansfield, and by most of the English nobles who had buildings to erect on their estates. In and near London those most remarkable are Caen Wood, the villa of Lord Mansfield, and Lansdowne House, formerly Bute House.* They took part in Parliament with the Whigs, which lost them the king's (George III.) office of architect. They represented the county of Kinross, as did a younger member of the family, who afterwards was Chief Judge of the Jury Court in Scotland. Of the Clerks, the father of Lord Eldin (Scotch judge) married an Adam; he was author of the system of naval tactics adopted with such signal success in the navy. Sir Howard Douglas has denied this as regards Rodney's battle in 1782

* Of the two brother architects, Robert and James, a good account is given in the fragment of a general biographical dictionary by the Society for the Diffusion of Useful Knowledge. The well-known façade of the Adelphi, off the Strand, has its name to commemorate the joint work of the brethren.

—his father, Sir C. Douglas, having been captain of the fleet. But the fact is undeniable that Clerk had brought his plan to maturity, and communicated the particulars to several persons, long before Rodney's action, and while Rodney was abroad; he having gone to the West Indies in January, 1780, and Clerk, as he states in the preface to his book, having gone to London in 1779, when he met by appointment Mr. R. Atkinson, Admiral Rodney's particular friend, and Sir Charles Douglas, his captain, to whom he detailed and explained every part of his system, for the express purpose of having it communicated to the admiral before his departure with the fleet. Mr. Clerk adds that such communication was made; that the admiral expressed, before he left London, his entire approbation of the scheme; and after his return openly acknowledged that it was Mr. Clerk who had suggested the manœuvres by which the victory of the 12th of April, 1782, had been obtained.

Clerk's system was followed by Howe, St. Vincent, Duncan, and Nelson, and with well-known success. The manœuvre is, in fact, the same that Napoleon practised on shore—the placing an adversary between the fire of two bodies. What makes Clerk's merit the more remarkable is, that he was not a professional man, and had never even gone a voyage to sea.*

John Clerk's intimacy was very close with the principal and his sister, who both had great confidence in his practical sense upon most subjects, when not perverted by certain odd prejudices and fancies. For instance, she being, like him, a warm advocate of exercise as a means above every thing for promoting health, used to quote him as saying, when asked, "What were you to do in bad weather?" "Why, run up and down stairs; there is no better exercise, or better fitted to bring all the muscles into play."

Once during the Reign of Terror, a fast-day sermon was preached, which we attended with him; and after morning service, when we were complaining of the preacher as having exaggerated by charging the Jacobins with sacrificing the priests at the foot of the altar—"Foot of the altar!" said

---

* See Appendix VII.

John, "that is only a way of speaking; but it lets the wretches off too easily. They never let them get to the foot of the altar, but murdered them in the streets or the prisons."

Dr. Adam was a teacher of the greatest merit, and a man distinguished by qualities very rarely found in combination with his literary eminence. The hardships which he endured from poverty in his early life have seldom been equalled, never exceeded. When he was endeavoring to educate himself, he for some years suffered from actual hunger, his only means of subsistence being the small sum of three guineas a quarter received from teaching, and out of which he had to pay fourpence a week for a miserable lodging, two miles out of the town, and his daily food was oatmeal-porridge and penny rolls. He dispensed with fire and candles: the former, by severe exercise when the weather permitted—when it was bad, by climbing one of the highest staircases in which Edinburgh abounds; the latter, by reading at the room of some fellow-student. His temper was never soured nor his spirits distressed; the zeal of studying and success in it sustaining him, and even making him feel happy. These particulars have been related by his pupils, among others the first Lord Meadowbank, but were very rarely even alluded to by himself, and only in general terms when illustrating in his class the value of industrious habits, and the comforts they bring under the most adverse circumstances. For it was one of the greatest merits of his teaching that he constantly lectured his pupils on moral and religious subjects, on their duties to Heaven and to their fellow-creatures, besides dwelling on the illustration of his remarks derived from their learning, classical, historical, and geographical. It is difficult to conceive a more useful discipline in all respects than his class afforded. But in no particular was his instruction more valuable than in opening the mind to the contemplation of characters, ancient and modern, and drawing from them the conclusions in favor of political virtue of every kind. He always spoke with great natural eloquence, and made very deep impression by the force and conciseness of his statements, and the rich illustrations from history, the constant reference to individuals, and the appeals to classical authority. It would be difficult to exaggerate the effects of his lectures, for such they were, though often consisting of a few sentences interspersed in the lessons as they went on. Among his favorite topics was inculcating the love of independence, the duty and comfort of making one's own fortune, and relying on one's self alone. Then he would chide a pupil's idleness or inattention; and if the lad was of the higher orders, "But *you* will get a post or a pension when others are working their way up-hill." Then the delights of learning in all its branches formed a constant theme, and the mischiefs of all obstructions in the way of its acquirement. "A tax upon paper is a tax upon knowledge," was a frequent expression. He was always extolling the ancient writers: it was his business. He would point out their beauties, and especially those less obvious, and would say—"It is too late to doubt of them; whoever should do so would find he had come too late; for all men's minds have long ago been made up on the subject." But he ever dwelt on their works having been the result of the greatest care, and of each being a monument of industry; describing Sallust, for instance, as passing his whole time in composition and careful correction. The eloquence of the old orators he would descant on by the hour, and show that its success was due to diligent preparation. With some exceptions he much undervalued the modern: of these exceptions Chatham was the chief, and he highly commended his method of bringing up his son, notwithstanding he had kept him from a public school. Of that son's eloquence he had formed an estimate strongly affected by his political opinions, which were those of the admirers of the French Revolution; and although he avoided the expression of them, it was pretty manifest how he leaned, even after its crimes had begun to stagger most of its partisans. I found when I had left his class that he was of those who very reluctantly admitted any faults in the Republicans. Whatever opinions he held on this subject, he always inculcated the most decided attachment to our own constitution. His taste in all matters of composition was sound and severe. If he admired Seneca more than was strictly just, he gave no preference to him over the purer models; and his liking plainly proceeded from the great store-house found in his prose writings of moral truths, those which he warmly inculcated. It must, however, be observed, that there are in many parts of Seneca's philosophical writings passages of great eloquence, in none more than the treatise on Providence, in that on the great question of the origin of evil, and that on the shortness of life.

The steady honesty of Dr. Adam, his devotion to his principles, his unwearied zeal and heartfelt enthusiasm in impressing them on his pupils, can never be forgotten by those who had the inestimable benefit of his teaching, and of learning, besides that which was the first and main object of his instruction, those other things with which it was connected, and on which no other teacher ever thought of dwelling. I consider myself indebted to him for whatever success has attended my life, whether speculative or practical; and a few of our fellow-pupils were so sensible of the great value of his general comments, and remarks on men and manners, that we made it a common practice to take notes of his observations, and to interchange, and correct, or extend them.

Moreover, he inculcated not only the expediency of written translations beyond those which were given in as our exercises, but of practising composition and speaking. Two or three of us used to meet of an evening and hold a debate on some subject which he had handled in his class; and having been taken by my tutor to hear a debate in a meeting composed chiefly of students in the University, but open to all who chose to subscribe, I tried my hand at composing an essay on the subject I had heard debated, "Whether prosperity or adversity was most favorable to virtue." On showing it to my father, I found a very severe judge, who thought the declamatory speeches I had heard misled me, and set me on other subjects that required argumentation and (being an old Etonian) classical allusions, and even quotations. The doctor was more lenient, and gave me encouragement; but I found by his questions that he substantially agreed with the judgment of the domestic forum. This excellent man had been a good deal thwarted by the authorities, provoked to personal altercation with unworthy antagonists, and assailed by a corrupt portion of the press. As to the authorities, his first work was a most excellent book on the principles of Latin and English grammar, designed to promote his great object of making classical studies a help to other studies, and not a hindrance—and he wished to introduce it in the school; but he found all the other masters, who had been accustomed to teach Ruddiman's Grammar, opposed to the substitution of his; and also the magistrates, patrons of the school, for the same reason, resolved to abide by Ruddiman's. After a severe contest, both in the courts of law and the town council, the latter issued a positive prohibition to the school to make use of Adam's Grammar, and he could therefore only indirectly urge his doctrines. I grieve to add that at one time the principal (Robertson) took part against him, who on all other occasions stood his warm friend, and obtained for him from the University his degree. But the question of extramural teaching, in after-times so much discussed, had arisen upon the introduction of Greek in the school by Adam as early as 1782; and the professors endeavored, but without success, to prevent this. The principal, who must have strongly disapproved of their opposition, yet yielded to it, probably on the ground of the professor of Greek depending entirely on the number of his pupils, from having no salary; and on the assumption that, with the frugal habits of the Scotch, few or none would send their sons to attend the Greek professor, if they had learnt a little Greek the year before at the High School.

The trouble which the doctor had with some of the masters under him arose from the improvements in teaching which he endeavored to introduce, at first with great resistance and only partial success—in the end, with their perfect assent. During the former period his chief opponent was Nicol, whose violence led to a personal quarrel, which had nearly ended in a duel. The man did not want talent or learning, but was of most intemperate habits and dissolute life. He was the intimate friend and pot-companion of Burns, some of whose best known and most popular bacchanalian songs bear traces of this intimacy. Of these the one most in favor with the Scotch begins with—

> "Willie brewed a peck o' maut (malt),
> And Rab and Allan cam to pree."

The Willie is Nicol, the poet is Rab; and Allan was one of the Mastertons, at whose school I learnt writing and arithmetic. Nicol's habits were well known to the boys, as were those of the other masters. They had an uncouth rhyme characterizing their masters. In this Luke is the teacher—Luke Fraser, under whom I was before rising to the rector's class; Frango was French, a most respectable and learned man; and Cruikshanks (a very able and successful teacher, as well as worthy man, under whom Horner and Murray were, until the former went to the rector's class and the latter to Westminster) is represented by Crukemshango:

"Sandy Adam loves his book,
And so do Luke and Frango;
Willie Nicol loves his bottle,
And so does Crukemshango."

I am pretty confident that the last line is owing to the rhyme and the contrast, and not to the fact. The attacks of the masters and their friends never gave Adam any uneasiness that had not long ceased when I was under him, and he never at any time made the least allusion to them in his class. The treatment of the press he had a good right to despise, when it came from the same disreputable quarter in which the principal was assailed. The history of Gilbert Stuart affords a remarkable and an edifying instance, perhaps a singular one, of great talents and considerable powers of work, though irregular, failing to obtain success, or to keep alive the memory of works distinguished by both learning and ability, owing to the malignant feeling under which they were composed, and their being devoted to its gratification. That these intemperate habits and irregular life would not have produced this effect, there are unhappily too many proofs in the history of authors. An able and learned work on the "History of the British Constitution," made the University of Edinburgh give him the degree of Doctor of Laws when little more than one-and-twenty; and he soon after published his "Views of Society in Europe," being an historical inquiry concerning laws, manners, and government. Immediately after this he was a candidate for the Professorship of Public Law in the University, and he fancied that he owed his rejection to the influence of the principal. Nothing could be more fitting than that such should be the case;

for the life of Stuart was known to be that of habitual dissipation, in the intervals only of which he had paroxysms of study. To exclude such a person from the professor's chair would have been a duty incumbent on the head of any university in Christendom, whatever, in other respects, might be his merits. But no admission was ever made by the principal's friends that he had interfered, or, indeed, that the opinions and inclinations of the magistrates, who are the patrons, rendered any such interference necessary. But the disappointed candidate had no doubt upon the subject, and he set no bounds to his thirst of revenge. He repaired to London, where he became a writer in reviews, and made all the literary men of Edinburgh the subjects of his envious and malignant attacks, from 1768 to 1773; the editors of such journals, as is too usual with persons in their really responsible situation, but who think they can throw the responsibility upon their unknown contributors, never inquiring whether the criticisms which they published proceeded from the honest judgment or the personal spite of the writers. It is the imperative duty of every one who conducts the periodical press to use his utmost diligence in preventing concealed enemies or rivals from using his paper as the vehicle of their attacks. He should lay down the rule never again to receive any contribution from a person who had deceived him by suppressing the fact that he had a grudge or an interest against the object of his former attack.

Stuart returned to Edinburgh, and set up a magazine and review, of which the scurrility, dictated by private resentments, was so unremitting, that it brought the work to a close in less than three years, when he went back to London, and recommenced his anonymous vituperation of Scottish authors through the periodical press. He also published in 1779, 1780, and 1782, three works: one on the "Constitutional History of Scotland," being an attack on Dr. Robertson's first book; another on the "History of the Reformation in Scotland;" and the third on the "History of Queen Mary"—being also an elaborate attack upon the principal. The ability and the learning of these works, and their lively and even engaging style, have not saved them from the oblivion to which they were justly consigned by the manifest indications prevailing throughout them all of splenetic temper, of personal malignity, and of a constant disturbance of the judgment by these vile, unworthy passions. The same hostility towards the person of the principal even involved this reckless man in a quarrel with his eldest son: it led to a duel, in which neither party was hurt—an accommodation having taken place on the field. I have heard Stuart's second say that he was obliged, knowing his friend's intemperate habits, to oppose the proposal—which he made with his usual want of conduct, and, indeed, of right feeling—that all the parties should dine together on quitting the field! That second (Mr. James Gray), an able and an honorable man, always admitted Stuart's unjustifiable conduct towards the historian, one of whose nieces he (the second) afterwards married. Stuart's dissipation continued unbroken, excepting by his occasional literary work; and he died of a dropsy in 1786, at the early age of forty.

Such was the man and such his fate who assailed Dr. Adam with a bitterness and pertinacity as signal as he had shown towards the great historian. His admirable grammar was received universally by the literary and didactive world (by the scholar as well as the teacher) with the approbation which it so well deserved; but it had one fault—it was on a subject on which Stuart's cousin, Ruddiman, had published a book. This was enough to enlist Stuart's ferocity against both the work and the writer. He published anonymous reviews without end, and he also published, under the name of "Busby," a bitter attack upon the personal peculiarities of Dr. Adam. Every one felt unmitigated disgust at such base and unprincipled proceedings, and the rector, like the principal, gave the unworthy author the mortification of leaving his assaults unanswered; nor did he even make any allusions to these attacks, though he occasionally expressed his regret at the prohibition of his grammar by the authority of the town council.

The moral inculcated by Gilbert Stuart's failure has been noted. The lesson of temperance and regularity of life is as remarkably taught by the doctor's personal conflict with one of the masters, Nicol, already referred to as the boon companion of the great lyric poet of Scotland. The temperate habits of our times make it hardly possible that a poet should nowadays attain eminence by bacchanalian songs, and even that ideas should be introduced that owe their point and force to drinking associations, as in the most pathetic of lyrics, "Auld Lang Syne." Even of professed drinking-songs there is this to be said, that they rarely tend to promote intemperance, and are for the most part only displays of wit and humor. They are chiefly perhaps to be excused, if not defended, in the same way that Voltaire pleaded in extenuation, if not justification, of his "Pucelle," that the most reprehensible passages, how offensive soever to decency and morals, had no tendency to inflame the passions, and were not prurient but witty, though indecent; a defense which no one of correct taste or sound morals can ever regard as more than an assertion that the matter complained of, though bad, might have been worse!

I don't recollect the doctor ever distinctly casting my horoscope, as he did that of some others; but the following letter from a daughter, who still lives, of one of the professors, mentions an odd guess of my own, like that of Erskine's mother, which he used to cite as an evidence of providential inspiration—for he never doubted that Providence acted by secondary causes.

The account given in the following letter of the reprimand is in one particular inaccurate. It was not for an essay, but for a message sent by the minority on a division in the Speculative Society, composed of Jeffrey, Horner, Kinnaird, and myself, and of which Jeffrey was the bearer to Professor Hume, whose class we were attending. The message was of an offensive, perhaps hostile description, complaining of his having said publicly, "Those young men, like their masters the French, are evidently skilled in political arts." Jeffrey, as instructed by us, asked if he had used these expressions; and said that if he had we felt bound to declare they contained a falsehood. We were all summoned. Jeffrey was out of town, Horner was ill, as well as Kinnaird, and I alone could attend. The reprimand was perfectly justified by our proceeding, and was most gently administered. The following is an extract from the lady's letter:

"I am sorry I myself was so young during Lord Brougham's college life as to have paid much too little attention to all that I might have heard. To me he was always most excessively kind, but it was the kindness of a young man to one who was comparatively a child. But I do remember one thing which made an impression on me: I heard that he and Horner and Lord Kinnaird had been engaged in the Speculative Society in defending an essay on some political subject, which essay (and its defenders) was on much too liberal principles for the tastes of the rulers of the day; and, in short, the three young men were sentenced (by the Senatus Academicus, I think it was) to submit to be reprimanded by the principal of the college for disseminating French principles and sedition. Of all of the three none were forthcoming but Brougham: Horner was ill or something, and Lord Kinnaird was absent, and Lord Brougham alone came before Principal Baird to receive his lecture. I believe the good principal's admonition was a lenient one, for he was a kind, good-hearted man, who did not in his conscience think the worse of the young gentlemen for their essay; and so Lord Brougham listened respectfully and made his bow, and all was over. This was an event that showed the spirit of the times; for the essay, I believe, contained nothing but what has become since the prevailing opinion and the law of the land. This is the story as nearly as I can remember it; but if there is any thing materially incorrect in it, I dare say Lord Brougham could tell you the exact way of it, if he or you think it of any consequence.

"There is a curious little anecdote which I heard from Mary Robertson at the time Lord Brougham was made lord-chancellor. She told me that when she and the Broughams were all children they were invited to a little ball at her uncle Mr. Abercromby's. We had a house somewhere about Coltbridge or Corstorphine (I do not know which), where the ball was to take place; and all the children, Robertson's and Brougham's together, were packed into a hackney-coach to go; but when they came to the toll-bar, not one of the party was found possessed of a sixpence to pay it; on which, after some consultation among themselves, Henry Brougham jumped up and said to the tollman, 'Oh, you surely will let us pass, for *I* am the lord-chancellor.'. Mary Robertson could not tell me whether he had at that time any idea of belonging to the law, but if it was a mere dash, it was a curious coincidence."

If it was not owing to chance that at Edinburgh I received

the care and counsels of the great historian, it was not to mere accident that I was indebted for my intimacy with the great advocate and orator, Erskine, and his brother Henry, only inferior to him in fame from his provincial position. The house in which we lived, on the north side of St. Andrew's Square, was under the same roof, and next door to Lord Buchan, eldest brother of the Erskines, a man of eccentric character and much underrated, but of considerable learning and talents, and so highly esteemed by Lord Chatham that he gave him a diplomatic appointment, which he was kept from filling by some quarrel about etiquette and rank; but Chatham continued his correspondent all his life, and I have seen his letters when I used to visit Lord Buchan at Dryburgh. They were on various subjects, public and personal; and I recollect the orthography was very indifferent, as, for instance, *does* being generally spelt *dos* or *doz*. He was exceedingly kind to us as children, and I continued his acquaintance afterwards, his phrase being, "Ye're min ain bairns of the hoose" (you are mine own children of the house). This led naturally to a great intimacy with his brother Henry; and when I was called to the bar, I had the benefit of his advice and instruction, as well as of profiting by the example of his advocacy, which had the highest merit, and placed him at the head of the Scotch bar. When I afterwards removed to London, the family friendship was continued by the celebrated brother, with whom my intercourse was constant and familiar. Both these eminent men impressed upon me, as the first of qualities in an advocate, that to which they owed their own great success, the sacrificing every thing to the cause, and indulging in no one topic, or any illustration, or any comment, or even in a phrase or a word, that did not directly and manifestly serve the cause in some material particular. This rule, perhaps, applies to all the departments of eloquence; but it is of paramount importance, nay, an absolute obligation, and of necessity to be obeyed in the conducting of a cause before any tribunal, even before a popular assembly. Both the Erskines had been educated at the High School, of which the younger all his life cherished an affectionate remembrance. The University he had not attended, having been at St. Andrews for a short time before he entered the navy. The care of his education devolved upon his brother (Lord Buchan), who was greatly his senior, and who most liberally, out of his moderate income, supplied all his wants. He died at his brother's seat near Edinburgh. Both these brothers inculcated their political as well as professional opinions very strongly on me at all times. They were staunch friends of liberty, and enemies of oppression, whether exercised over bodies of men or individuals; and I can bear testimony to the warmth of feeling, as well as the skill and judgment, which Lord Erskine showed at the end of his life in the great case of the queen. The remark made on Loughborough that his Scotch returned to him in his latter days (the phrase being that his English had run out of him by the effects of age), does not apply to Erskine. The taint of the High School of Edinburgh could not be perceived at any time of his life.

CHAPTER II.

EARLY LIFE—*continued.*

I leave the High School.—At Brougham with a Tutor.—Tale after the manner of Rasselas.—I enter the College of Edinburgh.—With Folkstone, afterwards Lord Radnor.—My early Efforts in Mathematics and Mechanics.—Optics, Chemistry.—Joseph Black, James Watt.—My first Speech at the Royal Medical Society.—I study Oratory.—I found the Juvenile Literary Society.—Become a Member of the Speculative Society.—Pedestrian Rambles.—Apollo Club, and High Jinks.—Feats of Edinburgh Burschen.—Heron's Play damned.—I go on a Yachting Expedition among the Western Isles.—My Fellow-traveller Charles Stuart (Stuart de Rothsay).—Islay.—Life at Sea.—St. Kilda.—Stornoway.—Cross to Elsinore.

HAVING finished with the High School, I passed the next fourteen months, from August, 1791, to October, 1792, at Brougham, where Mr. Mitchell was my first tutor—a man of excellent temper as well as sound learning, who intended to take orders in the Scotch Church. By his conversation on every subject it was impossible not to profit; and his moral maxims were as enlightened as his opinions on literary and scientific subjects. The time was principally devoted to Greek and Latin; and I was further instructed in such duties by my father, who retained his love of and familiarity with the classics; and, encouraged by him, I tried my hand at writing English essays, and even tales of fiction. I find one of these has survived the waste-paper basket, and it may amuse my readers to see the sort of composition I was guilty of at the age of thirteen.

My tale was entitled "Memnon, or Human Wisdom," and is as follows:

"Memnon one day conceived the useless project of being perfectly wise. There is scarcely any man who has not at one time or other let this folly pass through his head. To be very wise (said Memnon to himself), and, of consequence, very happy, one has only to be without passions, and (as we all know) nothing is easier. In the first place, I shall never love any woman; for when I see a perfect beauty I shall say to myself, 'These cheeks will one day be wrinkled; these fine eyes will be fringed with red; that plum (*sic*) neck will turn flat and flabby; that beautiful head will grow bald.' Now, I have only to see all this with the same eyes at present that I must see it with afterwards, and surely that head will never turn mine. In the second place, I shall always be sober. In vain shall good cheer, delicious wines, agreeable society, try to tempt me. I have only to figure to myself the consequence of excess—a heavy head—a disordered stomach—loss of reason, health, and time; and surely I shall never eat but to satisfy nature; my health shall be constant, my ideas always luminous and pure. All this is so easy that there is no merit in keeping to it. Then (continued Memnon) I must think a little of my fortune. My desires are moderate; my income is lodged in the hands of the Receiver-general of the Finances of Nineveh; I have wherewithal to live independent; and that is the greatest of earthly blessings. I shall never have the disagreeable necessity of paying court to any body. I shall envy no one, and be envied by none. Besides, here is another thing equally plain. I have friends; I shall keep them; so they can have nothing to dispute with me about; I shall never be out of humor with them, nor they with me. In all this there's no sort of difficulty. Having thus formed in his room his little scheme of wisdom, Memnon put his head out of the window. He saw two women washing near his house, under the plane-trees: one of them was old, and seemed not to be thinking about any thing; the other was young, handsome, and appeared much engaged. She sighed; she wept; and seemed to have only the more graces. Our sage was moved—not with the beauty of the lady (he was quite confident he never could be guilty of such a weakness), but he was touched with the affliction she appeared to be in. He went down stairs, and approached the young daughter of Nineveh, in the intention of consoling her with wisdom. The fair creature related, with an air the most natural and affecting, all the injuries she had received from an uncle whom she never had—with the artifices by which he had taken from her a fortune she never possessed, and all the evils she had to fear from his ill-treatment. 'You appear,' said she, 'to be a man of such good counsel, that if you'll only have the condescendence to step home with me and examine my affairs, I'm sure you'll relieve me from the cruel embarrassments into which I have fallen.' Memnon followed her without hesitation, for the purpose of examining, safely, her affairs, and giving her good advice. The afflicted lady carried him into a perfumed apartment, and politely bid him be seated upon a large sofa, where they both remained with their legs crossed, and opposite to each other. The damsel, while she spoke, cast her eyes on the ground, and sometimes dropt tears from them; and whenever she raised them, they always happened to meet those of the sage Memnon. The conversation was full of tenderness, which redoubled every time they looked at one other. Memnon took her affairs extremely to heart, and felt every moment more and more a desire to oblige so worthy and so unfortunate a personage. Insensibly they ceased (in the heat of conversation) to sit opposite to each other—their legs were no longer crossed. Memnon gave his advice so near and so tenderly, that neither one nor t'other could now speak of business, and they no longer knew where they were. While they continued in this situation, in comes the uncle. As may easily be imagined, he was armed cap-a-pie. His first words were that he proposed (as was reasonable) killing Memnon and his niece on the spot; and the last thing which escaped him was that he would pardon them, if he was well paid for it. Memnon was forced to give all he had about him.

"These were happy days when one could get off so cheap. America was not then known, and afflicted ladies were not half so dangerous as they are in our times. Memnon went home in shame and despair: he found a card inviting him to dine with some of his intimate friends. If (said he) I stay at home by myself, I shall think on nothing but my sad adventure. I shall eat none, and shall fall sick. I had much better go and make a frugal meal with my companions. The sweets of their society will make me forget the morning's folly. He goes to the place appointed; they perceive him somewhat out of sorts; they make him drink to drown sorrow. A little wine taken in moderation is a cure both for mind and body, so thinks the sage Memnon; and, so thinking, he gets drunk. They propose to play after dinner. A little play, well regulated, with one's friends, makes an honorable pastime. He plays, loses all his ready money, and four times more on *tick*. During the game a dispute arises; they turn warm. One of his particular friends throws a decanter at Memnon's head, and shuts up an eye for him. The sage Memnon is carried home, mortal drunk, with the loss of all his money, and half his eyes. He throws up a little of his wine, and as soon as his head is a little clear, he sends his servant to the receiver-general for money to pay his particular friends. He is told that his debtor had that morning broke fraudulently, to the alarm of half the families in town. Memnon, quite beside himself, sets off for court, with a patch on his eye and petition in his hand, to demand justice of the king against the bankrupt. He meets in the drawing-room several ladies, who sported, with an easy air, hoops of twenty-four feet in circumference. One of these, who knew him a little, muttered (eying him askance), 'How horrid!' Another, who was better acquainted with him, accosted him with a 'How do, Mr. Memnon? But, indeed, Mr. Memnon, I'm prodigious glad to see you. By-the-by, Mr. Memnon, how do you happen to have lost an eye?' And so she trifled on, without waiting for an answer. Memnon hid himself in a corner, and waited for the moment when he might throw himself at the monarch's feet. The moment came, and he kissed the ground three times, presenting his petition. His most gracious Majesty of all the Ninevehs received it very favorably, and handed it to one of his satraps to make a report of its substance. The satrap took Memnon aside, and said to him, grinning bitterly, and with a contemptuous air, 'You're a pleasant sort of a blinkard, truly, to address the king rather than me; and still more pleasant to dare to demand justice against an honest bankrupt whom I honor with my protection, and who, indeed, is the nephew of my kept mistress's waiting-woman! Leave off this business, friend, I advise you, if you value the health of your remaining eye.' Memnon, having thus in the morning abjured women, the excesses of the table, play, quarrels, and, above all, the court, had been, before night, duped and pigeoned by a fine lady, filled drunk, rooked at play, drawn into a quarrel, robbed of an eye, and had been at court, where he found himself laughed at. Petrified with astonishment and overpowered with grief, he moves homeward, death-sick at heart. He finds his house surrounded by bailiffs, in the act of gutting it on the part of his creditors. He stops half dead under a plane-tree; he here meets the fair lady of the morning, walking with her dear uncle. She bursts out a laughing at seeing Memnon with his plaster. The night came on; Memnon laid himself down on some straw near the walls of his house. A fever seized him; he fell asleep in the crisis of the disorder, and a celestial spirit appeared to him in a dream. It was clothed in resplendent light; it had six fine wings—but neither feet, nor head, nor tail, nor resemblance to any thing earthly. 'What art thou?' said Memnon. 'Thy good genius,' replied the being. 'Restore me, then,' said Memnon, 'my eye, my health, my money, my wisdom.' He then related how he had, in one day's time, lost all these. 'These are adventures for you,' said the spirit, 'which we never meet with in our world.' 'And where may your world be?' said the man of woe. 'My country,' said the spirit, 'is five hundred millions of leagues from the sun, in a little star near Sirius; as you see here.' 'Dear, what a nice country!' said Memnon: 'so you have no sluts who dupe a poor man; no particular friends who win his money and knock out his eye; no bankrupts; no satraps who laugh at you because they refuse you justice.' 'No,' said the native of the star, 'none of these things at all. We are never cozened by women, for we have no women. We never commit excess at table, for we never feed. We have no bankrupts, for with us there is neither silver nor gold. We can't have our eyes closed up, because we have not bodies made like yours; and satraps never do us injustice, because in our little star all the world is on a footing.' Memnon then addressed him: 'My good master, wifeless and dinnerless! how do you contrive to pass your time?' 'In watching over the other world intrusted to our care,' said he, 'and I am come here just now to console thee.' 'Alackaday!' replied Memnon, 'why didn't you come last night to prevent me from committing so many follies?' 'I was with thy eldest brother, Haspar,' said the celestial being.

'He is more to be pitied than thou. His gracious Majesty the King of the Indians, at whose court he has the honor of belonging, hath caused put out both his eyes for some petty indiscretion; and he is at this moment in a dungeon with his hands and feet in irons.' 'It's very hard,' said Memnon, 'when one has a good genius in the family, that one brother should be blind in one eye, the other in both—one lying on straw, the other in prison.' 'Thy lot shall change,' replied the animal of the star. 'It is true thou shalt always be half-blind; but then, this excepted, thou shalt be happy enough, provided always thou shalt not form the foolish project of being perfectly wise.' 'That, then, is out of the question?' said Memnon, with a sigh. 'As impossible,' said the other, 'as to think of being perfectly clever, strong, powerful, or happy. Even we ourselves are far from it. There is, indeed, one globe where all that may be had; but in the hundred thousand millions of others which are sprinkled over space, every thing is got by degrees. One feels less pleasanter in the second than in the first; still less in the third than the second; and so on, down to the last, where every mother's son is an absolute fool.' 'I greatly fear,' said Memnon, 'that our little terraqueous globe is precisely the little habitation of the universe about which you are doing me the honor to speak.' 'Not altogether,' said the spirit, 'but nearly so; every thing must have its place.' 'But stay,' said Memnon; 'some poets and philosophers, then, are in the wrong to say that every thing is for the best?' 'They are quite right,' said the philosopher of the upper regions, 'if we consider the arrangement of the whole universe.' 'Ah!' replied poor Memnon, 'I shall never be able to see that till I've got back my other eye.'"

We returned to Edinburgh for the college session in October; and I recollect, after passing through Carlisle, breakfasting at Netherby, where we saw Sir James Graham, then a child in his nurse's arms. The Bishop of Carlisle (Vernon, afterwards Archbishop of York) and I have often talked of the change which forty or fifty years had made on that infant.

Under Playfair I then began the course of mathematics. Nothing could be more admirable than his teaching. He was at all times accessible to his pupils for explaining things left short in the class, and removing doubts or difficulties that occurred in their reading at home. In this respect he was superior to the other great teacher of that time, Dugald Stewart, under whom we all derived the most solid instruction that lectures could afford, in the most attractive form of eloquence; but, probably partly from the exhaustion of his delivery, and partly from aversion to disputation, which such conferences were apt to occasion, he very often declined to see his pupils after the class rose.

Playfair's winter course was six months, and the summer three, at the second of which I attended with Lord Folkestone (now Radnor), whose intimacy, both personal and political, I have since constantly enjoyed, and a better man I have never known, to say nothing of his great abilities. Those who had the advantage of hearing him in the discussions in the House of Lords upon the distress of the country at the end of 1830, and on the Reform Bill the year after, when he delivered a speech of the most finished excellence, may remember my reference to a still nobler oration in the Duke of York's case in 1809, which no less accomplished judges than Windham, Canning, and Dudley, each severally assured me was one of the most powerful that they ever heard. One great merit of Radnor's eloquence was its being so plainly produced by strong and honest feelings. It proceeded manifestly from the speaker's heart, and it went direct to the hearts of his hearers.*

In 1794, on an exercise which I gave in, the Professor (Playfair) desired me to wait till the class rose, and then he said that I had hit upon the Binomial Theorem, asking me by what steps I had been led to it? I of course answered, as was the fact, that it had been by induction. But he said, "This piece of good-fortune ought to make you fonder of the mathematics than ever;" and as I wished to master the Fluxional Calculus, which he had done no more than explain the nature of, in that course, I desired to know what he would recommend me to read with that view. He said there were two works, either of which deserved to be studied, Lacaille and

* See Appendix VIII.

Bezout, but he preferred the latter.* I set to work with that, and in a few months showed him that I had profited by the study. My intimacy with Playfair continued all his life. I used to correspond with him on mathematical subjects, and I remember his letters in answer to mine from the north, observing that "I was as usual on our common subject, when in my aphelion." I recollect when we were volunteers together in an artillery corps. He was particularly diligent in superintending our ball-practice, and on the first occasion of it received great delight from the accidental success of his old pupil in levelling the gun, which shot through the centre of the target. "You see," he said, to those about him, "how we mathematicians carry the day." He would not allow it to be, as I admitted, a mere chance, and did not approve of my modesty being displayed to the detriment of science. The last time we met was in 1816 at Rome, where we passed part of the winter, the famous year when all the heads of London society were there—Jerseys, Hamiltons, Devonshires, Cowpers, Barings, Kings, Vernons, Westmorlands.

In 1794, '5 I was led away for a few weeks from the calculus by the interest I took in a problem proposed by the Academy of Sciences at Berlin for a prize—the deflection of a projectile from the vertical plane; and a solution having occurred to me, or a supposed solution, I drew up a paper (or memoir) and sent it. I never received the acknowledgment of it, and very properly; for I am certain, from what I recollect of it, that the demonstration was wrong, at least was inadequate, though I believe the theory was correct, which ascribed the deflection to the rotatory motion of the projectile, and its condensing the air.

But I recollect an experiment which, accompanied by my brother James and Reddie, I tried, in order to ascertain the effects of the rotation. It was to fire a bullet from a fowling-piece, placed horizontally, through a series of screens placed vertically. It was found that the bullet first deviated

* Nicolas Louis de Lacaille, who died in 1762, author of a host of books on astronomy, mensuration, and the higher mathematics. Etienne Bezout, author of "La Théorie Générale des Equations Algebriques," and of several other books chiefly directed towards the mathematical training of the several branches of the French military and naval force.

to the left, and then, on piercing the first screen, swerved to the right, and so at each screen changed its direction—indicating, as we supposed, that the direction of rotation was changed by the screens.

I, however, soon returned to pure mathematics, and several of the propositions afterwards mentioned in my paper on Porisms were investigated at this time. I was also diligently employed in experiments upon light and colors, and conceived that I had made some additions to the Newtonian doctrine, which I sent to the Royal Society in the summer of 1795. The paper was very courteously received; but Sir Charles Blagden (the secretary) desired parts to be left out in the notes or queries as belonging rather to the arts than the sciences. This was very unfortunate; because, I having observed the effect of a small hole in the window-shutter of a darkened room, when a view is formed on white paper of the external objects, I had suggested that if that view is formed, not on paper, but on ivory rubbed with nitrate of silver, the picture would become permanent; and I had suggested improvements in drawing founded upon this fact. Now this is the origin of photography; and had the note containing the suggestion in 1795 appeared, in all probability it would have set others on the examination of the subject, and given us photography half a century earlier than we have had it.

The experiments and propositions as printed in the "Philosophical Transactions" I have since considered as proceeding in great part from confounding colors made by *flexion* with those formed by *reflection*, for I am convinced that all the phenomena in my experiments may be explained without having recourse to the supposition of different reflexibility, by considering the colors as formed by flexion and then reflected. But there is a different reflexibility.

The Newtonian is another kind, not of the white rays being separated into their component parts by one reflection, but of the rays being reflected instead of refracted or transmitted; and I showed that this is owing, not to the different rays having different capacities of reflection, but to their having, in the first instance, been separated by refraction, the experiment being not of reflection without previous refraction, but after much refraction, and that their different refrangibility is in truth alone the cause of their apparent different reflexibility. I believe all opticians have admitted the correctness of my reasoning in this; and that the different reflexibility of the Newtonian system has long ceased to be admitted at all. In these papers I only had a query as to different flexibility, which Newton does not suggest; but in papers long since given in the "Philosophical Transactions," and in the "Memoirs of the National Institute of France," the existence of this property is fully shown by various experiments.

Besides the two optical papers (1796, 1797), there was one on Porisms, inserted in the "Philosophical Transactions" the year after (1798).

Great as was the pleasure and solid advantage of studying under such men as Playfair and Stewart, the gratification of attending one of Black's last courses exceeded all I have ever enjoyed. In my life of that great man ("Lives of the Philosophers") I have attempted to describe this pleasure.* Not a little of this extreme interest certainly belonged to the accident that he had so long survived the period of his success—that we knew there sat in our presence the man now in old age reposing under the laurels won in his early youth. But, take it altogether, the effect was such as can not well be conceived. I have heard the greatest understandings of the age giving forth their efforts in their most eloquent tongues—have heard the commanding periods of Pitt's majestic oratory—the vehemence of Fox's burning declamation—have followed the close-compacted chain of Grant's pure reasoning—been carried away by the mingled fancy, epigram, and argumentation of Plunkett; but I would without hesitation prefer, for mere intellectual gratification (though aware how much of it is derived from association), to be once more allowed the privilege which I in those days enjoyed, of being present, while the first philosopher of his age was the historian of his own discoveries, and be an eye-witness of those experiments by which he had formerly made them, once more performed with his own hands.

---

* See note, p. 29.

His style of lecturing was as nearly perfect as can well be conceived; for it had all the simplicity which is so entirely suited to scientific discourse, while it partook largely of the elegance of all he said or did. The publication of his lectures has conveyed an accurate idea of the purely analytical order in which he deemed it best to handle the subject with a view to instruction, considering this as most likely to draw and to fix the learner's attention, to impress his memory, and to show him both the connection of the theory with the facts and the steps by which the principles were originally ascertained. He would illustrate his doctrine of latent heat by referring to what is seen and felt, but passed without remark, in the boiling of a kettle, and the steam coming from its spout, of different heat at different distances; or would remind us of the surprise expressed by finding that boiling water is cooled far more quickly than could be foreseen upon the addition of a very little cold; or that a hot chestnut which the mouth can not bear is in an instant made bearable by the least drop of wine sipped with it, and the wine not becoming sensibly hotter. His experiments were often, like Franklin's, performed with the simplest apparatus—indeed with nothing that could be called apparatus at all. I forget whether he showed us the experiment of a bladder filled with inflammable air and rising to the ceiling, which he had often shown to his friends in private, and which was the origin of the air-balloon; but I remember his pouring fixed air from a vessel in which sulphuric acid had been poured upon chalk, and showing us how this air poured on a candle extinguished the light. He never failed to remark on the great use of simple experiments within every one's reach, and liked to dwell on the manner in which discoveries are made, and the practical effect resulting from them in changing the condition of men and things.

The scheme of the lectures may thus be apprehended—the execution imperfectly; for the diction was evidently, in many instances, extemporaneous, the notes before the teacher furnishing him with little more than the substance, especially of those portions which were connected with experiments. But still less can the reader rise from the perusal to any conception of the manner. Nothing could be more suited to the occasion: it was perfect philosophical calmness; there was no effort, but it was an easy and a graceful conversation. The voice was low, but perfectly distinct and audible through the whole of a large hall crowded in every part with mutely attentive listeners; it was never at all forced, any more than were the motions of the hands, but it was any thing rather than monotonous. Perfect elegance as well as repose was the phrase by which every hearer and spectator naturally, as if by common consent, described the whole delivery. The accidental circumstance of the great teacher's aspect, I hope I may be pardoned for stopping to note, while endeavoring to convey the idea of a philosophic discoverer. His features were singularly graceful, full of intelligence, but calm, as suited his manner and his speech. His high forehead and sharp temples were slightly covered, when I knew him, with hair of a snow-white hue, and his mouth gave a kindly as well as a most intelligent expression to his whole features. In one department of his lectures he exceeded any I have ever known —the neatness and unvarying success with which all the manipulations of his experiments were performed. His correct eye and steady hand contributed to the one: his admirable precautions, foreseeing and providing for every emergency, secured the other. I have seen him pour boiling water or boiling acid from a vessel that had no spout into a tube, holding it at such a distance as made the stream's diameter small, and so vertical that not a drop was spilt. While he poured he would mention this adaptation of the height to the diameter as a necessary condition of success. I have seen him mix two substances in a receiver into which a gas, as chlorine, had been introduced, the effect of the combination being perhaps to produce a compound inflammable in its nascent state, and the mixture being effected by drawing some string or wire working through the receiver's sides in an air-tight socket. The long table on which the different processes had been carried on was as clean at the end of the lecture as it had been before the apparatus was planted upon it. Not a drop of liquid, not a grain of dust remained.

The reader who has known the pleasures of science will forgive me if, at the distance of much more than half a century, I love to linger over these recollections, and to dwell on the delight which I well remember thrilled me as we heard this illustrious sage detail, after the manner I have feebly attempted to portray, the steps by which he made his discoveries, illustrating them with anecdotes sometimes recalled to his mind by the passages of the moment, and giving their demonstration by performing before us the many experiments which had revealed to him first the most important secrets of nature. Next to the delight of having actually stood by him when his victory was gained, we found the exquisite gratification of hearing him simply, most gracefully, in the most calm spirit of philosophy, with the most perfect modesty, recount his difficulties, and how they were overcome; open to us the steps by which he had successfully advanced from one part to another of his brilliant course; go over the same ground, as it were, in our presence which he had for the first time trod so many long years before; hold up, perhaps, the very instruments he had then used, and act over again the same part before our eyes which had laid the deep and broad foundations of his imperishable renown. Not a little of this extreme interest certainly belonged to the accident that he had so long survived the period of his success—that we knew there sat in our presence the man, now in his old age, reposing under the laurels won in his early youth. But, take it altogether, the effect was such as can not well be conceived.

One thing was very striking in his lectures, as also in his conversation, and it was equally remarkable in his friend and pupil, Watt—the great care, even to minute particulars of evidence, which he took to appropriate to every one his share in the discoveries of which he was treating. His love of justice was one of the most marked characteristics of his nature, as it was of the Duke of Wellington's. I well remember Denman saying, when he saw him rush forward to defend some officer unjustly attacked, or to obtain for him the share of commendation that he thought had been inadequately awarded, "Of all that man's great and good qualities, the one which stands first is his anxious desire ever to see justice done, and the pain he manifestly feels from the sight of injustice." This observation came with peculiar grace from one who in such attributes was the greatest judge of the day.

It is somewhat remarkable that both Black and Watt have

suffered more than almost any who can be named from the plagiarisms of others, and their unfairness, sometimes from national, sometimes from personal prejudices. They bore this with different degrees of equanimity. Black seemed never to regard it at all; indeed he was singularly exempt from either vanity or ambition, and only cared for the progress of science, by whomsoever it was assisted, though regarding as essential to that progress the due ascertainment and positive declaration of each person's merits. I have heard him with astonishment, in bearing testimony to the great merits of Lavoisier, both as a great discoverer and generalizer of facts observed by others, and bestowing praise unstinted upon his works, without even making the least allusion to the entire suppression in them of all reference to his name as founder of the new school of chemistry, by the discovery of latent heat and permanently elastic fluids; and this after he had received, years before, letters in which Lavoisier expresses his "zealous admiration of the profound genius and discoveries which had made such revolutions in science;" and the year after, "that he had for a long time been accustomed to regard him as his master, and only lamented not having been able to convey his admiration in person, and rank himself among his disciples." When Black saw that the discovery of latent heat was distinctly claimed as Lavoisier's own, after it had for twenty years been described in the professor's lectures, and been recognized all over Europe as his discovery, he was not a little surprised at the conduct of his correspondent. These strange proceedings of Lavoisier were, as we learn from Professor Robison, only treated with a silent contempt expressed for the flattery of his letters. Fourcroy gives Black the full credit of his discoveries, and distinctly states that they had been the foundation of the new system ("Elem. de Chym.," i., 30, 40; "Syst. de Cour. Chymique," i., 28, 40).

I remember the first time I ever was in his society. When I went to take a ticket for his class, there stood upon his table a small brass instrument for weighing the guineas given. On learning who I was, he entered into conversation in a most kind manner. He said he concluded I was not a medical student, as all but two or three of the class were; among whom were Messrs. Vogt and Watenbach, of Hamburg, and M. Kœnig, of Dresden. He asked what classes I had attended, and expressed himself much pleased with what I told him of the great interest I took in mathematics and natural philosophy, recommending the study of Newton's Optics, both for the substance and the method. When I was going away he said: "You must have been surprised at my using this instrument to weigh your guineas, but it was before I knew who you were. I am obliged to weigh them when strange students come, there being a very large number who bring light guineas; so that I should be defrauded of many pounds every year if I did not act in self-defense against that class of students;" and he particularly mentioned one class, describing them.

The qualities which distinguished him as an inquirer and as a teacher followed him into all the ordinary affairs of life. He was a person whose opinions on every subject were marked by calmness and sagacity, wholly free from both passion and prejudice, while affectation was only known to him from the comedies he might have read. His temper, in all the circumstances of life, was unruffled. This was perceived in his lectures, when he had occasion to mention any narrow prejudice or any unworthy proceeding of other philosophers. One exception there certainly was, possibly the only one in his life. He seemed to have felt hurt at the objections urged by a German chemist called Meyer to his doctrine of causticity, which that person explained by supposing an acid, called by him *acidum pingue*, to be the cause of alkaline mildness. The unsparing severity of the lecture in which Black exposed the ignorance and dogmatism of this foolish reasoner can not well be forgotten by his hearers, who both wondered that so ill-matched an antagonist should have succeeded where so many crosses had failed in discomposing the sage, and observed how well fitted he was, should occasion be offered, for a kind of exertion exceedingly different from all the efforts that at other times he was wont to make.

Against this Meyer he had no prejudice of a national kind whatever. One subject of his constant praise was Magroff, whom he held up as a great example of skillful and judicious analytical investigation, and placing him greatly above Potts.

Of Bergman he had by no means a great admiration, but Magroff was less ambitious in his researches, and Bergman claimed the place of a discoverer, which Black was unwilling to allow him, appearing to join with those who pleasantly said his greatest discovery was the discovering Scheele. It is needless to add that of Scheele he had the greatest admiration. In truth he placed him at the head of all; and except Sir Isaac Newton, I do not remember any name so devoutly revered by him as Scheele's. When, a year or two after, I passed in my Swedish tour one night through Koping, where Scheele lived, though a native of Pomerania, I well remember being haunted by the recollection of Black, an account of whose death had reached me just as I was setting out for Stockholm.*

Among others who have since been distinguished, Thomas Young and George Birkbeck were my fellow-students under Black.†

Long before entering the Speculative Society, and when only somewhat trained in the young Debating Society, after little more than one session at the college, I had an opportunity of trying my voice at a great meeting, that of the Royal Medical Society, a chartered body, to which almost all the medical students, and one or two others, belonged. The meetings were weekly, and between 100 and 150 were often present, including a small number of visitors. The subjects, of course, were almost always medical, or connected with medical science, but occasionally subjects were broached which had little or no connection with it. The business consisted of one or two papers which were read, each member being required, in his turn, to give in a paper; and the whole having been read, without debate, by the secretary, a second reading took place, at any part of which all present might introduce objections or discussion on popular topics, but of a scientific description. The debate was often of considerable length, and sometimes even adjourned. The subject on which I spoke was the much-vexed question of "liberty and neces-

* Charles William Scheele, the Swedish chemist, born 1742, died 1786.

† George Birkbeck, born 1776, died 1841, chiefly known for his exertions in the establishment of Mechanics' Institutes. George Young, celebrated for deciphering the Rosetta inscription, born 1773, died 1829.

sity," and, according to my recollection, I spoke after Mr. Woolcomb, subsequently an eminent physician at Plymouth, and a man of great learning and ability, universally respected through life; but whether my contention lay with him, or others who had espoused the same side—that of "necessity" —is not in my recollection. I, however, found that, after the first alarm had abated, I had no difficulty in making my way, and my speech was far better received than it deserved; the impression made being very much owing to my youth, which appeared very clearly from my person, and might have done still more from my topics. The Logic class which I was then attending furnished many of the terms used; as, for instance, I not only charged one of my antagonists with *petitio principii*, but had the pedantry to charge another with an *idolum theatri*,* Bacon's expression for a vulgar error.

It is pretty clear that, whatever merit the delivery or composition might have, or whatever town as well as college gossip it might give rise to, the argument was far from unanswerable; for it mainly consisted in an attempt to prove that a denial of free-will was inconsistent with the foreknowledge of the Deity, whereas the necessitarian side of the question is often supposed to be more aided by that topic. In truth, there is some difficulty in this view of the question; and that is perhaps best avoided by the assumption, quite well grounded, that with Omniscience there is no such thing as before and after, all times being alike present to the infinite and eternal mind.

The success of this attempt impressed on me more than ever the necessity of care and attention in preparing for any such occasion, and the necessity of going beyond books, and even not resting satisfied with the most important study of all, as preparation for eloquence—the oratory of the ancients. It became, therefore, my constant practice to hear all the speakers and preachers who were most admired. The Court of Session always, and the General Assembly in the month of May, were accessible; and I was not only frequently taken there by my father, but also went with one or two of my companions. At that time it was impossible to enter into the par-

---

* Ειδωλον θεατρον.

ticular merits of different speakers: little more could be learned than their excellence or defects of manner, with something of the difference between oratory as read or as heard. The great speakers and preachers left a lasting impression, and from some of the most eminent I really may be said to have brought away lessons or suggestions that have been turned to account. Even thus early I profited not a little from the great leaders of the bar, and somewhat from great preachers, both masters of declamation and of pathos. From one whose eloquence was remarkable, and in pathetic passages especially, I learned a use of the voice which was thus impressed on my mind when very young, and which I have often employed in after-life—namely, of dropping the voice at particular passages, to command general attention, or enforce silence. It was from the use of this expedient that some, as Abercromby (Dunfermline), used to talk of "Brougham's whispers," alluding to my power of whispering through the House of Commons to the very door and wall. The preacher from whom I learned this had a very feeble voice, which probably suggested it to him. I certainly had not the same reason. Of the great advocates, Hope had a most powerful voice; Erskine one of great variety, but of sufficient compass; Blair a strong but inarticulate one, his manner dignified, with his matter making amends for the defects of his voice. In those days, however, it was little more than the manner that was studied and remarked.

After my return from the Continent, I was admitted an advocate early in 1800, but I had for several years before been devoting myself to the practice of public speaking; having begun this by establishing, with some of my friends, a debating society, which was founded in December, 1792. I have now before me the original minute-book, in which the first entry is as follows:

"This society was formed in December, 1792; and at the first meeting, on the 22d day of December, 1792, received the name of the Juvenile Literary Society."

Then follows a list of the members, twenty-one in number, headed by my name as founder and first president. Among the first members were Horner, Henry Mackenzie (afterwards Lord Mackenzie), John Forbes (afterwards Lord Medwyn),

James Keay, who rose high at the bar; Andrew Wauchope, who distinguished himself in the Peninsular War; and Andrew Thomson, the eloquent preacher and leader in the Church courts.

The laws were very strict. Absence without excuse, to be inquired into by a committee, was fined. Coming late, half an hour beyond the time of meeting, was also fined; and occasionally, though very rarely, expulsion was inflicted for repeated breach of the rules. The laws were sometimes revised by a committee of inquiry, and altered upon its report. At the end of the session and commencement of the six months' vacation a commission was appointed, on the model of that in the General Assembly, to look after the affairs of the society. The meetings were on Saturday morning, when there were no college classes. The members presided in rotation, and an essay was read from the chair, and submitted to criticism. The questions were put into a list, upon the report of a committee. One was given out for each meeting, and a member appointed to debate it on each side; any other afterwards taking part in the discussion. Many of the speeches were read, but sometimes an extempore debate was had on a question proposed by the president, without any notice. The politics of the day were generally excluded; but from a letter from Forbes (Lord Medwyn), addressed to the secretary in 1794, there appears to have been an apprehension of their introduction.

I see one debate was on theatrical representations being injurious to virtue, and decided in the negative by four to one. On the question whether Elizabeth was justified in putting Mary to death, I stood alone against Elizabeth, which shows that the answer I gave at Edinburgh two years ago had not been an opinion recently formed. Having attended the drawing-room given by Lady Belhaven (his grace the lord high commissioner's wife) in Holyrood House, I was taken to see the chamber in which Rizzio had been murdered, and the queen's bedroom adjoining; and on my expressing the natural feeling of horror at the assassination, and the outrage also to her feelings, with some observations upon the conduct of Elizabeth, they said, "Then of course you consider Mary as innocent of all that has been laid to her charge." I answered, "Quite the contrary; I regard her conduct in the worst light possible as regards Scotland, my only doubt being upon her share in Babington's conspiracy."

On the question whether the lawyer or the divine is more useful to society, it was given in favor of the divine, *all the lawyers voting in the majority!* That Brutus was unjustifiable in killing Cæsar, was decided in the affirmative, as I well recollect, after an excellent speech by Horner on that side of the question. "Whether the prodigal is a worse member of society than the miser;" I voted with the majority, Horner the other way. "Whether man is happier in a rude than in a civilized state;" both Horner and I voted in the minority, I grieve to say, the decision being for the civilized state. "That benevolence is a stronger principle of action than interest;" Horner voted with the majority, I with the minority.

On looking over the rules and the proceedings of this society, it is very remarkable to find the extreme regularity with which the business was conducted and the order which prevailed; so that the example of these boys might be a lesson to their seniors in other assemblies.

Such of us as were destined for the bar afterwards entered the Speculative Society, which had been long established, and had a hall and library of its own in the college. Men older than ourselves were among its active members; but of our standing were Jeffrey (though a little older), Horner, Murray, and Moncrieff, Miller, Loch, Adam, Cockburn, Jardine—and there were several students who had come from England. Of these, the most distinguished were Lord Henry Petty (afterwards Lansdowne) and Charles Kinnaird (afterwards Lord Kinnaird), Lord Webb Seymour, and somewhat later the two Grants, Glenelg, and his brother Sir Robert. Political differences ran high at that time, and there was a personal quarrel with the professors, who had accused us of French principles. There was another quarrel from an attempt to exclude William Adam, when Charles Hope (afterwards Lord President) behaved, as he always did, most honorably, and with a total disregard of political differences. Notwithstanding these impediments, great progress was made in the practice of debating, which many of us showed in after-life that we had well learned; and I remember Lord Medwyn, when he came to

London during the session of Parliament, saying that when he heard the debates he recognized his old brethren of the Speculative, as well as their speeches there.*

It is fit to mention that the great lights of the Scotch bar at this time were Erskine, Tait, and Charles Hope, as speakers; Blair and Ross, as lawyers.† Admirable as Harry Erskine was in all respects, both as an advocate and a speaker, the person who struck me most, and gave me the first conception of an orator, was Hope. I had never been in London, and had heard none of the great speakers. The effect produced on me by Hope's eloquence was beyond any thing I could previously have conceived; nor have I ever forgotten it. He was a very powerful speaker in all respects, but his declamation was of the very highest order. Even his violent political opponents confessed this. I have heard Gillies and Malcolm Laing assert, that if he had been earlier introduced into Parliament, he would have proved superior to Pitt. Gillies himself had great powers as a speaker; and for close logical argument, Cranstoun (afterwards Lord Corehouse) was never surpassed. This was the opinion of all our lawyers who heard him at the bar of the House of Lords. Peel said he was the finest speaker he had ever heard, except Pitt —which was not a very happy comparison, as no two styles of speaking could be more entirely different. Indeed, Sir William Grant was the only Parliamentary speaker of the same order as Cranstoun.

Between 1795 and 1799, I generally (as my father did not care to return to Brougham) took advantage of vacations to make *walking* tours through different parts of the Highlands. These were wild scrambling excursions, but abounding in mirth and jollity; for we were young, active, and overburdened with high spirits.

My companions generally were, my brother James, John Russell, my cousin (his mother being a daughter of Dr. Robertson), James Ferguson, and Charles Stuart, my most intimate friend (afterwards Lord Stuart de Rothsay). I kept no journal of our tours; and only recollect that we visited the

---

* See Appendix IX.

† These will be found commented on in Chapter IV.

Falls of the Clyde, Stirling, Loch Katrine and its romantic scenery, and a large portion of the Western Highlands. We must have been indefatigable walkers; for I well remember, on one occasion, Stuart and I had not only walked the feet off our stockings, but also the soles off our boots. Some charitable friend near whose house we then were, but whose name I utterly and most ungratefully forget, re-equipped us, and then we went on to Inverness. These walking expeditions were the pleasantest times of my life; for I was then working very hard, and while in Edinburgh allowed myself no relaxation. And yet this is not strictly true; for there was a set of us guilty, at occasional times, of very riotous and unseemly proceedings. After the day's work, we would adjourn to the Apollo Club, where the orgies were more of the "high jinks" than of the calm or philosophical debating order; or to Johnny Dow's, celebrated for oysters. I do believe it was there that I acquired that love for oysters which adheres to me even now; so much so, that on coming to an inn, the first question I generally ask is, Have you any oysters? But sometimes, if not generally, these nocturnal meetings had endings that in no small degree disturbed the tranquillity of the good town of Edinburgh. I can not tell how the fancy originated; but one of our constant exploits, after an evening at the Apollo, or at Johnny's, was to parade the streets of the New Town, and wrench the brass knockers off the doors, or tear out the brass handles of the bells! No such ornaments existed in the Old Town; but the New Town, lately built, abounded in sea-green doors and huge brazen devices, which were more than our youthful hands could resist. The number we tore off must have been prodigious; for I remember a large dark closet in my father's house, of which I kept the key, and which was literally *filled* with our *spolia opima.* We had no choice but to hoard them; for, it is pretty obvious, we could not exhibit or otherwise dispose of them. It was a strange fancy, and must have possessed some extraordinary fascination; for it will scarcely be credited, and yet it is true as gospel, that so late as March, 1803, when we gave a farewell banquet (I think at Fortune's Hotel) to Horner, on his leaving Edinburgh forever, to settle in London, we, accompanied by the grave and most sedate Horner (æt. 25, or, to speak quite correctly, 24 years and 7 months), sallied forth to the North Bridge, and there halted in front of Mr. Manderson the druggist's shop, where I, hoisted on the shoulders of the tallest of the company, placed myself on the top of the doorway, held on by the sign, and twisted off the enormous brazen serpent which formed the explanatory announcement of the business that was carried on within. I forget the end of the adventure, but I rather think the city guard exhibited unusual activity on that occasion, and that we had a hard run for it. Looking back to those pranks reminds me of the inexhaustible fund of spirits we possessed, and how that *capital* foundation of never-tiring energy and endless restlessness enabled some of us to work on with unfailing strength to the end of life; and even now, writing at nearly ninety years of age, I can recall those, not boys' but young men's freaks with pleasure and even exultation; yet I agree with what the old beggar Ochiltree, in the best of all Scott's novels, says, "Aye, aye—they were daft days thae, but they were a' vanity and waur."*

I remember another occasion, which, however, had none of the riotous element, but was only a piece of sober fun. There was a man called Heron—at least I think that was his name—who was addicted to writing plays—execrable stuff; and yet he contrived, through some intimacy with the theatrical people, to get one of them put upon the Edinburgh stage. I totally forget the name of the piece; but I perfectly remember going with some of my merry friends to witness the first performance. It dragged wearily through two or three acts, the audience showing unmistakable symptoms of impatience, when, at a scene representing a dinner or supper, one of the actors after giving a toast said, "What shall we drink now?" To which I, from the middle of the pit, raising my lanky figure, replied, "We'll drink good-afternoon, if you please!" The effect was electrical; not another word of the play would the audience hear; and after vain entreaties from the manager that they would permit it to proceed, the curtain fell amidst shouts that must have well-nigh been the death of the poor author.†

---

* See Appendix X.

† See Appendix XI.

Late in the summer of 1799, I joined an expedition fitted out by John Joseph Henry, an excellent and enterprising man of large fortune in Ireland, nephew of Lord Moira, who afterwards married the Duke of Leinster's daughter. He had attended the College of Glasgow under Professor Miller, and occasionally came to Edinburgh, where I became acquainted with him. Charles Stuart, who was at Glasgow under Professor Young, also knew him, and joined the expedition.* Its purpose was to visit Iceland, and examine the various objects of interest in that island. But after cruising about the Western Islands, Iona, Staffa, St. Kilda, and others, it appeared to Stuart and myself manifest that the season was too far advanced, and that the voyage to Iceland must be given up, as in fact proved to be the case. While, however, we were among the Western Isles, I wrote the following letters to my kinsman, Lord Robertson:

"Islay, August —, 1799.

"My dear Sir,—Here we are safely moored in a comfortable berth, for which we gladly exchange our *good* ship and bad cabins. You must excuse various things in this letter—want of arrangement, poverty of matter, and bad, or at least careless style. As for the egotism of the epistle, debit it all to the traveller, and to my confidence in the interest which you are pleased to take in my rambles.

"We made a much longer stay in Glasgow than I either wished or expected. Gents of £16,000 per annum are always in a hurry, and do little—always busy, and lose time. However, I believe you will agree with me in thinking *my* time neither disagreeably nor unprofitably spent when I inform you that after a pleasant visit to Stirlingshire I passed the rest of the fortnight constantly with a set of ten or twelve military men, of long standing in the army, famous for knowledge of the world, and besides, in general, men of the best abilities and temper. The evenings (if sober) were diversified by visits to the Glasgow natives, whose golden brutality served to render our private society doubly agreeable.

"We came to Greenock for the purpose of superintending

---

* See Appendix XII.

our preparations several times; but as these trips were generally made in company of the above parties, and always in the night, our amusements were not interrupted.

"On Sunday last I went aboard, and our parties continued much in the same style. I must, however, out with *tout ce qui s'est passé* before we weighed. Our adventures prior to this period would have filled a volume. The only part of them which I look back on with regret is the *bottle* department; and over this scene I shall decline leading you, because I draw a curtain over it, and you'd run a great risk of cutting yourself in the dark among the fragments of innumerable dozens of empty bottles.

"A circumstance occurred to detain us two days after we went on board, but to me its tenor was so flattering as to compensate for the delay. Several applications had been made to Government, by Lords Bute and Moira, for a protection against pressing. These were point-blank and uniformly refused. I thought of writing to Sir J. Banks, who applied, and sent me notice by return. Next post came a second letter, stating his having obtained his request at once, on putting it upon the footing which I suggested.

"The protection accordingly arrived, to our great joy; and to mine in particular, as it was inclosed to me, with a very polite letter from Mr. Secretary Nepean.

"On Tuesday we dropped down, almost becalmed. A delightful day and charming scenery made us forget the slowness of our motion; and a gentleman, with your humble servant, performed the pleasant feat of dining in the maintop. We drank freely to our success, and *superintended* a salute fired on our land friends going ashore. I can not describe, with any degree of justice to the subject, the joyful nature of this scene. All our spirits afloat, a fine vessel, good crew, prospect of a pleasant voyage in *the bush,* and good weather *in hand,* enchanting scenery and agreeable company, rendered us completely cheerful. When in this humor, our passport, etc., before described, arrived from port, to *my* great joy. As soon as the new spirit of life which this imparted had subsided, a pleasant breeze again enlivened us; and scarce had our joy become, for a second time, calm, when, turning a point, the homeward-bound West India fleet arrived in full view and full sail. The setting sun showed us such a sight as I shall never forget; and while they passed us with a salute, slowly fired, I could not help thinking that if a romance-writer had wished to select circumstances for an outset to his piece, or indeed for any part of it, his fancy might, ten to one, have never conjured up such a collection of agreeable traits as conspired to illuminate our *début* upon the sea. This you'll think mighty romantic for one who at that moment was sitting aloft with a pint tumbler of claret in one hand and a sea-biscuit in t'other; but true it is and of verity we were all sympathetically struck. As we got down towards Govan, and the Channel, I went to deck; and after viewing the luminous track of the ship's wake, sometimes from deck, sometimes in the boat hoisted for me, I retired to the cabin, where we supped in perfect harmony. I took a last walk, and then slept for an hour aloft: this put me in mind of bed, so to bed I went. Turn the leaf, and you'll find fortune beforehand with you.

"At four in the morning I awoke, and found the vessel rolling and pitching, the wind blowing, the captain swearing, and the sailors, as is usual, all abroad. Force brought them to their posts, and fear, more than shame, kept them at work. We were making for the Mull of Cantire, the doubling of which is more dreaded than twenty West India voyages. This I knew, and had prepared for, keeping myself quiet and easy, by stripping naked in my berth, and taking *towels*, etc., to bed with me. By nine the storm increased. I seemed destined, within twenty-four hours, to experience every different feeling. Now all was confusion and bustle: the captain alone was calm as I am at present. I heard his orders in the wind: as things blackened he stripped, and became, if possible, more cool, as did the men. In this posture of affairs I heard him say, 'God! there's nothing for it!' but instantly the ship righted, though the rolling continued and the sea-sickness increased, all men vomiting but myself, who had taken care to shut my eyes for half an hour at first. Next night it grew calmer, and before that we had a *hot dinner*. The greatest of my foes was a cascade of rum, the cask being beaten through our cabin window! The immediate consequence was intoxication; but this soon went off.

"Making Islay at 11 o'clock, we landed; and after a little rough *admiration*, divided into two parties; one attended Shawfield to Islay House, the other went along the coast to view the country and see a wreck lying at some distance. You may easily believe I was of the latter division. The bay in which the brig was wrecked is nine miles long, and the finest I ever saw: we only wanted a storm to complete the scene. The vessel was cast ashore last November, and is quite dry at low-water. The sailors were all busy trying for the last time to float her round a point of land to Bowmore harbor, where we were landed; and in a few hours they actually succeeded. We saw the wreck raised along by a few barrels, though her bottom is battered to pieces, and her masts cut off by the maintop and foretop. She arrived at two in the morning, and we had her captain to see us all drink. After a botanical and mineralogical walk, our appetite reminded us of dinner; so a pot was boiled in tent, and a fine live salmon being caught was introduced. After a few turns in the warm water he became quiet—'vitaque cum gemitu fugit indignata sub umbras'—either the shades below, or the shade of our awning, or the uninvited guests (*umbræ*) who flocked round us. You have no idea, sir, how good boiled salmon is. To acquire this, three things are requisite—a stormy voyage, then a rustic entertainment without knives and forks, and chiefly the utter and absolute and animated freshness of the fish. I would turn up my nose at *your* CALLER Edinburgh fish. We concluded our meal, or rather *feast*, with some fine mutton; and then, on a green bank, and in a fine evening, with our faces towards the wreck and the Irish coast, Giant's Causeway, etc., quaffed goblets of the delicious nectar of Bordeaux and the Rhine—in other words, claret and old hock from our ship. A short walk up the country sobered us completely, and we returned to the village to tea. At supper we had the heads of the town, and (*inter alios*) a man who has written wisely against tea, and still more wisely against the Newtonian theory. It is amusing to find in this remote and barbarous corner a *carle* who holds Sir Isaac in utter contempt. Next morning, after visiting the ship, we went to Islay House, where we have remained ever since, to our vast edification. Every day we have made excursions through the island, and constantly found materials for gratification and amusement. The country is fertile, and only needed cultivation, which Shawfield is giving it in great abundance. The natives are a very simple and worthy set of men, and the women either very handsome or intolerably ugly. Shawfield's family is truly agreeable, and we all live together like brothers and sisters. We have hopes of seeing Lady Charlotte herself, should our vessel be wind-bound; but though the temptation is great, our eagerness to reach the main point is still greater.

"Monday evening.

"I must now think of finishing this long letter, and shall fatigue you further by giving you some idea of our plan. It may hereafter be modified by circumstances, but the outline will most likely remain the same. You may communicate this or any other part of the present letter to our folks, just as you please and how you please. We sail to-morrow or next day; and after touching at another island, St. Kilda or the Lewis, we make direct for the Faroe Islands, and reach them probably in eight or ten days. There is as much to be seen in them as at Iceland. Thence we go (perhaps changing our vessel) to Iceland; and after travelling there about six or eight weeks, we determine whether we return by the east or west, and this must very much depend upon the state of the privateering and the facility of obtaining neutral ships to convey us. If we go by west, we take a full view in the best season of the Hebrides, Orkneys, etc., and conclude all by going to Iceland for some time—perhaps for a considerable time. If we go by east—or if, instead of making Iceland, we go from Faroe to Norway, which is possible (and which, if you see my mother uneasy, you may tell her is the plan resolved on)—then our Continental tour must occupy a longer time, as perhaps the temptations of the season may draw us to Petersburgh. This, I confess, is my wish—winter is the time for Russia and Lapland. So good-night, and a *merry Christmas!* I shall write a line from our next point of *appui.* H. B.

"Should you be from home when this arrives, I leave you to judge whether it may not be proper to drop James a few lines, informing him that I am well, etc.; but as you please.

"H. B."

"Stornoway, August 14, 1799.

"MY DEAR SIR,—I am much afraid that you begin to be tired of my letters, but I trust more to the interest you were so good as to express for our success than to any chance which my details can possibly have of amusing you or giving any important information. My last was dated from St. Kilda, but you will not receive it for six or seven weeks. It contained little or nothing, was written in a pelting hurry, and more for the sake of the joke than any thing else. We had a most favorable run from Islay. During two days and nights the wind was fair, the sky clear, the sea calm; but my enjoyments were sadly damped by a very unwelcome guest—a seasoning sickness; it lasted all that time: and about fifty hours after our departure from Islay we came in sight of St. Kilda, or Hirta—the most remote, and, I think, most singular of all the British Islands. We put off a boat with several of our party, ordering them to hail the natives, and to send out a country bark, well-manned, to carry us over the neighboring surf. They got slowly to shore, and landed with difficulty on a very rocky coast, with a heavy rolling sea. We afterwards found, by their not making signal and some other circumstances, that we were taken for a French privateer, and avoided as such, all the inhabitants preparing their all for a flight to the mountains. We in the vessel stood round, and had a full coasting view of this most singular spot and its adjoining rocks and islets. A more awful scenery you can not imagine. The grandeur of the scenery was heightened by the fineness of the day, and still more by the idea that a single puff of wind might prove fatal to us, by raising the whole fury of the Western Ocean. At last came two boats, one belonging to the place and ours besides, but both manned by the *savages*. This alarmed us: we thought that our party must be lost or taken, and the arm-chest was instantly opened; but the boats approaching, we found the natives quite pacific, and several came on board—among others their priest, without whom nothing would induce them to venture near us. The worthy man partook of our cabin cheer, and we prepared to go ashore with some provender. We found him and his compatriots in a state of ignorance truly singular: they had heard of the war with France, but knew nothing of Lord

Howe's victory, nor any subsequent event; yet the proprietor's tacksman goes there twice a year: but we were told that he carefully conceals every event from them if successful, in order to keep up their *alarms*, which, we found, he turns to good account. We were amused with this miniature of what some in the great world are accused of doing, and still more diverted with the simplicity of these savages, who can thus be duped and made to believe their wretched residence and miserable possessions a bait sufficiently alluring to the 'grande nation.' Yet so it is, that they live in as constant dread of invasion as if all the wealth of London and Liverpool were stored up in St. Kilda. About eight o'clock we set off in the St. Kildian boat with above twenty of the natives and ten of ourselves. The sea was a little threatening, so we had to keep round by west. Our crew talked most infernally, and rowed very ill. Seeing that this proceeded from laziness and loquacity, I desired the first (who alone could speak a word of English) to promise them a dram if they rowed better, and to bid them be more quiet. The effect was instantaneous, and immediately the song arose, extempore in composition and far from unmusical in execution; of course pleasing in point of effect. I lay snugly wrapped up in my boat-cloak, which I beg leave to introduce you to as the envy and admiration of our whole party. We now weathered the gigantic rocks of Borera, which surround St. Kilda to the north and north-east; and as it was past eleven, I allowed myself to be lulled asleep by the cadence of the chorus and the oars. About half-past twelve I heard a little confusion, and found the steersman quitting the helm to give place to a more experienced one. Upon looking round, a scene presented itself which beggars all description. We were roughly and rapidly rolling through such a frightful pass as you can not form any idea of. On each side huge masses of broken and impending rock stretched up to a terrible height above our heads. These were towards their bases pierced with large, dark, rough caves, into which the sea dashed with stunning noise. Around our crazy overloaded bark lay huge masses of broken rocks, which rendered our course very serpentine, and every instant the keel grazed with a heavy and petrifying noise along the sunken rocks.

"A circumstance occurred which, if you ever were at sea, must add vastly in your mind to the charms of this fine scene. Every stroke of the oars was attended with a vivid and durable stream of fire, throwing out sparks on all sides still more bright. My attention was called from this grand spectacle to the ludicrous panic-struck pickle of our worthy doctor. 'Good Lord, sir!—Oh, sir—oh, sir!' 'Well, doctor,' said I, 'here is a fine scene for you.' ''Deed, my dear sir, I fear it won't do.' 'Look at that cavern.' 'We touch the bottom!' 'Is not this light delightfully horrible?' 'Hear! hear! how we touch the sides!' 'Only see, doctor, what a noble scene—the flashing of the water, the foaming of the sea, the majesty of the rocks!' 'Oh dear! I am sure our boat can't weather it.' 'Then, doctor, the craziness of the vessel, the shallowness of the water, the horrible gulfs near us. By-the-by, don't Mr. Burke reckon terror the basis of the sublime?' 'Mr. Brougham, sir—sir, I am just looking where we shall leap out, for a last chance, when the boat is dashed to pieces!' At one o'clock, after much perilous navigation, and a vast deal of grand scenery, we opened into a fine safe bay, and in half an hour more landed. We were conducted to the town (of which more hereafter), and entered the priest's house. A more wretched hovel never sheltered beast from the storm than this; and yet it is the only thing tenantable in the island, except the tacksman's. We refreshed ourselves a little, with his wife and mother; then, your humble servant being superintendent of stores and servants (*ex officio*), repaired with his train and provisions to the other house, was surrounded by many of the savages, ordered a fire, boiled a kettle, and blessed his *own* providence in the first instance for thinking of so charming and refreshing a beverage. I always make a point of landing in full uniform. My command over the stores and servants gives me vast dignity and patronage. Besides this, a joke goes about of giving us all nicknames. One is '*Lark*;' the doctor, from his crawling after weeds, stones, and puddles, is 'Toad'; and I, from some foolish mistake or other, 'Billy Pitt.' So that from hence wherever we go I am believed to be related to that 'excellent minister.' You can not conceive, therefore, how all these items procured me respect and worship; all the island was at my nod in a second. While tea was preparing, I marshalled them thus: servants at my elbow, for aids-de-camp; provender in the rear; male natives in front; female ditto at some distance from our gentlemen—a most necessary precaution to prevent jealousy. To each native I distributed a ration of tobacco and a dram—their two greatest prizes, though neither had been in the island for two and a half years. We then drank tea and fine milk till three in the morning. Several of ours went to bed; others slumbered over the fire. I sat up with the clergyman, whom I instantly put under the *question*, and talked over on all topics (insular ones) till near five o'clock, when we sallied forth to view the island in four different parties, the priest with us. And now for the first time we had a view of the *city*. Conceive, if you can, a sort of green bosom, at a quarter of a mile's distance, with steep green mountains, and on one side with a fine bay opening into rocky scenery; at one corner the dreadful pass, which I described before, and which appeared almost as bad by daylight. The rest of the scene is all ludicrous. The green bosom is divided into 400 'rip' or fields of barley and oats and potatoes—*twenty-five feet by three*! in the centre several green tufts of grassy sod, upon heaps of loose stones—these we at last discovered to be the houses, twenty-six in number: on the hills, more such molehills, rather smaller, for cutting peats. This is the town, or city of *Hirta*, or St. Kilda. It contains 100 inhabitants; and the rest of the island is only browsed by some sheep, horses, and cows.

"The view of this village is truly *unique*. Nothing in Captain Cook's voyages comes *half* so low. The natives are savage in due proportion; the air is infected by a stench almost insupportable—a compound of rotten fish, filth of all sorts, and stinking sea-fowl. Their dress is chiefly composed of a coarse stuff made by themselves, somewhat like tartan. They wear this chiefly in trowsers and jackets, with coarse brogues, also made by themselves. They make brooches of clumsy iron rings, with pins across: these are worn by the women to tuck up their plaids. Needles coarse in proportion; thong-ropes for ascending the rocks in quest of nests and birds; fish-hooks finer than the other articles; thread and horn-spoons are the remaining manufactures of this place—infinitely coarser and more clumsy, and made in smaller quantity and less variety, than those which navigators have found in any of the Pacific islands, New Holland in the south excepted. A total want of curiosity, a stupid gaze of wonder, an excessive eagerness for spirits and tobacco, a laziness only to be conquered by the hope of the abovementioned cordials, and a beastly degree of filth, the natural consequence of this, render the St. Kildian character truly savage. To all this our people added the leading trait of furtivity of disposition. 'We were in a constant jeopardy of pocket, so nimble-fingered are the savages. Bottles, sticks, etc., etc., all were seized; but so simple-minded were the filchers that we as speedily recovered the said chattels.' My dear boat-cloak fell, among others. I went in suddenly upon the suspected house, and drawing my sword, an instantaneous tremor pervaded the house, and I was told one of the servants had got it. The servants being called, and another flourish of the sword given, the simple men of St. Kilda lifted up a board, and tremblingly gave me back the dear stray. These apparently trifling traits in the character of these poor people will, I trust, be excused, as the best mode which my hurry and confusion can leave me of conveying to you an idea of the manners of a tribe which exemplifies most remarkably the old proverb, 'One-half the world don't know how the other lives.' We made several remarks on the state of the island, and the mode of management to which it is subject. Were its extent, fertility, and population of sufficient consequence, no better method of improvement could be fallen upon than to send a school-master, and then to abolish the present iniquitous method of collecting its produce. The tacksman (whom the people think a steward) resides twice a year there, to plunder under the name of *Macleod's factor*. He pays £20 sterling only to Macleod, and makes above twice as much himself. For this purpose all the milk of cows is brought into his dairy from May-day to Michaelmas, and all the ewes' milk together for the whole year. Every second lamb-ram and every seventh ewe go to the same quarter; and this sanctified to his use under the name of a *tenth*. The rest of the rent is made up in feathers, at the rate of 3*s.* per stone, and the tacksman sells them in the Long Island for 10*s.* He is quite absolute in dispensing justice; punishes crimes by fines, and makes statutes of his own account, which are implicitly obeyed. There are no murders ever known here; and the priest told us, innocently enough, that the only adulteress in St. Kilda is the steward's dairy-maid, who comes from the Long Island. There is no money current here—nothing like barter—and the rate of assessing the rent to Macleod is the only criterion of the prices of articles. According to this we found that a fat sheep is valued at 3*s.* 6*d.*, a cow at 30*s.*, a horse at 20*s.*, barley at 16*s.* per boll, and potatoes at 3*s.* per barrel, which may contain about eight pecks. The inland parts of the island (if it can be said to have any) are as fit for grazing sheep and cattle as almost any other places in the Western Islands; and several other spots besides the one where the town is appear equally susceptible of cultivation—*i. e.*, capable of producing no light or mean crops of barley. Upon the whole, I should suppose that with crops, with cattle, and with the vast resources of sea-fowl, eggs, and fish, St. Kilda is capable of supporting a population of 1500 souls with ease. The only mortals among the present inhabitants whom we found in any degree civilized above the brutes, were the priest and his family. He comes from the Long Island, and has been here fifteen years. He is a missionary, placed here with a salary (£25 sterling) by the Society for Propagating Christian Knowledge. If in the course of your calls you ever see Mr. Kemp (who corresponds with him once in an olympiad), pray give *Mr. Lachlan M'Leod's* respects to him, and tell him that he complains grievously of his short allowance. This will make me quit of my promise to him;—to say the truth, I think he has *quite enough*, unless that it requires some bribe to keep a man in St. Kilda.

"After a cheerful breakfast on good milk, etc., etc., we heard divine service performed audibly and fluently by our host in his kitchen, his only church. An altar stood *in medio*, viz., a kettle simmering on a fire. The savages stood round, and the priest performed in a corner. He read, sang, and spoke in Gaelic, if I can judge, better in point of harmony, fluency, and attic smoothness *et ore rotundo*, than any I ever heard. I sometimes thought he was reading Homer, and reading him with justice. I find this letter has run to such an unconscionable length that I must now beg to subscribe myself your most obedient servant,*

"HENRY BROUGHAM."

"Stornoway, August 19, 1799.

"MY DEAR SIR,—Again you hear from me. Since my last letter has appeared to be worthy of your notice, any anecdotes or remarks collected here must relate to the party more than the place, and an account of Lewis would only be a repetition of what must already have been printed. My reasons for writing, then, are truly selfish—to let you know what we have done to kill time, and to give you a further sketch of our plans. Every morning we shoot grouse, hares, snipes, and deer till five o'clock, then eat the most luxurious dinners of game and fish, drinking claret, champagne, hermitage, and hock: at night we are uniformly and universally *dead* (drunk). Your humble servant being in the chair (*ex officio*), does his best, and having a good capacity enough for wine, does odd enough things. Yesterday our mess fell off—Campbell and I and two natives set in to it, and among four had twelve port-bottles: the natives and Bob being stowed away, I finished another bottle and a half of port with an old exciseman, major of the volunteers. This morning I went out and found all Stornoway in full tongue at my astonishing feat; went to the moors, walked it off, and killed a brace of hares at one discharge (keeping their skins for shoes) above a hundred yards off, and a grouse soon after still farther; and to-night we give a ball. Now for business: my friend Stuart and I separate from the party at Faroe and try Iceland; after this go abroad for twelve months, and first to Sweden, Norway, and Denmark; live cheap, and study at Upsal; then take Russia. Now, could not you give us a letter or two of recommendation, either to your own or your father's friends abroad, or the colonel's? By-the-by, don't you know Mr. Coxe? Mr. Stuart is the late Lord Bute's grandson, and the Duke of Ancaster's nephew. He could get recommendations from his friends, but (like myself) is on a concealed march till he is forced to draw.

---

* See Appendix XIII.

"If any thing in my power can atone for this trouble, name it. I believe you can not. I have moved heaven and earth to send you a *buck* and some birds, but it won't do till the cold weather.

"With great respect, HENRY BROUGHAM."

"On board the Privateer Ullapool, Sept. 1, 1799.

"MY DEAR SIR,—You are, I dare say, not a little surprised to receive another letter still from me. My excuses for this offense are now so stale that I shan't any longer trouble you with repeating them; but, worse than all this, my epistles have been so frequent to you that I am really at a loss to remember where my last was addressed from, and in consequence am in some danger of plaguing you with repetitions. Taking it, however, for granted that you left me under way, or really so far from Lewis, I proceed to inform you that the captain accuses my friend Stuart and myself of having forced him to sea in a storm against the opinion of every man in the vessel. In truth we were now grown impatient enough on every account at our various and many delays, so I believe our remonstrances had some weight with the after-cabin council—*i. e.*, the captain and his mates. We then put in to the Birken [Orkney?] Isles, and failing to make anchorage from the running of ebb tide, we stood out again and got north of the Pentland Firth, into the much-wished-for North Sea itself. In the dead of night we were in a storm indeed. The sailors all expecting to see *Dairt* in half a *shake*, and the captain (who was twenty years a North Sea smuggler, and has been twelve times and a half wrecked) crying, 'I don't know what to do! As damned a tool this ship as ever dipp'd her gob in salt brine since Adam wrought at hemp-picking in Chatham dockyard—d——n his soul!' So he applied to the *doctor*, as the oldest man on board, for his advice—but, I before told you, a terrible *muck* (coward); and he voted for instantly making nearest port. We were still keeping to our course, if possible, and if she would not lie to it, we wished to run through the Pentland—any thing, in short, rather than turn. But the rest were of a different opinion, and the helm was tried. Happily she did not miss her stays, but obeyed rudder, and with a huge grin and volley of oaths the word was given. Thither we came, and here we have been again at the flesh-pots and shooting and drinking. Before departing, I beg to trouble you with this request, '*that any letters not yet sent for me, or any which you may procure previous to the next Baltic or Elsinore ships, may be sent in a small parcel to Ramsay and Williamson's at Leith, where they will be called for by a Northern friend of ours, master of a Baltic ship, and kept by our agent in Elsinore for us till we arrive. This you may tell also to our friends;*' and any obtained after that opportunity sails, may be sent per post to Copenhagen, not to Drontheim, by *the next ships*—I mean those that sail about the 20th of September. Your favors are so numerous, and my requests so well proportioned to them, that I am almost ashamed to say that a recommendation from *Sir W. Forbes* to *Mr. Reiberg* at Copenhagen would be worth its weight in gold to us all. You might, I think, procure this through the Russells (to whom my love, as to all yours) without letting my request be known. Again excuse brevity, troublesomeness, etc., etc. HENRY BROUGHAM."

The voyage to Iceland being thus abandoned, Stuart and I left the rest of our party in Scotland, and crossed over to the east coast, arriving there in time for the Baltic autumn fleet.

After a week's voyage with fine weather, except a gale in the Cattegat, on a bad lee-shore, when the wind, contrary to all expectation, shifted and saved us, we arrived at Elsinore on the 30th of September. We passed about a week at Copenhagen, where we saw a good deal of Mr. Merry, the Chargé d'Affaires in Lord Robert Fitzgerald's absence, and spent the early part of the winter at Stockholm. I kept a journal of this tour, which is as follows.

CHAPTER III.

VISIT TO DENMARK AND SCANDINAVIA.

Journal of Visit to Denmark and Scandinavia.—Landing at Elsinore.—Travelling in Denmark.—Copenhagen.—Objects of Interest.—College Library. —Palace.—The Town and the People.—The Theatre.—The Exchange.—The Constitution of Denmark.—Social Conventionalism.—Administration of Justice.—King Christian and his Court.—Journey to Helsingborg.—Travelling in Sweden.—Danish and Swedish Peasantry compared.—Scenery.—Adventures.—Stockholm.—Architecture.—Public Places.—Jealousy of Foreigners.—Science and Letters.—Sitting of the Academy of Sciences.—Swedish Artists and their Works.—Social Condition.—Immorality and Crime.—Gustavus III. and Gustavus IV.—Personal Anecdotes of Royalty.—Russia and French Influence, and Jealousy of Britain.—The Army.—Revenue.—Trade and Currency.—Language.—Police.—Religion. —A Clairvoyant.—Departure from Stockholm to Upsala.—Country Palace of Gustavus III.—Rural Affairs.—Reindeer.—Wild Animals.—Runic Antiquities.—Upsala Cathedral.—University.—Castle.—Journey continued towards Norway.—Visit by Lantern-light to the Falls of Trollhatten.—Göteborg, or Gottenborg.—Scots Residents.—A Ghost-story.—Winter Travelling.—The Frozen Fiords.—Sledging.—Glimpses of Social Life in Frederikshald.—Private Theatricals.—Voyage home.—Narrow Escape from Shipwreck.

JOURNAL.

1799. *Sept. 24th to the 30th.*—We had a slow, but agreeable enough passage of a week. The weather was bad, particularly in the Cattegat, where we were very near a bad lee-shore with a gale: the wind shifting, almost contrary to expectation, saved us; and after beating off and on, we made the straits of the Sound early on Monday, the 30th.

At 9 o'clock A.M. we saw the coasts on both sides of the Sound—the Danish seemed finely wooded to the very shore, on which several houses were scattered. At some distance we saw the town and castle of Helsingor, Elsingor, or Elsingoer, or Elsinore, or Elsineur, or Elsinoor—for it is spelt in each of these different ways. On the opposite side is Helsingborg, a Swedish town; and in sailing up to anchorage we observed on the Danish coast a neat white house, well situated among the woods, and surrounded by gardens and terraces, apparently in the English taste. The captain called it Matilda's Palace, and at Elsinore we found it was called by Englishmen Hamlet's Palace. It is said that the murder happened in the garden. It is now occupied by a ranger of the parks.

Sept. 30.—After having a salute for our convoy from the fort, we anchored, and dressed to go ashore. In the roads there were a vast number of ships, and several Danish men-of-war; yet we were told that the anchorage is often infinitely more crowded. No less than five boats came off to us, each asking less than the former one; so that from nine dollars their demands sunk to three. We remarked also the singular similarity that seemed to prevail among the natives. I don't think that I could easily have distinguished one face from another. No sooner had we landed than we found ourselves surrounded by a mob of merchants' clerks, who lay in wait for the ship, and tried to entrap each with the cry of "My dear friend, do you clear with us?" Our captain went to Howden's, and we accompanied him, delivering our letters from Hutchins. We then went to a tolerably good inn, kept by a man who was educated at Musslebro! After an indifferent dinner, but good claret, we paid our captain the enormous sum of twenty guineas for our passage, to which we added one for the men.

Mr. Howden called before dinner, and behaved very civilly. We drank tea with him, and went to the subscription-rooms, which are large and commodious. A hundred gentlemen, chiefly merchants, pay ten dollars per annum, and have the liberty of introducing strangers. After lounging in these rooms, seeing the gardens by candle-light, and looking at some billiard-play performed by English sea-officers, we were taken by Howden and his nephew, nicknamed "Caliban," to the subscription news-rooms, where we met a company of British worthies, and had a slangish conversation, adapted to the humor of the society. Howden then turned to us, and presented a dreadful account of Paul's customs about dress, passports, and the knout. Every thing showed us that this brute of a tyrant and tyrant of brutes wishes to keep his savage empire in a state of closeness and insularity as inaccessible as that of China.

Oct. 1.—After sleeping comfortably on English beds, we had coffee in our rooms, and went out to Howden's, whose civilities in procuring us letters to Copenhagen, and letting us draw for fifty pounds, and introducing us to Fenwick, the English consul, a gentlemanly and obliging young man, pleased us much. We found all the merchants croaking over the hardness of the times—the failures in Hamburg—the impossibility of selling their bills—sugars selling with difficulty at sixty per cent. under prime cost, and the other consequences of the Dutch expedition. Mr. Howden had to lament £700 worth of bills lying dead at Hamburg, besides being obliged to pay specie to Government from clearances.

After giving order to a Scotch tailor, we set off at twelve for Copenhagen in a stuhl wagen, or oblong cart, with a couple of seats across, on springs, and one for the driver in front. The horses are large and strong: two easily drew us and our luggage all the way. The road is indeed excellent—well raised, even, and smooth. We also took with us for half the way a ship's captain, at Howden's recommendation; and for the rest of it a young man who begged our permission. The day was damp, and rainy at intervals. The face of the country is delightful—disposed in ridges and flats, with clumps of fine trees, and some very thick woods. The cottages are situated in the most romantic spots imaginable; and were it not for the appearance of the houses, whose roofs are very upright and in several planes, and whose walls are studded with windows, one might suppose himself in the southern parts of England. The dress of the peasants is grotesque, and varies every league. It consists in general of a long wide doublet, usually red and laced; a waistcoat down to the knees, and leather breeches. The coat and vest are covered with a profusion of silver buttons, which constitute, in some measure, the peasant's wealth. We saw some ploughing in very broad ridges—the plough like the common English ones, only that some had two large wheels in front. The ground seemed rich and soft, and we saw some fields of grass, heavily manured, which in England would not be touched.

The mile-stones are large stone obelisks at every quarter

of a mile—that is, at every *English* mile. On the top part is a large crown, with the cipher of the king in whose reign it was raised, and with several ornaments. The business part of it—namely, the *number*, seems scarce attended to. We passed several gentlemen's houses, not remarkable, and also some manufactories, particularly a cotton-mill three stories high, with seven windows in a row, and a reservoir behind. We saw no river, few streams, and, of course, many windmills. The road, which scarcely makes any turn, runs beautifully through thick woods, and sometimes through a variety of moorish and wild ground, in which we saw one or two deer. The game-laws are very strict, and almost all the country is monopolized by the Crown. We arrived at Hirscholm at three o'clock, and as we were past the hour of dinner, we could only get cold things to eat. We had very good light Rhenish, which only cost three marks and a half. The landlord talked good French, and the inn was really a very good one. The village is neatly scattered among trees and water. Near it we passed the palace—a fine building, with coppice and gardens laid out by Queen Matilda, in the English taste. Near this lives Count Horn, the accomplice of Ankerstroëm: he is quite cut at Copenhagen, and tried in vain to get into society at Elsinore.

As we approached Copenhagen, the country got more open. About four miles from it, we passed the palace and fine gardens of Prince Carl. After a heavy rain, came in sight of the town. Saw the palace on the right; at the gates underwent a most strict examination of our baggage. The road comes to a point before arriving at the gate, where the different avenues break off, each planted with rows of trees. The ramparts are large, but out of repair. Coming to Rouch's Hotel, in the Great Place, were refused admittance. Same at Lubell's and Miller's; with a *laquais de place's* assistance got into Leoft's. All the people here ignorant of every language but their own, except a child who had been born in London. The landlady being at the play, we could get no supper till she came home; and then it was very bad.

Oct. 2.—Walked with our *laquais de place* to pay visits, having sent our letters. Only found Brown at home, but overwhelmed with business. Dined at Rouch's. Mr. Merry, the Chargé d'Affaires in Lord Robert Fitzgerald's absence, called in the evening, also Howden, who was croaking like an old frog, and read more Hamburg failures from his note-book; but he joined in Merry's tune of its being so much the better, as it must hurt the enemy.

Oct. 3.—Dined at Lubell's. Mitchell, the English consul in Norway, was there—a violent Ministerialist, and great advocate for the late King of Sweden, of whom he talked much. Said he was in a coffee-house in Stockholm at the time of the revolution.

Oct. 4.—Saw Thorkelin, who behaved in a very easy and agreeable manner to us, and showed us every civility, taking us about to the college and library. He is keeper of the archives, which he showed us all over, and told me, at the same time, to conceal it, as I was the first foreigner who had seen them.* There is a vast collection of treaties, well arranged and preserved: the principal ones which I looked over were those with Cromwell in 1651—Elizabeth—Joseph II.—Peter the Great; the Danish Corpus Juris, beautifully written in 1681; the Danish Magna Charta in forty articles, and on ten folio pages, dated 4th November, 1665; the famous Act of Cession, dated January same year, carefully wrapt up, wrote on two pages folio, with signatures on above twelve—sixty names and seals on each page, being the *tiers état.* To the charter is fixed a superb gold seal. Thorkelin, on our putting several questions to him, told me that we must not mention what he said, if we published our journals, and added that Coxe's imprudence had made every one cautious of speaking to strangers, and even of receiving them.†

The town stands on a flat upon the sea, which intersects it in several places, and has almost everywhere a stagnant and dirty appearance. The streets are in general narrow but even, and the houses high. The roofs being perpendicular, and in several planes, give them an ugly look. The

* Grim Jonnson Thorkelin, a celebrated Scandinavian archæologist, a native of Iceland. At the period of the visit he was well known in society in Britain, having spent several years in this country pursuing researches into the connection between the Scandinavian nations and the British Islands.

† In allusion to "Travels into Poland, Russia, Sweden, and Denmark," by Archdeacon Coxe.

single buildings, such as inns, offices, and chateaus, are very large and handsome, though built without any form except the oblong, and abounding too much in windows. The best part of the town is the Great Place, or market, in which is the theatre, opera-house, guard-house, and two very fine inns. But the finest building, of course, is the palace, which stands in another part of the city on a port of the sea. This, however, like the rest of the town, has suffered from the fire of 1795, of which one finds traces in every part. The streets are filled with rubbish. Every other house is building, and scaffolding is as common as walls. The consequence of this has been that few have sufficient capital to build. Lodging is extremely scarce. Mr. Merry could find none at first by any means, and even yet has got very miserable rooms, in which he is not settled. There are several *table d'hôtes*, but only two of any reputation. Rouch's we found to be a mere scramble, and frequented by indifferent people. Lubell's is more select and regular, being in the nature of a private dinner, at which the landlord and his family appear; but the eating was bad. There is also a club, or private society of merchants and others, which we were not present at.

The palace is a noble building, though at present nothing but the walls remain in the quadrangle; the inside is burnt or pulled down in consequence of the fire, which seemed to have attacked one side chiefly, as there the freestone facing is completely torn off from the brick of which the walls are built. The great quadrangle is five stories high (including the small ones between), and twenty-five windows in front. On each side is a circular sweep, and each sweep terminates in a circular wing, the whole ending in a noble gateway, to which an elegant bridge and street leads. The wings or sweeps have ninety windows in the row! The ornaments, which in general remain entire, are handsome. The style of architecture mixed—chiefly Ionic. In the rooms of the quadrangle poor families live, having built huts against the walls, and two of the front windows of the palace are filled up with the casement windows of these houses. In the front is a Latin inscription, bearing that the palace was built by Christian VI., in seven years, ending 1740.

The climate of Copenhagen is unhealthy. No one is to be

seen with a decent set of teeth or good eyes—either quite rotten or "sesquipedales." The people are fair and watery-looking. The streets uncommonly dirty; the mud has a putrid smell. The winters are so severe sometimes that Lord R. Fitzgerald told Mr. Merry he has heard them firing at deserters running across the ice to Sweden. The stoves in the rooms are iron, and not only look gloomy, but exhale a most odious smell, and are besides unwholesome. The diseases most frequent are gout and rheumatism, owing to the extreme dampness which prevails, except during frost.

The only public amusement here is a play three times a week. The theatre is about the size of old Drury—heavy, but rather grand. The ornaments are gilt upon an olive ground, which is the prevailing color. The house is dark, the light being all thrown upon the stage during the performance. There are only twenty lamps; eight more are let down from the roof over the pit between the acts. The band is good—about thirty performers. The acting appeared good and chaste. The people seemed critically inclined. They were in morning dresses, and sat as stiff as pokers: no flirtation nor gallantry. The play was, "She Stoops to Conquer;" and Tony Lumpkin was well done, though the song was omitted. The scenery was bad, but a ballet was given at the end, with some good dancing, and the dresses would have put the Bishop of Durham into fits.

The Exchange is an old building in the mixed Gothic style. The inside is filled with shops, through which are walks, and a reservoir at one end. Auctions are held in the corners. It was always crowded, and we saw in it several Polish Jews.

The University is an old and shabby quadrangle. We were present at an examination of the students, who were very mean-looking, and seemed to be questioned by the master, who sat in his chair, like boys at school. There are eighteen professors, the richest of whom have from 1500 to 3000 rix-dollars a year. The Royal Library is a noble institution. It contains about 25,000 volumes, and is unlimited for new purchases: it is kept in a fine suite of apartments in a wing of the palace. Two of these are called "*Bibliotheca Septentrionalis.*" There is a public reading-room, and every one may take home books with him. We looked over several of these, and found all sorts of works, some remarkably splendid. There is also a Royal Museum, but this we did not see.

The style of society was pronounced by Merry to be insufferable; and though we found reason to believe that he had exaggerated a little (from the nature of his situation), yet so dull is the place that the Russian general, Knox, who passed through lately on his way to Holland, staid only three days in Copenhagen, and a month at Elsinore. The visiting is confined to winter: in summer the merchants go to the country houses and boxes, and even in winter the parties are said to be dull: the Court is uncommonly so. At present the only ministers are the Russian, French, Dutch, and Swedish, all of whom live exceedingly private.

The government of Denmark is absolute, as every one knows. The Act of 1645, which made the crown elective, was abolished, and in 1665 the crown was made hereditary, and unlimited in power. The former Act being abolished, Dr. Thorkelin mentioned to me that no mention is made in it of the comparison with the government of our state; but I suspect he misunderstood my question. It has, indeed, every appearance of a despotic government. There are no states acknowledged, no control on the king's power. He names the privy council, who do all in his name. He levies taxes, makes peace and war, publishes edicts, alters, annuls, and makes laws. The titles are Graf, or Count, and Baron. But court employments or other great offices conferred by the crown constitute the great and almost the only difference of rank and station. These offices, it is true, are only given to such as are noble; but then letters of nobility are easily obtained. Thus the merchants who have made money become noble, and hold places. Mr. Selby is in this way a baron, and Mr. de Kônig is besides a councillor of state. The mercantile influence is very extensive, though Merry seemed to attribute a good deal more to it than was due. Certainly a government so much in want of money must depend much on the moneyed men; but how far these have a direct influence is another matter. However, Mr. Merry mentioned a circumstance which, if true, must prove that influence to be very great indeed. He said "that he was astonished at finding so many people employed secretly in trade; that every day he made discoveries of this kind; and he scrupled not to affirm that almost every body in Copenhagen was more or less concerned in commerce. The ostensible merchants who have the trade in their hands are few in number, and have the ear of the Court." Mr. Otto, on the other hand, seemed to laugh at Mr. Merry for ascribing *by his behavior* so much to his (Mr. Otto's) brethren; he said that Merry was constantly running up and down, and crying, "Why don't you join the coalition?" All these merchants are enemies to the present war—talk without scruple against England—and are peculiarly irritated by the Dutch expedition. Nothing can make them join but our success in Holland: while matters are doubtful, they keep on the safe side, and remain as they are. The Government is very poor. Last spring, when Hamburg was threatened, four frigates were equipped for the defense of Altona and Holstein. A fuss was made about a tax for this. The impost on land had been raised formerly, and was changed. Merry did not know exactly how it was raised; but, after all, it did not produce £200,000. This he finds from documents among the ambassador's papers. Notwithstanding the long peace which the country has enjoyed, yet there is little specie in it; what one sees is miserably adulterated with copper; but, except some small money, nearly all the currency is paper.

The want of states and other causes must render the Crown, in case of war, utterly dependent either on the rich merchants or foreign subsidies. The administration of this Government, execrable as is its theory, is in practice mild and gentle. Every liberty of speech and writing is practised, to a degree of licentiousness unknown in England, or known only to be severely punished. Of this the natives seem perfectly conscious, and laugh at English *liberty*, which they call a mere name. Two days before we were there, an instance of the Crown's power occurred. The press had grown so scandalously licentious, and even libellous, that an edict was published September 28th. This was, however, occasioned (in reality) by an advertisement appearing from a set of Jacobins, rather of the lower kind, who used to frequent Grouvelle's (the French minister's) house. It proposed that a literary society was to be formed, which was known to have politics in view. Paul instantly withdrew his envoy, and forbade in the strictest way all communication between the two countries. The edict was instantly drawn up and hurried through the council, then sent off by Baron Blum to St. Petersburg. It sets forth in a long preamble the evils of licentiousness, prohibits under the highest penalties expression against government or monarchy in general, and in fact destroys at once the liberty of speech and writing; but as every one knows that it is done to serve an end, people openly turn up their noses at it. Meantime a prosecution has been entered into against the editor of an obnoxious journal, but he is expected to get off, or at most to pay a trifling fine.

The criminal jurisprudence is mild in the extreme. There are, indeed, no juries, but the judges proceed with the greatest caution and inquire into the circumstances in the minutest manner possible. The sentence is not valid till ratified by the king, who can not make it more severe. Sedition is punished by imprisonment or a gentle fine. *Murder* and *treason* only are capital: the former happens not once in two years; the latter not since the time of Struensee, who was universally esteemed the victim of a party, and all the world sided with Matilda. For other offenses, the punishment is confinement with labor, and wearing chains. One sees several of these half-prisoners walking about in Copenhagen. The Danes think it does good in the way of example, a thing which admits of doubt in this case.

There are two courts of justice: one civil, called the Under Court, which is private, and does all business in writing; the other is open, and takes cognizance of criminals. The taxes are well levied, and easily for the people; they amount to one and a half millions a year, which does not come to more than 1*s.* in £20 at a medium, chiefly on consumption.

The army is beyond proportion: they call it about 70,000, but I believe the Government would find it difficult to produce a disposable force of 30,000. The pay is two skellings and a half per day, but the soldiers work for themselves, and have two reviews a year. They are no terror to the people, who indeed seem to care little either for the army or *noblesse.*

The fleet consists of about forty sail of the line, which lie in a very convenient dock in Copenhagen; but we did not go to see them.

The King of Denmark is an *idiot.* Dr. Thorkelin, however, talked mysteriously on the subject, and seemed to think that the ruling party kept his majesty *down* by this accusation. Mr. Merry said that ambassadors, etc., have to be drilled, as it were, beforehand, when they go into his presence, in case of his exposing himself. Lord Robert Fitzgerald used frequently to play at cards with him, and said he used to run out of the room suddenly and without cause. If any one answered him he was apt to be outrageous, sometimes spit in people's faces and boxed their ears. His own family never answered him. Mr. Otto told me an odd anecdote of him. A favorite of his had been removed by the influence of the Court, on which there was sent him, to light his fire, a common porter; him he created *a lord of the bedchamber*, and the man had to get a considerable pension to induce him to retire! Mrs. Howden saw him one day come to the garden wall, near the palace. He leaped over; but being told there was a gate near, he leaped back again and entered by it! In short, he is humored in every thing, and appears to be in truth an idiot.

In the mean time the queen-dowager and crown prince manage every thing. Count Schonneny, the finance minister, is said to be the most powerful of the ministry; but Selby (at Stockholm) told me that Bernstoff (the son of the great minister), who is only thirty, and a very able man, is in great influence. I rather believe, however, that he is only the organ of the Council. Indeed it matters not what he is at present, as the crown prince is to all intents and purposes prime-minister. The king signs his name and appears at court; he is, however, a mere puppet. The prince's brother is not in favor, and, I understand, does not appear at court.

The ambassador Grouvelle (who read the sentence to Louis XVI.) lives very retired.* I see, however, that he is popular among the prevailing powers, the merchants. I have heard young Selby excuse him by making him say that "if people knew all the circumstances they would not blame him so much." The Dutch minister also is popular. Lord Rob-

* Grouvelle, frequently mentioned in the "Moniteur" as "littérateur et diplomate," was sent as ambassador from the Republic to Denmark in 1713.

ert Fitzgerald is violent against both, and withdrew his name from the society at Rouch's. When Grouvelle came he handsomely retired; but as the others did not, the matter remains. Both the French and Dutch ministers were received at the society with open arms.

We were told at Elsinore that people were of late grown much less violent on politics, merely from being tired of talking so much on the subject.

Lord Robert Fitzgerald is apparently on *congé;* but his house and effects being sold, and Mr. Merry being settled here as consul-general and chargé d'affaires, he is now known to have retired for good till elsewhere provided for. He had been three years here, and his departure was supposed to be owing to a publication in the English papers relative to the Danish East India Company. It is evident that he was not used in the best manner possible at Copenhagen. Mr. Merry calls the literary men here "a set of the greatest Jacobins on the face of the earth."

Upon the whole, it appears that the mercantile government of Denmark is afraid of joining the coalition on two accounts; first, because its commerce is sure of suffering in the first instance; and, secondly, because the consequence must be an immediate increase of expense, which in its present situation it could not meet. What service it could render the common cause, even though it could be induced to take a side, I can not conceive. It must be subsidized by England for very indifferent troops, and for any assistance, which, in the present state of men's minds in Denmark, could not be hearty. At the same time the country seems quite in the hands of Russia and of England, so that the strictest neutrality is necessary.*

Oct. 5.—After writing letters and cursing the fleecing habits of this place, we set off to Elsinore in a decent covered carriage. Saw nothing worth notice on our way, except the corpse of a woman who had been drowned; it lay on the roadside, without attracting the least attention. After stopping for coffee at Hirschholm, got to Elsinore at ten, the night being very fine and starry, and went to the club, where

* See Appendix XIV.

we found the natives uncommon civil. Received more attention from Mr. Howden.

Oct. 6.—Early in the morning we got ready—by docking (of course) our tailor's bill—breakfasted with Mrs. Howden, who resembles much the Queen of Sweden. The quay as usual, for the Elsinorers keep no Sabbath. Had a pleasant passage to Helsingborg, a Danish mile over. It is a neat enough town, airily situated, and built wide. The inn is very bad: a villainous landlord, who had been two years at Sunderland. He has wagons of all sorts for sale, as people on leaving Sweden generally sell their travelling carriage; for these he asks the most extravagant prices, and I believe is generally sure of selling you, as people are not a little in his hands. For a very shabby uncovered one we paid thirty rix-dollars, and, after having it covered, could only sell it at Stockholm for ten! Our stay here was spent in running up and down after carriages and horses, and specie—for which we paid a premium of nearly five per cent. Near Helsingborg are the springs of mineral-water to which the Swedes resort every summer from Stockholm, and the town is said at this time to be very gay. After a bad dinner and much imposition, we set out. The road was good and smooth, so we drove pleasantly enough with one horse, the country generally flat, though rising here and there; a little cultivated. Saw some hay in stacks, but it seemed very indifferent. Some wood, however, was well scattered over the country; the rest appeared very marshy and damp. We met many carts of the peasants in different forms, all as simple as can be imagined, carrying casks, tubs, and boxes of wood and iron, made up the country. They were driven by peasants who put us in mind of gypsies. Many of the carts were drawn by oxen, and some by cows.

We got to Astorp after a chilly drive. It is a small hamlet of wood, pleasantly enough situated; indeed all the Swedish hamlets are romantic in the extreme. We were struck by the great difference between the peasantry here and in the places near to Denmark. We had tea, and dispatched the forebote, or *courrier en avant,* carrying our baggage, to travel all night, after having the *sedel,* a paper of instructions, written by a *learned* peasant, the only one in the parish. Had Swedish beds—that is, lay between two.

Oct. 7.—Got off between five and six to follow the forebote. The country as before—the roads also good. Met scores of natives, and cars of iron, wood boxes, etc. Saw some parties at breakfast on the road. Crossed a shallow lake, as all in this place are: the car drove into a large flat boat without our dismounting. Came to a more wild and rough country—also more woody—all natural. The houses are all wooden, the fires also. They are open, and set in a wide chimney at the corner of the room; a damper is let down as soon as the room is sufficiently warm. They use pine laths for candles, holding the light downward. Candles they also have, but exceeding small and very bad.

We went pleasantly on, sometimes taking two horses. The road winds through a variety of woods, some of them very thick. The trees are of different sorts, some firs; but the finest and most plentiful are oaks and beech, besides birch, aspen, nut, and alder. We saw also many heathberries, some cranberries, and a vast abundance of sloes; also *Osmunda regalis.* The cattle were chiefly pigs, running in the woods, and very lean, of course: cows and horses small, but fleet. We went on very quick, only stopping at the inns to get a crust of bread or an apple. At Markavid met a student of Lund (in Scania) who spoke German and French. After Markavid, saw many lakes among thick woods: these were universally very shallow, from the gentle slope of their sides and their general appearance. They had many islands, also wooded. We met several travellers. They rode, wrapped in surtouts, in open carriages holding one (sometimes two), driven by servant or self, and always smoking. At Travyd we got late. The driver had stopped to tie his spare horse to a tree before getting in sight of the next inn, a trick often played to save taking another spare horse next stage. Found the people here very civil, and got some sour milk and cold potatoes. The night cold, and a little rainy. Rode by a pretty large river to Hamnade, where by mistake the forebote had stopped, so we had to stop here. A miserable place. Coffee got, after much surprise at first, and honey for sweeting. Slept in one wretched bed, taking the precaution of showing pistols, and we afterwards found this was not unnecessary. On paying next morning the man made a charge for water!

Oct. 8.—A very wet day, at times raining very hard. The road lay over an open green turf all the first stage, and near the river. At Lingby found a Swedish servant who spoke good English. We breakfasted on blood-puddings, eggs, and milk. Next stage, two miles (Swedish), at a foot's pace, owing to the sulkiness of the driver: pouring the whole time, and no wood to shelter us, so got completely wet. Coasted a very large lake for two miles and a half without coming to the end of it. In the middle several islets; one large, with wood and houses on it. The houses in this part of the country are very neat, both outside and inside, and intermixed every now and then with church spires, constructed in a most fantastical manner of wooden billets representing tiles, which gave the landscape a very singular and romantic appearance. Passed what appeared to be a large shallow lake, with several houses scattered over it; but it proved to be only the overflowing of a river which runs through this valley. At Waramow found a good enough inn, compared to what we had been used to of late. Though it was now late, yet we resolved to go on. The road lay through impenetrable forests, and was so bad we could scarcely crawl along: it was perfectly dark, and we got shook to pieces, yet I slept through the greater part. From the next post we took the way by a shorter cut through a wood into the great road, which also lay the whole of the way through forests of pine, broken only here and there by an acre of land cleared, with a cottage on it. At midnight we came to a green break in the wood, where the inn of Skylingaryd stands. It was snug, and most agreeable to us: we had some potatoes, milk, and ham, with our own tea, a couple of good beds, and a fire, so that I feel myself rather comfortable while writing this, though I have more than half the journey before me; and so I shall proceed to note down a few observations on the country through which we have passed, the wildest and most unfrequented in the south of Sweden. The manners of the natives are the same nearly through this quarter—I mean through Skamaand and the greater part of Småland, towards Jonkopyichage.

1. The difference is striking between Elsinore and Helsingborg, the opposite side of the Sound. The peasantry, from the moment you enter Sweden, have a much finer appearance than the Danes. Their countenances more healthy, and without that watery white look which is so disgusting in Denmark. Neither have they that uniformity so remarkable among the Danes. They are much more agreeable in their manners, and, with the exception of the inn-keepers and people concerned on the roads, more honest.

2. Their dress is plain; none of those absurd ornaments before described are to be seen here. Their clothes are large and comfortable—of a warm woollen in summer, and sheepskin in winter. In Scania (province on the southern coast) we observed they were chiefly white; after that we came among blue: the poorest boys who drove us had good clothing, and stockings and shoes. At work they use wooden shoes, but we saw them always with leather when unemployed.

3. Their houses are all good and clean—magnificent, compared to those of the English peasantry, and much better than the Danish. They are built of logs, with white plastered chimneys and windows. They are generally painted red, and either thatched or covered with timber planks; and to preserve them from wet, they are raised on four small pillars of stone, sometimes of wood; sometimes, in the better sort, a dwarf wall is built a few feet up.

Almost every house, if it has offices, has a large may-pole; in many places parts of the flowers remain, and often a weather-index is placed at the top. The fires (of wood) are lit in a large stone chimney, opening into the room, in the corner. The damper is generally a movable plank, tied to a string which is pulled and fixed to a nail by the chimney, and as soon as the fire is *half* burnt out it is let down. In many houses the damper is fixed on a pole, which moves round on a prop between two uprights, and is pulled up or let down by another pole. All this is on the outside, and has a singular appearance enough. The consequences of letting down the damper too soon are often dangerous, both in these houses and the ones heated by stoves.

4. The food of the peasants is chiefly a soup of gruel made of meal, beans, peas, and turnips chopped small; to this meat is sometimes added. But oftener their food is hog-puddings, either made of the blood or of meat and the inside, like a haggis. They don't seem to feed so much on the flesh, at least the peasants and servants; they eat a great deal of cold boiled potatoes and boiled milk. Their bread is of rye and barley, made either in hard cakes or in thin flat loaves, with a hole in a middle for hanging them up. They are baked twice a year, but keep quite well, and the beams in the roof of the houses are studded with them; they have them also thick, but not for keeping, They preserve blueberries and cranberries for sauce, and stew apples and pears. Their meal is very good, and they use it for porridge. They make a drink of warm milk, of which they are very fond; and the better people use beer and eggs. Their *brandwein* is extremely fiery, and resembles gin or whisky; but they can make it very good, and season it with seeds; this the better sort of people drink in Stockholm. On the whole, the peasantry live more comfortably in every respect than in England.

5. They all work in iron and wood; in the former clumsily enough, in the latter very neatly: they use the adze for every thing. They make neat boxes, and vats of a large size, hooped and tipped with iron. These we met in whole caravans on the road, and the boxes often filled with cheeses, all going to fair and market.

6. The number of lakes is very striking, but still more so farther to the north. We saw few rocks the first two days, but the third we found great blocks here and there among the woods. The country was in general flat during all these days, and seems favorable to inland navigation.

7. The roads are excellent; they are made of gravel, and kept up by the proprietors through whose ground they run. Everywhere we saw stuck up by the roadside something written, which we afterwards found to be the name of the peasants or proprietors who were bound to keep that part of the road in repair; so that the governor or road-surveyor can challenge the faulty person at any time. The consequence of the goodness of the roads is, that the least roughness or steepness, which in England would be disregarded, is here deemed

impassable, and the least rising of ground is labored up as if it were a steep hill. The horses are very tractable, and easily driven: the peasants drive very skillfully, but crawl up the least rising, and then go down at full gallop as soon as they reach the top.

8. The peasants are obliged to find horses, and both they and the inn-keepers are under the strictest *nominal* discipline. If a *holcar* (man who gives the horses) asks drink-money, he is to receive so many lashes; if an inn-keeper imposes on the journey, he is to get lashes; more for the next, and, for the third offense, he is to be sent a slave to a fortress. Like all severe regulations, these are never enforced. Yet there is a book printed which has these regulations at the beginning, and is distributed to every inn, with blanks for the name of the passenger, the date, hour of his arrival and departure, number of horses, where from and whither going, also for his complaints against the people, and theirs against him. Once a month the surveyor examines this; but we observed that, except in the remote provinces, the people did not seem to care about it. The price is eight skellings (eight pence) a Swedish mile per horse, of which ten make a degree, or near seven English. They drive, and seldom ride, their horses.

9. In these southern parts we saw chiefly growing rye, barley, beans, and a few peas and oats. They dry these grains in three ways. That which we saw in the south was simple enough: it consisted in piling up the sheaves loose upon long poles stuck through them; these are scattered round the house or barn, and have a singular enough appearance. Another method is that of placing three sheaves triangularly, leaning against each other at the top; on this they placed a fourth, tied tight at its upper end, diverging over on the others like a beehive, so that the rain runs off as if it had been thatched. The third is chiefly used in Finland: a barn is built of three floors, with a division in the middle for threshing and laying out the grain; on the ground-floor, on each side, is built a large oven of stone, reaching up a few feet into the second; it is lighted and made quite hot, while the wet grain is laid loosely on the floors. Nobody can enter it for some time after it has cooled, but it dries effectively. All this we heard afterwards.

10. The agriculture of the south, where we have passed, seems backward. The fields slope often to the very middle, and the furrows are so broad that they seem in most cases merely intended for footways or divisions: when they are meant for drains, they are often laid in the most injudicious way possible, sloping and slanting across the rising. The plough had one handle, and was in some respects good enough: they chiefly use oxen.

11. The fences of the first kind in Scania are very good, and indeed peculiar to the country. They are composed of every sort of wood easily raised; turn a corner, or mount and descend again with equal facility. They appear so frail that no beast will attempt climbing over, and are too high to be leaped. They are easily repaired.

12. The mile-stones are more simple and useful than the Danish, and quite conspicuous: a pile of stone roughly hewn and neatly put up, on the top a flat iron plate or stone with the number of miles; but these are confused in one respect, that they don't all count from town to town, but often from mile to mile.

Oct. 9.—Our journey had been through forests, only interrupted here and there by pieces of cultivated plain, and occasionally great masses of rock, the inns being generally bad. At one of them we had our pistols broken, and one of them stolen. The excuse was that they had been left out, and that there were many passengers beside ourselves. But as our writing-desks and the rest of our luggage had been in our bedrooms, and we never absent except for half an hour while our supper was getting ready, and while we were in the kitchen to hurry them with it, we therefore never thought of examining desks or luggage, and only found next day (October 10), on our arrival at Jönköping (a singular-looking town half fortified on the Wettern Sea), that our desks had been opened and the greater part of the money taken. October 10 was spent in going to the judge to have a proclamation published, offering a reward through all the churches, and in our writing to Copenhagen to have the bills which had been taken stopped; so we did not leave Jönköping till eleven at night. Our carriage having now got a canvas covering on it, we resolved to travel all night as soon as a driver could be found; and in the state of our broken arms, we were comforted by being told that a Jew had been robbed and murdered not far from the town. We concluded it would not be very cold, from having killed a viper on the road as we came. Nevertheless, after a little travelling, it grew bitter cold, and we could only go at a foot-pace, the horses being knocked up. I, of course, fell asleep, and my dreams experienced a singular change as soon as the cold and the breeze began. I first thought I was on board a ship in a piercing wind, and tried in vain to get into the cabin below. I awoke for a minute or two, and again was asleep. But now I was walking on the pier of Leith in a cold day. Then I was in rooms where there was no fire, and all the windows open, so that the wind blew through one's very body. I again woke, but soon slumbered again, and then I was near a blacksmith's forge, and going in for the warmth of the fire. The bellows were turned against me and blew cold wind, and then, unable to struggle longer against the elements, I gave up all further attempts to sleep.

Oct. 11.—Arrived at the end of the stage, we had to wait till half-past eight, and then proceeded pleasantly enough, the day fine, and the road showing a charming view of the lake—the banks woody, and also very rocky. On this day the country was well cultivated, often indeed very rich; barley, oats, rye, flax, and young wheat. Some places had been thickly wooded, but cleared now; the roads remarkably bad. On the road to Uncta met great crowds of market people, some well-dressed, substantial-looking farmers. At Uncta found a crowd, all drunken and smoking; the scene was odd enough. We then rode on, in a charming moonlight, through a cultivated country to Esta, where we had to wait till half-past twelve, and then to Mölby. During the intervals of sleep, consoled ourselves with the idea of comfort there, as it is the best inn on the road. At three we arrived, after the variety of a horse restive and running away, but met with grievous disappointment, owing to the people absolutely refusing us any grog whatever. The kitchen had a fiery furnace lit for baking. In about an hour and a half a dozen damsels turned out of one bed in the corner. We found that the house was brimful of a General Quilfelt and suite from Stralsund. After much waiting, got some of our own tea made. The suite were soon all astir to set out about four. Stuart went to one of their beds, while I bullied, and made tea by main force; then had a long conversation with the general, whom I found very gentlemanly.

We dispatched a forebote, and ordered our horses at nine to Shrobick, where we expected to meet the general again to-morrow night—I ought to say to-night, as I am writing between four and five, just going to bed in one of the aid-de-camp's nests.

Oct. 12.—After napping in the nest, scarce cold from the aid-de-camp's carcass, got up at eight, and breakfast being discussed, remarked the odiousness of the hogs here: they perform the office of scavengers *orally.* Stuart was literally hunted by them. Mölby is situated on a quick-running river of considerable size, on which are a great number of mills; indeed no room is wasted, the rocks in the river being joined to the bridge over it by a small lateral passage, all of wood, and mills constructed on the same: from this number of mills the town receives its name. We set out to follow our forebote, and travelled slowly (the roads being very heavy) through a flat, cleared, and cultivated country: the remarkable feature of rocks continued in the flattest ground. All this day it struck us much that, instead of being abrupt and high masses, as before, these had gradually become low and smooth, appearing in single patches in the middle of the fields.

Here and there were seen also some more abrupt and rugged blocks, chiefly among clumps of trees. At the first inn we came to, were kept two hours for horses. Drove on very quick, through fine woods. Passed a plain where a few works were thrown up. Supped at a place for exercising artillery and reviewing. Came to Lynköping, a pretty large town with some good houses in it, and one or two large public buildings. By the merest chance in the world found our luggage, the forebote having stopped. Met a very civil young man (Mr. Wenman) who was stopping here in his way to England. He had been there for two years, and spoke English; was very civil indeed in getting rooms. We set off, leaving Ned to follow with the baggage when horses should be got. The country again fertile. The roads this stage were under repair. Every twenty or thirty yards we saw the country carts unloading, which they do by taking off one side. They don't put any bottom, so that the roads are very soft in damp weather. When the road is much broke in woody country they throw in pieces of wood, and sometimes we saw ledges of plank at the side for the water. At Thumble we arrived by moonlight, and had a bad supper of eels, and pig, and milk. Such a devil of a landlady I never saw. Were joined by some travellers to Carlscrona, who rode on with us to our next stage. Ned coming up, we continued—I driving for pleasure, as the night was charming and mild. Every half English mile, a lake—woods now and then—several gentlemen's seats—a village or two—passed also a few rivers. At Brink got cattle immediately; indeed we afterwards learned that General L. had ordered horses for us all the way as he passed. Continued to Nordköping. The scenery much the same, though more woody. Passed two very fine chateaux: one, of freestone, with two wings and large offices, belongs to Count Fersen. No gardens nor pleasure-grounds apparently; all rocks, wood, and water.

Oct. 13.—At one o'clock in the morning arrived at Nordköping, the largest town we saw between Copenhagen and Stockholm; indeed it is the third in Sweden in point of importance, and the Göttenborgers say it is larger than Göttenborg. It stands on both sides of a very rapid and noisy river of considerable breadth, over which is a good wooden bridge. The houses are chiefly of wood, and well built, many of them covered with copper. There are a vast number of streets, some of them very long and not very narrow: a great number of mills on the islands, as at Mölby. The horses not being ready, we sported the courier, and got on with the last ones to Aby. It began to grow foggy and disagreeable. My drowsiness got the better of my driving, which became rather ticklish, and frequently had near played the devil; however, got safe to Aby about half-past two, but with the loss of our whip in an unlucky nap. I slept on to Shrobek, giving up the whip. Found we had missed the Koll by one hour, he having set off at five. In our way on from the next inn we met the provost-clerk with several funerals, the first we had seen here. The coffin and mortcloth was laid in a peasant's cart, like the gravel, and as we saw two or three coffins at the same funeral, supposed every club to bury on a Sunday in preference. The country is of the same kind to Nyköping, where we arrived at two, hungry—nay, ravenous, having gone all night, since six o'clock in the evening of yesterday, without food. Ate a hearty dinner in a large and good inn, where the rooms were indeed handsome. This town is large and handsome, the streets are wide, and there is a fine exchange or town-house. The country round is very well cultivated. Indeed this is the best province in Sweden in point of fertility.

The agriculture from Mölby, or even Jönköping, improves vastly, though the furrows are still too wide, and not always raised enough. Great quantities of cervises were growing wild these two days, the first I ever saw. Continued to ——, where we stopped to refresh ourselves with milk and the first good beer we had seen.

The baron forebotized for us, and was very civil, as indeed we found every body except the road people. Stuart had a very rough ride from hence in a post-wagon. I went thus too, after trying to get on in the gig. The night was very fine, and the woods and lakes thick as usual. Found the people growing more imposing and insolent as we approached the capital.

Oct. 14.—At the two next stations there were no houses inhabited, so we had to wait in the cold for the horses. Södertelge, the most rascally kennel we ever saw: all accounts agree in this. Left Ned to follow, and went on slowly to Fitja, where we had coffee, and were obliged to wait till eleven for bed. Met with a clergyman and some officers who talked bad French. Were much surprised at the demands of the Södertelgean for additional hire, but afterwards found the case not peculiar to South Sweden. At Fitja is a very fine piece of water on both sides the road. It is finely wooded down to the very brink, and has islands also wooded: we saw several sails on it. It grows very wide in view, but is still quite land-locked. All the stage between Fitja and Stockholm is absolutely barren — nothing but woods and rocks; a house now and then looks like nothing less than the approach to a capital. Stockholm appeared at first like a village scattered among rocks and rising grounds, but grew somewhat better as we approached. Crossed a bridge to the gate, where we underwent a very close examination of every article. More rocks, only inclosed, and a few oaks scattered. Again thought the town abominable; but were much struck with the fine show of iron, chiefly bar, at the dépôt. At two we arrived at our inn, to our infinite joy. This inn is very indifferent, in a bad part of the town, and has a very large *table d'hôte*, where we dined for two or three days till we were introduced to the society.

As we went to the play this evening (though we were too late), we saw enough of the quay, palace, buildings, etc., to raise our opinion of Stockholm.

It is a large, well-built city, and contains above 80,000 inhabitants. Its situation is strikingly romantic—more so, indeed, than that of any other capital in Europe. It stands upon barren rocks intersected in every quarter by the sea or the Meler Lake, which here runs into an arm of the Baltic with considerable rapidity. The heights around are all rocks covered with firs; and two sheets of water, part of the Meler above, and part of sea below, are remarkable features in the view. The city of Stockholm, properly so called, stands on an island. The streets in it are for the most part ill built and narrow; but it contains the chief public buildings, and a very noble quay of hewn stone (granite) of great length, and in such deep water that vessels of any burden may lie touching it. The custom-house stands here, and is a large building of hewn stone, with pillars at the door rather heavy, and an inscription purporting that it was built by Gustavus III. The quay continues in this direction the whole length of the island; and then, interrupted by the bridges, it is again continued on both sides in another direction. The Exchange is also in Stockholm. It is an older building; but large, and with a handsome front. The business place is a spacious room with a wooden floor, and a small apartment off it. There are two busts in the large room—one of the architect, the other of a remarkable citizen. Above stairs are rooms where subscription-balls and public dinners are held.

Near the palace is a large old church, with an inscription bearing it to have been erected where a very high tower formerly stood (Turris stupendæ altitudinis). It has a very fine organ, and one or two large pieces of sculpture on the monuments. The desk and pulpit are also very handsome. The palace is a superb structure, much larger than the Copenhagen one. It consists of a quadrangle with wings, and a bow behind. In the empty space, or between the wings to the quay, there has been a sort of garden, forced upon bare rock. It was the work of the regency. Under the stair which leads from the quadrangle out to the gardens is a marble statue of Venus (de Medicis), a good deal damaged, particularly in the fingers of the right hand. There are four staircases, all very splendid, formed of Swedish granite, polished, and in vast massive pillars, banisters, and porticoes. In the interior of the staircase there is also porphyry. On the balustrades along the garden, between the wings of the quadrangle, there are some china vases belonging to Charles XII., with his cipher on them.

There is a court for the parades of the Guards. It was here that the late king addressed them on the morning of the Revolution.* They are paraded here every morning, and the king frequently attends himself.

There is in the palace a very fine collection. After two or three rooms full of pictures, chiefly by Flemish masters, and several by Swedes, thrown together in confusion—but some of them very good—you are led into the long room where the drawings are kept. These are indeed extremely valuable. They are in ten large volumes—in the whole, between three and four thousand—by the first masters of all the schools. There are also several fine pictures in this room—as *Venus blinding Cupid,* after which the common print (Strange's)† is engraved. There are two galleries of statues, brought from Italy by the late king, disposed with great taste and effect. The most remarkable of these is a *Sleeping Fawn,* placed at the bottom of one of the galleries, and the principal figure in it. It is of very great value. The remark which struck us all on viewing it was the masterly representation of *sleep,* without any appearance of *death.* This

* The Revolution accomplished by Gustavus III. in 1772, when he overthrew the constitution and became absolute. He charmed the soldiers and people by addressing them in their own language.

† Sir Robert Strange, a distinguished engraver, born in one of the Orkney Islands in 1721.

gallery itself is very fine, having two rows of pillars, between which are statues of the Muses. The Fawn is the only one that fronts in the area. An inscription bears that the building was finished in 1796 by the regent.

The library is a spacious room, lined altogether with white-wood. It is, however, a contemptible collection, only 35,000 volumes, which were a present from the king, though, from the privacy of the establishment, it appears that he gave very little away in making the gift. In a separate gallery on one side is a collection of manuscripts, and another of classics. Here, too, are the only remarkable books in the whole—viz., the *Great Bible,* called *The Devil's,* from a book on magic being affixed to it; the exercises of the late king when a boy —one of these is a little singular, being an ode of Rousseau's violently in praise of freedom, and abusing tyrants in a very pointed way; and lastly, a beautiful manuscript copy of the evangelists. The rooms of the palace are large and elegantly furnished, containing a variety of superb mirrors, the floors of wood curiously inlaid, the prevailing furniture blue velvet and satin with gold, and, above all, many fine pictures, chiefly Flemish, though there is a vast crowd of inferior ones. We remarked particularly *Venus and Adonis,* by Vandyke; *Mercy,* by Rubens; and the *Judgment,* by ditto; an old *Hermit,* by Rembrandt, also his mother.

In the king's sitting-room there are two statues (small), one a Venus, representing a lady actually living at Stockholm; the other a male statue, both by Sergell. There are also several busts, particularly one of the queen-dowager, by the same. We regretted not having seen the large room called "*La Salle des Chevaliers,*" where the States assemble, and also the private chapel, as both of these are said to be very fine. On the north side of the palace there are two bronze statues of lions, but this part is not finished. In the *Place des Nobles* stands the Salle des Nobles—a very singular-looking old building, oblong, with a light coach-roof, a statue at each corner, and plain pilasters. There is a title on it, "*Palatium equestris ordinis,*" and a Latin inscription in a line running along the top of the front, . . . *Majorum consiliis atque sapientia virtute et felicibus armis.* The staircase in the inside is very broad, above twelve feet, with massive rails and lamps. The large room is about sixty feet by thirty, with a wagon-roof, on which is a large painting, seemingly laid on and not projected. The walls are completely covered with coats of arms, every head of a noble family having his arms here. I reckoned above two thousand, but there are not half the number at present. This building, as may easily be imagined, is now of very little use since the dissolution of the Senate. Indeed we were present at a concert held in the large room.

Close to the Salle des Nobles are two other public buildings, also old; one is the town-house, where the courts are held.

The mint is a large and rather heavy building, with four fluted pillars of great bulk.

In the place before the Salle des Nobles there is a pedestrian statue of Gustaf Vasa, with an inscription purporting that it was erected by the Order of Nobles soon after the Revolution. From Stockholm west to Rytterholm a bridge leads, handsome though not large, built of hewn stone by Gustaf III.; the balustrades of polished granite, of which and of the porphyry there are some fine slabs, particularly the one which has the inscription. The only building of consequence in Rytterholm is the Cathedral church, which is very old, and by no means fine, though the best in Stockholm. It is only remarkable for the bodies which it contains. Gustavus Adolphus is below ground, as are the greater number, but the coffin of Charles XII. is above. It is of black marble, and has no inscription—only a crown and a lion's skin. Once when we saw it, the king had very lately been inspecting the body in an inquiry concerning the manner of his death, and the workmen were repairing the lid, which had been broken, so that we saw the small coffin of red velvet and gold lace. In the same aisle (which is a handsome circular building on the outside, with pillars and a crown and cushion of stone on the top) there are two other coffins above ground —I believe those of Queen Ulrica and Frederick Adolphus. Gustaf III. is in the vault. Marshal Torstensen is buried in his family aisle in the same church, and several other men of fame. In the island north of Stockholm is the *manège* and stables, which hold one hundred horses; some of these, particularly the Spanish, are very fine; but we were much surprised at the very rough and bloody way in which they are trained.

The communication between the island and the city is at present by two wooden bridges; but that one which leads to the palace is to be taken away, and the handsome stone bridge that leads from the north island to the north suburb is to be continued to the palace. This bridge was built by Gustaf III.

The Nortmalins Torg (or market-place) is a large open area, in the middle of which there stands an equestrian silvered bronze of Gustavus Adolphus, erected by Gustavus III. On the right of it is the palace of the late king's sister, the Abbess of Quidlenberg, who does not reside much here; and opposite is the opera-house. These are exactly alike, and form the east and west sides of the place. They are large, handsome buildings, though plain, of white freestone, with pillars of an oblong form.

The opera-house was built by Gustavus III., and has the inscription—"*Gustavus III. Patriis Musis.*"

In the inside it is very large and splendid; has a pit, amphitheatre, and four tiers of boxes. The band is numerous, but at present there are few good singers and no remarkable one. The *figurantes* are far superior to those in London, but there is no very first-rate dancer. However, as several of these are exceedingly good, and as the scenery, decorations, and, above all, the number of performers, surpasses any thing of the kind to be found elsewhere, it may be reckoned one of the first institutions of the kind in Europe, if not the first. The expense is beyond all proportion to the other establishments, being 80,000 rix-dollars per annum.

It is now altogether in Swedish; but the late king had a French opera also. He was himself the manager; and was so imprudent as to say "*that it cost him more trouble to govern his opera than his kingdom.*"

We had an opportunity of seeing the opera to great advantage at the queen's lying-in; indeed the operas given on this occasion were the only solemnity which accompanied it, except above a thousand guns which were fired the very moment she was delivered. She was brought to bed about two in the morning; and the king and court repaired immediately to the Ryderholm Church, where a Te Deum was sung. The baptism was a very fine show, in the private chapel of the palace, every one attending in court dress.

Dido was the opera given at the lying-in; Panurge, at the reception, which happened a few days after we left Stockholm. At the former we were present, though privately (owing to the particular circumstances). The spectacle was truly grand; the pit and amphitheatre being joined by boarding, benches were placed there for the court, the king and queen-dowager sitting in the middle. They were superbly dressed, particularly the king, in cloth of gold. Next to him the Duke of Sudermania, and next to the queen, the duchess. Behind, the officers and the knights and nobles in gala dresses. On the right side, behind, sat the foreign ministers: in the boxes, the ladies and gentlemen, all in court dresses. The duke had a helmet, and a vast plume of feathers; so had the king, but his was borne for him. There was a *garde d'honneur* also with these large plumes, which resemble opera dresses, and have a very singular effect. It was only in the upper gallery that any middling people appeared, and even these dressed. The splendor of the whole, the quietness and politeness of the behavior, were very striking indeed. The opera was exceedingly splendid, but the singers were indifferent, and the singing itself is a patchwork; the music in general psalmodic, though there are some very pretty airs.

The arsenal is now removed to some distance, and is a large, old, and plain building, more remarkable for the antiquities it contains than for any thing else. In the first room are several exquisite figures of armor, which had been really worn; among which was that of Gustavus Vasa and Gustavus Adolphus. There is also a wax figure, in a glass case, of the late king, very disagreeable and mean-looking; also the dresses worn by him and the duke at Sacuthend and Wibog, with the duke's sword, and both having several shots through; also the dress worn by the king when he was shot. The wound was through the back, a little above the rump, and went into the bladder. In a little adjoining room are various sorts of old armor, chiefly rude cannon and pistols, those which the late king and Charles XII. had to play with when children. In the next and last rooms are a vast number of colors, particularly all those taken by Gustavus Adolphus and his generals, by Charles XII.—one taken by his own hand—and by the late King of Sweden. Here is also the boat which Peter I. built in Holland, and which was taken coming to Russia. In a suite of rooms leading off to the left are a number of articles, horse-furniture for Queen Christina, etc., etc.; a vast number of rich vests from Turkey and Algiers, particularly a fine large piece of gold cloth, with many diamonds and rubies, etc., and a vast multitude of pearls, quite covering it; and a very handsome gilt *traineau* of blue satin, a present to Gustavus III. from the Empress of Russia. But the most remarkable things here are the dresses; the clothes worn by Charles XII. when he was killed. It is a very plain blue doublet, with large round brass buttons; waistcoat and breeches of the same; also his shirt, belt, and sword-handle. The small cocked hat has also the mark of the ball on each side. We saw also one of the daggers made to assassinate Gustavus Adolphus; also his dress in which he was killed, almost hacked to pieces, the shirt all cut and bloody; also his horse stuffed.

Near the opera-house is the theatre, an old building, formerly the arsenal, square, with four turrets. The performers are neither numerous nor good—unequal—though there are two or three very excellent ones, particularly one who has the faculty of making himself so like the great King of Prussia that an officer who had served under him cried when he saw him, as Seton told us, who was with him at the time. The piece where he appears in this character is called "Kammar Page." The theatre is very small and ill lighted; all the light is thrown on the stage, as at Copenhagen. There is very little variety of scenes; but the house is elegantly fitted up.

On the quay above the bridge stands the club-house: it belonged to one of the oldest of the Swedish nobles, Count Bondè, and is the best and largest private house in Stockholm. The upper floor is let to the club; and this is the best institution for strangers, and even for natives, which the town offers. It is indeed reckoned without its match in Europe. The club was originally composed of the foreign ministers and such as they introduced; but it has become now much enlarged, and the number of members fixed at three hundred, each of whom can introduce a stranger, who has then the run of the rooms for two months. The regulations are very good, and the scheme excellently managed. The rooms are very large and handsome, consisting of a reading-room, where the Swedish and foreign papers are received, with maps and periodical publications; a drawing-room, with sofas and tables; a large ball-room, where cards are played on common occasions; billiard-room, card-room, and dining-room; besides dressing-rooms and apartments belonging to the *maître d'hôtel*, who is a Frenchman, and keeps six or seven servants. There is a most excellent table in the French style, where you dine for thirty-two skellings, or about two shillings—or forty-four skellings with claret. The thirty-two was lately raised from twenty-four. At this society all the most fashionable men in Stockholm attend. Some of the first merchants subscribe, but seldom or never go there. Those who go seem to spend their whole time chiefly in billiards and card-playing. The bulk of the company are officers. Sometimes as many as sixty dine. They play very well at billiards, almost always Carolina; and a good deal of gambling goes on at this as well as at cards, the favorite games at which are Ombre and Dummy.

When we first came to Stockholm the club was not so well attended as afterwards, owing to families being out of town, and no visiting taking place. Indeed at best there is very little of it here, and none for strangers, except among the foreign ministers, your banker, or any other citizen to whom you have an introduction, and who gives you one formal feed.

The Swedes are a very polite people, the officers particularly, at least as far as bowing and etiquette; but of real politeness we saw very little, owing to their extreme rudeness to strangers. The Court's fear of being thought dependent upon any foreign power descends to individuals; and at the time we were there every stranger complained. The only way to avoid this state of *coupée* is to cut all the diplomatic people; for, with one exception (the Spanish secretary, who had been here fourteen years), not a soul among them is associated with.

MEN OF LETTERS, ETC.

There are three learned societies here—the Swedish Academy, the Royal Academy of Sciences, and the Academy of Belles Lettres. The first is wholly for the improvement of the Swedish tongue. It was founded by Gustavus III., and is at present engaged in a dictionary; but the members have been rather remiss, and only a few of them have finished their letters. The other two publish their memoirs in Swedish.

I was present at a sitting of the Academy of Sciences. They have a large house in the city, where the office-bearers have also apartments. Their museum of natural history is far from rich. There are, however, a considerable number of snakes, and a room full of South Sea dresses, etc., brought by Mr. Sparman, who went with Cook. The *Hortus siccus*, too, is well filled. The library is very small, being of very late date. The Academy met, when I saw it, in a plain, good room, hung round with pictures of its most eminent members and encouragers. There were twenty present, who sat all round a long table; and the unfortunate visitor was obliged to sit *solo* beyond the circle, at the wall. A number of the members (indeed the greater part) had orders, and were noblemen. The chair was filled by an old gentleman who had been minister for foreign affairs. The subject of conversation was, "The propriety of extending the knowledge of Lapland;" and the plan for the purpose was carried by a ballot almost unanimously. A paper was also read giving an account of a new steam-engine, invented by a gentleman who resided many years in Russia and Sweden, and is now counsellor of mines. The talking was carried on rather too quickly, and without much distinctness or any order. I was made acquainted (by Mr. Sparman) with Mr. Swanberg, the professor of astronomy; he lives at the Observatory, and was very obliging in assisting me with letters for Torneo, of which place he is a native, though I was surprised to find he knew little or nothing of Lapland. He was up last summer at Torneo examining the measurements of the French Academy, as the Academy here means to repeat these on a great scale, taking in two degrees. This work they are already preparing, and think to begin the summer after next, though want of money is a great obstacle. Mr.

Sparman is a very worthy creature, and, I believe, skillful enough in his profession, but his scientific knowledge seems confined altogether to natural history. He complains that Vaillant (whom he calls *charlatan*) has copied his map, and says that Lieutenant Paterson used him much better. He is a Swedenborgian. Mr. Sjostrom is one of the secretaries, and a great electrician. He lectures in the Academy's great hall, where they meet in summer: it is very handsome, and he has a good apparatus. He has translated "Cavallo's Electricity" into Swedish; and is busy with a discovery he has made lately, and which he explained to us. He finds that all parts of the body which do not perspire sensibly, will show evident signs of electricity by being pressed hard and the electricity suddenly raised.

To Mr. Melanderhjelm I was introduced by Mr. D'Asp;* he is an old man of about eighty, but with his faculties entire. His delight is mathematics, and he had published various works and papers on this subject, particularly a treatise of astronomy. There is no university at Stockholm, but several lectures are given. The learned men are not on the whole much esteemed or well known, and are stigmatized as peculiarly Jacobinical; indeed the number is not considerable. There are two sets, one belonging to the Academy, the other (perhaps those of most merit) are private. There is a review written by one of these, said to be very severe and much dreaded by the Academy; also a periodical miscellany, called "Lävingegen Blandäde." It is a collection of translations and original pieces, some of them very exact. We particularly admired a Swedish translation of "Alonso and Imogene." There are a great number of pieces translated from the "Wealth of Nations." All that class of men are freethinkers.

The fine arts are in a flourishing state here, considering how few amateurs there are among the rich. There is an Academy of Painting and Sculpture founded by the late king. Mr. Fredenheim is at the head, a gentleman of taste, who has travelled much and has several good things, particularly a fine col-

---

* Daniel Melander, incremented to Melanderhjelm on his being ennobled in 1778, born at Stockholm 1726, died 1810. A list of his works and a reference to biographical notices of him in Swedish works will be found in the "Nouvelle Biographie Générale."

lection of coins, chiefly Roman, *inter alia* a Niger. He is son of Melander, the late Archbishop of Upsal. The Academy has produced a set of young artists of great merit in drawing and modelling. The terms are very reasonable.

The first artist here is Mr. Sergel, a statuary.* He was some time at Rome, and was obliged to leave it owing to the jealousy of the artists, and to one (supposed to be Canova) of whom only he was inferior. His last work, not yet finished, is the bronze statue of Gustavus III., which the citizens of Stockholm have caused to be made, and it is to be placed upon the quay, before the palace, on a pedestal of Swedish porphyry. This is a most superb statue, fourteen feet high, weighing thirty tons with, and twenty-four without, the knobs. The attitude is that of the Apollo Belvedere. His left hand is leaning on a rudder, round the top of which is a laurel wreath. In his right is an olive-branch, rather too small. He is supposed to be returning from the Finland war with the peace, and stepping from his boat to the palace. We could not help remarking the extreme dissimilarity of the two sides of his face. The left has more slope and less angle than the right, in the cheek; and the left brow falls away flat and hollow, the skull becoming round and large on the opposite side, to which it looks twisted; the forehead large, and the expression of the face fine. It resembles the bust of Mr. Fox between the eyebrows, and the nose is somewhat aquiline. It is strikingly like (as D'Asp told us, who was constantly with the late king); only Sergel said the twist in the face was rather greater in the original. This is the first thing of the kind that has been done at Stockholm, and succeeded perfectly well. It took a fortnight to cool. In return for this statue there is an obelisk erecting in the space between the palace and Exchange, commemorating the loyalty of the inhabitants of Stockholm during the Finland war.

Mr. Sergel has several good statues; two particularly at the end of the room, besides vases, a dying Octriades, and a fawn,

* Johan Tobias Sergel, born at Stockholm in 1744, died 1814. He endeared himself to his countrymen by declining munificent offers from Catherine of Russia, that he might spend his days and exercise his art among them. The most easily accessible account of him is perhaps that in the "Biographie Universelle."

after that in the palace, are the best of his own above stairs. Below is his theatre, where we saw his two masterpieces—*Mars holding Venus,* wounded by Diomede, and *Love raising Psyche.* The body of Venus is finely expressed. There are also medallions of Gustavus III. and IV. extremely like, and casts of Trajan's column of the real size, executed by Sergel at Rome, by order of the late king, for whose temple at Haga most of these things are intended.

The best painter here is Mr. Breda, a pupil of Sir Joshua Reynolds, and one whose works are known in London. He painted the Turkish ambassador, which was exhibited in London, and then engraved. It is now here; but he has several others better.

Mr. Martin is an R.A. of London; his *forte* seems to be caricature-painting, for his landscapes are daubs. One of his pupils is a most wonderful drawer of figures, but nothing in landscape.* Mr. Belanger is a most excellent landscape-painter, both in oil and water-color.

The manners of the people in this capital are extremely dissolute, particularly of the people of fashion. The instances of profligacy about Court almost exceed belief in so northerly a situation. The women of fashion carry on their amours in the most scandalous and public manner. Madame de L——, whose husband is minister at the Hague, lives openly with Baron D'E——. Her sons, two of the most fashionable young men in Stockholm, are very intimate with the baron, and with the minister too. She is daughter of the late Count J——. On her husband complaining to him soon after his marriage, he asked him, "Have you any paper, any writing, any title-deed, by which to plead exemption from the common lot of husbands?" This kind of instance might be multiplied to an endless extent. This profligacy seems to descend to the lower orders. Their manners are growing corrupted too. While we were at Stockholm several instances happened: a man killed his wife because she would not assist him in corrupting his

* This Martin can not be David Martin, the portrait-painter, celebrated for the picture of Lord Mansfield, which he afterwards engraved, as he died in 1797. Nor can it be John Martin, celebrated as the author of "Belshazzar's Feast," and others of the like character, for he was only ten years old at the period.

own daughter. Three men were hanged for forgery (one of them a nobleman). They continued forging notes even while in prison. A gang of thieves robbed a noble's house with the assistance of his servants. Another gang formed a plan to rob and murder indiscriminately, throwing the bodies into the sea; and this they actually perpetrated on several. The causes of this profligacy among the lower classes may be partly owing to the state of the currency and dearness of provisions. The conduct of the late king gave rise to the profligacy of the Court.*

Gustavus III. endeavored by every means in his power to render Stockholm a second Paris. He increased the splendor of the Court, invented the Court dresses, and encouraged the arts, besides erecting a number of public buildings. He introduced and encouraged effeminate habits, and pursued a system of favoritism that led to his own destruction; for we were told that the real cause of Count Horn's joining in the conspiracy to assassinate him—nay, of his originating the conspiracy itself—was his loading with honors and making governor of Stockholm a young man who, from some cause, had made Horn his implacable enemy.† The highest office under the Crown is Governor of Stockholm: but this has been kept vacant since the death of Gustavus.

The consequence of the present king's utter want of economy has been that the country is quite drained of money, and from this the greatest inconveniences arise, besides the real loss. They have notes down to twelve skellings: each skelling at par is above one penny sterling, there being six rix-dollars to the pound; but when we were there the medium of the exchange might be reckoned six rix-dollars thirty-two skellings to the pound sterling, or a plate equal to one

* It must be held as corroborative of the accuracy of the account here given of the amount of social immorality and of criminality in Sweden, that a like picture is given of the country by an acute traveller there nearly forty years later—see "A Tour in Sweden in 1838, comprising Observations on the Moral, Political, and Economical State of the Swedish Nation;" by Samuel Laing, Esq. The popular Swedish novels of Miss Bremer let their reader into the secret of social life by her reference to those sins which prove sore temptations to the heroines whose virtue overcomes them.

† Gustavus III. was shot dead at a masked ball on the 10th of March, 1792.

shilling, and a rix-dollar to three shillings. It is perhaps a consequence of the fluctuating state of the money that there is the most surprising uncertainty in the prices of articles. There is no sort of level or standard. In the same part of the town you find in different shops the same article different by half the price almost. This remark Mr. Hailes made in *the most positive manner*. There is no such thing as tracing a lost note, for the numbers are not always changed in the new yearly issue. To get specie you must pay a heavy *agio*, which at that time was about fifty per cent., so much was the paper depreciated. The states of the kingdom are the security for this rix-gelt, and the bank for the banco-gelt, which is of the same value with specie. The king is allowed to issue a certain number of notes; but as he issues to supply the waste, there is no check upon him in this respect. It was for the purpose of obtaining the diet's sanction to the last issue that the meeting at Gefle was held: the king, also, wished to have the *bank* into his own hands, but this he could not accomplish. The late king made specie somewhat plenty by borrowing from Holland near a million specie, which he circulated; but this is now drained off also. The old plates (of copper) went to Denmark chiefly.

At this diet bribery was exercised in a very open way, though on a small scale. Thus pensions were given of a rix-dollar per day. Indeed the late king ruled very much by corruption, which, from the poverty of the nobility, he found no very difficult thing. One of the engines of bribery was *orders:* of these are four.

1. The *Seraphim* or *Blue Ribbon*, which is held by a few only.

2. The *Sword*, a military order of merit—a yellow ribbon, distributed with immense profusion to almost all the army above captains. It is this which Sir Sidney Smith has.

3. The *Polar Star*, a black ribbon given to civil officers, learned men, etc.

4. *Vasa* or the *Wheat-sheaf*, a green ribbon given to eminent merchants, agriculturists, etc.

The *Sword* and *Vasa* were invented by the late king, and distributed in great profusion, as well as the Polar Star and letters of nobility in the way of *douceurs*. Indeed this continues, as we saw at the queen's lying-in, when three columns of the newspaper were filled with a list of creations.

The dissimulation of the late king was consummate. He retired to Upsal for two winters, and cultivated the acquaintance of the learned men, attended lectures, etc., while in fact he was busy planning the Finland war, which surprised not only Russia, but all Europe.

He came to dine at Ekolsund, and seemed quite *dégagé*. Walked about with Seton, and pointed out the improvements required about his place. That afternoon he set off, and travelling with his usual dispatch, two Swedish miles an hour, arrived at Hedmora in the morning, where he harangued the Dalecarlians, and raised them for the relief of Göttenborg. This rapid mode of travelling he always used. He had his bed in his coach, and undressed regularly at night. He used, if going too slow, to put down the window, and ask the coachman (Mölman) "whether he was carrying eggs to market." That evening Seton asked one of the lords who was with him where they were going; but he told him, "we know nothing more about it than you do." He laughed much at English liberty, and hated the English, admiring and copying the French in all things. When setting off from Ekolsund, happening to talk of the safety of travelling in Sweden, he said: "By-the-way, Seton, how can the King of England possibly allow highway robberies? Were I there, I'd order three or four regiments of horse to patrol the roads; but oh! that would be reckoned an infringement upon liberty," with a sneer and laugh.

De Lisle, the French consul, saw him at Göttenborg (in 1788), just as the accounts had come of the order for assembling the States General in France. He said in a very sad way to him, that it would not end there—that a revolution dreadful to all Europe was at hand—and spoke as if he knew it otherwise than by mere conjecture: he added, "I must hasten to finish my revolution before this begins, and before it becomes dangerous to call together the states."

The most extravagant accounts are given of his eloquence—of his uncommon powers of persuading and talking people over, and his irresistible faculty of producing tears in his audience. Yet he did not understand Swedish as well as

French, and used to write his speeches in the latter, and then have them translated. He contrived, by his address and eloquence, to ingratiate himself wonderfully with the people, whose power he wished to balance against that of the nobles.

While he was in Finland he was himself outwitted by the Danes. General Mansback (whom we saw and conversed a great deal with at Friedric's Hald) was sent over on a message of compliment to him, and staid a week entire with him, but in fact to be a spy on his intentions; and the king's constant tone was, "I am sure Denmark will do nothing against a peace so necessary," etc., etc. But all of a sudden the general (Mansback) and the prince royal broke into Sweden, and had well-nigh taken Göttenborg, had not the English minister (Elliot) threatened to bombard Copenhagen. The present king is totally unlike him, both in person and character. He is wholly managed by a junto, who direct every thing, to the great discontent of the rest of the nobility. Of this junto the chief are Count Uglas, governor of the province of Stockholm; Count Fersen, who commanded the regiment of the Swedes (Sweders Ronol) in France, and made a very narrow escape from the guillotine for his zeal in assisting the royal family's flight in 1791; and Admiral Rosenstein.

Some are, however, of opinion that the king's abilities will break forth, and indeed there is some reason to think that he will endeavor to imitate his supposed father; at least he recalled all those whom the regent had displaced, and has lately appointed the wife of Armfelt governess to the young crown prince, which makes people expect that he himself is to be recalled. The regent by his conduct displeased every body, particularly by his choice of Reuterhölm for his minister. He is a man of very inferior abilities; and instead of his brother's determined spirit, his government was marked by timidity and indecision. He was never popular even before, and his loss of the Swedish fleet at Wiborg had greatly incensed the people against him. He displaced the chief favorites of his brothers, some of them openly, others more indirectly. Thus D'Essen threw up his offices, and quitted the court, on some *economical* regulations being proposed in his department.

The dismissal of Munk was another act of his, and has been much misrepresented. In the course of Gustaf III.'s extravagance and constant want of money, he had borrowed a considerable sum from Munk, who was a particular friend of his. Munk wanted his money very much; and the king, to pay him, ordered him to get a sum nearly the double of what he owed. Munk got this done openly in the king's name by an artist in town, and, being paid out of the sum, the king got the surplus. The notes were sent to Finland by a Jew, and drained that country of money. Munk, having got no order under the king's hand, on his death was ordered to leave the country, and the estate in Finland, bought with his money, was confiscated. He went to Italy and bought an estate in the Cisalpine Republic, whence, of course, he is now driven, and lives at Hamburg on a small annuity, which he still has. The lenity with which all Gustaf's murderers (except Ankerstrom) were treated, and the duke's connection with the masons of higher orders, of which he was master, has given rise to a report, doubtless unjust, that he was privy to his brother's murder. I read a book in Stockholm where this is roundly asserted ("Assassinat de Gustave III., par un officier Polonais").

Mansback (who is a great mason) told a story of the duke and himself having met in a church in Stockholm, and being about ghost-raising, when the duke approached the wall, seeing a spirit, as he thought, on it. When going to address her, she asked an indecent question, to the extreme confusion of the party, who did not recover it for a long time. It was, in fact, a woman of the town who had got into the church.

The assassins are now much scattered. Horn is in Iceland, Ribbing is said to be in Paris, and Lilienhorn is a school-master in an obscure town in Poland. It is thought to have been very lucky for the peace of the country that the king lived some weeks after his brother, as, had he died without making the proper arrangements, there is little doubt that the discontented party would have taken the opportunity of attempting a revolution. The power of Russia, of course, keeps them in awe. The antipathy of the people is very violent; in playing at cards (for instance) they call in joke your adversary "the Russian." This antipathy swallows up any pique against the

Danes, with whom they would willingly join against Russia. The Court, however, must bend to their power. Accordingly the late proclamation was written to please it. This absurd piece was written with the king's own hand.

The present *politics* of Sweden are very singular: a *fear of dependence* seems the great spring of all the Court's motions; yet the favor shown to the Russian ambassador, who is treated on every occasion with peculiar distinction, seems inconsistent with this principle. He alone is allowed to sit at table with the royal family; and at the opera-house he was placed in a place quite separate from the other ministers. It must, however, be observed that he is the only *full* ambassador now in Stockholm. The king was to have been married to one of our princesses (Mary), but the match was broken off, for fear of dependence on England. Then he went in person to Mecklenburg, where every thing was ready for his marriage with one of the princesses there; and when all was arranged and publicly notified, he suddenly broke off, for fear of English influence. He went to Petersburg (forced to break off the other, it is said, by the emperor) and was waiting there in expectation of being married to one of the grand-duchesses, but he seized the opportunity of the empress's death and returned home. He then married the Princess of Baden (who at first disliked him and the country), and with whom (except her beauty) he got nothing, neither friends nor money; but then her insignificance secured his apparent independence.

The people, especially the merchants, are violent against the English; laugh at our liberty, which they call gilded slavery; talk of Pitt as a monster, and the war as the greatest of all curses. They indeed smart from it, and declare that their trade is ruined. The successes of France always increase the public prejudice in her favor; and on these depend also the motions of the Government. It is supposed that the king has a mind to follow out some of his father's plans, especially with respect to a Russian alliance.

The governors of provinces have the whole district also almost completely under their power; the different chancellories, or the parliaments, being wholly under their direction, while the bishop governs the Church.

Finland and Pomerania are distinct and separate governments. The raising of taxes is left to the governors of the provinces, and is done as follows: Every province is divided into hundreds; and formerly there were subdivisions of tithings, a distinction now lost. In each hundred the governor selects a jury of nine—three nobles, three ecclesiastics, and three peasants. These meet in the chief town of the hundred and fix the sum to be paid annually by the district. When a general tax is to be laid on the nobles, it is by an assessment laid on the ploughs of land, into eighty thousand of which the whole country is divided, as England formerly was into Hydes and Knights' fees, and as many parts of Germany now are, into "whole-farmers" and "half-farmers."

The people in office are in general very poor, and their influence in no way formidable. It is a great deal if they can support a trifling household upon their appointments, and offices (at court) are so poor and yet so eagerly sought for; yet scarcely an officer of State has sufficient influence to give away a place of a hundred rix-dollars a year. The same poverty extends through every department of State, though magnificence is aped by having a multitude of officers with small salaries in order to oblige many dependents. Thus there are four secretaries of State with £200 per annum salary, though quite in want of employment. The minister for foreign affairs has £400; the postmaster-general, £150. The judges have £100; but this is so taxed that they do not get above £80: the consequence is bribery. The diplomatic men are well paid—indeed beyond all proportion. Thus the Swedish minister in London has £1500 per annum. The nobles, whose fortunes are extremely unequal, but in general very small, are reduced to the necessity of oppressing their peasantry, of which we saw the effects in our journey to Stockholm; though in the North, we are told, where the peasantry hold of the Crown—in Bothnia, Jutland, Angermanland, and Helsingland—the contrary is observed, for there the peasantry are rich and independent. The Court itself shows a curious mixture of poverty and state. For while they pay 80,000 rix-dollars for the opera, they and the town were afraid to have an illumination at the queen's delivery, for fear there would not remain enough of candles. The queen's state-coach is an old one formerly belonging to an English minister. There are so seldom court days that strangers are presented in a private way after the parade, otherwise they must wait eight months; and a regiment of two hundred and fifty uncommonly tall men (Swedes) were obliged to be disbanded very lately, literally because the expense of feeding, etc., was too great. Though there is scarcely a party given in a whole year by any individual nobleman, yet they have *piques-niques*, at the expense and profusion of which a stranger is surprised; and occasionally great *fêtes* are given by the society, most remarkably splendid—for instance, one (while we were gone to Upsal) where five hundred people were present, and a most magnificent entertainment; but not above £200 were allowed them monthly for expenses.

The partiality for a French alliance exists yet; all the men of property and consequence wish that, whatever government is established in France. The old alliance may be established between France, Poland, Prussia, Spain, Turkey, and Sweden, as a bar to Russia on the one hand, and England and the emperor on the other. For England they do not conceal their hatred; and though their ships have been seized by both sides, they are silent as to the one, and load the other with abuse. When the fleet (said to be worth half a million sterling) was lately seized and condemned, to the great loss of the mercantile interest in general, and the utter ruin of one, the commander of the convoy who gave them up was tried and condemned to be shot, and, though pardoned on the place of execution, yet sent for six months to the fortress of Sveaborg. The King of Sweden, too, wrote a letter with his own hand to our king, who (some accounts say) left it all with his ministers and judges; others, that he gave no answer at all. One of the accusations against Mr. Hailes was, his having appeared on 'Change the very day the news of the capture came. D'Asp was recalled from London, it is said, because our king turned his back on him, which the King of Sweden pointedly did to Hailes, and treated him with every mark of disrespect. The people were furious, crying that he deserved to lose his crown if he did not take vengeance.

Bonaparte's return occasioned a dinner of a large company, composed of some respectable people, and others, as clerks, etc., to drink his health; Suwarrow's was drunk in cold water; and the French consul, who presided, gave the fraternal embrace once round, and then again; and being asked a third time (as the story goes), was so fatigued he could not. A singer (Dupuis) was immediately sent out of the country for having sung there, but was to have been pardoned; but coming on the stage one night when the king was there, the first sentence of his part happening to be, "I don't go, but stay here," was prodigiously applauded as being *àpropos*. The king said to the officer who sat with him, "But he *shall* go." Accordingly the man was sent off, but a great subscription made for him, and loaded with presents, and impostures were practised to get more from the king. The French consul, too, sent to make his apology to the minister of foreign affairs.

The wives of ministers are not received at court unless they wear the Swedish court dress. The only one who has submitted to this is the Portuguese minister's lady, Madame de Correa, who does not find herself a whit better received than before. This dispute about the dress originated with a minister of the emperor, whose wife was literally turned out of a ball-room by order of the late king.

The population of Sweden does not exceed three millions, of which one must be allowed to Finland and Lapland. The last has now only 10,000 inhabitants.

The army nominally amounts to 80,000 men, including militia: they support in time of peace only enough to garrison the forts, and for the guards. The greater part of these standing troops, including two yeomen regiments, are divided between Stockholm, and Pomerania, and Finland. The most important garrisons are those of Sveaborg and Marstrand—the former in Finland, the latter on the frontiers of Norway. These are esteemed the keeps of the empire, being both built on inaccessible rocks, at the distance of three or four miles from the coast, and Sveaborg commands a fine harbor.

The rest of the army is rather a militia, but upon a singular footing, and, I believe, unparalleled in Europe. Each province furnishes a regiment, which is called after its name. The men, who are all peasants of the place, have no pay, except at stated times when called out. Besides this, they are obliged to parade every Sunday at the church-door of the parish. They are found in a house, and a small portion of ground, which the proprietor is obliged to take care of when the holder is in the field or at exercise.

In this way each estate is burdened with a certain number of men. Their houses are marked by a square board, with a number inscribed on it. The children of soldiers in general become soldiers too, and, being trained to the musket from their youth, do not differ from the soldiers of other armies. The officers have farms in the same provinces with their regiments—the captain in the midst of his company, and the colonel in the middle of the province. The same plan is extended to sailors who are quartered along the coast; but this does not answer so well, and it makes the navy full of old men, as the young take care to get employed among the merchants, who are obliged, however, in time of war, to furnish a certain quota of men to the navy. The army in Sweden is thus extremely economical. The king's guards themselves are only paid twopence per day when on duty, and at other times have to work for themselves. However, the soldiers are often supported by the public works, in some of which they are the chief laborers, as at Trollhatta. The officers are for the most part very poor, though men of family. Thus, a lieutenant has only one hundred and twenty rix-dollars per annum. The chief officers at present in the Swedish service are Count Fersen; Platten, the governor of Pomerania; and Shlimpston, the commander-in-chief in Finland. The navy is powerful in proportion to the other establishments: forty sail, chiefly frigates, of which the greater part are at Carlscrona, one of the finest harbors in the world, though some are laid up in ordinary at Stockholm. Many of them are old and ill-built; but those which have been laid down of late are on the most beautiful models made by Admiral Chapman, who lives at Carlscrona, and is one of the first naval architects in Europe. The last time the king was at Carlscrona, a frigate was launched, and the keel of an eighty-gun ship laid down. Though beaten at Wiborg by the Russians, they perfectly retrieved their credit by a victory at Suensk-sund.

The revenues of Sweden amount to about two millions sterling, but are rather on the decrease, from the expension of the mines; and they are burdened with about eight millions national debt, the interest of which they find it difficult to pay. The commerce, particularly up the Gulf, is greatly increasing: several ports have been opened of late.

Stockholm is situated very advantageously for shipping, not only from the excellence of the harbor, but its distance (six or eight miles) from the sea, so that ships have to be warped up between narrow channels almost all this way. The staple articles are flax, hemp, iron, and deals; and chiefly flax and iron, of which last particularly there is a magnificent dépôt at Stockholm.

Gefle is a large trading-town up the Gulf, and is reckoned the fourth in Sweden; it fits out ships of seven or eight hundred tons burden. Sundsvall, Hudiksvall, Havösund, Lulea, and Tornea, and several large places up the gulf, have lately been made free towns, and have added very considerably to the commerce of the country. In the West Indies, Sweden has some small trade, from the possession of St. Bartholomew, ceded by France. It is a barren rock, and now literally a dépôt for smuggling. The governor had behaved so ill to the inhabitants, that deputies were arrived in Stockholm, while we were there, to complain of his conduct.

Their trade in the East Indies used to be very considerable, and Göttenborg the head-quarters, though at present it is in a bad way, the India House being actually shut up, as we heard then, and the people complaining most dismally that their trade is ruined. The consequence of all this is, that coffee has been forbid, in order to encourage tea, to the great annoyance of the people. Indeed, while Lord Henry Spencer was our minister at Stockholm, so violent an altercation arose on this subject among the ministers, that several are said to have been obliged to quit the court, and Lord Henry sent on the subject a courier-extraordinary to England. French brandy was also forbidden; but (from some instances of discontent which occurred) it was found better to take off this prohibition.

The great obstacle to commercial improvement is the depreciation of the rix-dollar, which introduces endless confusion, as well as loss. Thus, in retailing, if a person wishes to buy an article whose price is not expressed by any note, he must either pay more than the price or give specie, by which he loses; for, if you give away specie in common dealings, the *agio* is not allowed, which you paid to get it. Thus, too, all officers under Government are paid in the rix-dollar, so that, since its immense fall, the value of the salaries has fallen in proportion, while the price of provisions rises. Besides rix-dollars and banco, they have lately issued a note of very singular kind—viz., a piece of copper intrinsically worth one-sixth of a skelling, which is made worth a half-skelling, and is called a *pollet.* It is singular enough that a number of prices remain so much the same. Thus, that of posting was not different in 1736, as we see by Duther's voyage—and how long before I know not.

It seems not improbable that some violent convulsion will take place from the state of events.

The language of Sweden is evidently sprung from the Teutonic, and that it is a very pure remnant of that stock may be inferred from a curious circumstance.

Almost everywhere else we find in names of *persons* and *places* remnants of dead language, and not to be understood by the present natives, though easily understood by knowing the roots of the ancient local tongue. But in Sweden the case is quite different; all the names are modern Swedish, and any one moderately acquainted with that language as it is at present spoken there can easily discover the meaning of each appellation. For instance, one can form a very good guess at the situation, etc., of a place before seeing it. Names of persons can almost all be traced as easily; and this is connected with another peculiarity. No one but a noble can properly have any surname, though merchants, etc., do take them. Then, in courts of law these names are not acknowledged—they are called in deeds and citations, James, *James's son*, and Anne, *James's daughter*.

The lower classes, as peasants, have actually no surnames at all, being constantly called by their Christian names. Thus a parish register is an unintelligible list of Christian names with the fathers' affixed. When a gentleman hires a servant, he often wishes to distinguish him; this he does according to his fancy: thus Seton calls his coachman always "Preston," after his Scotch estate. This prevails also in Iceland and Norway. The people have thus derived their names from circumstances; thus one of the oldest families is called

Bondé (a peasant), and *Vasa* is a *wheat-sheaf.* When the clergy take a name, or continue their father's, if he had one, they add the termination "*us*" to it: thus the Archbishop of Upsal's father was called *Troil,* he himself *Troilus,* and when ennobled became *Von Troil.* Almost all the names ending in "ander," as *Dryander, Polander,* etc., come from the province of Småland. There are, of course, various dialects in Sweden. That spoken by the common people in Stockholm is by no means good; and I perceived the greatest change in the dialect of Western Gothland, where —— could not always make himself understood. I believe it softens down more and more as you get into the Danish provinces. The purest Swedish is spoken in Wermeland, in Dalecarlia: the natives speak a dialect quite different from the rest of the Swedes, who can not understand them; but they also speak Swedish, and are shy of using their own tongue except among themselves. It very strongly resembled Anglo-Saxon, and many words which we heard repeated in Dalecarlia are quite good English. Besides, they retain the *th* and *w,* which none of the other languages except the English do. The manners of these people are as different from the other Swedes as the language. They are by much the best of them, and the bravest as well as simplest. Gustavus III. was peculiarly anxious about cultivating their good opinions, but he never succeeded well. The Swedish language has been much cultivated by the natives—at least they have many more authors than the Danes or other Northern nations, perhaps from their being more insulated and having less intercourse with foreigners. The history of their own country has been written by their two best authors, Dahlin and Lagobring. The latter, being written according to a clear method, and without the tedious prolixity of the former, is esteemed the best. The Chevalier Ihre, famous for his knowledge of Northern antiquities, has published a work of great labor and information, "Dictionarium Suedo-Gothicum."* Their chief poet is Kelgren, who, besides several

* Johan Ihre, born at Lund 1707, died 1780. The Dictionary referred to was published at Upsala in 1769, in two volumes folio. A list of his works will be found under his name in Adelung's Supplement to the "Allgemeines Gelehrten Lexicon" of Jöcher.

poems and imitations, is celebrated for his opera of "Gustaf Vasa," in the composition of which the late king is said to have had a share. The poetry is said to be extremely fine; and the decorations, etc., are splendid in the performance, beyond conception. But probably much of its merit consists in its being a grand national subject. Besides, I am told, it is a good deal imitated from Richard III. Their other chief authors are Leopold, who has written some small poetical things; and Silvertalp, a satirist and author of the "Ser Review." There are, besides, a multitude of translations from English, French, and German, and many authors of political pamphlets, which they are at incredible pains to get transported into Russia, as the difficulty of procuring such publications there makes them sure of a ready sale.

The law of Sweden is founded partly on the civil law, partly on the old Gothic constitutions. The code is small and very distinctly drawn up, occupying only one small volume. The criminal code is extremely mild, and (except Ankerstrom's) no execution had taken place at Stockholm for twenty years. One happened while we were there, that for forgery (*vide supra*), and was performed in a cruel manner. The culprits were hung up by the middle, their head and heels almost touching; then the executioner gave each a kick on the neck, so that the numerous spectators actually heard it break. They were so shocked at the spectacle that it was feared for some time after a tumult might take place.

The police of Stockholm is very bad indeed. The *lieutenant de police* was turned out of town by the late king for infamous practices. The rogues about town are chiefly soldiers, and it is extremely unsafe to walk at night in any but the most frequented parts of the town. Thieving is universal.

The religion of Sweden is Lutheran, though they admit bishops who are for the most part ennobled, and prelates of orders. *Von Troil* was created Archbishop of Upsala—the only Lutheran archbishop in the world—by Gustavus III., rather as one whom he could make sure of in his political intrigues, than for any shining talents. In 1789, when the Act of Security was to be signed, Troil was so much intimidated by the nobles, that he durst not consent—on which the king desired him to have a *fit of the gout*, which he complied with, and the Bishop of Lynköping (the next) signed. He has since had the gout in earnest, and was confined with it when we saw him at Stockholm. His revenue is £1500 per annum, and some patronage of small livings, a great thing in Sweden, where there exists literally scarcely any such thing as patronage at all.

The inferior clergy are for the most part selected at Upsala, Lind, and Abo, the three universities, from the poor students. The livings are small, and the parishes very extensive.

In order to have an opportunity of seeing the rural economy of this country, and also of visiting Upsal, we accepted the invitation of Baron Seton, a Scotsman, and spent several days with him, both in going to Upsala and in returning. Seton had been well acquainted with Gustavus III., and ennobled, some said from the king's love of a joke, his name being Baron, which he changed for an estate left him by his uncle, called Seton. I remember seeing on one of his window-shutters a few words written by Gustavus, importing that on such a day he had come there from the revolution: of course the date was 1772. There was then at Stockholm a great sculptor, Sergel, whose works were well worth seeing, and who had many anecdotes to relate of former times.* It must be added that nothing we heard of Gustavus III. tended to raise our opinion of him in any respect, but for his talents. His public conduct is well known; but he had left a very indifferent impression in society of his private and personal character.

This was the opinion of others, as well as ours, of whom he mentioned Edward Daniel Clarke, and his pupil Cripps. They came to Stockholm while we were there on their Scandinavian tour, which they extended to Greece; and Clarke has published a full account of it.† We became acquainted with one who proved another author of "Travels" some years after—Acerbi—who with his friend Beletti had come from the Milanese, and was afterwards in Marescalchi's mission to Paris. He amused us with an account of a famous *clairvoyante* who

---

* See above.

† To be found in the six volumes of "Travels in various Countries of Europe, Asia, and Africa," well known as Clarke's Travels.

had operated upon his friend and him with different results. When the question was put to Beletti, "Doit-on aimer sa patrie?" he answered, "Quand on en a une"—which Acerbi said was *clairvoyante's* power, not only in getting an answer from one in a trance, but such an answer was above his friend's capacity in his natural state. Lombardy at that time was neither Austrian nor French. Napoleon only two years after made Melzi vice-prefect before he assumed the iron crown himself.

The country between Stockholm and Ekolsund is rocky and woody — some lakes; and the road lies chiefly along branches of the Mälar. After the first stage, however, you get into cultivated country; indeed, the whole province of Uppland is plain and fertile. The house and estate belonged to Gustavus III., having been given to him by the States as a provision when prince. It consists of two large wings joined by a low colonnade of offices. The house is very elegant, and well furnished; but so much too large that Seton is wishing to sell it.

The estate is one of the largest, perhaps the largest, in Sweden. The grounds are laid out in the old French style, of straight avenues, mazes, etc. We saw the rooms which Gustavus's court occupied. He was very fond of the place; and on the windows are some inscriptions written with his own hand. One in particular, dated September, 1772, "Jag komt hit ifran Revolutionen."

The ground is uneven where the house stands, and high, well wooded, with a very extensive avenue. On one side it stretches down to the Mälar, which gives an easy communication with Stockholm; on the other side it overlooks an extensive and cultivated plain, in which the chief part of the estate lies. On the lake he has a large brick and tile work. A great part of the land is let out to tenants on long leases, which he has introduced here from Britain. Some is let out for life on quit-rent, and a third portion remains in his own hands—no tenants at will. The part in his own hands he cultivates to the best advantage, and on a very extensive scale. The land is pretty equally divided in the cultivation of wheat, barley, peas, etc., nearly as in England. But it is remarkable that the plough which they use, and have used for two hundred years—called the Helsingland plough—is the very same which the Agricultural Society lately introduced into England. They chiefly used yoked oxen, which work through land lately cleared of wood, and studded with large stones and roots in a surprising manner. They raise their furrows very imperfectly in the middle, making cross-cuts and sweeps to carry off the moisture, which does it very imperfectly. The climate is well adapted for reindeer. One of these we saw at Ekolsund, where he has been kept some time, being bought from some Laps, who sometimes come as far south as Stockholm. It is a dark brownish-gray, the horns pointed, two flat lying back, and two forward; he is the size of a fallow-deer, and stretches up his head, when he runs, in a singular manner. His pace is a rough trot, and his hoofs almost as large as those of an ox, with dew-claws, spreading when he runs, to prevent him from sinking in the snow. The accounts of his speed are much exaggerated. He can go seventy miles a day for three or four days, but is sure to be killed by it. After three or four hours they tire; the least weight annoys them. The sledge is more properly a boat in every respect, and the common rate is about *forty miles*. In the woods here, besides game of all sorts, except wild boar, there are bears, and abundance of wolves. While we were there, a flock of six or eight came so close to the house that the watch shot at them; and they constantly destroy the dogs, etc., if they go any distance from home. The elk is sometimes met with, a creature of great size, though harmless. In the king's menagerie they have one, twenty hands high to the back. There are also lynxes of two sorts, both beasts of prey, and valuable for their furs. Of game-birds we have here cocdubois, a large and excellent bird; the snoripa, moor-game, and, above all (from the North), the xerpar, a small bird about the size of a chicken, quite white, and exceedingly delicate, sometimes carried as far as Paris, and sold for two guineas a piece.

At Ekolsund there is a runic stone with an inscription, bearing that it had been erected by Gotho, widow of an ancient hero, to his memory; also that the same hero had been the founder of Ekolsund, by its old name of *Harvista*. Besides several runic remains scattered up and down the country, they still make in Norlad the runic sticks, or almanacs, which were formerly used, and which represent the properties, etc., of the month by *hieroglyphics.*

Ekolsund was built by Count Jott, one of Gustavus Adolphus's generals.

From Ekolsund we went up to Upsala in a carriage lent us by Seton, and accompanied by Mr. Halsted, who was educated there, and knew every body. After travelling through a flat country, we arrived at Upsala, and sent our letters, waiting for that night in a snug though poor inn enough, called the *Cellar*, or *Skellar.* In the next room, where a great number of the students have an ordinary, they sung the whole time almost—some of them extremely well, but in general without words. The "Marseillaise" was the most conspicuous tune, and oftenest repeated.

The town stands in the middle of a very fine plain, on a river small but bright, the hill on which the castle is situated standing almost alone. The town counts about five thousand inhabitants, is built chiefly of wood, and interspersed with gardens. The four principal streets meet in a great square. The cathedral is a very large pile of building, though of brick; it has two towers of copper, which make a fine appearance. It contains the tomb of Gustavus Vasa (whom the king lately exhumed, and found well preserved), St. Eric, the families of Geer and Stuve; Archbishop Menandi, a very elegant one, erected by his son, M. de Fredenheim; and Linnæus, lately put up. It is composed of one block of Swedish porphyry and a medallion of the great man. The altar-piece is very fine.

We then saw the public hall or theatre, where an oration was holding, by Professor Götling, on the birth of the prince, in Latin, written by a professor. Then the library, which is a large collection, but disappoints one in point of rare old books, when one considers that Gustavus Adolphus pillaged from the German libraries, and all the treasures of these were lodged here. We saw, however, the celebrated *Silver Book* (Codex Argenteus), or Gothic Testament, which has made so much noise. It is the only Gothic book extant, except the Codex at Wolfenbuttel, to which, however, it is infinitely superior. It is written in silver letters on purple vellum, and the boards are silver. The letters, however, in many places have eaten through the vellum on which they were written. We saw a remarkable manuscript of the Edda, which has been the subject of a controversy between Professor Schlozer, in Germany, and the late Chevalier Ihre.*

In the same room with these manuscripts is placed a very large and valuable chest, carefully locked with several locks, chained and sealed, containing all the private papers of the late king, which he ordered here before his death, and left to be opened fifty years after his death.

We then dined with the family of M. Wetterstedt, the governor of Uppland, he himself being at present at Stockholm. After dinner, went to see the collection of Professor Thunberg, the Japanese traveller. He is in bad health, and very old, so we did not see him: he lives in the house that formerly belonged to Linnæus.† We saw also the garden and green-houses, where there is a small collection, not in bad order, formerly arranged by that great man. The green-house and garden are to be transferred to the chateau, where handsome buildings are already erected; but as only a certain sum yearly is allotted, the work goes slowly on. In the evening we went to see a literary curiosity—a traveller, M. Ödman: he has not stirred out of his room for sixteen years. His sole occupation is abridging voyages, of which he has published above one hundred volumes in Swedish. He talked French so ill, that it was difficult to converse with him. He lies lounging on a bed, from which he seldom stirs. He has a family, and tolerably good appointments. We then went to the reading-room, where the students go; it is uncommonly well stocked with foreign newspapers, and Swedish, of course.

Next morning we went to see the collection, chiefly mineralogical, of the Royal Society of Upsala: this we found in a neat small house well filled up: in one of the rooms the Society meets. Among other specimens are some very good native silver ores from Sala, and in general a complete collection of Swedish mineralogy.

* See above, p. 135.

† Carl-Peter Thunberg, the great Swedish botanist, born at Jönköping in 1743; died at Upsala in 1828. A list of his works will be found under his name in the "Nouvelle Biographie Générale."

The shells are also numerous, and there is a large flora. Professor Lilieblad, who showed us the place, has published a "Flora Suecica."

We then went a second time to the chateau, a long and inelegant red building not finished, having a round tower at one end, and not the other. We called on M. Adam Afzelius, lately returned from London, where he resided some time under D'Asp in a diplomatic capacity. D'Asp introdueed us to him by letter. He was a long time in Sierra Leone, and has brought home a large collection of rarities from thence: he has not arranged them, but means to publish an account of his voyage. The castle is built on the site of the old fortress, of which the ruins still surround it. We saw the cell where *Steen Sture* was murdered by Eric II: The king stabbed him in the arm; he drew out the dagger and kissed it, then returned it to Eric, who in a fury of rage dispatched him.

From the castle there is a fine and very extensive view. Gamla (or old) Upsala is distinctly seen half a Swedish mile off. This is only remarkable for the *Mora Stein* on which the ancient kings of Sweden were crowned; besides a number of barrows, under the most remarkable of which it is thought that *Kjalman*, one of these, is buried. I visited also the professor of chemistry, who lives in the house and laboratory of Bergman, who arranged his mineral collection. The laboratory seems very excellent, but I did not see the collection.

The University is not in so flourishing a state as formerly. There are six hundred students, who are divided according to their provinces or nations of Sweden from which they come: each nation is under the care or inspection of one professor. The morning after we arrived, each nation received a private reprimand from its professor for having showed indecent violence in politics; and particularly for having composed indecent songs ridiculing the birth of the prince. Two weeks after this, the king came to Upsala himself, resigned the chancellorship after a violent speech to the professors, etc., accusing them all of Jacobinism, and ordered them to choose another. They pitched on Count Fersen, with which the king was well pleased.

The students here are for the most part extremely poor: very many of them are farmers' sons. The professors here seem of a rank superior to the common run of those on the Continent. There are several travelling pensions or bursaries, and we saw many who had been in Lapland with these, even the length of Enaratraok.

The Society publishes the Upsala "Acta Eruditorum;" and corresponds with the Societies of Abo, Stockholm, Göttenborg, and the Physiographical Society of Lund. They have many leading members—Thunberg, Lilieblad, Afzelius, Götling, Moravius.

The University is much split into parties, the professors always quarrelling. Ihre was much annoyed by some of them. His retorts are much talked of, for he was a man of wit. One of them meeting him on the bridge, said, "I never go out of my way for a knave." "But *I always* do," said he, stepping aside. The students, instead of fighting as in German universities, are rather given to drinking and singing, but not to great excess. They seldom have strangers, and are extremely civil and kind to you; this we experienced from the professors and the governor's people very universally.

After taking another view of the theatre, where a Swedish oration was this day held (ladies being admitted) on the same subject, we set off for Ekolsund, where we arrived at ten o'clock at night, after a very cold and slow ride, the roads being exceedingly heavy. At Seton's we found Baron Schwerin, a poor nobleman.

Dec. 16.—Drove rapidly through woods, our path good; waited at Höfve near two hours, then through one of the most extensive and thickest forests I have seen to Haslerör. While sitting waiting for horses, I amused the people by an involuntary feat, the carriage running back about a dozen yards down a slope, but received no hurt.

The horses are not changed at Mairiestadt, as towns are always avoided if possible, from the difficulty of finding horses. However, as I wished to see the quarters of the man who had committed a recent murder, I stopped a little; was told, however, that he was still whole in prison, as a robber, murderer, and incendiary. Went to the inn, and, seeing a small *table d'hôte* laid, had the curiosity to wait to sup at it.

However, I had to eat alone, as the company kept walking up and down, to the number of eleven, while I fed. Their staring amused me a little; but I met with the utmost civility. Some herrings which I ate here, from Wencon, tasted exactly like those of Loch Lomond.*

This town stands on the Wennern Sea, and is a pretty large place. I saw several genteel people enough.

In passing on, one of the horses fell at his length. The driver, swearing he was dead, would stop us. After getting it round, found the cause of the fellow's noise was my Russian brute's having threatened him with his sword if he did not drive quick. After satisfying the one and terrifying the other of our cattle, got on.

Dec. 17.—Got on through the next three stations, Biörsäter, Enebaken (good), and Kollänger, without dismounting, sleeping chiefly. Passed through Lidköping without stopping. It is a good-looking town on a bay of the Wennern, with a stream running past it, and vessels. There is a large, neat square in it, with some good buildings.

At Mölby, stopped to get some refreshment from the soup, etc., being sadly galled and torn, and continued to Tañg. This forenoon the road went through a country where wood was not to be seen. The road, striking off to Trollhatta, becomes execrably rough, and now from the frost peculiarly so; and near that place it is even dangerous. On the right is a fine rocky hill, with columnar top, much wood behind.

Arrived at Tañg at four, and before horses and guide could be got it was quite dark. Dined in a very snug inn, and then went out by the light of a lantern to see the works and hear the falls. The view, though obscure, was quite satisfactory, and even sublime. The road of scaffolding being all a sheet of ice, the ladders and planks also, by which we had to crawl up the sluices, we had a very difficult business to keep ourselves safe. After crawling up and down for above an hour, we returned to our inn, highly pleased, though much fatigued.

After coffee, and looking over the traveller's book at the inn, and adding a note, set off at ten, and had a very slow and hazardous drive along the rocks which form the road. It

* Probably Loch Fine.

was bright moonlight, and the night agreeable. At the first station, had to wait an hour and a half for horses. In going to the next, were overtaken by a storm of snow, and had to crawl; were stopped at the next also.

Dec. 18.—At the second had coffee, and, as it was morning, proceeded through the most rocky part of Sweden I had yet seen. Remarked particularly a valley and a vast plain, with a river running through it (almost frozen), and all surrounded by masses of absolutely bare rocks, some of them of very considerable size. The valley turns, and continues apparently well cultivated; the rocks ranged on each side, with a few trees scattered over them, and several clumps up and down the valley, and some neat gentlemen's seats and boxes. There is a good wooden drawbridge over the Gotha, which is here very broad, and at the end appears Göttenborg. The day being now fine, the prospect was very pleasant. Several streams and one considerable river cross the road and fall into the Gotha. Entered Göttenborg at two o'clock, along a canal with trees planted on the sides, and the boxes of the merchants.

Göttenborg. — The merchants who compose the body of this place are all croaking at the times, the effect which the war has had on the country. The India House is actually shut up, and the Exchange almost deserted. A few houses engross all the trade, while there is a multitude of small merchants and traders almost starving.

The principal merchants are British, chiefly Scotch, who unite the English style of living with the Swedish way of drinking. The town is large, and chiefly of brick — some pretty good buildings. It was built by the Dutch, in the style of Rotterdam, with canals and trees. The inhabitants are in great discontent with the present state of their trade, and have lately shown marks of it. The use of French brandy having been forbidden, the distilling of Swedish spirits became extremely unpopular, particularly at Göttenborg, from the quantity of grain consumed in it. The mob rose and destroyed the works, warehouses, etc. The governor employed conciliatory measures, and the mob was appeased. The king was furious, and severely reprimanded the governor by letter for not having made the soldiers fire, for which there was no pretext. The popularity of the governor is excessive among all ranks.

Dec. 19.—We set out from Göttenborg at nine, determining to make for Norway, in the almost certain expectation of finding a vessel there for some port in Scotland. After driving up the valley, and crossing the river by the drawbridge, we came to a ferry under the Castle of Bohus, now in ruins, but which must have been a place of no small strength. Its ramparts are of stone, and very high. It is built on a rock, and surrounded wholly by the river's branches. The view from it is extremely romantic; everywhere around are huge rocky masses, with a few trees scattered about. The valley on one side; on the other the river's branches meeting under the neat town of Kongelf, and disappearing among the rocks. The wooden bridge here was destroyed by the Danes in 1787, the stumps only remaining, so that a ferry is now established; and we were stopped for about two hours, in the most intense cold, till the ice could be broken. At Kongelf we stopped to eat some of our cold provisions, and then continued our journey in the dark. The carriage being shut, we were not actually frozen, but the road was execrably rough, and we went on a foot's pace; besides, it was more hilly than is usual in Sweden. At one in the morning, arriving at a decent inn, we decided to stop for the night, and found a couple of comfortable rooms.

Tired with the cold of yesterday, I was glad to take advantage of a hot bath before I turned in. And here a most remarkable thing happened to me — so remarkable that I must tell the story from the beginning. After I left the High School, I went with G——, my most intimate friend, to attend the classes in the University. There was no divinity class, but we frequently in our walks discussed and speculated upon many grave subjects—among others, on the immortality of the soul, and on a future state. This question, and the possibility, I will not say of ghosts walking, but of the dead appearing to the living, were subjects of much speculation; and we actually committed the folly of drawing up an agreement, *written with our blood*, to the effect, that whichever of us died the first should appear to the other, and thus solve any doubts we had entertained of the "life after death." After we had finished our classes at the college, G—— went to India, having got an appointment there in the civil service. He seldom wrote to me, and after the lapse of a few years I had almost forgotten him; moreover, his family having little connection with Edinburgh, I seldom saw or heard any thing of them, or of him through them, so that all the old school-boy intimacy had died out, and I had nearly forgotten his existence. I had taken, as I have said, a warm bath; and while lying in it and enjoying the comfort of the heat, after the late freezing I had undergone, I turned my head round, looking towards the chair on which I had deposited my clothes, as I was about to get up out of the bath. On the chair sat G——, looking calmly at me. How I got out of the bath I know not, but on recovering my senses I found myself sprawling on the floor. The apparition, or whatever it was, that had taken the likeness of G——, had disappeared. The vision produced such a shock that I had no inclination to talk about it, or to speak about it even to Stuart; but the impression it made upon me was too vivid to be easily forgotten; and so strongly was I affected by it, that I have here written down the whole history, with the date, 19th December, and all the particulars, as they are now fresh before me. No doubt I had fallen asleep; and that the appearance presented so distinctly to my eyes was a dream, I can not for a moment doubt; yet for years I had had no communication with G——, nor had there been any thing to recall him to my recollection; nothing had taken place during our Swedish travels either connected with G—— or with India, or with any thing relating to him, or to any member of his family. I recollected quickly enough our old discussion, and the bargain we had made. I could not discharge from my mind the impression that G—— must have died, and that his appearance to me was to be received by me as proof of a future state; yet all the while I felt convinced that the whole was a dream; and so painfully vivid and so unfading was the impression, that I could not bring myself to talk of it, or to make the slightest allusion to it. I finished dressing; and as we had agreed to make an early start, I was ready by six o'clock, the hour of our early breakfast.

[*Brougham, Oct.* 16, 1862.—I have just been copying out

from my journal the account of this strange dream: *Certissima mortis imago!* And now to finish the story, begun above sixty years since. Soon after my return to Edinburgh, there arrived a letter from India announcing G——'s death! and stating that he had died on the 19th of December!! Singular coincidence! yet when one reflects on the vast number of dreams which night after night pass through our brains, the number of coincidences between the vision and the event are perhaps fewer and less remarkable than a fair calculation of chances would warrant us to expect. Nor is it surprising, considering the variety of our thoughts in sleep, and that they all bear some analogy to the affairs of life, that a dream should sometimes coincide with a contemporaneous, or even with a future event. This is not much more wonderful than that a person whom we had no reason to expect should appear to us at the very moment we had been thinking or speaking of him. So common is this, that it has for ages grown into the proverb, "Speak of the devil."

I believe every such seeming miracle is, like every ghost-story, capable of explanation.

There never was, to all appearance, a better authenticated fact than Lord Lyttleton's ghost. I have heard my father tell the story; but coupled with his entire conviction that it was either a pure invention, or the accidental coincidence of a dream with the event.

He had heard the particulars from a lady—a Mrs. Affleck, or some such name—during a visit he made to London about the year 1780, not very long after the death. The substance of what he heard was, that Lord Lyttleton had for some time been in failing health; that he was suffering from a heart complaint; that a few days before his death he related to some female friends who were living in his house in London an extraordinary dream, in which a figure appeared to him and told him he should shortly die; that his death, which really took place a few days after the dream, had been very sudden, owing, no doubt, to the heart disease. My father was convinced that the female tendency to believe in the marvellous naturally produced the statement that the moment of the death had exactly corresponded with the time as predicted in the dream. The story was told with corroborating circumstances—one of which was, the attempt to cheat the ghost by altering the hour on the clock; and the tale obtained a surprising degree of credit, considering the unsubstantial foundation on which it really rested.

On all such subjects my father was very skeptical. He was very fond of telling a story in which he had been an actor, and, as he used to say, in which his unbelieving obstinacy had been the means of demolishing what would have made a very pretty ghost-story.

He had dined one day in Dean's Yard, Westminster, with a party of young men, one of whom was his intimate friend, Mr. Calmel. There was some talk about the death of a Mrs. Nightingale, who had recently died under some melancholy circumstances, and had been that day buried in the Abbey. Some one of the party offered to bet that no one of those present would go down into the grave and drive a nail into the coffin.

Calmel accepted the wager, only stipulating that he might have a lantern. He was accordingly let into the cathedral by a door out of the cloisters, and then left to himself. The dinner-party, after waiting an hour or more for Calmel, began to think something must have happened to him, and that he ought to be looked after; so my father and two or three more got a light and went to the grave, at the bottom of which lay the apparently dead body of Mr. Calmel. He was quickly transported to the prebend's dining-room, and recovered out of his fainting-fit. As soon as he could find his tongue, he said, "Well, I have won my wager, and you'll find the nail in the coffin; but, by Jove! the lady rose up, laid hold of me, and pulled me down before I could scramble out of the grave." Calmel stuck to his story, in spite of all the scoffing of his friends; and the ghost of Mrs. Nightingale would have been all over the town but for my father's obstinate incredulity. Nothing would satisfy him but an ocular inspection of the grave and coffin; and so, getting a light, he and some of the party returned to the grave. There, sure enough, was the nail, well driven into the coffin; but hard fixed by it was a bit of Mr. Calmel's coat-tail! So there was an end of Mrs. Nightingale's ghost. This grave afterwards became remarkable for a very beautiful piece of sculpture, by some celebrated artist, representing Mr. Nightingale vainly attempting to ward from his dying wife the dart of death. My father always instanced this as the best piece of monumental sculpture in the Abbey.* After this long digression, it is time to return to my journal.]

Dec. 20.—Up at six; and after coffee—which, as usual, was served as tea and *eggohl*, a sort of caudle of eggs, sugar, ale, and milk, much used by travellers in Sweden, and excellent for keeping one warm, we set out slowly, the road being bad, and a good deal of snow having fallen. The country similar to that which we had of late been in—namely, more hilly by a great deal than the rest of Sweden. The natives quite different in their appearance from the other Swedes we had seen; very ugly, and dressed differently—loose jackets, boots, with trowsers; apparently all having to do with the sea, as fishermen or sailors. The inns were better; but the people of all kinds more insolent, and very greedy. In short, I never saw so strongly-marked a difference in so short a space.

The road wound up and down some very steep hills, overhung by high rocks covered with snow, but much varied by firs perfectly green, and sometimes by purple birch, which had a very pleasing effect. We went extremely slow, and arrived at Qvistrum about eight. The landlady is the woman mentioned by Mrs. Wollstonecraft, but we could not discover her wondrous beauty.

This day we passed Uddevalla, situated on a firth of the sea, which was quite frozen, and had people skating on it. It is a neat town; the houses tiled, and built in a way quite different from the usual Swedish houses. There are some good shops and houses; and the shipping is considerable, though now laid up. All this day very mild indeed—I suppose from the neighborhood of the sea.

Dec. 21.—Ready at six; pass the bridge where the battle was fought, or rather was said to have been fought. Mrs. Wollstonecraft tells a lie upon the subject. We heard from Mansback how Armfelt, a cavalry officer, was posted at the

---

* The celebrated monument to Mrs. Nightingale in Westminster Abbey is understood to be the work of Roubilliac.

pass beyond the bridge, to defend it, with about seven hundred Swedes. Mansback offered a deserter of his own, who knew the country, his life, if he would carry him by another road through the hill, which he did; and then he surrounded Armfelt, and took him. For this Armfelt was broke. Mansback thinks this very harsh, and says he was not at all to blame. As for the bridge, he said he could have passed the river easily, half a mile above, in twenty places.*

Dec. 21.—The bridge and pass are very romantic, the rocks, trees, etc.; indeed, all the day the road went through a great variety of the finest rock-scenery, often through flat, cultivated country, and sometimes in sight of bays of the sea, all frozen, but chiefly among vast masses of rock quite bare, rising abruptly, and whole hills, perhaps three hundred feet high, of not an inch but these masses, some of them as flat as a wall, others rough, and in general each is one undivided block rising out of a plain, or the sea. We proceeded with little refreshment. Once I tried the *brandwein* with water, and found to my cost that what I had heard was true (of its being impossible to take it diluted from its emetic tendency); for, though I only sipped a little, I was really sick and ill the whole night.

Dec. 22.—All the night the road was over very steep and dangerous hills, so that we were obliged to get out every now and then to walk. This we did not regret, as the scenery was always interesting. Once we were overturned, though luckily on level ground, and not hurt; the carriage, however, was much damaged, so that we could not descend or climb a hill with it safely. At the custom-house at Svinesund we were stopped for examination of passport, dues, etc., etc. It stood at the bottom of a tremendous descent. The scenery around is inexpressibly grand, the river or firth being on each side surrounded by high rocky masses, with a few trees scattered. Got over the ferry (at twice) which separates the two countries; on the other side stopped only to get a little milk, the landlord speaking good English. Had another hill to climb

* A good English account will be found of this eventful period of Swedish history in a Life of Armfelt, by the late Thomas Watts of the British Museum, in the fragment of a General Biographical Dictionary issued by the Society for the Promotion of Useful Knowledge.

equal to what we descended before; and after being considerably fatigued with the long and heavy walks, slept on to Helle, where we breakfasted, and by the charges, etc., found we were really in Norway.

Hence to Frederikshald, our bags on sledges, the scenery growing more and more mountainous: arrived at ten.

Frederikshald is a considerable town: it stands pleasantly on a firth, with a river. It is very neatly built, chiefly of wood. Some of the houses are very large and elegant, and the rest comfortable. The sea was all frozen, and the shipping laid up, but the commerce is very considerable—almost wholly with England, in deals and iron. The castle commands the town completely, stands very high upon huge rocks, and is formed of fine stone works, absolutely impregnable on the side of the town, and commanding the neighboring hills, which are indeed inconsiderable heights. The inn was wretched, and the charge most exorbitant, being six rix-dollars for two nights—breakfast and bed. It has a good view of the water among rocky heights; on these people were skating and driving *traîneaux* to a great distance. Mr. Nils Anker calling, we, after dressing, returned his visit, and were taken by him to Mr. Dank, junior's, where we dined with a very large and elegant party, among whom the Governor-general Mansback, some officers, and all the principal natives—no ladies except the mistress of the house. We were amused with the custom of drinking thanks after dinner, which runs round the table. "Tank, tank," "tank for mit" (thanks for meat). After coffee, went to a private play, where all the ladies and gentlemen of the place were assembled. The theatre was very small, and a sort of make-shift—the play a Danish translation of Kotzebue's "Brothers," and acted in general ill; but one actor played very decently, and the company seemed much pleased. After the play some of the men retired to billiards and smoking, and the theatre was immediately cleared into a ball and sandwich room, where waltzing and eating went on till four in the morning, without fiddling, however, as it was the regimental band. We remarked that not one of the officers belonging to the place were there. Indeed there exists, as is but too common, a complete division between the natives and soldiers. The women struck us as very pretty.

Dec. 23.—Having last night met with Mr. Paulus, the late French consul at Christiansand, I went to breakfast (by invitation) with him and his daughter, in the same inn with ourselves, and was kept so long there in conversation that we could not go to the castle. Dined at Anker's with a large party, chiefly of the same class as yesterday, but much more select. Afterwards the men smoked in a room *per se*, then cards (with *chasse café* on the table), then sandwiches—a visit of ten hours. Were much disgusted with the barbarous way in which the master and mistress seem the *whole time* the very slaves of the company, running up and down, etc. The mercantile gentlemen talk English for the most part.

Dec. 24.—At nine o'clock went up to see the fort, and the spot where Charles XII. was killed, having had an order from the governor. However, we were detained some time at the gate.

He was standing near a stone looking over a small rail, and a cross two feet high is upon the spot instead of a low pyramid formerly placed there. On the cross is cut a rude inscription—" C. XII. fell. Dec. 1718."

It is about four hundred yards from the part of the castle whence the shot is said to have been fired. There are two rising grounds, one on the side of the cross, and within pistol-shot of it; and if he was assassinated, it must have been from one of these. The mask taken from his head after death (a cast of which is at Brougham) represents the wound in a different place from the one supposed to have been inflicted by the shot from the fort.

Frederikshald, Dec. 24.—The inhabitants of Frederikshald enjoy great immunities from their patriotism on this occasion, when they burned their houses to prevent them from falling into the hands of the Swedes. The example was set by the family of Colbiönzel, whose antipathy to the Swedes is noted. The story of Anna Maria Colbiönzel is well known. She detained a regiment of Charles's (up the country), by giving notice to the Norwegian troops, and detaining the enemy in her house. We met with the only lineal descendant of this celebrated woman at Mr. Dank's, at Frederikshald.

The Norwegians, in their poems and conversation, talk of Charles XII. as a victim to their liberties sacrificed on the altar of Frederikshald, and say that there was no prospect of his succeeding in his attack on Frederikshald, or in his expedition, even if he had taken it. This, however, is assuredly not a just view of this case.

Dec. 24.—Set off, after breakfast, at eleven o'clock, and travelled all day on the snow, the trainage being completely established. Passed the river frozen, but had to unharness the horses and leave our carriage, as the ice was not sufficiently strong. Had to regret not seeing the celebrated cascade.* Passed an inn kept by one Alexander, a Scotsman—miserable indeed. Came through some woods, in which we remarked that there was much more underwood than in Sweden. The day was very dark and bad, snowing copiously. Had to wait at one station two hours for horses in this disagreeable evening, and came on very heavily, owing to our wheels. At Moss we arrived at eleven, and found a very good inn, kept by a Frenchman, with supper and beds all ready, thanks to the forebote.

Dec. 25.—Moss is a considerable town, the houses neatly built of wood. There are a vast number of saw-mills, the water of which, being almost all frozen, had a very singular effect — the icicles, iced cascades, etc., being innumerable. The magazines of timber are immense, and there is also a great iron-work belonging to General Anker. As a great quantity of snow had fallen during the night, we were obliged to put our carriage upon a sledge and pack up the wheels. The natives were driving about very finely in their small *traîneaux* to church, it being Christmas. We passed through an extensive forest on very high ground, then came to cultivated country, which lasted most part of the way. The inns which we saw were all uncommonly good, and we were everywhere invited to eat, according to custom. The last stage being very hilly and bad, we did not arrive till twelve at Christiania. During this day we did not feel it very cold. Found good beds, a very good inn, and comforted ourselves with wine, as we could only get a sandwich for supper.

Dec. 26.—Called on Squire Haygerup, the mayor, Mr. Lee, the English vice-consul, and Mr. Matheson, a merchant. The

---

* Of the Glommen.

governor and Mr. Anker and all else being out of town, as is the custom at Christmas, experienced much hospitality. Dined *en famille* with Mr. Haygerup, and heard the Norwegian song. Supped at Mr. Lee's.

Dec. 27.—Went to buy books and maps, and found the town miserably provided in these—very few, and enormously dear. The furs we found equally scarce, but saw some uncommon fine lynxes. The town is very regularly built. A considerable part of the houses are of brick, and some very large and handsome. So regularly are the streets built, that one can not easily find his way. At the meetings of the streets are placed large square cisterns or reservoirs of water, supplied by copious streams. These were smoking to-day like boiling caldrons. The streets are spacious and even; the houses built chiefly of timber, though many of them are of brick and stone, covered with a rough coat of stucco. Among the public buildings we noticed the school or university, the prison, and the fortress—which is separate from the town, called Aggershuus—the old name of the city, and the name of the province to this day. The town stands on an arm of the sea, far indeed from the ocean, and so retired as never to feel its storms. At this time all was frozen, and sledges with any burdens could pass over the bays; but the ice in these firths is extremely treacherous, for a sudden change of wind or weather carries off in a few hours every flake of ice from masses which appeared before immovable.

The valley of Christiania is extremely beautiful; but we quite agreed with Mrs. Wollstonecraft in wondering how Mr. Coxe could discover *glaciers*, as the flat is surrounded by rising grounds so gently sloping and so trifling in height as hardly to deserve the name of hills. Among the houses which we remarked as splendid were those of Mr. Anker and Mr. Collet. Mr. Anker's is a large building, disposed in a quadrangle, with every convenience of outhouses and offices, and with all sorts of sumptuous and luxurious accommodation—as we afterwards experienced. After dining on tolerable venison, we received an invitation in the most polite terms, by express, from Mr. Anker, who was then spending the Christmas holidays (according to the custom of the place) at the country-seat of Mr. Collet, fifty miles up the country. Our letters of introduction had been sent off from the town that morning, and we received the letter of invitation at five in the evening—no bad example of expeditious travelling.

Dec. 28.—At seven o'clock in the morning a couple of single sledges, with most excellent horses, were ready at our door. After fortifying ourselves with coffee, we set off, each sledge having a servant to stand behind and drive. We flew rather than drove through the town, my sledge soon breaking down from the rapidity of the motion; but we soon mended the broken parts, and got on as swiftly as before. The trainage was most excellent; and I reckoned, by comparing our pace at this time with the slower rate of travelling we afterwards went at, that we did not take more than three minutes to the mile — indeed the motion was disagreeably rapid, the horse sweating, and myself obliged to shut my eyes, and even then complaining of pain and oppression. The hill ground to the west of the town relieved us; but we were surprised to find that it did not retard our pace more than we wished. Without attending at all to the road, our guides sprang up the sides of the knolls, and kept the sledges from stones, hollows, and stumps, by dismounting and balancing with their feet and hands.

Admired the fine situation of Christiania from these heights; changed horses without stopping; and then, at the next station, came out to warm ourselves, as is usual, every now and then, in this mode of travelling. We had come hither chiefly through woods. Now we went on the ice the other two stages. The river Glommen being well frozen and smooth, we whisked along quickly, though now and then the ice broke—*i. e.*, the surface-ice without water. Passed immense timber magazines belonging to Mr. Anker; came to the lake, a mile broad and three long, and soon were at Mr. Collet's, at Flädebije. The house is a large one, roughly built on an eminence, and bitter cold, but only used twice a year—now and in the hunting season. We here met with every civility, kindness, and hospitality that can be imagined, and so much of the style of living and manners of the natives. The party was quite on the frolic and "*vive la bagatelle.*" The most unbounded liberty was allowed—the young people constantly mingling in all sorts of innocent freedoms; indeed the quantity of kissing grew quite tiresome, every game ending in a kissing-match. The party consisted of twenty-nine, without us two; and was afterwards increased to thirty-one, but afterwards amounted to thirty-five in all. The host and hostess (*obervert* and *obervertina*) never seemed at all different from the rest of the company, except that their healths were drunk at dinner. A couple was appointed to the office of host and hostess for each night, the order being arranged at first, and each couple with a few others performed a small dramatic piece contrived or imitated by themselves. The theatre is the end of the sitting-room, loosely and roughly fitted up, as nothing but paper is allowed to be brought from town. The *parts* are studied, but the *words* are left to the occasion, except in one instance, where there was a French drama from the "Taming of the Shrew," by De la Toenaye, a French traveller, one of the company. At the end of the play, the couple invite the company to spend the next day with them; and accordingly, during the whole of it they act as host and hostess, sitting at the head of the table, ordering and arranging every thing, etc., etc. The day is chiefly spent as follows, but every one enjoyed the most perfect freedom of doing exactly as he pleased, without any one so much as asking where he was:

After breakfast (which is not a formal meal, but continues two or three hours as the company drops in), we walked out, conversed, read, rode in sledges, called at each other's rooms, and some took the amount of the slee, others (chiefly the old gentlemen) played at Ombre and Boston, and smoked. After luncheon, as a whet before, dined at two, and sang constantly, drinking toasts at the same time—such as *Halletelskop*, "the whole company;" *Benskip's skaal*, "friendship's health;" *Piger's skaal*, "girl's health;" *Norge's skaal*,* etc. In the middle of the table was placed an emblematical figure of some kind, having a reference to the subject of the last play. Round the dining-room and in the ceiling are hung a vast number of these figures, collected for thirty years past, during which time this custom has continued in the family. After dining, and drinking a claret and burgundy, bishop

* Norway's health—a toast.

(Bischoff), retired to the next room, each gentleman leading his own lady; and after the ceremony of kissing hands, coffee and pipes, then tea, some game of romps, or a dance, cards and pipes, supper, play, dance, and cards; and the evening ended with the last host and hostess (*vert* and *vertina*) sitting in the middle of the room and being kissed—he by all the ladies, she by all the men. The last night, a rude masquerade instead of the play; and some of the servants danced the *Haling dance*, a very curious wild dance from the interior of the country, of immense difficulty, requiring great strength and agility, on the heels and toes chiefly, round the room, whirling the partner round, and leaping and twisting over her. This one of the *ladies* danced with a footman!

In autumn Mr. Collet has the same sort of party for the chase, which may be carried on here, as there is a great deal of flat ground. There are not many bears in this quarter; but Mr. Dank's (of Frederikshald) father killed eleven during his life. There is a considerable number of wolves. The game is hares, of which we saw one or two, as white as the snow; ceders (the coryctu verus, our capercailzie), rupo (partridge), and hierpati. We eat reindeer-venison also, exceedingly fine, and far superior to our other deer-flesh. Mr. Collet's house here stands above the lake; around it are woods and cultivated grounds, but no pleasure-grounds, of course. We went to see his saw-mills, and brick and tile works—both on a very large scale. Drove on sledges—very cold, indeed, and believe it was from this that I got a boil on my cheek, which proved exceedingly troublesome.

The following is a list of the company who were at Flädebije: Mr. and Mrs. Collet—[illegible]—and Lady Anker, Miss Collet, Miss Klaason, —— and —— Kaas, Mr. and Mrs. Julstoup, Mr. and Mrs. Julin, Miss Talma (sister of the great actor), (the governor of the province), Miss Kaas, Miss (Young Ankers), Captain Nilson, Lieutenant Carlson, —— (——), —— (——), Cadet Keaason, Mr. de la Toenaye, General Anker, Mr. Gram, Mr. Collet, Mr. Anker, Mr. Maribeau; among other chance visitors, Mr. Rozencraz.

The arrival of Bonaparte in France, and his proceedings at Paris, had been known at Stockholm before we left it, and the expectation of a revolution entertained. But the event of 18th Brumaire (9th Nov., 1799) had not been known, and the first account we had of it was at Flädebije. De la Toenaye was determined to return to France if the emigrants were allowed; and instead of the *promenade autour de Scandinavie*, which he meant to add to his former travels in Great Britain, he had to be content with a *promenade autour de mes Foyers*. He even doubted whether the return of the emigrants would be allowed.

The sleigh is much used here. The skates are above six feet long and turned up at the ends, requiring the balance to be thrown before by bending the knees forward. A pole, with a round plate at the end, is also held in the hand to balance by. Accidents often happen, either from falls or splitting up, by the feet running off separately. They go in this way very quick down any steep, and take great leaps off eminences. They have a regiment of (I believe) seven hundred men on these snow-shoes, of which they are very proud. This troop once drew a Swedish force of cavalry down a steep, where it was either cut to pieces or destroyed by the fall. The people are all extravagantly fond of sledging. The common people enjoy it in a great degree, and seem to feel the greatest pleasure in the motion and driving. Children and boys either skate or go upon a small double patten of two pieces of wood shod with iron, on which they sit and run down hills or descents, etc.

We set out for Laurvig late in January, at which port a vessel to England was expected to sail. We were kept a week or ten days there, and embarked on a timber-laden ship, happily for us, as to this cargo we owed our safety. The weather being very good, indeed a calm, though it was February and in the North Sea, when we had our pilot on board at Lowestoft, on the coast of Norfolk, the vessel, a few miles from shore, struck on a sand-bank, the rudder was carried away, and such a leak sprung as kept us at the pumps for three or four hours; but the leak defied all our efforts, the ship became water-logged, and was only prevented sinking by our cargo. We made signals of all kinds, and fired guns to make them put off boats for our assistance; but the sea had increased, and the only one they tried was swamped! so we had to remain at the mercy of the only anchor we had, the captain considering that his old and crazy vessel would hold together unless it came to blow hard and to drive us on shore, or the wind shifted and we were driven out to sea, in neither of which cases could she hold together. It was no small relief to us, therefore, when a Newcastle collier came in sight and she approached near enough to learn our condition. She threw a rope on board and towed us into Harwich, where we slept, and next day came to London. There I only stopped to take the mail for Edinburgh, where I arrived safe.

Here my journal ends.

CHAPTER IV.

THE SCOTCH BAR AND THE "EDINBURGH REVIEW."

My Opinion of my Friend Charles Stuart.—Death of my Brother Peter.—I am admitted Advocate.—Profession distasteful.—Correspondence with Sir Joseph Banks.—Work at "Colonial Policy."—Leading Men of the Scotch Bar.—Harry Erskine.—Blair.—Charles Hope.—Maconochie (Lord Meadowbank).—Cranstoun (Lord Corehouse).—James Reddie.—Walter Scott. --Jeffrey.—The "Edinburgh Review."—Sydney Smith's Account criticised.—Jeffrey's and Horner's Account.—My own History of it.—The early Contributors, and their Contributions.—Progress of the "Review," and its Influence on Politics and Literature.—List of Contributions to the early Numbers, and Names of their Authors.—Anecdotes of Jeffrey and his Coadjutors.

It was observable that during our shipwreck, Stuart, who was an old traveller by land and by water, and never for a moment was disconcerted or lost his presence of mind, yet had a much worse opinion of our chances of escape, and was much more impressed with the dangers of our situation than I, a mere novice in travel. I was sanguine because I was inexperienced. During our whole intimacy for seven months, I had constant occasion to mark, more than I had ever done before, those great qualities which distinguished him, and carried him to the head of his profession in most difficult times. It is enough to say that the duke placed in him the most unbounded confidence when he was our minister in the Peninsula, and when he afterwards succeeded him at Paris. He is the most remarkable example I know of the great evils attending our political system, at least in its administration—the conferring all the important offices in the State on persons who possess the debating power. Stuart, but for his never having cultivated that faculty, would have filled the highest place in the conduct of our affairs during the many long years that the party ruled to which he was, both hereditarily and personally, attached. I speak of his great and good qualities after constant and cordial intimacy of much above half a century.

1800.—In this year happened the greatest misfortune of my life—greater than any, save one, that has ever yet befallen me—my brother Peter, the most beloved, the most highly prized of all our family, was killed in a duel by Campbell, of Shawfield. Even at this distance of time I feel as if it were a recent affliction. At the time I was nearly distracted; indeed, I verily believe my mind was for a time unhinged, for I left Edinburgh and wandered about I know not where. My prevailing idea was to avenge his death. As the duel had taken place at St. Salvador, on his way to India, Campbell was far beyond my reach; but I vainly thought he ought to be indicted for murder. I must have written to this effect to my uncle, Mr. Lowndes, who then lived in London; for I find by a letter of his that such must have been my hallucination.

Early in 1800, Peter had got his commission as ensign in the 85th Regiment, and was ordered to embark at Portsmouth with troops under the command of General St. John. On the 31st of March, I had written to Stuart, then living at Whitehall, to tell him of my grief at parting with Peter, and that I felt more than ever disinclined to remain in Edinburgh and work at my profession:

"I still continue more and more to detest this place, and this cursedest of cursed professions. He (Peter) will see you as he passes through London, and I really wish you could manage to procure some letters for him. He does not know what station his regiment is to go to, and has a number of recommendations on chance already. One or two more in the same way (I mean whether he knows and can tell you where he is to go or not) will do quite well."

I have said that I was so distracted by this dreadful blow, that I wanted to have Mr. Campbell brought to justice. My father would not hear of any such proceeding, and my uncle was equally against it. He wrote to me as follows:

"London, 1st November, 1800.

"My dear Henry,—No one can lament more sincerely than I do the very unfortunate event which is the subject of our correspondence. If I had not known Peter, I should undoubtedly have lamented his death, and commiserated the feelings of those more near to him, but I should soon have thought little of the subject; but having known him, and, knowing him, loved and admired him, my sorrow for his untimely end will be very lasting, and often will he have a tear to his remembrance.

"With such sentiments towards him, therefore, I am sure you will believe that the advice I am about to give is the result of consideration and regard to the memory of your brother.

"That advice is, to let the matter drop, and not to bestow one thought more upon a public prosecution."

I acted upon this advice; and after a time I resumed my legal studies, as it became necessary that I should prepare myself for the examination in Scotch law, and also for the public examination preparatory to my call to the bar, which took place early in the month of June, 1800.* I went the summer circuit, attending the Assizes held in the counties of Berwick, Roxburgh, and Selkirk—my chief, I may say only, business being to defend prisoners who were too poor to pay for professional assistance. I had an invincible repugnance to the profession I had chosen, and constantly wrote to Charles Stuart, then settled in London, expressing my desire to escape from it, and that if any opening could have been found for me in diplomacy how gladly I should have accepted it. It had occurred to me that my father's old friend and school-fellow, Sir Joseph Banks, who had on several occasions expressed an interest in my welfare, might have it in his power to help me. I have, through the kindness of a friend, been furnished with the copy of a letter I wrote to Sir Joseph, with whom I had been in correspondence on some matters relating to science, and also on the subject of my future career. The letter is as follows:

"Edinburgh, Dec. 10, 1800.

"SIR,—I was honor'd with the receipt of yours in course. I beg you will believe me when I express my satisfaction at your prospects of speedy recovery. I am only afraid lest

* See Appendix XV.

your goodness towards me may have led you to exert in writing before it was quite safe, still more before it could be convenient. It would surely be superfluous to return my warmest thanks for the new proofs which your letter contains of the interest you are so kind as to take in my trivial and humble concerns; but I avail myself with pleasure of the liberty which you give me to trouble you once more upon the subject.

"My resolution is still unaltered to attempt an opening in the political line. The difficulty, however great, is not sufficient to deprive me of some hopes that such an opportunity may occur. I believe I mentioned in my last that perhaps some private connections of your own might afford you a chance of hinting something in my behalf. I did not venture to expect that you would set about finding such opportunities. I only begged of you to have me in your eye should any occasion offer. More active exertion on my behalf was beyond what I had ever hoped. In the mean time, I am endeavoring, by cultivating as much as possible the duties of my profession, to secure a retreat for myself in case the other plan should fail. My aversion to it as an *ultimate* object continues the same —not to mention that it exposes one to the worst part of party politics, and that to succeed in it requires almost as much interest as to rise in the diplomatic line. I beg you will not put yourself to the trouble of writing sooner than your health and convenience permit. I should not have answered your last at this time, had it not appeared necessary that you should be put in possession of my *resolutions*, in case of chances offering, at the present very singular crisis. With great respect and esteem, I have the honor to be, sir, your most obliged humble servant, HENRY BROUGHAM, Junior.

"Right Hon. Sir JOSEPH BANKS,
"Soho Square, London."

All this, however, resulted in nothing; and so I continued to work at my distasteful profession, in hopes that some day or other business might come to me. But much of my time was occupied with literary and scientific pursuits, and chiefly by compiling a work upon the Colonial Policy of the European Powers. I was employed upon this during the greater part of 1801 and 1802, relieved only by weekly discussions at the Speculative Society, where I was a pretty constant attender and debater; and during a portion of the time by arranging with Smith, Jeffrey, and others the establishment of the "Edinburgh Review."

The Scotch bar afforded the amplest occasion at that time for profiting by the example of great talent and professional learning. The violence of party and exclusive spirit had considerably abated; and although there was both in society and on the bench still a tendency to discountenance those who were on the wrong side of the question, there manifestly was felt a great improvement upon those times. Harry Erskine had been removed from his place at the head of the profession (Dean of Faculty) for merely attending a public meeting to petition against the Sedition Bills (called the Pitt and Greenville Bills). I attended that meeting, and can answer for it that he strongly urged them to disperse quietly; and there was nothing like violence of any kind in the proceedings.

Of professional business there was now pretty nearly an equal distribution; officially, all was of course in the hands of the Tory or Dundas party. The learning and talent were almost equal in both parties.

Harry Erskine, both in society and in public, was the most popular advocate—indeed the most popular man. His education was entirely confined to Edinburgh, but he had none of the accent or other provincialisms of the place. His taste was well cultivated, but far from severe; and, like his brother's, his acquaintance was confined to the English classics. His speaking was of a very high order. The language was admirable, expressive, wholly without affectation, fluent, never verbose, and his manner perfect, both in action and delivery. It was impossible to have more variety, or to suit the style more perfectly to the subject and the occasion. In statement and explanation he excelled, and his illustrations were copious.

His wit was renowned, and, as it made him the life of society, placed him as the first favorite of the courts; but it also was used in excess, partly owing to the audience whom he addressed, the fifteen judges, who required to be relieved in their dull work, and, as soon as he began, expected to be made gay. Hence a very great mistake was committed by by-standers, or generally by those who either heard, or heard of, his speeches, and fancied they were all joke, all to amuse the court, or at best to turn his adversary and his arguments into ridicule. He was a most argumentative speaker; and if he sometimes did more than was necessary, he never for an instant lost sight of the point to be pressed on his audience by all the means he could employ, and which really were every weapon of eloquence except declamation and appeals to the tender feelings. Of course a great cause placed him more under restraint, and more called forth his exertions; yet it was singular how much he would sometimes labor even the most ordinary matters. However, if I were to name the most consummate exhibition of forensic talent that I ever witnessed, whether in the skillful conduct of the argument, the felicity of the copious illustrations, the cogency of the reasoning, or the dexterous appeal to the prejudices of the Court, I should without hesitation at once point to his address (*hearing in presence*) on Maitland's case; and were my friend Lauderdale alive, to him I should appeal, for he heard it with me, and came away declaring that his brother Thomas (Lord Erskine) never surpassed — nay, he thought, never equalled it.

Gillies was a speaker of a different cast, but of great excellence. He reasoned clearly and powerfully, but he also had great resources of declamation and of sarcasm. I heard his speech on the great case of Sir John Henderson, the first occasion on which he distinguished himself for mere oratory, and which drew from Hope and others the expression that they had been taken by surprise. The cause was remarkable —Sir John taking occasion to throw out a challenge to Hope, who said he trusted he had the courage to refuse as well as accept such a defiance. Indeed, he had fought, a few years before, a duel with Wylde (afterwards professor of civil law), for whom Burke had conceived the greatest admiration in consequence of his book on the French Revolution, cried up as a triumphant answer to Mackintosh's "Vindiciæ Gallicæ." It was one great drawback upon Gillies that he saw all things with the eyes of the Edinburgh Whig party, a thralldom from which Harry Erskine (as well as his brother, in the southern sphere of that party) had emancipated himself. I have never observed so great capacity as a speaker, generally so much cramped and enfeebled, as in Gillies's case.*

William Tait was one of the most accomplished lawyers of his time. John Clerk had as profound a knowledge of law, especially the feudal, in all its branches, and not merely in its theory, but in its most minute details of practical application; and would argue points of the greatest difficulty, and propound original views which sometimes at first startled himself, but by degrees won his assent and were obstinately persevered in. But he had not that acuteness which distinguished Tait, nor that marvellous fertility of resources, nor that singular clearness of concise statement, when his legal points were urged one after another, which I recollect led Moncrieff to describe his argument as a bundle of the best-polished and sharpest-pointed spears; nor that manner which was a model of graceful delivery. With all his merits, Clerk was in manner and language singularly defective.

Of Matthew Ross, the subtlety and extensive ingenuity with extraordinary learning could not be exceeded; but he seldom gave oral arguments; and the display of his unrivalled acuteness and rich stores of legal fancy was confined to the papers which, under the old system of the Court, contained almost all the arguments of counsel; while Tait's penetrating acuteness, almost preternatural—and quickness, of which he was sometimes himself the dupe—were, in spoken argument, constantly remarked with wonder.†

Blair was a speaker of a very high order, without those qualifications which distinguished Tait. Of a bold and masculine understanding, extreme sagacity, and profound reflection, with little fancy in inventing topics, and no great nimbleness in meeting or escaping objections, he yet always

* Adam Gillies, brother of the historian of Greece, raised to the bench as Lord Gillies in 1811. A notice of him will be found in "Peter's Letters."

† William Tait, admitted a member of the Speculative Society in 1776, died in 1800. Was sheriff of Stirlingshire, and in Parliament for the Kinghorn burghs, in Fifeshire.—*History of the Speculative Society*, p. 131. Of Clerk, see above.

brought to bear upon his subject a plain and homely vigor, to which almost all difficulties yielded, and before which almost all antagonists gave way. His style, too, both of reasoning and diction, bore the impress of his nature; they were plainly suited to the man; they were racy and they were apposite. The hearer never for a moment doubted that the speaker thoroughly understood the whole matter in hand, and was perfect master of it. Despising the vulgar arts of ordinary advocates, he unfolded the subject to all exactly as he saw it himself; and his comments had so much force, were so plain, yet so strong, and clothed with so much dignity of expression, as well as presented with so much gravity and yet earnestness of manner, that his discourse seemed rather judicial than forensic, and he appeared to decide the cause he was pleading. So earnest a manner is generally an abatement of dignity, yet in this speaker it proved not so. His vehemence, even though not sustained by fluency, and set off by less felicity of diction, never for an instant led the hearers or the spectators to undervalue him and withhold respect, as is wont to happen when, in the fervor of declamation, the orator, seeming to lose command of himself, is nearly sure to lose the sway over his audience. We have spoken of his fluency as inconsiderable—but this had no bad effect; for, as you saw a mind struggling with the topic, you perceived that the ideas were too many to find easy utterance. There was none of the unpleasant anxiety attending a hesitating speaker, and which is unpleasing because it gives alarm. The thoughts were there and struggling for birth, and, in one way or another, were sure to reach the audience. Occasionally he rose to a higher pitch than merely the height of argumentation, if indeed any higher pitch there be. No one who had the advantage of hearing his noble speech in the case of Heriot, the descendant of the founder of the hospital, will easily forget the fine burst of impassioned and indignant eloquence with which he denounced the cruel injustice of disputing the founder's wish for his kindred: "What avails it, my lords, that a great benefactor of his species should generously devote the hard earnings of a long life to the sacred uses of charity, if no sooner laid in the grave than all he most fondly favored are repudiated, all his cherished objects cast into oblivion, all his darling plans scorned?"*

The person who made the greatest impression on my mind of all these eminent advocates was Charles Hope, from whom my first idea of eloquence was derived—that is, of oral as contradistinguished from written eloquence. He had the advantage of an English education, which kept his pronunciation pure: his voice was magnificent. His professional knowledge; his manly and vigorous understanding, which despised trifles, and loved to grapple with the main body of the subject; his bold and self-possessed manner, to some judges unpleasing, but to the best not distasteful, and his nervous eloquence—seldom equalled, perhaps never surpassed, whether we regard the language or the tones in which it was conveyed—soon placed him in the first rank of advocates. That I am not using too strong an expression in thus characterizing his oratory, I may venture to give two proofs. Few men had less party or personal leaning towards another than Laing (the historian) and Gillies (afterwards the judge), and no one will question their capacity to form a judgment of eloquence; the latter, indeed, was himself a first-rate speaker. Both gave it as their opinion, and at a time when party ran high in Edinburgh, that Charles Hope's declamation excelled all they had ever heard; and they made no exception whatever, though they had often heard all the great speakers in Parliament: and these men were very far from prizing as of any value mere declamation, unaccompanied with argument or statement. The other fact to which I appeal is the admiration expressed, both by Mr. Pitt and Mr. Fox, of his speech in defense of himself and his conduct as lord advocate in 1804, when Mr. Whitbread brought it under the review of the House of Commons. Of the opinion expressed by these two great orators there is no doubt; but the circumstance to which I allude is, that several persons present, who had heard him on former occasions—that is, in Edinburgh—regarded his speech in the House as a failure, so much impressed had they been with the merits of his eloquence from their recent

* Robert Blair, lord president of the Court of Session in 1808, died suddenly in 1811. Notices of him will be found in "Peter's Letters," Lockhart's "Life of Scott," and Cockburn's "Life of Jeffrey."

recollections of it. I sat with Horner in the gallery, and, greatly prejudiced against him as he was, owing to Edinburgh party politics, this was his clear opinion with my own. But noble as was Hope's oratory, and richly as any account of it might be illustrated by examples of its success, facts are known to me which illustrate qualities far above all excellence, parliamentary or forensic. When the party to which he belonged came into office in 1804, he was, as before, lord advocate; and when the place of justice-clerk, the highest judicial place but one, was as a matter of course offered to him, he declined, insisting that Henry Erskine should be appointed, and was himself the bearer of the communication, in order that the party feelings of that excellent man, but staunch partisan, might be consulted. Fully sensible, as he ever after proved, of this generous conduct, the advice of the party made him decline, and it was not till then that Mr. Hope was raised to the bench. His conduct made, as well it might, a deep impression on Harry Erskine: towards Hope and his family he ever after retained the warmest feelings, notwithstanding the hostility, personal as well as political, in which they had passed their lives.

Nor was this trait in the fine character of the man confined to his riper years. I remember Dr. Adam telling me an instance of self-sacrifice and noble feelings; that when he was a pupil, and had risen, in the first year of his attendance, to be first (*i. e.*, dux) of his class, a blind boy of the second year being next to him, Hope yielded his place, but would suffer no one else to pass him, and had himself the first place the year after. The doctor used to dwell on this trait as marking a feeling and generous nature, and it obliterated in his mind all recollection of the wide difference in political principles which at the time separated them, and the acrimony which then prevailed. One can plainly see that the same boy was the man who afterwards acted the like part to Harry Erskine. The latter's disqualification for the highest place was certainly not natural, but still was decisive; it was the belonging to a party that had not the choice, which Hope's party and himself alone could exercise.*

* See Appendix XVI.

Allan Maconochie (afterwards Lord Meadowbank) was perhaps the most thoroughly grounded in legal principles, and indeed had received the most general legal education, of any man at the Scotch, perhaps at any bar; for, besides being deeply versed in Scotch and civil law, he studied and attended court, and kept terms, with a view of being called to the English bar, particularly studying under Lord Mansfield: he also, for several years, attended the French courts of law, the Parliament of Paris. His general education, under the advice of his kinsman, Dr. Robertson, whose ward he was, had been carefully conducted, and he was the only private pupil that Adam ever had. He made him a distinguished classical scholar. He had even attended lectures on divinity and Church history, and was so familiar with medical subjects that he lent assistance to an eminent physician (Dr. Gregory) in preparing his thesis on taking his degree. He was professor of the law of nature and nations, and prepared an elaborate course of lectures on the subject. In business, which he had to a great extent, he was distinguished by his great learning, his close reasoning, and his clear, lucid statement of facts. But his great fame is in his judicial character, having proved one of the very best judges that ever sat on any bench; nor on Scotch cases is there any one whose authority weighs, to this day, more in the Lords.*

Among those of less standing at the bar in those days, Cranstoun (afterwards Lord Corehouse) stood highest. He was a most accomplished lawyer in every branch of jurisprudence, and his arguments were admirable in all the qualities most fitted to that kind of speaking. It was strictly and purely a legal argument of unbroken fluency; not so devoid of ornament, but more various in illustration than Sir William Grant's, which had copious illustration, but taken almost entirely from legal topics. Cranstoun's mind was enlarged by general education, as well as disciplined by intercourse with speculative men, especially with Dugald Stewart, who had married his sister, and with whom he lived in constant and familiar intercourse. He was allowed to be not only at

* Allan Maconochie, born 1748; raised to the bench by the title of Lord Meadowbank in 1796; died 1816.

the head of legal arguments after Tait had left the bar, but to be alone in his particular line; for his arguments, though never departing from the subject of Scotch law, were illustrated by appeals to general maxims of law. Out of the profession his wit was eminent, and it was refined; but he hardly ever took advantage of it even as far as a sarcasm upon, or *reductio ad absurdum* of, an opposite argument. When on several occasions he was heard at the bar of the House of Lords, he created such a sensation as I never recollect among the great English conveyancers. I heard Preston rising into enthusiasm in his admiration at what he said possessed every one merit of argument. A lay-hearer gave a less judicious testimony to his merits. Peel having once heard him, said he was the first speaker since Pitt—which was not much more happy in discrimination than if he had said he was the finest speaker since Catalani or John Kemble; for assuredly the two things, though each greatest in its kind, were so absolutely different as to admit of no comparison. They did not profess to effect the same purpose; they were incommensurable quantities.*

The rare accomplishments of Meadowbank for the profession have been mentioned. Next to him I am not aware of any one who had so diligently prepared himself for it as Reddie. I knew him intimately from the time we were together at the High School, under the same masters — Fraser and Adam.

At Fraser's class, during the four years we were in it, he was without intermission constantly at its head, no one ever dreaming of entering into competition with him. In the rector's class, where he only remained one year, his modest nature kept him back; and Wishart, whose second year it was, not he, left it at the head, no one ever conceiving it possible for a one-year's boy to attempt that place. Next year, which was my second nominally (I having been detained at home by illness all the first but six weeks), he had left the school, else there can be no doubt neither Keay nor I would have had a chance with him. At college he applied himself

* George Cranstoun, raised to the bench in 1826; took the title of Lord Corehouse.

to scientific and literary subjects diligently, and then to the civil law and general jurisprudence. He passed some time under Professor Miller at Glasgow, and very few men ever came to the study of the Scotch or English municipal law after so ample a preparation, by having examined the legal principles common to all systems. He began his professional life without any patron or party to rely upon, or any recommendation but his own great learning, solid, though not brilliant, talents, and a sound judgment, which well fitted him alike to advise a client and to conduct his cause. In the course of two or three years his extraordinary merit became known, notwithstanding his modest and retiring nature; and Mr. Hope, then lord advocate, afterwards lord president, distinguishing him among his contemporaries without any regard whatever to the differences of his political opinion, contributed greatly to his professional success. It was in some prize causes which involved the questions of neutral right, so much agitated towards the close of the first Revolutionary war, that he became first known in the courts, and showed himself not more deeply versed in the doctrines of public (sometimes now termed international) law than capable of close and logical reasoning in their application. His argument on the right of search, connected with the case of the Fladoyen, was very long remembered at the Scotch bar, and at once pointed him out for advancement in the profession.

Nor can any doubt be entertained that, had he continued at the bar, the highest place both in practice and ultimately on the bench would have been within his reach. This was held by all men (save one) of every party as an incontestable proposition; but his own modest and little adventurous nature led him to prefer an humbler path, and he listened to the suggestions of some friends at Glasgow, whom he permitted to propose him as a candidate for the respectable and very important office of town-clerk, the assessor of the magistrates, and presiding judge in the town court, the principal civil court of that great commercial city. As soon as it was known that he was willing to take the office, the other candidates—six in number, all professional men of eminence—one of them sheriff of the county, another professor of law in the University —retired from the contest, and he was chosen unanimously.

He entered upon the duties of this office in 1804; and until 1822, when, by the appointment of a resident sheriff, many causes were removed into that court, the number that came before him, including the small debt jurisdiction, was nearer six than five thousand a year, of which many were of great importance in principle as well as value, the jurisdiction being unlimited in amount, and in every kind of personal action. The satisfaction which his judgments gave was almost unexampled; they were rarely appealed from—most rarely altered upon appeal. In affirming one of those which ultimately came before the House of Lords (1833), the lord chancellor observed that it "well became even the most eminent judges upon the bench to approach with the greatest caution and deference a judgment upon a point of law pronounced by so distinguished a lawyer;" and this remark met with the universal concurrence of the profession.*

The great professional success of Jeffrey was owing to extraordinary abilities carefully cultivated, and his literary superiority was helped by the opportunities which the Scotch bar affords of cultivating letters without interrupting its practice. The law is not so jealous a mistress there as with us in England: the literary reputation which would inevitably prove fatal in Westminster Hall, rather aids than impedes the lawyer's progress in Edinburgh. So at least it was in Jeffrey's time; but I am not aware of any other in which great eminence was attained in both departments. Sir Walter Scott had no success at the bar; and the works of Monboddo and Kaimes were rather the fruit of their leisure, when they had been raised to the bench, than of the intervals between session and session while struggling at the bar. Jeffrey had studied partly at Edinburgh, partly at Glasgow, and was for some time at Queen's College, Oxford. He had well grounded himself in the principles both of the civil and the Scottish law, and he had diligently applied his great talents to the cul-

* It is to be regretted that every thing about the personal history of Reddie is lost after his leaving the Edinburgh circle. Those who remember the portions of that circle remaining, between thirty and forty years ago, will remember his name often referred to in the same tone of high praise. He died in Calcutta, where he was first judge of the Court of Small Causes, 28th Nov., 1852 (obit. Gent. Mag.).

tivation of eloquence, as well in speech as in written composition. His classical education was that of an accomplished scholar. With all the poets especially, whether of Greece or of Rome, he had a most familiar acquaintance; and his skill in these languages remained unimpaired through after-life, insomuch that to the last he read, for relaxation, the Greek classics almost as easily as the Latin. It was probably from his natural love of poetry that he somewhat undervalued the great orators of the Attic school; partly, too, from a proneness to paradox, allied with the extraordinary ingenuity of his mind and his disposition to grapple with great difficulties. In the Speculative Society he bore a most distinguished part; and its members never can forget the brilliant display so often made in that seminary, of his singular readiness in debate, the subtlety of his reasoning, and the extraordinary liveliness of his fancy—a fancy ever under control, and used always for the purpose of aiding the argument, or arriving by a short route at the conclusion. I well remember a speech in which the resources of the Russian empire having been largely dwelt upon as proving its foreign influence, and the mild course of criminal justice under the Empress Elizabeth, as showing how a despotism might be administered in mercy, he gave such a picture of the colossal body as, without reducing its dimensions, made it viewed without alarm, and such a sketch of Elizabeth's clemency as rendered the Siberian journey more horrible to contemplate than the passage across the Stygian ferry. The picture of Russia was so full of fancy, the comparisons introduced so various, so happy, each more unexpected than the last, that we all listened in breathless silence and wonder, until our feelings of admiration and astonishment, reflected upon the speaker, for a while suspended his utterance. On another occasion, the question regarding the obligation of representatives to obey the instructions of their constituents, his argument was the usual one, but urged with a closeness and a force amounting to seeming demonstration, by carefully concealing the fundamental error of assuming the representative to be only commissioned to *speak* for his constituents, and not to *deliberate* for them. A most conclusive answer was given by Henry Mackenzie, perfectly well reasoned, and happily turning into ridicule the meeting of men to debate, when fettered by the orders under which they assembled—a meeting which was utterly absurd, if it did not at once end in a vote without a word of discussion.

He had been eight years at the bar, and had during the more recent of those years obtained a fair share of practice. He married in 1801—a bold step—for his father was unable to assist him; his wife (Miss Catherine Wilson) had no fortune, and his professional income did not exceed £100 a year. They took a house—or, to speak more correctly, a third floor or flat—in Buccleuch Place; but in May, 1802, they removed to an upper story in Queen Street.

This brings me to a subject on which I naturally feel deep interest—the history of the "Edinburgh Review." A somewhat inaccurate and even fanciful account of the origin of the Review is given by Sydney Smith, as follows:

"Towards the end of my residence in Edinburgh, Brougham, Jeffrey, and myself happened to meet in an eighth or ninth story, or flat, in Buccleuch Place, the then elevated residence of Mr. Jeffrey. I proposed that we should set up a review: this was acceded to with acclamation. I was appointed editor, and remained long enough in Edinburgh to edit the first number. The motto I proposed was, '*Tenui musam meditamur avena*'—We cultivate literature on a little oatmeal. This was too near the truth to be admitted, and so we took our grave motto from Publius Syrus, of whom none of us had ever read a line. When I left Edinburgh, the Review fell into the stronger hands of Jeffrey and Brougham, and reached the highest point of popularity and success."

Now nothing can be more imaginary than nearly the whole of the above account.

In the first place, there never was a house eight or nine stories high in Buccleuch Place, or in any of that portion of the new town of Edinburgh. No house at that time exceeded three stories.

In the second place, Smith *never was appointed editor.* He read over the articles, and so far may be said to have edited the first number; but regularly-constituted editor he never was—for, with all his other rare and remarkable qualities, there was not a man among us less fitted for such a position. He was a very moderate classic; he had not the smallest knowledge of mathematics or of any science. He could no more have edited—that is, sat in judgment upon Playfair's article on "Mascheroni's Geometry," No. 17, p. 161; or on Delambert's paper on the "Arc of the Meridian," No. 18, p. 373; or on Bentley's "Hindu Astronomy," No. 20, p. 455, than he could have written the "Principia."

He was an admirable joker; he had the art of placing ordinary things in an infinitely ludicrous point of view. I have seen him at dinner at Foston (his living near York) drive the servants from the room with the tears running down their faces, in peals of inextinguishable laughter; but he was too much of a jack-pudding. On one occasion he was the high-sheriff's chaplain, and had to preach the Assize sermon. I remember the bar, who were present in York Minster, being rather startled at hearing him give out as his text, "And a certain lawyer stood up and tempted him!" But I am bound to say the sermon was excellent and much to the purpose.

Whatever faults he may have had, he had too much good sense to be ashamed of his name; he used jokingly to say, "The Smiths have no right to crests or coat-armor, for they always sealed their letters with their thumbs!"

I think we owed the motto for the Review to the painstaking and solemn Horner, who, being as incapable of understanding a joke as Smith was of writing the "Principia," discovered in Publius Syrus, a comic writer of the time of Cæsar, the motto which we adopted, and which Horner thought better than Smith's "oatmeal" suggestion. Smith left Edinburgh in 1803. He had negotiated with Manners, one of the firm of Manners & Miller, booksellers in the Parliament Close, Edinburgh, who at first undertook the publication, but afterwards gave it up, on seeing that some works were attacked which their firm was engaged in publishing.

Smith then made an agreement with Longman, who was his relation, to act in conjunction with Constable, who was fixed upon as printer and publisher in Edinburgh. The following extract from a letter from Jeffrey to Horner will throw some light on the subject:

"Edinburgh, April 9, 1802.

"DEAR HORNER,—I have been cutting at my quill for these five minutes, pondering with the most intense stupidity what apology I should make for not having written to you before. The truth is, though it is any thing but an apology, that I have written none of my reviews yet, and that I was *afraid* to tell you so. I began to Mounier, however, this morning; and feel the intrepidity of conscious virtue so strong in me already, that I can sit down and confess all my enormities to you. I must first tell you about the Review, though, that you may be satisfied that it holds the first place in my affection. We are in a miserable state of backwardness, you must know, and have been giving some symptoms of despondency; various measures have been tried, at least, against the earliness of our intended day of publication; and hints have been given of a delay that I am quite afraid would prove fatal. Something is done, however; and a good deal, I hope, is doing. Smith has gone through more than half his task. So has Hamilton. Allen has made some progress; and Murray and myself, I believe, have studied our parts, and tuned our instruments, and are *almost ready to begin.* On the other hand, Thomson is sick: Brown has engaged for nothing but Miss Baillie's plays; and Timothy has engaged for nothing, but professed it to be his opinion, the other day, that he would never put pen to paper in our cause. Brougham must have a sentence to himself; and I am afraid you will not think it a pleasant one. You remember how cheerfully he approved of our plan at first, and agreed to give us an article or two without hesitation. Three or four days ago, I proposed two or three books that I thought would suit him: he answered with perfect good-humor that he had changed his view of our plan a little, and rather thought that he should decline to have any connection with it.

* * * * * * *

"Very faithfully yours, F. JEFFREY."

Now, my reason at that time for declining to be of the connection was, that no security was given me for the sole and undivided management being in Jeffrey's hands. It was not made clear to me, in the first place, that the booksellers were to be *mere instruments*, entirely in subservience to us, and exercising not only no control, but no influence of any kind; for this was the fundamental object of the Review. Next, all former works of this description had been notoriously, more or less, under the influence of the publishers of books, who were certain to shape their course according to their interest, so far as not merely to suppress or make mention of their publications, but even, in many instances, to distribute praise and censure at their instigation. Lastly, it was possible that Jeffrey's control might be interfered with by certain of our body, in whom the same confidence could not be reposed, either as regarded their opinions or their discretion. In the course of the summer, ample security being afforded on all these three points, Horner accordingly thus wrote, early in autumn, as follows to Allen, who was then at Paris with the Hollands:

"1st September, 1802.

* * * * * * *

"Our Review goes on tolerably well. In consequence of Constable's own arrangement, it is not to appear till the 1st of November; but more than half the first number is already printed. I wish you would advertise the publication in some of the Paris newspapers or journals in the manner that you shall judge most likely, if there is any chance to excite a little curiosity about it. Jeffrey has written three or four excellent articles, and Brougham is now an efficient and zealous member of the party. We regret your loss to a degree that I shall not express to you, though we do not altogether despair of receiving a few short critiques on such foreign publications as you happen, at any rate, to read with care. I particularly wish we had from you a review of Ware's strange paper on the blind boy restored to sight. Brougham has selected from the same volume of the "Philosophical Transactions," Herschel's discovery of the sympathy between the spots of the sun and the prices of wheat in Reading market.

* * * * * * *

"Yours ever, FRA. HORNER."

These preliminary difficulties being thus explained and disposed of, I now proceed to give some account of the establishment of the Review, of its early supporters, and their contributions.

I can never forget Buccleuch Place, for it was there, one

stormy night in March, 1802, that Sydney Smith first announced to me his idea of establishing a critical periodical or review of works of literature and science. I believe he had already mentioned this to Jeffrey and Horner; but on that night the project was for the first time seriously discussed by Smith, Jeffrey, and me. I at first entered warmly into Smith's scheme. Jeffrey, by nature always rather timid, was full of doubts and fears. It required all Smith's overpowering vivacity to argue and laugh Jeffrey out of his difficulties. There would, he said, be no lack of contributors. There was himself, ready to write any number of articles, and to edit the whole; there was Jeffrey, *facile princeps* in all kinds of literature; there was myself, full of mathematics, and every thing relating to colonies; there was Horner for political economy, Murray for general subjects; besides, might we not, from our great and never-to-be-doubted success, fairly hope to receive help from such leviathans as Playfair, Dugald Stewart, Robison, Thomas Brown, Thomson, and others? All this was irresistible, and Jeffrey could not deny that he had already been the author of many important papers in existing periodicals.

The Review was thus fairly begun; yet Jeffrey's inconceivable timidity not only retarded the publication of the first number (which, although projected in March, was not published till October), but he kept prophesying failure in the most disheartening way, and seemed only anxious to be freed from the engagement he and the rest of us had entered into with Constable to guarantee him four numbers as an experiment. Various other minor obstacles (such as Horner's absence in London and Allen's in Paris) arose, which for a time almost threatened the abandonment of the undertaking; but at length a sufficient number of articles were prepared to be revised by Smith, and the first number came out early in October, 1802.

The success was far beyond any of our expectations. It was so great that Jeffrey was utterly dumbfounded, for he had predicted for our journal the fate of the original "Edinburgh Review," which, born in 1755, died in 1756, having produced only two numbers! The truth is, the most sanguine among us, even Smith himself, could not have foreseen the greatness of the first triumph, any more than we could have imagined the long and successful career the Review was afterwards to run, or the vast reforms and improvements in all our institutions, social as well as political, it was destined to effect. The tone it took from the first was manly and independent. When it became as much political as literary, its attitude was upright and fearless: not a single contributor ever hesitated between the outspoken expression of his opinions and the consequences these might entail on his success in life, whether at the bar, the pulpit, or the Senate.

The great importance of the Review can only be judged of by recollecting the state of things at the time Smith's bold and sagacious idea was started. Protection reigned triumphant—parliamentary representation in Scotland had scarcely an existence—the Catholics were unemancipated—the test acts unrepealed—men were hung for stealing a few shillings in a dwelling-house—no counsel allowed to a prisoner accused of a capital offense—the horrors of the slave-trade tolerated—the prevailing tendencies of the age, jobbery and corruption.

To the improvement of some, and the removal of others of such evils, the "Edinburgh Review" has not a little contributed. To Sydney Smith much is, therefore, due. The share he had in this good work has never been sufficiently appreciated. He was a very remarkable man, a great lover of freedom, but a still more fervent lover of truth. He was not led away by the false appearance of liberty which the dangerous and mischievous doctrines of the French Revolution too widely spread. He looked upon all that had been going on in France with calm good sense; and in all his writings, while he was the unflinching advocate of every sound principle, he earnestly protested against the dangers to which true liberty was exposed by the mistaken zeal of its first worshippers.

I consider that the Review owed much of its continuing success to the wise advice which Smith administered to Constable at the conclusion of his short reign as *quasi* editor, and during the discussion of the arrangement about to be made with Jeffrey. The substance of this advice was, that a *permanent* editor should be engaged at a liberal salary, and that *every* contributor should be paid ten or twelve guineas a sheet.

Constable, who, as I have stated, was the publisher in Edinburgh, was more liberal-minded than any of his craft, and he had the sagacity to see the good sense of Smith's advice. From the great sale of the first two numbers, he justly calculated upon a considerable increase in future; but he knew that this could only be secured by inducing the best men to enroll themselves as contributors, and that however agreeable to their vanity *anonymous* fame might be, yet the solid gratification produced by liberal pay would be quite as effectual. I think the editor began at £300 a year, and the contributors at ten guineas a sheet; but before long these payments were raised. The sums paid to the writers was left entirely to Jeffrey.

Even as late as September the progress was very slow, although by that time part of the first number had been printed; but articles did not come in as quickly as Smith expected, so that, hard-worked as I then was with my "Colonial Policy," I was obliged to write several articles in addition to the two ("Olivier's Travels" and "Wood's Optics") I had prepared as my contribution. To these I added "Horneman's Travels, "Acerbi's Travels," "Playfair on the Huttonian Theory," and an article on the "Sugar Colonies."

In September, 1855, John Murray was staying at Brougham.* We were talking one day of the selections I had recently been asked to make from my articles in the "Edinburgh Review," for publication by Messrs. Griffin, when my brother suggested that Murray and I should sit down and put the names of their authors to all the early numbers, he and I being the last survivors of the first contributors. We worked at this for ten or twelve days. Murray sent to Edinburgh for some contemporary notes he had; and these, with our own recollections, enabled us to make a very full and correct list.

Referring to this, I find that the writers in the early numbers were—Sydney Smith, Jeffrey, Horner, Murray, Thomas Brown (successor to Dugald Stewart), Hamilton (afterwards

---

* John Archibald Murray. See Appendix XVII.

Professor of Oriental Languages at the East India College, Hertfordshire), John Thomson* (afterwards Professor of Surgery in the University of Edinburgh), and myself; afterwards we were joined by John Allen* (then Professor of Physiology, afterwards Lord Holland's family doctor), Walter Scott, Emsley, Playfair, Hallam, Malcolm Laing,* Sir William Drummond, Sir John Stoddart, John Eyre, Lord Aberdeen, and Dr. Duncan. When we got beyond the twentieth number we had other contributors—such as John Leslie, Malthus, Mill, Bloomfield, and Mackintosh.*

To the four first numbers Smith contributed eighteen articles; namely:

No. I. Art. 2. Dr. Parr's Spital Sermon.
" 3. Goodwin's Reply to Parr.
" 9. Rennel's Discourses.
" 12. Bowles on the Peace.
" 16. Dr. Langford's Anniversary Sermon.
" 18. Public Characters of 1801–'2.
" 20. Nares's Sermon.
No. II. " 2. Sonnini's Travels.
" 6. Lewis's Alfonso.
" 10. Necker's Last Views.
No. III. " 2. Collins's New South Wales.
" 6. Fiévée, Lettres sur l'Angleterre.
" 14. Percival's Account of Ceylon.
" 17. Delphine, by Madame de Staël.
" 22. Sturges on the Residence of the Clergy.
No. IV. " 2. Catteau, Tableau des Etâts Danois.
" 4. Wittman's Travels.
" 10. Edgeworth on Irish Bulls.

Jeffrey, sixteen; namely:

No. I. Art. 1. Mounier, Sur la Revolution de la France.
" 6. Baldwin's Egypt—jointly with Brougham.
" 8. Southey's Thalaba.
" 13. Herrenschwand's Address.
" 19. Bonnet on Revolutions.
" 22. Mackenzie's Voyages.
No. II. " 3. Paley's Natural Theology.
" 8. Denon's Travels in Egypt.
" 14. Hunter's Poems.
" 22. Madame Necker: Reflexions sur le Divorce.

* In reference to the names in the text, see Appendix XVIII.

No. III. Art. 1. Gentz: Etât de l'Europe—jointly with Brougham.
" 5. Hayley's Life of Cowper.
" 21. Thelwall's Poems.
" 23. Sir John Sinclair's Essays.
No. IV. " 1. Miss Baillie's Plays on the Passions.
" 21. Works of Lady M. W. Montagu.

Horner, seven; namely:

No. I. Art. 7. Irvine on Emigration.
" 11. Christison on Parish Schools.
" 14. The Utility of Country Banks.
" 25. Thornton on Paper Credit.
No. II. " 16. Canard: Principes d'Economie Politique.
No. III. " None.
No. IV. " 11. Lord King on Bank Restriction.
" 18. The Trial of Peltier for Libel.

I contributed twenty-one, and four jointly with others; namely:

No. I. Art. 5. Olivier's Travels.
" 6. Baldwin's Egypt—jointly with Jeffrey.
" 21. Horneman's Travels.
" 23. Wood's Optics.
" 24. Acerbi's Travels.
" 26. Playfair's Illustrations of the Huttonian Theory.
" 27. Crisis of the Sugar Colonies.
No. II. " 9. Politique de tous les Cabinets de l'Europe.
" 12. Woodhouse on Imaginary Quantities.
" 15. Herschell on the New Planets.
" 17. Bakerian Lecture on Light and Colors.
" 23. Transactions of the Royal Society of Edinburgh: Ivory's Solution of Kepler's Problem, and Wallace's Algebraic Formula.
No. III. " 1. Gentz: Etât de l'Europe—jointly with Jeffrey.
" 3. Shepherd's Life of Poggio Braccioline—jointly with Perceval.
" 8. Wollaston on Prismatic Reflection.
" 9. Wollaston on the Oblique Reflection of Iceland Crystal.
" 10. Hatchett's Analysis of a New Metal.
" 11. Guineas an Incumbrance to Commerce.
" 13. Ritson on Abstinence from Animal Food—jointly with Jeffrey.
" 26. Stewart's Life of Robertson.
No. IV. " 6. Transactions of the American Philosophical Society.
" 8. Dallas's History of the Maroons.
" 12. Walker's Poems.
" 15. Davis's Travels.
" 16. Fuseli's Lectures—jointly with Dr. Parry.

This last article was written by Parry; but I was requested to put a little *salt* into it.

I find that in the first twenty numbers Jeffrey wrote seventy-five articles; Smith, twenty-three; Horner, fourteen; and I, eighty.

The great success of this publication, three editions being immediately exhausted and a large permanent circulation established, and the influence of the work in after-times, are matters well known and universally felt. The first effect of our Review, absolutely independent of the trade and of any party in the country, local or general, was to raise the character and to increase the influence of periodical criticism. The purpose to which this influence was devoted was the promotion of sound and liberal opinions upon all questions in Church and State, leaving the doctrines of religion untouched, and assuming the duty of submission to the constitution as fixed and permanent, the frame of our government only being subject to decorous and temperate comment or discussion. The severity of the criticism on books and their authors was much, and often justly, complained of; but no one could accuse it of personal malice, or any sinister motives. The rule was inflexibly maintained never to suffer the insertion of any attack by a writer who was known, or even justly suspected, to have a personal difference with the author, or other sinister motive; and if any person had been found to have kept concealed such cause of bias upon his critical judgment, no contribution would ever afterwards have been received from that person. So, if any one had practised the deception of concealing the real authorship, he was placed under the ban of prohibition. The first two or three numbers were given gratuitously, and neither the writers nor the editor would receive any remuneration. Afterwards, as I have before mentioned, for five or six years, the editor had a salary of £300 a year, and the writers received ten guineas a sheet of sixteen pages. These sums were in the succeeding years raised, the editor to five hundred, and the contributors to twenty; so that upward of ninety thousand pounds must have been paid for the publication of this work. There may have been occasionally some difference in the rate of payment of different writers, though I have no reason to believe in any such. But one rule was absolute—no one was allowed to refuse payment at the usual rate. Professional men, or judges in the receipt of the largest incomes, or private gentlemen—Romilly, Denman, Drummond, Aberdeen—were as much required to receive their payment as any writer who made letters his profession.

It was one benefit conferred upon literature and science, that men were led to work at the production of dissertations, often of treatises, interesting and popular in their composition, who might never have otherwise engaged in such works. Men who would not think of publishing a book had a place ready to receive their writings, and a place of respectability in which their works appeared in decent company. If they desired concealment, their secret was inviolably kept; but so many were well known as members of society, and mixing with it daily, that there was the responsibility, the want of which is often complained of in periodical publication. The work was really in one important respect unlike former Reviews; it contained what these only very rarely had—dissertations on the subject, as well as accounts of and criticisms upon the works reviewed; and this, doubtless, was carried so far as to interfere with the main object of a periodical article. I remember Sackville, Lord Thanet, saying he waited to see the Quarterly pamphlets before he made up his mind on such and such a matter; for the rival journal pursued the same plan. But this contributed largely to turn men's thoughts towards engaging in written discussion. That most of the writers to whom payment was little or no inducement thus became authors, there can be no doubt. Horner often said that his dissertation would in all probability have been in his portfolio had the Review not existed; but this was one of the instances in which, as Denman observed, our good friend, being wholly incapable of deceiving others, now and then deceived himself; for there were no such writings found among his papers; just as Hallam charged him with being the author of a self-denying ordinance, as he called it, that no man at the bar should ever take office, and soon after our friend himself did so—contrary to the advice of his oldest friends. He afterwards, on giving up his office, described it as the cause of his having no success at the bar—an exaggerated view, undoubtedly; but certainly he had much less success than his talents and learning deserved. Those talents were of a very exalted cast, and his powers of labor, while his health remained unbroken, were fully equal to any demand upon them. His merits in spotless integrity, perfect temper, sound judgment, and devotion to his principles, have been often and fully acknowledged even by political adversaries, and never exaggerated by the partiality of friends. But some of the most zealous (Cockburn, for example) have greatly underrated his talents, and really suppressed some of the most extraordinary instances of their successful display.

To return to the Review, it may be observed that, besides the exception taken to occasional vehemence of the censures on works, there arose some doubts upon the orthodoxy of the opinions in religion, and objections to the undeniable bias against the existing policy and ministerial arrangements. The attacks on the Methodists by Sydney Smith gave great offense to a large and powerful body, the Evangelical party, especially in England. They complained, and most justly, that he had confounded the Calvinistic with the Arminian Methodists, charging the former with all the views of the latter, which such men as Wilberforce and Henry Thornton, Babington, Stephen, and Macaulay were just as incapable of falling into as Sydney Smith himself.* The Review suffered not only from this great mistake, but from the tone of levity on sacred subjects almost unavoidably assumed by any one arguing against great and manifest errors, sometimes of a ludicrous description. There were frequent complaints in Edinburgh, much strengthened by the known, and indeed absurd, opinions of Sir William Drummond, who was a frequent contributor, though only upon classical questions. A worthy and pious friend having taken exception to some passages not written by Drummond, the latter used to call him the "reverend lord." I recollect Ward, a person not remarkable for the decorum of his language on religious subjects, quoting on his friend Dry (the nickname of Drummond)

* The article is in the Review for January, 1808, in the form of a review on "Causes of the Increase of Methodism and Dissension," by Robert Acklem Ingram, B.D.

"*Nemo novit Deum, sunt etiam qui de eo impure male existimant.*" This was about the time of Drummond's taking the title of the Crescent, which he had received at Constantinople while ambassador—an assumption which Ward announced to us by saying, "Drummond having a devil, now calls himself Sir William."

Whatever objections men might take to the secular or the spiritual opinions of the Review, or to the causticity of the criticisms, from the charge of being a party tool, or of ministering to personal feelings, it was always free. The works published by its conductors were either not reviewed at all as was the case with my own work on "Colonial Policy"), or only, when the subject required their being inserted, referred to without any comment. The decided part taken on some great questions, especially on slavery and the slave-trade, unavoidably gave rise to warm panegyric of certain individuals, and invectives against others; but these persons were wholly unconnected with the journal; and as often as they adopted views, or espoused a course of policy different from that maintained by the Review, their merits on subjects in which the reviewer agreed did not at all mitigate its censure when they differed, of which Stephen afforded a remarkable instance, his *Orders in Council* calling down upon him a censure as strong as his great services in slavery always obtained most just applause. If I rightly recollect, Wilberforce himself was visited with censure of some severity, at the time of the Yorkshire contest in 1807, in consequence of the part he had taken upon the constitutional question, which occasioned a change of ministry, and the dissolution of Parliament.*

Jeffrey's labors as editor were unceasing, and I will venture to say, if we had searched all Europe, a better man, *in every respect*, could not have been found. As a critic he was unequalled; and, take them as a whole, I consider his articles were the best we had. As an instance of the care he took in revising and preparing contributions, I remember an article

* In the number for July, 1812, there is an article on "A Letter to H. Brougham, Esq., M.P., on the subject of Parliamentary Reform, by William Roscoe, Esq." Among other instances of the costliness of elections is—"The committee which conducted Mr. Wilberforce's election for Yorkshire in 1807 state their expenses at fifty-eight thousand, with every resource of the most rigid economy and great voluntary assistance in labor" (p. 137).

on the Memoirs of Prince Eugene was sent to Jeffrey by Mill. Jeffrey gave it to Dr. Ferrier, of Manchester, to revise; and when he got it back from Dr. Ferrier, he himself corrected it, and added the moral reflections and the concluding observations on the new Paris edition of the work!

The great and increasing success of this journal, while it mightily raised him in the public estimation, in no way interfered with his progress towards extensive practice at the bar. He was afterwards dean of faculty, lord advocate, and a judge, and one of the ablest and the best that ever sat on the Scotch bench.

It was the custom to say he had failed in Parliament. I recollect meeting Sir Robert Peel the night he made his first speech; and in answer to my inquiry as to its success, he said that Jeffrey had fired over their heads, and was too clever for his audience.

After the July number came out, I received the following letter from Jeffrey:

"Edinburgh, August 5, 1804.

"DEAR BROUGHAM,—I am very sorry that your letter of the 24th ult. should have arrived while I was in the country, both on account of the delay which consequently took place in delivering the inclosure for George Street, and because I find by your subsequent letter, which I received this morning, that there is but little chance of my being able to reach you by letter within the four seas. I believe I have never thanked you enough for your great and exemplary services in the campaign which is just terminated. I was so hurried while it was going on, that I really had not leisure to estimate them properly; and it is only since the number has been out that I discovered myself to have been indebted to you for no less than six sheets. I have been prevented, too, from the same cause, from deprecating your indulgence for the liberty I took in suppressing and altering a few sentences in the beginning of your Lauderdale. They did not bear at all upon the argument, and I was really anxious that there should be no pretext for complaining of any thing personal or contemptuous in the manner.* I have not yet seen any of the other Re-

* Referring to a review of "An Inquiry into the Nature and Origin ot Public Wealth, and into the Means and Causes of its Increase," by the Earl of Lauderdale.—"Edinburgh Review" for July, 1804, p. 343.

views; but it will give me great pleasure to find that the confutation, which must, I think, be the most masterly and convincing, is also the most temperate and polite. It will amuse you to hear that I was presented to the peer, and spent an hour in conversation with him, the very day on which the Review came out. I was anxious to see him afterwards, but though I remained till yesterday in his neighborhood, I never had an opportunity of meeting with him. He seems to have shut himself up immediately on receipt of the book, and had not emerged when I left that part of the country.

"I forget what I said to Horner, but I am sure I excepted Lauderdale from the sentence of mediocrity.

"Of that article he knew my sentiments long before its publication. I should ask pardon of you and John Playfair for the phrase, however, even after the exception of it had cased it with vigorous propriety; but all I meant was, that there was scarcely any article that was likely to make a noise, or to become very popular, which, if it be true at all, is in many instances the fault of the subject.

"I am glad you think my 'Slave-trade' passable. You see I have not ventured an inch beyond you, and have aimed at nothing more than a clear and popular exposition of the most striking parts of your pamphlet.

"I am sorry that you think P. so very objectionable. I was a little staggered with the colonization of India, but that project was the very text and spinal marrow of the article, and could not possibly be separated from it; besides, I think the public is too quiescent and timid in its ignorance of such subjects, and I can not help thinking you a good deal too decisive. India can not be colonized, indeed, like a country that is thinly or barbarously peopled; and that distinction ought to have been considered.*

"But it may be colonized in a sort by intermarriage and the constitution of small landed estates. I do not believe P. is very profoundly prepared to answer objections or follow out his scheme in detail; but the suggestion, I think, may do some good, and in my heart I believe that the poor youth had

* Alluding, apparently, to an article in the Review for July, 1804, in which colonization is suggested.—See "Edinburgh Review," iv. 305.

no *wicked* designs whatever in indicting this article. What designs, may I ask, are imputed to him by the chairman?

"As to pious interpolations in Chatham, I utterly deny the charge. The only alterations I made in that article were an abridging what you say of Granville, and investing some of your vital Christianity with a more profane phraseology. It is very edifying to see your surprise at your own goodness.*

"You are very much mistaken if you suppose that I countenance Wilberforce or his principles. I have much respect for his talents, and great veneration for his character. I shall read his book 'at a convenient season,' but scarcely expect to get the length of W—— or King Agrippa. In the mean time, I am very much flattered by the favorable opinion of such men, and should be sincerely sorry to do any thing to scandalize them. I have no doubt you may have Washington, and it will be better, perhaps, to let it get to a greater length before it be cut down. I am told it is dolefully tedious and ill-written. I shall venture a response on Sir W. if no Oriental competition presents itself. I have better hopes of young Hamilton. You say nothing of Borrow's China. I hanker after it; not because I have read it or heard any thing very prepossessing about it (for I have neither), but chiefly because I wish to be put upon some tack that will force me to make up my mind about that absurd people. I shall also, if you wish it, try to give an abstract of your 'Colonial Policy,' short and simple; and if the time be not past, I have no objection to say a word or two to Stephens opportunely. This will be enough for my share, I think. I thank you heartily for your recruiting services. It is after the former failure of your R. S. men I am afraid to depend upon them after you are out of the way of dunning them. Might I entreat you to remind them yourself, and to point out the necessity of being early, as I may otherwise be obliged, in prudence, to fill all the places. I am greatly elated with the prospect of a paper from W——. I wrote, in a pacific and friendly epistle to Dr. Reeves, my hope that his indignation was abated, and his resolution to desert us was withdrawn. He has made me no answer, whether out of scorn and abhor-

* Review on "Chatham's Letters," July, 1804, article 9.

rence or to get time to consult his friend, I know not. I have done my duty. If he fail, I shall want a medical reviewer. Do you have any such in London? We shall take no more of Dr. R.'s. I think I must have a man that can write—if Fowler, of Salisbury, were willing, he is very able. I think I shall set M—— upon him. By-the-way, is any arrangement made with W—— or G—— about S——'s book? We must have some scientific pot-hooks this time for the refreshment of the Bailie. May I depend upon the account of L——, and has L—— himself fixed to do Volney or any thing else? You see of what importance you are to me, by the number of questions I am obliged to ask when you are going away. What are you going to do in Germany? Do not stay longer than three months, for God's sake; and give us a glimpse of you here in your transit to the South. I wish you all sort of amusement. Try and establish the Review somewhere on the Continent. Get a Hamburg journalist to puff it, and, above all, write often to me what you are doing. If you will send me an address, I shall write you as long letters as a Turkish spy. God bless you, my dear Brougham! and learn never to take any thing amiss that I say or do to you.

"Ever most faithfully yours, F. JEFFREY.

"P.S.—Murray is in Argyleshire, and most of the faithful scattered."

CHAPTER V.

A TOUR THROUGH HOLLAND AND ITALY.

Notes of a Ramble on the Continent.—Closed to the British, and necessary to obtain American Papers.—The Voyage.—The Helder.—Traces of the British Expedition.—Amsterdam.—Utrecht.—Delft.—Dutch Appreciation of the "Colonial Policy."—Ryswick.—Discussion on the Slave-trade.—Projects for Co-operation in Abolition.—The Hague.—A sitting of the Legislative Body.—Haarlem.—Dusseldorf and its Picture-gallery.—The Rhine.—Venice.—Pictures.—Journey through Italy.—Naples.—Pompeii.—The Grotto del Cane.—Rome.—St. Peter's and the Vatican.

In the autumn of 1804 I determined to go to Holland, where I hoped to obtain much information on the subject of the slave-trade, with the intention of afterwards proceeding through Germany, if I found that could be done without much difficulty, and thence to Italy. Jeffrey had written to me in July remonstrating; he complained of my absenting myself at that period of the year, and throwing the labor of preparing for the October number of the Review upon his shoulders, for Murray and many of the others were about to take their holiday, leaving him alone in Edinburgh. To make his mind easy, I contrived to send him four or five articles before I left England: one was upon the means of rendering Great Britain independent of foreign corn, with other plans of national improvement.

The state of the Continent made travelling there difficult for any one—for an Englishman, *impossible;* so I went as an American, furnished with an American passport and papers.

I left London early in August, and after a very quick passage, rather blowing, with execrable provisions and accommodation, two sick women and a stupid younker, made Camperdown in thirty-nine hours after our departure from Gravesend, and arrived at Helder on the 8th of August.

It blew a very hard gale on a lee shore as near as possible, and a brig went ashore. We weathered it, however, and at 5 P.M. cast anchor between Helder and Texel, as the searchers could not come off in the gale. At 5 A.M. went off in a Dutch boat to the "Admiral," a fine 80-gun ship, in beautiful order, and quite clean. Most civilly treated.

Helder, Aug. 9.—Helder, an ill-built large town about size of Gravesend, all clean and neat. Met many French officers, who behaved most civilly. At Helder went to the Roodelieuw, or Red Lion, and found the French commissary and commandant had quarters in it. They civilly interpreted for me, and I passed for a Frenchman, I believe.

Battle fought on the sand-hills here.* Seven hundred French and two thousand Dutch soldiers are in the camp and outposts, well clothed and armed, with dépôts—fine-looking men. Supped and had a bath, which, after thirty-six hours passed on shipboard, was a great luxury.

Aug. 9.—I hired a sort of phaeton, with two good horses, and set out to Alkmaär: sandy roads—country all sand-hills, but improved after the first two hours. Passed the field of battle and the camp.

Conversed with my driver, very intelligent, and picked up some Dutch. Find, if he can be trusted, they don't like the French, and still less the English. Common Dutch and French soldiers at constant daggers-drawn, but officers on good terms. The Dutch like Americans better than any. This is so natural in Dutchmen, that I take this as truth, though on sorry authority. The horses being troubled with flies from the extreme heat of the day, I jocularly called them Frenchmen, and said the English were the whip that drove them off. The man said, the Dutch preferred the trouble of feeding the fly to the pain of the lash that drove it off. We stopped twice on the road at neat little villages, and our route lay through a delightful country of meadow and canal. Little or no wood, except here and there a corner cut off to make a young shrubbery for the neighboring house, though in no form or taste. The hedges are good. Lüst-houses on all banks, sometimes *on* the canal—a box like a bathing-machine, with one or two

* In reference to the capture of Helder by the force under Abercromby in August, 1799.

rooms; sometimes a row of these together. Last stage from Alkmaär is called Schooldam, all battered by shot, still to be seen.

We saw fishing in the canal two rival priests of the town, the Catholic and Protestant. Every one, especially the French, civil to a degree. Near Alkmaär, a delightful country, and more wood; surrounded by thirty to forty windmills, which, however, also go by water. The churches have a fine, lofty appearance from a distance, and are really superb buildings; the town neat, and even pretty—canals and trees running through it; a large fosse and walls, with a handsome new and a fine old gateway. No trouble entering; no one ever stopped or spoke to us. A meadow of half a mile square on the north side, filled with little gardens and hedges, and crammed with lüst-houses, surrounded with a ditch almost stagnant. They appear to the number of two in twenty yards, all along the outside, and have a singularly Hollandish appearance.

I am just waiting for my dinner, which I have made shift to order in my bad Dutch. A very comfortable dinner, with exquisite hautboys in abundance, and good claret, prepared me for the rest of my journey. I first saw the cathedral—fine, one hundred paces long; two organs; the nave lofty. Proceeded at four through narrow, soft, winding roads, in one continued grove of young trees; every now and then a break showing a meadow of great extent in various crops—sometimes nothing but green grass as far as the eye could reach. Now the smell of beans from large patches, and then cows and canals. The first Dutch mile brings a view of Burwyk, and larger woods; villas thick-set; large avenues, walks, fountains, temples, and fine houses; thick and nice-trimmed hedges, dark walks, parterres, and all the richness of Dutch gardening. Every proprietor a "Koofman." People all civil to excess, both French and Dutch. All smoking, and drinking claret and coffee. Appearances of industry and ease universal. Came to a plain of vast extent, with Amsterdam in the distance, salt-water lake, and sea far off. Haarlem church to the right, row of sand-hills at a distance, behind; meadows studded with spires, and clumps of farm-houses; road along a dike for ten English miles. Dam at Spardam gave a dreadful idea of power of sea breaking in; at gates at 9½ exactly, as said;

went over nervous bridges, etc., rumbling on the piles. Then to "The Arms of Amsterdam," a superb French hotel, where by accident I found Galiffe lodges. Excellent supper, and most refreshing Rhenish Madeira and Seltzer. Sound nap.

Amsterdam, Aug. 10, 1804.—Kindly received by Vander Hoeven, Galiffe, and Melville. Monstrous bustle on all hands. It is easy to lose one's way in Amsterdam, as one always finds the same trees and canals in every street of any size. Hollow sound of piles, and stink of canals. Houses huddled together as if falling. Some obviously so; one or two here and there actually zigzag. No plainness, all in bad taste; clumsy cut-out tops and ornaments.

Stadthouse a massive square, about four hundred and sixty windows, five stories, and twenty-three windows in front; finest hall of marble I ever saw—about one hundred pilasters fluted. Hall of Capital Condemnation, small, strong, and gloomy, but well ornamented. Exchange most extensive; each pillar and compartment numbered and named from country, and even town. Grand bustle and fine room. All the people very horribly dressed. *Table d'hôte* excellent. Two courses and dessert, with half-bottle good claret, for one florin and a half.

Amsterdam, Aug. 11.—Went to call on Elliot—not in town. Went to Hôtel de Ville, or Stadthaus.

Dined very pleasantly at Melville's, and in the evening went to see the Dutch play and the famous actress Vatir, who astonished me. Two good men actors. A pretty house, well lighted and fitted up. A ballet, very good, but most indecent. Even the *figurantes* danced extremely well. The orchestra very good. Tea handed round between the acts.

Amsterdam, Aug. 12.—Went to Mr. Vander Hoeven's chateau, three and a half hours' journey, in a carriage and pair: dull country, duller day, and some heavy rain. Found his lady at home—a very pleasant little Brabançonne, though an invalid. He out fishing on his water; went to him—no sport. The carp, tench, and eels, as well as perch, are very fine; the villa excellent, extensive; less uniform than any I have seen, somewhat *à l'Anglaise;* but the country quite sandy, like all the district near the sea. Every thing bespeaks the national character of making a pleasure of business, and being precise as in an office, at all times. In the theatre the seats are marked, so that each man in the pit has one place. In any applause, a single *hist* may stop it all. Very fond of amusements like this; extremely punctual; never kept waiting, or disappointed, or cheated by tradesmen. Best attendance possible at inns, and by drivers, who carry you to a very second.

Sweated by France; pay seventy-three per cent. on income; fit out ships for France, and, when not needed, have to buy them back. Do not love the French at all.

No paper money, except bills and actions; all silver, copper, and good gold, which bends between the fingers.

The wealth and credit of some traders here is astonishing. Hope has placed £100,000, some say £200,000, of bills in one morning at "'Change." No one, however, comes near him. Payments above a certain sum must be made in bank money, which bears a premium of only two, three, or four per cent. at present. Though there are no notes in retail trade, there are bonds of foreign loans as low as one hundred guilders in constant circulation. The colonial bonds not lower than £100.

Water is very bad at Amsterdam, so that the only water used for drinking comes from Utrecht, where it is famous. The price is four stivers a bottle, almost as dear as the worst kind of claret, which one may buy for six stivers.

Utrecht, Aug. 13.—Set off with a small valise for this place at 1 P.M. in the treckschuyt. Day at first dull, then stormy and wet, yet the view rich and fine; villas in various forms and sizes. Our dinner, cold fowl, bread, and wine, as is the custom; women drinking tea the whole way. We were forty in all, besides those on the roofs. Passed Maarsen, a neat, clean village, inhabited chiefly by Jews; only one horse all the way; stopped twice, once to drink a cup of tea and light pipe. Arrived here at 8.30 with the usual precision of the country, and found a most comfortable hotel, the Castle of Antwerp.

The French troops treat the people here with great harshness, and are detested by all ranks, ages, and sexes. There are fourteen French generals under Marmont, the *général-en-chef*. One of them said to him that Utrecht had suffered nothing since the Revolution, and that it ought to pay now. The general, therefore, seized some of the best houses for quarters for his *état-major*. The municipality remonstrated, and were driven out with contempt. Since that the French have done as they pleased in the town.

I saw to-day (Aug. 14) a pamphlet, published at Utrecht in 1802, to prove that it is the part of a good citizen to undertake any office that might be offered him, whether he likes the Government or not. It has had some effect. Previously none but the scum could be found for the public departments.

The rent of land is from twenty to forty florins the Dutch arpent. Very bad land at ten to fifteen. An instance of fifteen per cent. for money vested in land is quite rare; seldom more than five; average two to four. Since the Revolution, land has risen in value, because no one trusts the public securities, and all wish to invest in land. Loans almost impossible to be had by private people, and in trade they either gain a great deal or nothing at all. This, by the way, always operates, and has been too much neglected by economists; it is the *extreme*, and not the average, profits which tempt.

TO THE HAGUE, PASSING THROUGH ROTTERDAM.

Hague, Aug. 20, 1804.—Breakfasted with Crawfurd; then went to Roquette's and drew for £20. Dined with M. Van Yzendoorn's married sister, and set out with him on the roof for Delft; found it delightful. A Dutch gentleman was on it, from whom procured much accurate information in return for simply explaining a few passages and references in my second volume, which is now being translated into Dutch.*

Land near towns lets sometimes for so high as one hundred and twenty guilders per margen (about two English acres); and this is for the vegetables and milk sold in towns. In country from ten to thirty guilders, and no more. Three per cent. for money vested in it is the ordinary average rate, and two and a half is very frequent; all owing to the heavy expenses of draining, which requires a mill-machinery, and of dikes, repairs, houses, duties, imposts. In an income of £120 per an-

* De Staatkunde der Europeesche Mogendheden
nopens het bestuuren van Volkplantingen.
onderzocht en beöordeeld door Henry Brougham, Jun.,
Uit het Engelsch door P. Van Yzendoorn.
Te Amsteldam, 1804.

num, perhaps twenty goes to land-tax, income-tax being paid from the rest.

The surface of the ground, to a depth of seven or eight feet, is cut for peat—excellent fuel. This is then flooded, and clay soil remains of excellent quality. It requires a public authority to cut turf, for fear of inundations.

Legislative body can not initiate; Senate must propose; they only originate. Foreign ministers received by foreign secretary. No man can hold two appointments. East India Company lost one hundred millions of florins by the American war; on making up their accounts, they lost in last war not less; no dividends for several years before its abolition, nor since.

All the old nobility, the patrician families, and those not noble, but who have long been in Government offices, the peasantry, and the proprietors, and especially the rich yeomanry, are for the stadtholder. The merchants, the army of course, most of the functionaries, especially Amsterdam, from old jealousy, are against him. Towns often jealous of each other.

The schuyt set us down at Delft, and we landed to view the fine old spire, and monuments in the cathedral; a noble one on William the First's tomb, two hundred years old; four bronzes of Justice, Religion, Prudence, and Liberty; a fifth of Fame, balanced on one toe, and movable, though 220 cwt.; the rest marble, white and gray. There is a modern one of Grotius. The chime the finest in the world.

Took a carriage, and, the moon shining very bright, came through a most rich succession of seats, the best I have seen. In this delicious light, this most beautiful wood, buildings and streets in the scene struck me much; and I believe, as to the country, a moonlight is best adapted to show its beauties by hiding its petty defects.

Aug. 21.—After breakfast went to the parade of about one hundred and seventy foot, fifty horse (beautiful), and sixty artillery, all Dutch, with a good band. The French Government keeps no troops here.

Then to the French coffee-house with Van Yzendoorn; then to the *Society* or Club, an institution where only members of the Government high in office, ambassadors, and strangers introduced by them, are admitted: was introduced to several eminent men—Van Keyser from Java, of the East India Company; Van Omphal, a legislator, and others. Complimented by all on my book, which they seemed to know as well as myself. Lionized to all the state-rooms of the old palace, rich with the Spanish trophies—the chamber of the Admiralty, etc.; chairs with the Orange arms, and curtains—the stadtholder's rooms, now those of the Legislative Body, and library—the palace of the Senate, etc.; some of the rooms very superb, and all elegant. Gobelins tapestry beautiful.

Those public buildings are in one chateau, with gates, surrounded by a moat.

At the Senate palace, a fine public garden, with all sorts of walks, arbors, and "lüst-huyses."

Saw the squares, which are noble, and the houses, hotels of embassies, palaces, etc., all scattered about in profusion. Bentinck House, with fourteen large windows in front. All the places of vast breadth, no canals, and trees very large.

Dined at the Deuxvilles *table d'hôte*, frequented only by the Club Society; had much instruction from Omphal about the policy, etc., of Holland.

Walked afterwards to see two fine villas beyond Ryswick; passed the villa on the site of the treaty chateau; drank tea, etc., at a lüst-house, and returned with Van Yzendoorn to the Society.

The people in communes of sixty thousand choose electors, who choose the legislators. These are now in an assembly extraordinary: having discussed the deficit of sixty millions, they imposed a capital tax of 2½. In public the debates not interesting, but much in committees. Saw them break up, and the soldiers in the square salute the president, who walked out in plain hat cocked like the rest, and black knôt.

SLAVE-TRADE.

Van Yzendoorn said he believed if England abolished they would directly follow.

Roquette—same, though less strong.

Gentleman in West Indian Department said there is no fear whatever from insurrection in Dutch colonies.

Crawfurd and others all misapprehend abolition question, and talk of emancipation.

Yzendoorn, etc., talk of dangers of mooting the point now.

Omphal talks of necessity of having supplies to make the colonies yield any thing.

French papers full of attack on Pitt on the slave question; every word of the debate, and especially Wilberforce's speeches, with comments, all violent in favor.

Notice of the Congos forming a white party.

See my ground clearly, and find it will probably do. Have prepared all to-day.

Van Yzendoorn is to translate the pamphlet on the trade and the memorials, and give all manner of facilities. Luckily all have read my book, and it is in great favor.

Aug. 22.—All morning working at memorial. Dined at the Deuxvilles — thirty-five people. Tea with Van Yzendoorn. After seeing the rest of the palace — viz., Hall of Holland: a most splendid room, indeed—walked and spent the evening with Van Edelbat, controller of colonial finance: two years in Caraccas—nine in Cavasson (?); well informed; has just views on slave-trade and colonies.

Cavasson very valuable; takes sixteen millions of florins per annum, chiefly from Spanish contraband; eighteen thousand negroes, four thousand mulattoes, and three thousand whites. Negroes well treated, but driven with overseer from 9 to 1 with whip; keep up and increase without importation, so that there is a constant exportation to Spanish Main and elsewhere; increase about three per cent. per annum.

In 1798, just before capture of Surinam, etc., a great debate here in Legislative Body on slave-trade. Many opposed its continuance, particularly De V., who proposed abolition and emancipation; carried by a narrow majority in favor of the present system, and for encouraging the trade. But no details of the plan to this effect were entered into till two years ago, when the new Council took it up. The plan is now organized, and only waits a peace for full execution. The duties formerly laid of 10 florins on importation of negroes taken off, and a bounty granted of 5 on males, and 2½ on children and women. All goods for Africa go duty free, and if they paid a duty on original importation, it is drawn back. Thus, nails and muskets from Germany pay 2½ per cent. *ad valorem*: this is drawn back if they are sent to Africa, and they are free from the 2½ on exportation, which they would pay elsewhere.

Trade to West Indies free to all Dutch in Dutch vessels. Pay 2½ per cent. *ad valorem* out, which must come back in produce there and 3 per cent. at home. No abolitionist in Council and Senate. Vickers, leading man, is for the system, and so is Bexieu; Van Edelbert not; and all limit their support to their own supply. He is to speak to Vickers. Van Yzendoorn was for long time on commission on Java's laws; says they tried to alter them, but he against. The law of settlement exists in great force. No one can be maintained under one year and six months' residence. Tax-paying not specified, because every one must pay in excise. If he resides that time he can't be removed; before it he may, until he proves his town, and that becomes bound to support him when poor; till then he may be turned out, though in full health. This is very old law, and not much acted on, but it has its effect: Amsterdam alone has abolished it, and is eaten up with poor.

The Hague, *Aug.* 23, 1804.—After finishing and dispatching the memorial, went to the Maison du Bois. The wood is enchanting, being large and irregular—in short, a fine forest in any country, and, after the Dutch-cut walks, truly refreshing. A coach and footway winds irregularly through it. On the right is a deer-paddock, with a few head of cattle, and at present some artillery equipages. In middle of the way found a tent with pipes and all sorts of liquors; refreshed with a glass of lemonade, and continued.

Aug. 24.—Finished the French memorial, and sent it to Van Yzendoorn, who has a friend very confidential, having been a captain in navy, whom he sometimes uses to copy in very private business. He is to take a copy for himself, to be very prudently used.

Attended the sitting of the Legislative Body—a president and twenty-four present, and one was sworn in and took his seat. The room long and vaulted, with a good, sombre light from twelve windows. The president knocked with an ivory hammer after each point was done. The secretary read the minutes and orders of the day. All the members in full dress, plain black. They sat the whole time like jurors, with pen, ink, and paper before them; a few spoke a little, in a plain, discussing manner, but sitting all the while. The session ends to-day. They have given the prince five million guilders for his privy purse, though this is secret; and have imposed a tax of 2½ per cent. on capital.

Went with Van Yzendoorn to Count Hogendorp's to dinner. A pretty campagne two miles off—a large and most select company, it being the stadtholder's birthday. His health was enthusiastically drunk. These were his firmest friends. The most interesting of the company was M. Vander Hein, formerly secretary or minister of the department of the Maes, in the Admiralty, which was represented like the East India Company, though now he has retired in disgust. He is grandson of the pensionary Heinsius. I got much information from him. He informed me that in the years 1792 and 1793 a proposition to abolish the slave-trade—or rather, first to discuss if it should be abolished, and then how, was made in the States General, in imitation of England; but being referred to the states, towns, and admiralties, as such, a thing required by the constitution, they began to examine the question; then came the troubles, before any further progress was made.

Dutch law allows no execution but for theft in goods publicly exposed, housebreaking, and murder. Forgery, punished by the right hand cut off, is very rare. No man hanged without confession, and this is extorted, but not till after conviction by other evidence, and not so as to hurt the health. If he still stands out, he is imprisoned for life: not applied once in fifty years, and never to burgesses, who are tried by civil process, and may be hanged.

Haarlem, Aug. 25.—Had much conversation at *table d'hôte* with M. Costeris of the West India Council. He belonged to the anti-stadtholder party, and was a leading man. He arrested the princess in 1787, and fled for seven years.* He is tolerably acute, but ignorant, and confounded abolition and emancipation; very angry at surrender of the Cape, and, enraged at seeing Batterbury, who commanded the troops, sit-

* This refers to the rising against the house of Orange, which caused the Prussian invasion of 1787. The princess was Frederica Louisa, the daughter of Frederick the Great.

ting opposite to him at the *table d'hôte*, cut him. He is to be tried, and it will go hard with him. Gave him my views in general on the abolition, and he seemed influenced by them. I think the members of Council and Government are prejudiced against abolition, and that France would prevent it. The Council very mixed: one Rypel is in it, who has been in prison six years for trying to effect a counter-revolution, and if judged by military council would have been shot.

Haarlem, Sept. 4.—After the museum, went at one to the organ. It was truly superb, though I scarce believe, as I was told at Hope's, that if played full it would break the windows! It was well played both for the soft and full. The swell was sublime beyond description. It should be heard from a distance. There were many notes of the *vox humana* execrable.

In the Place, near the cathedral, is a good statue of Laurence Coster, erected in 1722 in the Physicians' Garden, and in 1801 removed from thence. It has this inscription:

> "Viro consulari Laurentio Costero Haarlemensi
> Artis imprimendi vero inventori."

He holds a letter-block in his hand, and leans on the branch of a tree with the other.

On one side of the base, the above; on another, a printing-press, in form nearly resembling a modern one; on the third, a figure of Coster, cutting a letter out of a tree; and on the remaining side, a tolerably good Latin inscription, to the effect that he is crowned with laurel, not as a warrior for deeds of arms, but as the benefactor and civilizer of the human race by his immortal invention.

The representation of Coster cutting a letter on a tree refers to the tradition, commonly believed in Holland, that he amused himself by forming letters upon the bark of trees in a wood near Haarlem; that he followed this up by cutting single letters on separate blocks of wood, which he united in lines, and from them took impressions upon paper.

Although this story may not be perfectly credible, there can be no doubt that Coster was the first who cut letters on wood, and that he must be allowed to share with Mentel, of Strasburg, and Faust and Guttenberg, of Mentz, the honor, if not of inventing, at least of suggesting what led to the art of printing. For if metal types were first cast at Mentz, their wooden origin had its birth at Haarlem. The Haarlemites contend that their townsman first printed in 1430—that his workman, Guttenberg, stole the wooden blocks, carried them off to Mentz, and there, in partnership with Faust, printed first with wooden blocks, and afterwards with metal types. Coster died about 1442.

From Haarlem return to the Hague, and from thence went to Düsseldorf, where I arrived Sept. 14. Saw the remarkable *chef-d'œuvre* of Gerard Douw. It has all the beauties of a fine miniature, with the expression of a full-sized picture. Said to have cost 500,000 florins, of which he received 75,000 himself. There is also a masterpiece of Raphael, "St. John in the Wilderness;" also a Correggio, "Jesus from the Scourging." Nothing can be more melancholy than the effect of this. The grief and pain in the face is devoid of every sour or angry feeling. A pity of others tempers his agony. But the masterpiece is Guido's "Assumption." I was told that £100,000 had been refused for this picture.*

Proceeded up the Rhine to Cologne and Coblentz (Sept. 17). Passed many boats near Bonn, carrying trees of liberty, with tricolor flags. Took in many of Bonaparte's Guards, Italians. Visited Ehrenbreitstein, quite demolished by treaty, never taken; stands nobly over Coblentz, which is a remarkably neat town, with some large buildings. Vineyards constant, rich and beautiful. Scenery, if possible, finer; regulation of vineyards on both sides the same, which is, that there are fifteen days before the vintage (Oct. 16) when not even the *proprietor* can enter a vineyard on any account; that is the time when the grapes are quite ready for the press. On the 15th of October drums give notice, and all rush in; then they can eat their fill.

Passed Mentz, but did not venture to go into it. After leaving the Rhine, I worked my way through Switzerland into Italy, arriving at Verona, where I slept on the 5th of October.

No need of being called—was roused by a horrid tooth-

* The celebrated Düsseldorf Gallery was afterwards removed to Munich.

ache, and rose before five. Cured it in two hours with tobacco-leaves. Road to Vicenza one rich vineyard; a few mulberries. The vines make garlands all the way between the elms, and each garland is weighed down with innumerable clusters of black grapes. Generally clover and grass between the rows; sometimes corn and maize. Peasants all gay, being Sunday and the Emperor's name-day. Road level, some part steep from high bridges. Three or four rivers, large, but utterly dried up; one had a good road along its course; but in a few weeks, perhaps days, they will overflow. One or two bits of road I can't conceive passable in the dark.

Regaled on grapes. Arrived at midday at Vicenza (Oct. 6), and agreed for room. Sent letter to Greathead, and dined excellently. Fine Braganz wine for six liris; never drank any thing better. After dinner took *siesta*, and told it is gone out of use. Awoke by Colonel Roche, who got my card, etc., by mistake: very polite.

Oct. 13.—Got to Venice.

Venice, Oct. 14.—Went to the Galleries. "The Presentation of the Virgin," by Titian—thirty-two figures: chief is a most lovely woman, turned towards us, with red silk and satin robe, or rather gown; enchanting sweetness of face; and a peasant, with egg-basket—*i. e.*, old woman sitting below, looking half up—face and hands inimitable. Sky and trees cold and harsh, as usual, but grouping all fine.

Then to the Palazzo Pisani—Moretto (Bonvicino). On stairs, "Icarus and Dædalus," Canova's *coup d'essai*, and excellent for such. In one room, "Death of Darius," by [*illegible*], good and horrid; his body is dreadfully convulsed and discolored. Noble Veronese in next room, "Alexander receiving the Family of Darius:" chief figures are Darius's queen, profile, in grief, and kneeling; and Alexander, in red under-dress, standing in an attitude of inimitable grace, ease, and dignity, beautiful and youthful. Darius's daughter is dressed in a straight gown, quite modern. On the whole, the piece is fine. It was painted in the house.

But in the Barbarigo Palace is the *chef-d'œuvre* of collections. In one room some excellent pieces by Titian's scholars; in next, twelve first-rate Titians, besides other small ones—viz., portrait of Barbarigo, very capital, dated 1492, painted when Titian was only sixteen years of age—all these done in the house. "St. Sebastian," head alone finished: Titian died while doing it. "Christ crowned with Thorns," livid complexion, very striking. "Redeemer," with finger lifted up, and globe in hand; sublime face: mouth peeling off. "Madonna and Child," coloring fine, but expression vulgar, and face rather fat. "Christ bearing the Cross," dark. "Venus and Adonis," she turning her back, naked, and throwing arm round him to retain him; looks coarse at first, but, examined, is very sweet; her face and his excellent; above all, *the* Venus, naked to middle. Near are two cupids—one holds glass, in which she is looking, turning slightly round, almost profile; color exquisitely delicate, and full, and mellow; hand and body noble, and the greatest beauty I ever saw, which for elegance and softness is lovely indeed. An Apollo, by Giovanni Bellini, worthy of accompanying its neighboring picture by Veronese.

Oct. 15.—Morning spent in study at St. Mark's and shopping; in evening, at the usual hour of nine, got into my gondola and *drove* to theatre; very fine; staircase noble; company numerous and good; acting first-rate—Orestes, the character by Deblairis, one of the best I ever saw; his horror at discovering his parricide was far superior to any *male* acting I ever had seen. Rather effeminately dressed; arms and neck shown naked, and his part a little over-acted. Accent said to be foreignish. The action rather more than just, but a foreigner can't judge well in the country of gesture. Women, gods, and Ægisthus and Pylades excellent; latter's concealment of his friend first-rate. I never felt so animated as by the applause and bravos.

Oct. 16.—Day very bad. Spent it in St. Mark's, and had a long spell from three to half-past twelve at night.

Oct. 17.—St. Mark's. Learnt that Venturi is now ambassador from Italian Republic to Berne. Went to Sassi's collection now on sale; some fine sketches, some good pictures, especially two Schiavones advertised as Titians, and a noble Correggio.

At night, the weather being as usual divine and moon bright, went to Square of St. Mark, and saw the resort which holds here nightly. All nations here meet; you have Jews, Poles, Turks, Greeks, all in their costumes; the Turks elegantly dressed, always smoking long pipes, and sitting at doors and on low seats under piazzas. One coffee-house, called Florian, is the resort of all the fashion and English; they sit in the rooms and drink coffee, lemonade, etc.

Some have long collections of seats standing under an awning, and extending to the Place. Busy scene.

Went on the water in an open gondola, and enjoyed a delicious two hours, quite still; moon shone with a full glow on the cupolas and palaces. Ships look fine; coasted round the lagune to the outer or quarantine roads, then round the islands. The canal Giudecca, nearly half a mile broad and two long, in a sweep, with cupolas of San Giorgio Maggiore at one end and the Salute on other side; it is a noble view.

Oct. 18.—St. Mark's. Shop of pictures; a good Veronese, smaller than usual.

At night to the theatre; Mareschini, a new tragedian; for the first time "Idomeneus's Return to Crete," founded on his vow to kill the first he met, as a sacrifice to Neptune for his safety from the storm. Mareschini a very fine actor; same nudity; liked him better, because chaster, than Deblairis. He was so applauded as I never saw before; three times called, one after another; made neat speech; name of poet called, and he came forward and acknowledged it; others all called and applauded; very interesting. Had spell again at Review for Jeffrey, the subject being, "On the Military Character of the different European Armies."*

Oct. 19.—St. Mark's. Ducal palace; inside of square very rich architecture; two colossal statues of Neptune and Justice, brought from Athens. Golden stair whereby ambassadors ascended to the Hall of the Grand Council, which assembled every Sunday to the number of eight hundred; long benches, plain, and in rows; grand Tintoret of Paradise, contains above two hundred figures; largest I ever saw—occupies whole end of Hall; other end a Veronese; Palma's, Bassano's, and Tintoret's on side, chiefly battles and historical pieces connected with Venice; on ceiling a fine Veronese, "Venice crowned." Hall of Council of Ten, plain; best

* See "Edinburgh Review," January, 1805, p. 451. Review of a French Pamphlet, "Caractère des Armées Européenes," etc.

Veroneses away at Paris. Hall of Inquisition, all the roof by Tintoret; best pictures were the Veroneses in the Grand Council Hall.

Saw hall in which were four doors, each with two marble pillars, brought from Greece in the best times of Venice. The whole by Palladio, rather loaded. Ponte dei Sospiri between Council of Ten and Prison.

In the Church of the Salute are some good Giulio Romanos; an altar-piece of the Advent by Titian. Sacristy has four of his; three on ceiling, superb.

Having finished my article for Jeffrey on the 20th, I took a gondola for two or three hours to enjoy the lagune. Returned, and at two went to the post-office; had coffee and refreshments served, and, when all was ready to depart, the courier retired, while I went to *high mass*. There was something solemn in the thing. A small chapel and altar in the upper hall of office for the purpose. The priest of the parish officiated, with all the robes and ceremonials, but with a courier-like velocity.

Set off near three in a covered boat; night delicious; good mattresses and pillows; the noise of the oars did not prevent us from sleeping till eight in the morning; when I awoke, found we were alongside of a wall, five or six miles from Chioggia, of huge stones, hewn, strongly cemented. It shelves up to the top by steps, and is above twelve or fourteen feet high.

Oct. 22.—At Chioggia changed boat and had refreshments; then up the Adige, which is here a noble river: the sail was used, and it was delightful. From the Adige, by a canal and lock, to the place where we left boat (Savia). Commandant of the place (a French officer of Polacks) had me brought up for examination, not understanding my American passport; he was excessively civil, apologized, and gave me Rosolio, with many compliments, after signing my passport.

At Pesaro, Oct. 23.—Arrived at Foligno (24) at six in the morning—never remember being so fatigued. Horrid toothache—no sleep. Went over very rough road; bones almost broken by the constant practice of galloping through towns, where the pavements exceed all others in hills and valleys. All the towns of the Campagna di Roma are on hills, steep on both sides, rising out of a noble plain full of vineyards. Quantity of villas with gates highly ornamented. Came to Spoleto—"Spoletum, Umbriæ caput"—a most ugly town, but ancient, with striking wall of Gothic thickness. Went on without stopping by the Via Flaminia, arriving at Rome (Oct. 25) at eleven. Fatigued and jolted to shivers by the Via Flaminia—a causeway twenty miles long. Not so sore as yesterday. Last night the train continued as before. Passed through Terni. From thence to Narni, which stands in a striking situation on the brink of a precipice, which looks over a beautiful valley. Thence over hills of great height, with dreadful precipices on one side; and when in the midst of one descent, there began the grandest thunder-storm I ever saw. It lasted an hour, and the lightning was the most vivid I ever witnessed. The flashes disclosed at each time a prodigious gulf on one side so clearly that I could have counted the trees and stones. The thunder echoed over the Apennines. Afterwards the lightning continued to flash at intervals, but distant.

Nothing very particular happened till, with scarce any sleep from the jolting, we came in sight of the Eternal City. The distant view is fine; but all Campagna di Roma (this district of Romagna) is absolutely a waste of waving ground in heath, lean grass, and scattered, stunted vegetation, with a cottage, church and chapel, and crucifix here and there. Met, both yesterday and to-day, vast flocks of sheep and lambs. The shepherds seem an odd race of peasants, covered with hairy skins; dogs all crossed with the wolf. View of Rome at a distance very fine, from the unevenness of its foundations and the number of cupolas. St. Peter's looks like St. Paul's, only on a gigantic scale. Passed the Tiber—red, rather than "flavus Tiberis"—by an old bridge. Passport civilly looked at at the Porta del Popolo—fine obelisk. Came through the Corso; passed Trajan's pillar and some fine buildings; arrived here in the Venetian house of the minister and couriers—a very large, good palace surrounded by others, some of which have eighty-four windows on a side.

After dining at the Café di Venezia and sleeping, which was necessary to remove a fever which was oppressing me, went to the opera; neat, but small. An opera buffa, and a comedy in one act. Music very pretty. Tiers of stage-boxes are called after the great composers. Actors very submissive, as usual—bow when applauded.

Rome, Oct. 26.—Went out to hunt for an English *compagnon de voyage* to Naples, having resolved to go thither at once. Agreed with courier. Went to see sights. Church of Sant' Andrea della Valle—noble—frescoes and architecture by Domenichino. Antoninus's pillar much inferior to Trajan's, which was excavated by a former pope. Grand fountain of Trevi—water comes as from the rock. Effect of Michael Angelo's architecture of the Campedoglio is superb. Colossal foot of Apollo wonderful.

Cardinal Borgia received me very graciously at dinner, made me come in, and invited me to stay, but I refused till my return. American consul very civil. Evening spent at the Colosseum, Circus, and Forum. Then set off after regaling on ices, which you have here *excellent* in every coffee-house.

Two guards well armed attended on horseback; being soldiers of the pope, I had no confidence in them. The courier of Naples was robbed a month ago here. The road sometimes fine, at one place twenty miles in a line with rows of trees. Terracina and other towns finely placed on hills, as usual.

After losing great-coat and handkerchief from the horrible machine, arrived here and saw Vesuvius, with dull, solemn light; am told it was not visible last night, and obeys the wind.

Oct. 29.—Day delicious. View of mountain and smoke fine; with glass saw the lava as it flowed down, issuing from one small hole in side in fine white clouds.

Oct. 30.—Went to Pompeii.

Temple of Isis—plain: communication for priests with the oracle's part, and a good room behind. Hence you cross to the main part, I think, of the whole, over vineyards planted on lava above the town. Here you are in the midst of the town—a broad street and two narrow leading off its end. Houses compact on each side, and shops. On each side of causeway are ruts of wheels just size and width of Christian carts and sedias. Thence over more vineyards to a villa—fine house, rooms, paintings, bath, etc.—magnificent, though not at all large. Fine terrace behind looking into garden, exactly use of this day. The depth of the shower of ashes is from six to eight palms, very heavy and close; fine soil above is from two to four, excellent for vines, but plains better for grain, etc.

Walked two miles off road to the main stream of lava. Fine sight of desolation. Twenty-four feet high, and more in some places; hot; frequent parts of yellow, red, and brown sulphur; and as you ascend you come to hotter parts, and these are almost all sulphurous, and give out much hot sulphurous-acid gas; many parts even, near bottom, very hot. Went up through the desolated villa, and visited houses overthrown; many parts, as I ascended, burning hot. Walked over parts, and saw where a stick, etc., took fire. At night is quite red. Almost knocked down with fumes.

The views of Naples and bay most striking. The large, even, flat walls of the houses here are made for the spot, and the quantity of villas and islands in offing, with English men-of-war and three Neapolitan (fitted out against the Algerines), add much to the effect.

At Naples almost famished. The Neapolitans take the *siesta* regularly. They shut up shop at midday, then regularly undress and go to bed as at night, till four, when they begin again. Six is at present Ave Maria, or night, and all hours reckon from it; but they know the hours of our computation.

They call them "di Spagna," sometimes "di Francia;" in some parts of Italy, the latter. The title don is frequent here with all ranks, since the Spanish times. It is used with first name; second little used. Lazzaroni are very numerous; have all houses if they please, but prefer streets and porticoes.

Naples, Nov. 1, 1804.—Went in *calèche* to Avernus. Grotto, on going out of Naples, is astonishing—a mile long, a hundred feet high. Four carriages can go abreast. Solid rock arched out. Continued in one line of road through vineyards, till came to Baiæ. A finer bay is not in Europe. Bridge of Caligula a quarter of a mile long; had fourteen arches—ruins visible; thence could go to Baiæ by bridge of boats. Capreæ in offing. At Puzzoli took a cicerone; was pestered with offers of cameos, found on shore and in ground. First saw temple with three fine pillars—good deal cut away at top—vast square; tepid-water accommodation for the priests; rings for victim remain, and parts of cornice and capitals.

Went to Lake Agnano in *calèche;* found guide with party of English, including two or three of royal navy. Lake is a dull and very deep-looking water, a little like Avernus. Fowls abound on it. Grotto del Cane at one side, road between. The grotto is about three yards long, eight feet high, and five broad—uneven floor; just a hole inside of hill and rock; an old wooden door at it for benefit of cicerone, who hires and rents the key. When our sailors were trying to force the door, came the cicerone with dogs, who seemed to know quite well the process, and not to relish it at all. One had fifteen times tried it, and could hardly be brought up; was laid on his side and held fast; gasped, and fell into convulsions. This was very unpleasant, from his being large. We had him brought into the air; he became quiet, and then he recovered and howled a little. He was not dipped into the lake; this is a vulgar error. Lighted torch extinguished suddenly and thoroughly; difficult to light again; I fancy this is from the humidity. I had brought a large bottle of pure water, and I emptied nine-tenths of it carefully at the deepest part of the air, which had not been much agitated; then corked and agitated for a minute. Rapid absorption; much more than with common carbonic-acid gas. Took from the grotto a full mouthful, and tasted nothing but heat.

Air of grotto not at all bad; the heat great. If you look along the stratum, you see a very singular appearance. At a certain height—very unequal, for the ground is unequal—you see a *level* of mist, one definite line between the good and bad air; the latter being like steam, and hot. It lies like water in a cup, and the heat does not make any mixture.

Baths of St. Girolamo in neighborhood on banks of lake: modern building, with chimneys, which steam like smoke. The vapor is very hot, and is sulphurous and hydrogenous. In one part, if a light is held, it smokes black, without flame.

At other times, was told, it flamed. Suppose this depends on proportion of water and sulphur. In some places it is acid, and forms acidulous sulphates, which abound in great masses; most frequently acid and sulphurous, and hydrogenous.

Returned to Naples. Mountain had a dull red light over it; rather fine; and the passage of the grotto was in a high degree picturesque. Torches were necessary.

Nov. 2.— After breakfast, went to the Monte; ascent gradual, among villas and views of the bay. One odd conceit —a large painting placed to represent a villa or box; not bad, for it actually passes in the crowd of real ones. Entered a locked villa, and wound along its slope. Came near grotto of Posilippo, but high up in air, on a tremendous precipice of wall. Over the entrance of the grotto, and, between this and that, hollow corridors deeper still; over that stands the tomb of Virgil; our picture* like it, but not quite like the situation, from not taking in its chief features—the precipices on both sides. In the inside, inscription on stone opposite not much defaced, and only lost four words—date 1504.

A Russian gentleman and company dined in the tomb, which is a decent little room with a good, flat floor, but the window overlooks the precipice of the grotto road. Climbed up and cut pieces of the laurel shrub, which has a delicious smell.

I went along the brow, and had a noble view of Vesuvius, the bay, and city; then wound up the hill about a mile to the gate of a high villa on the other side. Enjoyed a noble view of Mysenum, Baiæ, and flat between.

Nov. 3.—Took a *calèche* to Portici, with an order to the Museo Reale; very well worth the trouble. Indeed all Pompeii and Herculaneum are thus surveyed in the very best manner. Every portable thing being brought away, every portion of the palace is devoted to this superb purpose. The

---

* By Buonaria, now at Brougham. The picture was brought, with several others, from Italy by my father's grandfather, who visited that country very early in the last century. He returned to England so imbued with Italian taste, that he rebuilt a large portion of High-head Castle in the Italian style, and brought workmen from Italy to decorate the interior. The household accounts at Brougham show that he spent £10,000 on this work—an enormous sum in those days.

floors are all made of ancient mosaic, disposed exactly as found. You find it in every form: small bits, two, three, or four inches; large pieces, figures, and blocks. In one room are manuscripts unrolled, like burnt cylinders. All sorts of antiques. All the cameos are still at Palermo.

Nov. 4.—Set out from Naples on my way back to Rome.

Nov. 5.—Left Capua, passed Terracina, and arrived at Veletri on the 6th.

Nov. 7.—Set off from Veletri after chocolate, and arrived after dark at Albano, where breakfasted at a Trattoria. The best bread imaginable, made in half-pound rolls, each costing four bajocchi. On leaving this finely-situated town, had a splendid view—on one side the sea, in front the great plain of the Campagna, stretching before us all the way to Rome, which looked to be at no great distance. The town, domes, palaces, and ruins, backed by the distant Apennines, had the finest effect possible. The whole plain covered with endless remains of aqueducts—at every step a ruin. Along the road, tombs and temples of all forms, then a ridge of earth, beyond which, aqueducts as far as the eye can reach. Last of all Rome itself, as the ruins thicken. We enter by St. John Lateran, a beautiful piece of architecture, but in parts too much ornamented; then the Colosseum, then the Forum; arches, Titus and Severus. On arriving at the Casa di Venezia, found the places already taken, and so sent adrift. The route to Florence blocked up by the plague, and a cordon round Tuscany. Same difficulty, apparently, in the way of Ancona. Doubtful what to do. Went to San Pietro, in Montorio, as soon as I had dressed. View superb, commanding the whole plain from the platform at the foot of the church-stairs, which is very high, and commands all Rome. St. Angelo, a noble object. Dome of St. Peter's, rising above the ruins, has a fine effect.

The court of the church was a round temple, built over the spot where St. Peter suffered martyrdom. The church is nothing, except that it once held the "Transfiguration." Below is an excellent St. Sebastian, a fine Flemish piece; and a number of marble figures, small and large, by Michael Angelo.

From thence to the Vatican.

The entry in front of the great circle is finer than can be

conceived; the massive pillars, the church, the great centre object, then the noble fountains, have an effect not to be described. On entering the church one is struck dumb and almost blind. Nothing but grandeur; yet all is ornament—no littleness, but every inch well wrought. All marble and gold, the roof dazzling, and the dome, with the grand altar, are exquisite as well as sublime.

St. Paul's differs as much from it as size does from size, combined with splendor and elegance, and beauty of every sort. The paintings are all mosaic. The chief piece is certainly the "Transfiguration;" and I fancy the original, now in Paris, is not *much* finer! The light on Christ's figure is radiant. His attitude is a little constrained. The hill is too petty; but Christ's head, the attitude of Moses and Elias, and the stupefaction of the dazzled apostles, are miraculous indeed. His hands and feet, and the feet and hands of the two former (Moses and Elias), are like bas-relief. One can't possibly think it flat mosaic. A number of other mosaics, both in the roof and altar. "Christ walking on the Sea," his baptism, and that of Constantine, are the most striking. The repairs of the outside of this great temple make it look new and small; but perhaps the former effect counterbalances the latter, as in point of size it has much to spare. The Vatican rather fell short of my expectations, chiefly from the frescoes having suffered much from damp and time. The four rooms (the stanze), with vaulted roofs, all designed by Raphael, and all but one painted by him, and that one by Giulio Romano, are indeed noble, in spite of slight defects. The most striking appeared to be the "Disputes of the Doctors," done when he was twenty-three, and had been only one year in Rome. This is full of his peculiar genius. All his drawing and imagination are there in full force. The School of Athens has suffered considerably. Socrates's countenance is taken from Christ in the "Transfiguration." "St. Peter delivered by the Angel"—said to have reference to the deliverance from captivity of Leo X., after he was taken prisoner at Ravenna. This fresco is remarkable for the singular lights, quite uncommon in this master: the angel outside the window throws his light through the bars—the effect prodigious. The armor of the sleeping soldiers is thus illuminated. One soldier, awake, has a torch in his hand, and the moon is shining behind. One part of the soldier's helmet reflects the torch-light, the other part the moon-light, which at the same time is illuminating the landscape behind. All this is very singular for Raphael, and most marvellous in its excellence.

In the corridors round the courts of the building are a profusion of the finest frescoes. Each arch has four. These are small, but most brilliant, though exposed to the air for three centuries, and are much better, in point of preservation, than the rooms. The frescoes in the Loggia are by different hands. Raphael designed one side, containing about fifty paintings; he finished one, and his scholars the rest. Zucchero did the other three sides. In Raphael's part each subject has four pictures; the finest and *freshest* is the "Creation." He finished the first part, "Chaos, and the Deity making Light." He is soaring wildly with purple robes among fire-clouds, and sweeping his hand, which produces the light; it is a divine piece. Then the land and water; He is still flying and tracing with his finger. Then the sun and moon, less exact; and then the beasts—fantastic, for you see them making by bits — first a horse's head, and so on — which is not the idea. The figure of the Deity standing here is very fine. "Moses striking the Rock," noble.

The stanze suffered much during the sack of Rome by the Constable Bourbon. The troops lighting fires in the rooms greatly injured the paintings, which were afterwards carefully cleaned by Carlo Maratti about the end of the seventeenth century.

Left Rome, and arrived at Terni on the 11th of November; at Pesaro on the 13th. Fano and Sinigaglia, 16th and 17th, fortunately escaping the plague quarantine, which I expected would have detained me at Ancona. By sea to Trieste, and thence to Vienna. On the 8th of January, visited Presburg, returning to Vienna, which I left, and arrived at Prague on the 23d; and from thence to London.

CHAPTER VI.

VOLUNTEERING PROJECT, AND MISSION TO PORTUGAL.

Narrative of Projects as to Volunteers and Militia.—Reception of them by Government.—Estimate of the Efficiency of such a Force in comparison with Regular Troops.—Notices of the younger Pitt.—Lady Hester Stanhope.—Lord Liverpool.—Lord Castlereagh.—Fox.—Designs of Napoleon on the Spanish Peninsula.—Condition of Portugal.—Special Mission to Portugal.—My Share in it.—Lord St. Vincent.—Lord Rosslyn.—General Simcoe.—The British Fleet in the Tagus.—Project for the Seizure of the Royal Family, and the Removal of them to the Brazils.—Anecdotes of Lord St. Vincent.—Death of Fox.—Ministerial Rumors.—Conclusion of the Mission.

The following is a brief and exact statement of certain proceedings which took place last August in Edinburgh relating to my efforts in attempting to organize a volunteer corps. The facts can be proved by the original papers and correspondence which I sent to Wilberforce, in Old Palace Yard, on the 17th July, 1804.

A large body of gentlemen, between the ages of twenty and thirty-five, who from particular circumstances happened not to be attached to any volunteer corps, considering the danger of invasion imminent, desired exceedingly to form themselves into a battalion of infantry, to serve without pay, and to clothe themselves. They accordingly met, to the number of above two hundred, about the end of July. My intention at that time was to serve in the militia of the northern counties of England, with which I was chiefly connected, and I had actually taken steps for obtaining a company in the West York militia. I was, however, applied to by the leading persons among those above mentioned; and having the honor of enjoying a very unmerited share of the confidence of the body, I was requested to attend a meeting which they purposed to call. This meeting did me the honor of appointing me the chairman of the association, and of desiring me to charge myself with the superintendence of their concerns. I mention these particulars to show the reason why I feel it my duty to retain some interest in the manner in which they were treated, and to take this opportunity of doing them justice. I must also add that the body in whose name I write these lines was composed of all the young gentlemen of family, fortune, and talents in that part of Scotland who happened to be in no volunteer corps. They were about two-fifths Scotch, two-fifths English, and one-fifth Irish. Some of them were residing at Edinburgh for pleasure, others attending the University, and some belonged to the place, being engaged in the professions of the law and physic, or members of independent families. All of them, at every meeting, showed the utmost zeal for the service of the country; and their eager wishes to form an effective corps induced me to give up for the time my intentions of entering the militia, and to remain with the rest of the body, to our very great inconvenience, in Edinburgh during the whole of the season.

It was resolved, with the countenance of the University, the magistrates, the lord-lieutenant, and the commander-in-chief, to form a battalion of light-infantry of five hundred and eighty-eight men, who should serve everywhere without any expense to Government. We immediately enrolled a large proportion of that number, and knew that in a month it must be completed, as our letters from the country showed that many others only waited our establishment to join us; and our plan was set on foot at the very worst possible season of the year. We obtained the hearty concurrence of all the constituted authorities above mentioned, and acted in every step by their special advice—that is to say, I communicated almost daily with the commander-in-chief and lord-lieutenant, and these proposed regulations to the association, which were uniformly carried unanimously and eagerly. Our offer of service was drawn up, signed by me at their desire, and transmitted in the form pointed out by the persons above named, accompanied with an obligation signed by the whole body, and forwarded to Lord Hobart by the lord-provost of Edinburgh, as lord-lieutenant of the city, and the Duke of Buccleuch as lord-lieutenant of the county, both very warm friends of the plan. I should add that our design was, instantly on being formed, to march into quarters for six weeks, in order to complete our discipline during that season of the year; and my decided opinion is, that if our offer had been accepted, there would at this moment have been in his majesty's service a light-infantry battalion of six hundred spirited young men in the highest state of discipline, instead of the same number of gentlemen attached to no corps, and certainly not very keen "*to die with the levy en masse.*"

It remains to mention the reception with which it pleased Lord Hobart to honor the hearty and unqualified offer of our most zealous and active services. He returned *no answer:* he *never even acknowledged the receipt of our papers.* We waited in Edinburgh, to our utmost inconvenience, the whole summer, many of us belonging to very distant parts of the island, and every post expected to be called out. The lord-lieutenant wrote repeatedly in our favor, and so did the commanding officer. They received no answer, any more than we had done. In November, I tried to set on foot a new corps after Lord Moira's arrival; and so disgusted were those *hundreds* now, whom I could have persuaded with a word to march to Land's End three months before, that only eleven would put down their names. This was the true way to encourage "the *volunteering system,*" and "*call forth the energies of the country.*"

I am no advocate for that system, nor for the militia system, except as subservient to the recruiting of the only defense of any modern and civilized state—a *regular army.* On the contrary, I hold every other means of defense to be barbarous in the extreme, and utterly repugnant to the whole principles of political science; and as for balloting, I think it is not a jot different from a *poll-tax* falling in the way of a lottery, while the principle of volunteering is worse than that of supporting the state or the poor by voluntary gifts. Therefore it is not as an advocate of the system that I feel the bad consequences of the above conduct, but as an enemy to gross inconsistency in great state affairs, and as a friend to conciliatory measures in great emergencies of the public fortunes. I have drawn up this narrative to satisfy those who did me the honor of putting themselves and their zeal under my direction. It is a duty I owe them, and they will be more than recompensed for the INTOLERABLE insult which was formerly thrown upon them, if their efforts are made known to those distinguished persons whom it is their first and best wish to please.

TO JOHN ARCHIBALD MURRAY.

"21 Craven Street, April 2, 1805.

"MY DEAR MURRAY,—I won't begin by a number of excuses for not answering sooner your very agreeable letter, but seize the present moment to tell you how angry I am at your not coming up this spring. I am almost afraid that fate, the enemy of all wise and good men, may continue to make us miss one another, as I have some intentions of a pilgrimage to the shrine of Jeffrey during the autumn, and you, I'm told, have thoughts of looking towards the South. Nevertheless, I highly approve of your London plan, disinterestedly speaking; for there is always good society at the empty period of the year, and you'll be able to enjoy it in great style, besides seeing something more of the country than birds on the spring flight generally look at.

"I entreat you to bear with me while I give you a commission. Jeffrey seems to have thought I was out of humor in my last letter to him, which he must have entirely mistaken, for I never was less angry in my life than when I wrote it. In fact, the whole Lord L. business has not once made me feel sufficient interest in it to feel any approach to passion. I have only time to write this by the present post, and wish much that Jeffrey should not for a day mistake me so much as to suspect such a thing.

"But chiefly, I want to explain my opinion about the notice printed in No. IX. of the Review. It tied me down to publish the answer, which I would not otherwise have done, when I found there were so many scruples about giving it the plural form. I also thought that it was as much as possible committing the Review against Lord Lauderdale to talk of *our rejoinder*, and to cut Lauderdale by the very style of the notice. But I feel much indebted to the notice, upon the whole, from another consideration, which I certainly only discovered upon reading Horner's article on the Corn Bill. The very unnecessary introduction of L.'s book there, in a manner which gave a most erroneous idea of H.'s general opinion of the book, must have had the effect of making L. conclude that he had succeeded in his end of obtaining a favorable verdict from the reviewers in general. The notice tended to counteract this. I own I was the more astonished at the remark in Horner's article, from the circumstance of his having told me repeatedly that my review erred in not being severe enough —that he himself would have been more bitter — that he wished to review the observations in the next number, and that he meant to have a former compliment to L. erased in No. II. Hence, again, I must say I feel obliged for the notice in No. IX.*

"All the world talks all day about the tenth report: it is more universally enjoyed than any publication I ever remember to have seen, and not a voice is raised in Melville's behalf even by ministerial people.† If fame may be credited, Pitt has written him a dry letter, and the doctor‡ means to vote against him. But I give you this only as the talk of uninformed persons. The general question seems to me very short and clear. Whether the public lost or won—whether Lord Melville gained or not—whether even Trotter gained or not—I have no reason to inquire. A statute provides to the public money security against risk, and a high officer in a station of great trust acts in the teeth of that provision. The public has incurred *risk;* and if you were to prove that it had gained instead of losing, I would only say, 'So much the more dangerous is the precedent.' If it is argued that Lord Melville served the State with the navy money on pressing emergencies, the answer is plain: he should have applied for

* See "Edinburgh Review," October, 1804, art. 15. "On the Bounty upon Exported Corn," at p. 205, is this passage: "The different employments of national capital, and the progress in which they naturally succeed each other, or alternate, form a subject on which we are not yet in possession of a complete theory, though a beautiful sketch was drawn by Dr. Smith, to which many original remarks have been added by Mr. Brougham in his work upon Colonial Policy, and some happy illustrations by Lord Lauderdale in the last chapter of his late publication."

† The tenth Report of the Commissioners of Naval Inquiry, ordered by the House of Commons to be printed, Feb. 13, 1805—the foundation of the impeachment of Lord Melville. See State Trials, xxix., 550 *et seq.*

‡ The doctor—*i.e.*, Addington.

a bill of indemnity. But, in truth, such a bill could only have been got for a part of the transaction so extremely trifling that the application would have ruined his cause.

"But though the above is clearly the naked *State* question, I am far from viewing the facts of profit and loss as indifferent. It is something that such sharks should be brought to justice; and it is much, much indeed, that an attempt is made to wipe off this *first foul stain* which the country has ever received from the conduct of its rulers. Dirty fingers will absolutely not do in England.

"All people of any character here seem to *feel* much upon the occasion—and well they may, upon national grounds.

"But those who love Dundas with *the pure affection which I bear him*, must feel a mixed sensation—a little sorrow for the country, and an infinite satisfaction for the fate of the men. I feel truly savage upon the whole affair, and only lament most sincerely, as every admirer of Pitt must do, that he has been so long coupled with such a nasty dog. The city (who say they used to feel the fellow in the stock-market) are going to petition for his removal; and though he will gain a great victory, most likely, in Parliament, I venture to prophesy that he will soon be little heard of.

"The capture of our West India Islands comes in to puzzle ministers a little further, and I have no doubt that a few days will bring the worst news from the East. Every man who knows how to estimate the importance of Mr. Pitt's security to the country at present must feel inexpressibly annoyed at all this. Indeed, I must be impartial enough to say that nothing has surprised me more than the strength of the tide now setting in against him. But he will gain some great victory, and scatter all his enemies, except those *eternal existing circumstances*, which I fear he is fated to be undone by, and which he seems once more to hug as close as ever. Pray tell me what Edinburgh folks say of Lord M.'s business. I agree in all you say about Fox's impolicy. What a pity that the first man in *the world* should be incapacitated from ever ruling in this country by so trifling a defeat!

H. B."

Although on more than one occasion I had heard Pitt

speak, I never had an opportunity of making his acquaintance; but many years after his death I received from my friend William Napier so graphic an account of a visit he had paid to Pitt in 1804, that I wrote down nearly the whole of Napier's statement in the very words he had used in relating to me the impression left on his mind by his visit to the great minister. Napier received through his friend Charles Stanhope, Pitt's nephew, an invitation to pass some time at Putney. When he arrived, Mr. Pitt received him cordially, and welcomed him with such gentle good-nature that he felt instantly not only at perfect ease, but that he was in the presence of a friend with whom he might instantly become familiar, to any extent, within the bounds of good-breeding. All this produced a strange sensation, for Napier had gone to Putney determined to hold fast by his Whiggish principles even in the presence of the wicked Tory minister, however polite and condescending he might appear to be; for he had been reared among Whigs, and accustomed to hear Mr. Pitt abused with all the vehemence of their sneering virulence. So he looked upon Pitt as an enemy of all good government, and had always heard his father, who was no Whig, condemn the war with France as an iniquitous and pernicious measure. Thus primed with fierce recollections and patriotic resolves, he endeavored to keep up a bitter hatred of the minister; but in vain. All hostile feelings gave way to unbounded surprise at finding such a gentle, good-natured, and entertaining companion, for such he proved to be long before the visit was at an end.

Lady Hester Stanhope was there: he found her very attractive; and so rapid and decided was her conversation, so full of humor and keen observation, and withal so friendly and instructive, that it was quite impossible not to succumb to her, and to become her slave, whether laughing or serious.

She was certainly not beautiful; but her tall, commanding figure, her large dark eyes, and varying expression, changing as rapidly as her conversation, and equally vehement, kept him, as he expressed it, in a state of continual admiration.

She had little respect for the political coadjutors of Mr. Pitt, and delighted to laugh at them. Lord Castlereagh she always called "his monstrous lordship;" but Lord Liverpool was a constant theme for ridicule and contempt. Thus, speaking of a design which had been approved of by Pitt, of conferring military decorations, she said it had been stopped by the meddling folly of Lord Liverpool, who insisted upon being consulted on the texture and colors of the ribbons; whereas, she said, she thought, as a young woman, she was more capable of settling such a question than an old woman like Lord Liverpool. But he would not give way, and ended by sending her four thousand yards of different ribbons, all, as she said, to be paid for by the public; and this collection he proposed to examine in concert with her, for the purpose of selecting the most suitable. Lady Hester declined the partnership, and so there was an end of the plan for military decorations.

Some years afterwards, and after Mr. Pitt's death, she told Napier a more melancholy story, in which Lord Liverpool played a part. A young fellow of Deal had been engaged in smuggling, and got involved in a fray in which a sailor was killed, but not by him; and there were, besides, circumstances of extenuation: however, he was apprehended, tried, and condemned to death. His old mother went to Lady Hester, beseeching her aid; and Lady Hester without hesitation went to Lord Liverpool, stated all the circumstances, and made out, as she fully believed, a case for pardon. Napier said she described her interview with the most bitter sarcasm. His maudlin lordship, she said, listened with great interest to her story, admitted it to be a case for commiseration, and that the plea she had urged in the man's favor was very powerful, but added that, before he could give an answer, he must consult his housekeeper! He went down stairs, remained half an hour with his adviser, and, returning to Lady Hester, told her "they had wept together over the sad case, but that the man must be hanged!" All this seems incredible, but Napier assured me it was positively so stated to him by Lady Hester, and that she had told him many other stories about this houskeeper, and of her marvellous influence over Lord Liverpool. Of Sir John Moore she always spoke with great admiration, and said that Mr. Pitt had so high an opinion of him that he never received from him the most ordinary note without showing it to whoever was then with him, and pointing out the grace and felicity of the expressions.

Mr. Pitt used to come home to dinner after his cabinet work a good deal exhausted, and requiring port-wine, of which he generally drank a bottle during dinner in a rapid succession of glasses; but as soon as this stimulus restored his strength, he drank no more. His conversation then became gay, good-natured, and humorous, and he would tell all sorts of amusing stories: some of them about the colonel of Napier's regiment—the 43d. This was General Smith, an uncle of Sir Sidney; and certainly a humorist, as appeared by the stories Mr. Pitt used to relate of him. One was that, during the fears produced by the apprehension of the French invasion, the general sent by extraordinary express a parcel supposed to contain important news, but which turned out to be the night-cap of a member of the Government, who had left it behind when on a visit to the general. Another story was that, when he commanded on the south coast, he sent a dispatch to Pitt announcing that *two* French ships were then actually landing troops in *three* places!

Mr. Pitt liked practical fun, and used to encourage it. One instance, which Napier gives, shows Pitt in a point of view singular, and little to be anticipated of so generally solemn a personage. They—Lady Hester, James Stanhope, and Napier—had resolved to blacken his face with burnt cork, which he most strenuously resisted. Early in the fray, a servant announced that Lord Castlereagh and Lord Liverpool had called, desiring to see him on important business. "Let them wait in the outer room," said the great minister, instantly returning to the battle, catching up a cushion and belaboring his attackers, who proved too many for him, and, after a prolonged struggle, got him down and began daubing his face—when, with a look of well-assumed confidence in his powers of still resisting, he said: "Stop—this won't do: I could easily beat you all, but we must not keep these grandees waiting any longer;" so they were obliged to get a towel and basin of water to wash him clean before he received the grandees. Being thus made decent, the basin was hid behind the sofa, and the two lords ushered in. Then a sudden change and entirely new phase of manner appeared, to Napier's great surprise and admiration. Lord Liverpool's manner was, as usual, mean-looking, bending, nervous, and altogether pitiful. Lord Castlereagh, Napier said, he had well known from his childhood; had often been engaged with him in such athletic sports as pitching the stone, bar, and so on; and he had looked upon him as a model of calm grace combined with great strength. What, then, was his surprise when he saw both him and Lord Liverpool humbly bending as they approached the man who had so recently been maltreated with such an excess of fun! But it was Mr. Pitt's sudden change of manner and look which most entirely fixed his attention. His tall, ungainly, bony figure seemed to grow up to the ceiling—his head thrown back, his eyes fixed immovably in one position as if gazing into the heavens, and totally regardless of the two bending figures before him. For some time they spoke, and he made now and then a short observation; but finally, with an abrupt, stiff inclination of his body, but without casting his eyes down, dismissed them; and then, turning round with a laugh, caught up his cushion and renewed the fight.

Napier described to me another instance of what he called Mr. Pitt's power of countenance. Some time after the visit to Putney, while walking across the parade-ground of the Horse Guards, he saw Mr. Pitt talking to some gentlemen, evidently upon business which interested him. Napier caught his eye while still some forty yards distant. Pitt gave him a smile and nod of recognition, but on Napier advancing, laughing, towards him, his countenance assumed a commanding fierceness of expression difficult to describe, but unmistakably saying, "Pass on: this is no time for foolery."

Napier concluded this account of Pitt, which I have given in his own words, by telling me a good deal about Fox, whom he had frequently met, not only at his own father's at Clifton, but in Fox's own house, or, more frequently, at the Duke of York's, which then stood on the present site of Stafford House, where Fox lived when he was prime-minister. I much regret that I did not make more copious notes of what he related to me, as I had done in the case of Pitt. But I well remember that he told me that Fox's manners were totally different from Pitt's; always agreeable, gentle, kind, and good-natured; but not attractive for young people, inasmuch as he never appeared to take any interest in them, but rather to bear with them than to like them. Such was the clear impression he made upon young Napier; whereas Pitt's manners were joyous hilarity and delight at having the opportunity of unbending his mind, and relieving himself from public cares, where he could do it safely; and this Napier declared was very attractive.

Between this time and the autumn of 1806, when I accompanied Lord St. Vincent and Lord Rosslyn to Portugal, I have nothing of any interest to record. I now proceed to give the history of that mission, and the circumstances connected with it, much of which will be explained by the correspondence and dispatches which follow.

The intention of the French Government—that is, of Napoleon—to invade Portugal had for some time been made manifest in various ways during the summer of 1806, and it appeared to the English Government that the situation of that country was becoming critical. It was felt that if France should succeed in establishing a peace with the Northern Powers, she would probably attack the only remaining ally of England upon the Continent, and might even succeed in making herself mistress of the Portuguese dominions. Portugal, from its long alliance with England, was regarded by Bonaparte almost as a part of our dominions, both in a commercial and political point of view. Considerable as were the benefits we derived from its trade, and great as was our preponderance in its councils, he certainly formed an exaggerated estimate of both; seizing upon Portugal was like a direct defeat of England. He was smarting under the recent defeat at Trafalgar, and had found not the least facility in his plans of invasion; so that any thing like a territorial advantage over us would be a gratification, if it did not amount to a compensation. The possession of the Tagus was intimately connected with our other great naval victory at St. Vincent; but though the importance of that event in rescuing us from the most complicated and almost inextricable embarrassments must have been well known to him, he cared little about any thing that had happened before his own reign, so entirely did personal vanity form a part of his character—more entirely than of any other person of great renown. To be able to boast that he had driven the English into the sea, captured their only stronghold on the Continent, and dethroned those who held it by and for them, was his main object, and probably nearer his heart than any substantial injury done to us, or any real advantage gained to himself.

The Courts, too, both at Lisbon and Madrid, were feeble beyond all description; their Governments, both civil and ecclesiastical, as bad as possible; the Queen of Spain and the Prince of the Peace more likely to assist the French in destroying Portugal than to oppose any obstacle to its destruction. Since the peace of Presburg, Bonaparte had nothing to occupy his attention, nor had any thing occurred to postpone the project of subduing the ally of England and winning the last stake England had to lose on the Continent of Europe.

Early in August, 1806, the English Government had received intelligence of the intention of France to invade Portugal with an army of 30,000 men, then assembled at Bayonne. From perfectly reliable information, it was believed that it was the object and intention of Bonaparte to dethrone the royal family, and to partition Portugal, allotting one part to Spain, and the other to the Prince of the Peace or to the Queen of Etruria.

The ministers thereupon resolved to send an army to the Tagus, to be there met by a competent naval force, the whole to be intrusted to the command of Lord St. Vincent and Lieutenant-general Simcoe, with full powers, conjointly with Lord Rosslyn, to negotiate with the Court of Lisbon.

I received from the Foreign Office the following letter:

"Downing Street, August 12, 1806.

"SIR,—I am directed by Mr. Secretary Fox to inform you that his majesty, having been pleased to appoint the Earl of Rosslyn, the Earl of St. Vincent, and Lieutenant-general Simcoe to proceed on a special mission to the Court of Lisbon, you have been selected to accompany them as secretary to the said mission. You will, therefore, join the Earl of Rosslyn and General Simcoe, who are proceeding without delay to the place of their destination, where the Earl of St. Vincent will be already arrived, and place yourself under their directions;

and you will exert yourself to the best of your ability in the execution of all such matters as may be intrusted to you.

"(Signed) BENJ[N]. TUCKER."

I was further informed that, to avoid multiplying places unnecessarily, I was named secretary, but in all respects I was to act as a fourth commissioner. General Simcoe was taken ill on his passage out, and grew so much worse after his arrival in Lisbon, that he was compelled to return to England, and shortly afterwards died. The work of the commission thereupon was carried on by Lord St. Vincent, Lord Rosslyn, and myself.

Lord St. Vincent was ordered to proceed with as little delay as possible to Lisbon, to be in readiness to execute the secret service communicated to him by Lord Howick. He was directed, after having placed the ships off Brest under the officer next in command, to proceed, without a moment's loss of time, to the Tagus, taking with him such of the ships then under his command as he should judge necessary; and to remain in the Tagus until joined by the troops which were about to be employed in this special service.

The object of this move was to counteract the expected French invasion of Portugal by the army then assembled at Bayonne.

In executing this service, Lord St. Vincent was especially directed by Lord Howick to keep the following in view: First, if he should find the Portuguese Government willing and resolved to make effectual efforts for their own defense, either singly or in co-operation with Spain, he might intimate that England would be ready to afford substantial assistance, the preliminary step to this being the presence of an English squadron in the Tagus. Second, if the Portuguese Government, believing resistance to be impracticable, should resolve, as had been conjectured, to remove their ships, forces, stores, etc., to the Brazils, then that he should co-operate with them for that purpose, by affording the aid of the British fleet under his command. Third, if the Court of Lisbon should appear too undecided to adopt either of the above resolutions, that he should take such steps as should prevent the accession of force, particularly of naval force, which the enemy would receive were they allowed, without resistance, to possess themselves of the port of Lisbon, and which must at all events be prevented, and such means adopted as might enable him to bring away the Portuguese ships of war, Brazil and other ships, and also the persons, ships, and property of the British factories, and, above all, the Court itself.

In the event of this last contingency arising, the troops which were embarked had been ordered to follow him with the least delay possible. But he was especially cautioned to be most careful not to give any information, before they actually arrived, that they were expected by him, and above all to do nothing that might alarm the French minister at Lisbon, or give the smallest hint to the French party there, that might lead to any measures being taken to counteract or defeat whatever steps he might ultimately be compelled to take.

Thus it will be seen that the object of our mission was to provide with the Portuguese Government for the defense of the country; to show them that an invasion was intended, of which we had abundant proof from the diplomatic intercourse with Paris, as well as from the preparations actually in progress on the Spanish frontier; to require adequate preparations on their part, with the co-operation of our naval and military forces, and whatever aid in subsidy might be required; and if it should be found that either they would make no effort in self-defense, or that their means, with all the help we could afford them, were wholly inadequate, then our object was to urge the transfer of the Government to the Brazils, assisting by every means in our power this important operation, which implied the removal of the royal family, the ministers, and the principal nobles, as well as the substitution of the metropolitan for the provisional or colonial system. The three commanders were as well selected as possible for this difficult and delicate service. The admiral's name, renowned all over the world, was peculiarly an object of veneration in these countries which had witnessed his great exploits: of the generals, Lord Rosslyn had served in the country, and was distinguished by his great knowledge and talent for business; and the third was General Simcoe, son of the general who had been sent to Lisbon at the time of the great earthquake with the liberal grant of money given to relieve the distresses which it had occasioned. The greatest weight of authority was possessed by the head of the commission, and the most favorable disposition prevailed towards the other members. My intercourse was with Lord St. Vincent and Lord Rosslyn, because General Simcoe, as I have before stated, died before we began our operations. On the voyage, however, he (Lord Rosslyn) and myself had a great deal of discussion upon the objects of our mission, and the extraordinary difficulties which we expected to meet from the strength of the forts, should entrance into the Tagus be refused; and in that case we were to remain with the fleet off the coast till the troops arrived; though these conversations turned chiefly on the formidable nature of the service we were undertaking, and particularly on the great means of naval defense on the river, in case we should have to force a passage and a landing. For the first three days of our voyage we had been constantly signalling strange sails, and, receiving no answers, were often on the point of preparing for action; so it seemed as if we were destined to have a hostile encounter either at sea or when we reached the Tagus, and we all felt desirous that it should end one way or another. When we arrived, however, there was no prospect of the kind. We found none of the fleet off the coast; it had all entered without the least opposition, or any delay whatever interposed; and then we found the great admiral's plan clearly explained.

I could not but recollect who this illustrious man was, with and under whom it had become my lot to act: not only his achievements, of which I had heard Pitt, when in the act of moving a censure upon his naval administration, "extol the vast renown," declaring that they "shed a new lustre on our national glory, and made his name a tower of strength in every naval capacity,"* but his other great qualities, of which, on the same occasion, I had heard Fox, in his factious co-operation with his rival's proceeding, profess his unstinted "admiration, when he found him possessing in so high a degree what he truly described as so much more rare than gallantry in the field, civil courage and decision."† Thus impressed

* House of Commons, 15th March, 1804. † Same debate.

with a deep sense of his genius, both in war and peace, I felt the greatest deference for his judgment, no less as a statesman than a warrior; and it may well be supposed how closely I observed his proceedings, and how anxiously I cultivated his friendship. I soon found that, like all great men, though having entire confidence in his own judgment, he received patiently, even kindly, any doubts or objections proposed by those for whom he entertained respect, not even rejecting the suggestions of others, or their information, without duly considering what was offered; and only showing impatience when subordinate persons required to be assured that his resolution was taken, and in peremptory terms announced. His objection to the word *impossible* he did not conceal; indeed he could never comprehend its meaning, even before his mind was made up—and nobody dared to use it afterwards.

On our arrival in the Tagus, we found that his first step had been, as soon as he anchored, to cut off all communication between his fleet and the shore, which he effectually did by proclaiming an eight days' quarantine. When his colleagues in the commission joined him, he still prohibited all his officers and men most strictly from landing; but threw open the ships to the inhabitants of the place, whose multitudes never ceased pouring through the vessels, lost in admiration of their beauty, their force, and the discipline of their crews. His intercourse now began with the Court, and we soon found, what might, indeed, have been expected, that his name, independent of the armament, made his influence supreme. But our attempts were vain to convince the Court or its ministers that an invasion was prepared, and that they must expect the French army to cross the Pyrenees immediately.

I have already stated, generally, the instructions of the commissioners. It happened, however, when I fully considered the position of Spain in all respects, that there was a fair prospect afforded by our expedition of detaching her from the French alliance—in fact, of inducing her to make some efforts at this particular time for recovering her independence, supposing that the full powers which we had with respect to Portugal were extended to Spain, both in respect of pecuniary and military assistance. Her grievances were at their height. Her abject submission, and the great losses which it had inflicted, were rewarded not only by the seizure of the last of the Bourbon dominions in Italy, but by an attempt to obtain the cession of Sicily from England in return for the Balearic Islands and Porto Rico, parts of the Spanish possessions. But, independent of just cause of offense, the danger was manifest, indeed imminent, of an invasion from France. A French army was assembled on the frontier; and though the pretense was to invade Portugal, yet even that operation implied its march through Spain, which must prove the next thing to an occupation of the country. There was every inducement to make the effort, and the moment was favorable; indeed, was in all probability the last opportunity the Spaniards ever would have. In Germany there was a great and general agitation occasioned by the French armies continuing on the right bank of the Rhine, and which was there increased to exasperation by the acts of violence committed, especially the murder of Palm, the Nuremberg bookseller. The indignation of Prussia at the establishment of the Confederation of the Rhine was extreme; and the hostility to France was stronger in the Prussian territories than in any other part of the German states. The exasperation was increased by the discovery that Napoleon had proposed to give up Hanover as part of his terms with England, allowing part of the Hanse towns as a compensation. Every thing seemed to portend a rupture with France, which of course meant an invasion of Germany. The Emperor Alexander had, by his ambassador, concluded a treaty entirely favorable to Napoleon; and nothing prevented Russia from breaking with him but the negotiations still pending with England; and the ratification of the treaty was delayed. All these things had been known to our Government before we left England, in consequence of Lord Yarmouth's communications, acting as our minister at Paris previously to Lord Lauderdale's more formal appointment; and I conceived the plan of opening a direct intercourse with Madrid. This was laid in detail before my colleagues in the commission, who all, especially Lord St. Vincent, entirely approved of it, as did the Government at home. The chief minister (Godoy, prince of the peace) was applied to for passports, that I might proceed to Madrid and carry on the negotiation there directly. A week's delay in sending them was proposed, and I proceeded during that time to the North, charged to examine the preparations pretended by the Portuguese Government to be making on that frontier against any attack, though the ministers were, or affected to be, satisfied that none was intended. But before I went, our conversation with the Government had been most unsatisfactory, not only as to their disbelief of any peril, but also as to getting them to make preparations against a design which they persisted in considering, or at least in representing, as very remote. That their means of defense, as far as we could ascertain them, were very inadequate, was but too manifest. It was very fit that we should examine their preparations in the North, if it were only to have a test of the accuracy of their statements. But, on the best consideration we could give to the whole case, it appeared that the passage of the Pyrenees by the French army must at once seal the fate of Portugal, whatever assistance we might be able to render them; and that therefore we should be driven to the other alternative as soon as that passage was effected—viz., the prevailing on them to transfer the seat of government to the Brazils. But we plainly perceived that this was quite as hopeless as to make them prepare effectually for their defense. I had repeated discussions on this great question with Lord St. Vincent, and he never for an instant imagined that they would voluntarily accede to the proposition. The reluctance to remove was universal and deep-rooted, wherever the subject was broached. Those at the head of affairs, as often as we approached it, plainly showed us that no result of an invasion, no terms which a successful enemy could propose, would be more hateful than their banishment for life across the Atlantic would be to those whose excursions had hitherto been confined to a journey between their town and country residence at home. But the admiral, well aware of this resolution, without letting any one entertain the least suspicion of what he was about, arranged every thing for the voyage of the royal family and its attendants. In talking over the matter, when both of us dwelt upon the absolute necessity of the strictest secrecy, I remember his saying, "You know there is but one way of keeping a secret—to tell nobody." I said, "Of course our colleagues must know it." "Certainly," he said; "but not their families, as they call their aid-de-camps." And General Simcoe being exceedingly ill, it was agreed that I should mention it to Lord Rosslyn as soon as the preparations were completed, before which time it was unnecessary to trouble him. As soon as every thing had been prepared, and all communication between the fleet and the shore cut off (I forget on what alleged ground), the admiral only waited till the proper moment came to execute his plan. The success appeared quite certain. His design was to have one or two boats with crews of picked men, then a few of his most able and trusty officers, and a number of men on whom he could rely, not in any order or arrangement, but scattered about, and ready to assist when they received directions either from himself or the officers, who were to be dispersed among them. He had rehearsed with them what he expected would be done, and no one had the least suspicion of the service in which they were to be employed, all supposing, probably, that these evolutions were merely a piece of discipline connected with landing and embarkation, as the arrival of our troops was known to be expected. As soon as the moment came, and the operation was resolved upon, the admiral was to propose that the regent and his attendants of rank should drive to the harbor to view the Hibernia (his flag-ship), dressed out on occasion of some English festival. They had frequently done so before, and their repairing now to the spot would not be objected to. The regent was of course likely to be accompanied by many of his Court, and Lord St. Vincent himself would attend him. I recollect his saying, in answer to my question whether he would invite him to a collation as on former occasions, "Certainly not; for, considering what was intended, it might be thought contrary to good faith." I replied that I conceived the plan to be so little grounded on good faith, as to make this distinction somewhat of a refinement. But he said that was as one happened to feel it, only they would cry out the more against the whole proceeding.

When we had with the utmost possible respect attended the regent to the boat, he expected that there would be a positive refusal to go on board, which he meant to urge in the most humble and submissive terms. He laid his account with the resistance being greater the more he pressed, and took for granted that either a peremptory refusal or a return to the palace would be declared as the suspicion entered their minds of what was in view. He then was determined to take the prince's arm, while one of his officers (I think it was Sir Pultney Malcolm, who was in the secret, and on whom he had entire reliance) took the other arm, and the men joining them, the prince and his chief attendants were to be forced into the boat as gently as possible, but at once, and conveyed on board the Hibernia without their having time to give any warning to their servants, all of whom were to be detained by the men surrounding the boats. On their arrival at the Hibernia, the regent would find the most ample preparation for accommodating them, and as many as they chose to send for. But they were to sail for Rio Janiero that evening, after issuing a proclamation to declare the Seat of Government transferred. Lord St. Vincent had no doubt that, great as the ill-humor and even indignation might be, yet a few hours' conversation would obtain this proclamation. All communication with the shore being cut off, and the commission having the power of placing the whole affair in whatever light they pleased, he believed the regent and those about him would consent, and care would be taken to send for his favorites, in whose hands he was known to be entirely, as we had found from all our sources of information, including Lord Strangford, who had been for some time *chargé d'affaires* in the absence of our minister, Lord Robert Fitzgerald. Aranjo, the chief minister, was to be allowed, if he chose, to join his master; but we had no idea that any thing would have tempted him to quit Europe, particularly in these circumstances. The unhappy condition of the queen would have required that she should be conveyed on board in the night; but the regent would have been made to give the proper directions, and one of the other ships being ready for part of the Court, she might have been embarked in that. To have left her behind would furnish the invading army with the means of misrepresentation, and even of acting in her name.

As every part of the execution of this plan depended upon

the admiral himself, the only risk I could perceive of its failure was if any attempt against him had succeeded. But this must have been at the very first; and in case any troops should have been suddenly brought together from their accidentally being near the spot, the marines were to be landed, so as at once to overpower them; for part of the plan was to have them repeatedly landed as for parade or review. But the obtaining possession of the regent's person, and the consequent acting in his name, rendered any such emergency extremely unlikely. The picked men, who were to man the boats and to mix with the crowd, afforded abundant security against every thing except some chance attack upon the admiral's person.

There could be little doubt that Lord St. Vincent had borrowed his plan from Cortez's seizure of the Emperor Montezuma (at least the leading features of it), and I told him he had been reading my great kinsman's account of that transaction. He did not deny it, but said there were material variations in his plan. There was force, though gentle force, if necessary, at the beginning of his plan, and there was no maltreatment or cruelty at the end. He expressed the greatest horror of Cortez's cruel, blood-thirsty, and sordid conduct, not only towards Montezuma, but in all his actions and designs; and on my entirely agreeing with him, he said that miscreant had not been enough abused. Your uncle, I think he said,* has not abused him half enough; in which I entirely agreed. Our discussions on the matters connected with this plan took place at different times before I went to the Northern provinces. It formed a frequent subject of our conversation. It plainly occupied his thoughts a good deal; and I recollect when at Cintra, where we had gone for a day to escape the heat and the offensive atmosphere of Lisbon, after his rubber of whist, which he made me play with his old hostess, Mrs. Dacy, and Dr. Cope, our physician—when she and the doctor retired, he would fall a-musing on the subject, and putting questions for consideration.

---

* Of this expression I may have some doubt, for he was in the habit of saying "your uncle," in reference to another, Mr. Meux, who had married my father's sister, and with whom Lord St. Vincent had been at school, and always kept up some intercourse, and had him occasionally on board his ship. He used to speak of "my old school-fellow, your uncle Dick."

It was on such occasions, as well as on board the Hibernia, that he dwelt on many things which were most interesting in his former life. Thus he described the means which he adopted for putting down the mutiny in the vessels so often sent to him for that purpose; and he was very indignant at the complaints which were sometimes made of his cruelty, or at least his severity, when in truth it was only his humane determination to prevent mischief and spare life by vigorous action that were the ground of complaint. An instance he gave of this, which I shall not easily forget, was when the fleet lay off Cadiz, and a seventy-four, I think she was, joined him in as bad a state as possible. He soon found that the mutinous crew were all but in possession of the vessel. "I knew well enough," he said, "that all would be right, and the authority of the officers restored, were they laid alongside of an enemy; but of that there was little chance, to all appearance:" so the officers were, one after another, quietly withdrawn, and two vessels of superior force suddenly directed to place themselves one on each side of the mutinous ship, with orders to sink her after distinct announcement of the fixed intention. I don't recollect whether this notification was to be made by calling for some of them on board, or by sending some men to her, but the notice was clearly conveyed, that disobedience to orders would instantly be followed by the extremity of punishment. Lord St. Vincent well knew that what actually happened was certain to take place—submission, as soon as the mutineers saw the men in the other ships at their guns with matches lighted. I think it was the day after this mutiny was quelled that he ordered a court-martial to try the ringleaders; and some of the worst being singled out for punishment, an officer waited upon him to know at what hour it was to be inflicted. He said, "To-morrow morning at eight." The officer begged leave to remind his excellency that the morrow was Sunday; to which his excellency did not return a very gracious, but a very short, answer. "The foolish man," he said, "did not perceive that, an execution never before having taken place on a Sunday, I was determined to make it have ten times its ordinary effect, and to avoid the necessity of making more examples than would suffice."

So on a much more recent occasion, when he was first lord of the admiralty, he related how he had been attacked for the harshness of his proceedings when our fleet, after having been long at sea, and expecting to be paid off upon the peace in 1802, was suddenly ordered to sail after the French expedition fitted out against St. Domingo, and a general and alarming mutiny broke out. Courts-martial were held, and men condemned. The fleet was drawn up in a half-moon; signals were made for each ship to man a boat for attending execution. The next signal was for the convict in each ship who was to suffer to be hanged up; and the third signal was for all the fleet to sail, which it did while the punishment was barely over—I rather think he said, before the men were cut down. But certainly there never was a whisper of discontent on the whole voyage. It is easy to understand how a less decided course might have had the appearance of being less harsh, and might also have kept the fire of discontent alive for a length of time, caused great injury to the service, and led to loss of life both in quelling the mutiny and in the punishments necessary to be inflicted upon its ringleaders.

One of the most remarkable instances of his prompt decision, as well as his ignorance of the word "impossible," was that which really gained the battle of St. Vincent, and had all the important effects of both quelling the mutiny and relieving us from the apprehension of invasion. Intelligence was brought overland to Lisbon, where he lay with his fleet, that from clear indication the Spanish fleet was immediately to sail. He ordered his fleet to be instantly got ready; and when his captains who were assembled said that, under five or six days, this could not be done, he said it must be done in six hours, and he would not hear of a moment longer. They were in great consternation, but they knew their man, and that the fleet must put to sea in the time specified. It did so; and the victory was gained with less than half the enemy's force. A day or two later and the Spanish fleet would have escaped them, raised the blockade of Brest, swept the Channel, and led to the invasion of Ireland. This was the plan which Napoleon afterwards complained of Villeneuve for having failed in enabling him to execute, when he drew off the army of England (as he called it) to gain the victory at Ulm.

When I, in one of our conversations, referred to his great and prompt decision, and to the breaking up of the Addington ministry in 1804, immediately after the joint attack upon his naval administration, expressing my wonder that he had not taken the king's offer to stand by them and dissolve, if necessary—his answer was, that he certainly should have insisted upon this course being taken, but he knew that there were friends of the besieged in the garrison ready to open the gates to them. He particularly named Perceval and Eldon, whom he believed to be in league with Pitt. On my saying he had the professional dislike to lawyers, he added that Hawkesbury also inclined to Pitt, and perhaps Castlereagh, but of Eldon he was sure. But he denied having the least prejudice against our profession, and, on the contrary, said he had some most excellent friends who were at the head of it, particularly Erskine, for whom he had the greatest regard, and had sometimes taken him on a cruise. Indeed I always found he had a kind of professional pride in Erskine, from his having been, as he said, "bred to sea." In mentioning Addington, he said he had been much underrated, and in some respects was a considerable man, especially for his political courage, which, he said, would have borne him out in resisting the coalition had it not been for the enemy within his garrison.

I found him to be less adverse to the Catholic question than was supposed; but he greatly disapproved of Pitt's manner of conducting it, with the knowledge which he had of the king's strong prejudices; and considered that the whole matter might have been settled with a little temper and firmness. He had frequent occasion to come upon the subject of the Catholic system and its gross abuses, which he always maintained that sensible men like Aranjo and Souza viewed in the same light as we ourselves did; while the mere courtiers and the royal family, especially the regent, were in a state of deplorable bigotry, and were ruled partly by their confessors and partly by their servants. I recollect his going to see the ceremony of a woman taking the veil; and on that occasion he showed very little respect for the solemnity when the part of it came which shows the individual to the world for the last time unveiled, and he had been expressing his pity beforehand on so sad a thought as a young creature shut up from the world. We were a good deal amused at his expense, for it turned out to be an old woman not in any respect interesting. We afterwards accused him of emitting exclamations far from benedictory, and not altogether suited to the place.

He was one day referring to something which I had published, and on his saying "you authors," I said you used to say, you lawyers, when you denied having any prejudice against our craft, but still less ought you to take exceptions against authors, being one yourself, and of a celebrated work. He asked in what way? I told him that when I was lately in Scotland, his health, I found, was given at political dinners as the author of the "Tenth Report."* He said he quite understood what that meant—it was on account of Lord Melville; and that he was extremely vexed at the use to which the party had turned it, and at the very great exaggerations which had been made as regarded Lord Melville, though it was impossible to exaggerate the other abuses which the inquiry had brought to light. He ascribed Pitt's hostility in part to the inquiry but I think erroneously, because the attack on Lord Melville had really not been begun till a year after the motion against the Admiralty.

The only subject on which we differed was the slave-trade, upon which I well knew he had very strong prejudices. Like most seamen, he had imbibed these in the West Indies, military men being generally the other way; but he also had conceived false notions of the leaders in that great cause, whom he regarded as among the righteous overmuch; and some of them, by the language they held rather than the topics they used, gave him an unfavorable impression. I well remember the strong opinion of the abolitionists against Lord St. Vincent. It was a common joke of Wilberforce and Stephen that we, on carrying the abolition, should allow two slavers especially—one for him and the other for Thurlow. When on board the Hibernia in the evening, I have talked with him

* See above.

about the power of sleeping at any time, which, like him, I possessed. Once, when leaning on a gun, he said he could sleep close by it and not be awakened by its firing the morning and evening gun—that is, after he had been, as he called it, several days afloat. I have continued writing after he turned in, as he phrased it, and this about eight or nine o'clock: when I asked how early he intended to get up, he would say, "At eleven or twelve," meaning that after three or four hours he would be up and working. He never paid the least regard to time, but was most exact in requiring all under him to do so.

He often mentioned his peerage, and one day said, "See that desk? I chucked the patent into it when it came out after the 14th of February, and would not even open it, knowing its contents by letters received." Some time after came the letter remitting the fees and perquisites, which he considered a necessary part of the honor, for no man cared less about money; and then he opened it, and took his title.

In his great dining-room, where he could have above sixty at table, it was observable that Nelson's dirge was always played by the band on great occasions, and I well remember that the tears stood in his eye, hating as he did all displays of feeling. He never mentioned Nelson's name without emotion, and would have been inexpressibly hurt had he lived to see those letters which Lady Hamilton so basely published, and in which Lord St. Vincent, and indeed every person mentioned, except Sir William and Lady Hamilton, are attacked, though never any one more venerated another than he (Nelson) did his great master, or more gratefully felt his great kindness, and the extraordinary exertions which he made in fitting out the fleet which he gave him to command, and which gained the battle of the Nile. But it was a kind of disease with Nelson not to bear any person being in authority over him, even as a puisne Lord of the Admiralty.

When the delay of the passports for Madrid led to my quitting Lisbon and proceeding to the North, I was satisfied, from what I then saw, that there were little means of defense, and that no preparations were really intended. On my return from Lisbon, I found that our fleet had suddenly been ordered home, and that I was directed to remain until the passports came from Madrid. These were again delayed; and it was evident that, the Prussian army under the Duke of Brunswick having marched into Saxony, at Madrid they were waiting to see the consequences of the rupture with France. But though Godoy was afraid of the open quarrel with Napoleon, which must have resulted from my being received at Madrid, he had concluded a secret treaty with Russia to join against France as soon as the French armies should have sufficient occupation in Germany; and before the first battle had been fought, he had, with the greatest imprudence, published a proclamation, manifestly hostile to France, for assembling all classes, and making soldiers repair to their regiments. The battle of Jena, a week after, destroyed all hopes of a successful resistance, and the proclamation was explained away by the pretense that the object of the armament had been the apprehension of some attack in Africa from the Moors. I was, however, still kept in suspense, by Godoy wishing to have communication with England, unknown to Napoleon; but as he sent no passports, I refused to wait after November, and returned to England, considering all prospect of Spain being detached from France as at an end, by the conquest of Prussia, and the completed dependence of Germany, which would probably enable Napoleon to prosecute his designs in the South. The Government which I represented had no wish to maintain a protracted negotiation at Madrid, even if what had passed there with Russia had led to her supporting Prussia, and renewing the war with France. The folly of the Spanish Government had led, after the defeat at Jena and the entry of Berlin, to the more entire subjugation of Spain, and to the abandonment of the half-begun resistance of Portugal. But even had the contest in the North been foreseen (which ended in the peace of Tilsit), it was impossible to expect that while it lasted the powers in the Peninsula would do more than remain passive till they saw how it was to end; and, in fact, Spain did not even so remain, but allowed Romana to join Napoleon with a considerable force, the penalty which he made her pay for the premature demonstration, denied as soon as it failed. The battle of Friedland and the peace of Tilsit were the final consummation; and it was Napoleon's insane aggression upon Spain which threw away all the advantages he had gained, and ended in the liberation of the Peninsula, with our assistance, and in his own downfall.

The following I give from my dispatches to Lord Rosslyn:

"Oporto, Sept. 21 (Sunday), 1806.

"My dear Lord,—It is unnecessary to trouble you at great length with any account of what has been done here since my arrival. I shall only state that I find every moment greater reason to be satisfied with having come, and to be convinced that the service never could have been completed without the presence of one of us on the spot.

"Mr. Warre has been induced to enter very warmly and effectually into the business in contemplation. He may be said to have joined us with his whole forces; and these are indeed very considerable, both in connections and in correspondence.

"As no time was to be lost, we took measures on the day of my arrival for dispatching a proper person to Bayonne. He received full and repeated instructions, and I was with him for above an hour immediately before his departure.

"He is in every respect a judicious choice, if I may be allowed so far to flatter myself. He has orders to correspond with Mr. Warre through *two* channels, either of which it would be next thing to impossible to detect. He is at this time well on towards the frontier, and is to remain at Bayonne and San Sebastian till further orders.

"Another person will probably be dispatched by a different route this day; and the renewal of the reports of preparations from different quarters seems to demand that a third person should also be on the spot. This is the more necessary from certain circumstances respecting the arrangement of the affair which I can not now explain. This person is now in readiness. Upon the whole, the difficulties attending this business have been greater than could be conceived, and of a nature rather unexpected; but I trust they are now nearly overcome.

"Mr. Warre, on receiving my first letter, had dispatched a proper person to Ferrol, Bilbao, etc., and we expect his return in a few days.

"I have arranged matters for securing in a couple of posts

an extensive correspondence with persons residing along the bay at Bilbao, St. André, etc., etc. These will give us a warning in case any new arrangements for intelligence should become necessary, and they will also check the other information. Mr. Warre's own communications with different parts of the north of the Peninsula are various and important. He is to improve and extend them immediately with a view to the affair in hand; and I shall not fail to suggest whatever may seem important, both respecting his own inquiries and his correspondence with Lisbon in future.

* * * * * * *

"The French consul here and his family positively deny the Bayonne preparations. They seem to be sincere, if I may trust my own observation; and this is the general opinion in the place.

"Pray let me know by your answer what news you have from England, especially about Mr. Fox. Should any thing private occur, you may cipher with the dictionary. But letters sent by the channel which this goes by are perfectly secure. Mr. Warre trusts it in all matters, though otherwise fully suspicious on such subjects.

"When you write, I think a compliment to Mr. W. for his zeal and judicious conduct, and for his *present* extensive correspondence, would have a good effect, besides being quite well merited.

"I remain ever, my dear lord, most faithfully yours,

"H. Brougham."

"Oporto, Sept. 24 (Wednesday), 1806.

"My dear Lord,—* * * I purpose, as soon as I have put the last hand to the business here, to go to Beira, where, by means of Colonel Prior, I hope to have a military man of much confidence immediately employed in the service. I shall return here with all speed—say, on Monday—and expect to receive your answer to my last at that time. You will certainly have time to send my English letters here before I leave this place, as that can scarcely be before this day week. Pray think if any thing further can be done while I am here, and command my services for any private commissions which you may have to execute. The accounts of Mr.

Fox's situation are truly afflicting. I view the event, which must before this time have taken place, as the most deplorable which could at present happen. The advices from Gallicia look like peace and quiet. You will find from Mr. Warre's letters to Lord S., in which I have made him write most fully every thing that he learns, a number of reports from the side of ——; but they prove nothing at all, except that the people there, as elsewhere, deal in reports respecting the other parts of Spain. A gentleman from the neighborhood of Finisterre arrived yesterday, and, having passed through the whole province of Gallicia, positively denies the existence of any thing like preparations in any part of that province.

"With my best compliments to Lord St. Vincent, I remain, in haste, yours faithfully, H. BROUGHAM.

"Pray hint to Lord Strangford that if he gave the merchants here somewhat less reason to think the present crisis would end safely, it might be as well. I think his last letter held out too fair hopes."

TO LORD ROSSLYN.

"Viana, Sept. 29 (Sunday), 1806.

"MY DEAR LORD,—I have been here since Friday night, and have had the wished-for success. But it is only necessary that I should trouble you with a notice of some fresh information which I have obtained to-day. Hearing that a Portuguese vessel had arrived here on the 26th from Bayonne, after an uncommonly quick passage, I used every means in my power to examine the captain, and to check his information by that of his crew. The result of my attempts is as follows: The vessel is a port-schooner, the St. José Diligente. She sailed from Bayonne on the 18th, entered the Port of Passage on the same day, and arrived here on the 25th. There were two Italian regiments at Bayonne, and a French invalid regiment. It was reported that more troops were expected there, and that they would be encamped about the town. News were also circulated of a rupture with Russia, Prussia, and Sweden, and of Bonaparte having already marched his troops on that account—so far the captain. A sailor adds that the troops expected at Bayonne would amount to thirty-five or thirty-eight thousand men, reported to be destined for the invasion of Portugal. A strong dislike of the present Government is also mentioned; and it is added that, before the schooner arrived at Bayonne, a *riot* had been apprehended, the troops ordered out, and tranquillity restored by this means. The two Italian regiments had not been long there. I conceive that if the riot story is true, these regiments may have been marched thither in consequence of it. At any rate, this account quite confirms our former information as to the non-existence of actual preparations. Letters received in this place last night from Gallicia state that considerable bodies of troops were assembling at Corunna and Ferrol, supposed to be destined for South America. This is given on the authority of respectable Spanish houses in those parts of Gallicia.

"A schooner from Russia has just arrived here. She came from Riga and touched in Denmark, having had a very quick passage. I have as yet heard no certain account of her intelligence, but have desired that it should be collected and transmitted to-morrow. They say she talks of Prussia having marched 100,000 men to Holland.

"Ever yours, H. BROUGHAM."

TO LORD ROSSLYN.

"Oporto, Friday morning, Oct. 3, 1806.

"MY DEAR LORD,—I thank you for your letter of the 24th. I received your courier yesterday afternoon. The cause of the delay is as follows: Your courier arrived here on Tuesday, late at night, which was shamefully long. I was at Viana, and Mr. Warre dispatched a courier to tell me of the arrival of yours. I set out instantly, and had a painful journey hither, where I arrived at one in the morning. I read Morland's note, and found by it that I must come speedily to Lisbon, though for what reason I can not certainly tell. I rather suspect, from all accounts, that we are going home. I should have liked better to sail by convoy from hence; but, as I am quite uncertain what may be your commands, I must just set out for Lisbon, and run the risk of not finding you there. I shall accordingly leave this by day-break to-morrow. I should have gone on this morning without doubt, but for a sprained ankle, which prevents me from mounting a mule. If it be no better, I must go by a litter. At all events, I shall lose not a moment, and shall possibly be with you on Tuesday morning, if I can get change of mules to go by night; if not, certainly on Wednesday evening. I send back your courier with this in the mean time. My business is completely and most satisfactorily finished in this quarter. In Bracança, Valença, and the rest of the Northern frontier, I had an opportunity of seeing much with my own eyes that may serve present purposes, and can't fail to be useful, at any rate, hereafter. Respecting my main object, every thing is on the very best footing. We have now in Bayonne and Ferrol two proper agents arrived; and for Bayonne several others, of the very best qualifications, on their way by different routes through Spain. All that can be desired from correspondence in various quarters must be obtained, and in many different ways. This branch of the business is in such hands that it may continue, so long as there are British merchants here and in the North. Information from the Spanish frontier, on the side of Almeida, is settled in a way equally satisfactory, and for no expense whatever. The expenses of the commissaries are as limited as possible; and should Government not choose to defray them, I will take them on my own head. For this purpose, I have advanced all the small sums necessary out of my own credit, and, where it was necessary, have extended that credit by the assistance of friends. The whole has been arranged with the utmost secrecy; and even Mr. Warre only knows of what has been done by himself. Should it be necessary, now or hereafter, to send a still better observer, I have an officer of very great trust and experience ready at an hour's notice. He has assisted me much, and was zealous to go himself, but I declined it for the present. He is a quartermaster, and the fittest man for the service. One of the emissaries is a military subject, an elève of his. I have arranged matters for improving in various essential respects the general correspondence of the consuls in the North, and have in general taken all the steps that seemed to me best adapted for organizing such a state of communication with France and Spain as will secure us at all times the best and earliest intelligence. The present crisis may soon pass over, but the expense will cease with it; and the same communication may at any moment be renewed by writing a few letters. I think that, until something definite occurs, no counter-orders should be given to the emissaries. Had we possessed such means of information ten weeks ago, our expedition and mission to Lisbon would have probably been saved.

[Private.]

"I lament most sincerely the fatal news of Mr. Fox's death. Though I had almost made up my mind to expect it, I own I felt it as if it had been a surprise. Next to that calamity the worst news is the piracy in South America. If Popham is not shot, we deserve to be conquered everywhere, both on sea and land, and in negotiation. Might it not have happened that, while he was buccaneering in the king's name, we had orders to promise Spain the safety of her colonies as an equivalent for her aid in Europe? May this not be better *still* in the event of a new coalition? If Popham had only taken a place in the common way, and there been shot or hanged, no lasting harm would have been done. But he has begun a rebellion all over America; it may reach Brazil, and must spread over Spain and America; and how can we undo what he shall thus have done? I heartily hope he will be punished as severely as the popular feeling in England will permit. I don't detain your courier longer than to assure you how happy I shall be to join you in Lisbon, and to congratulate you on the happy termination of our mission.

"Believe me most faithfully yours,

"H. Brougham.

"P.S.—Should you have sailed before my arrival, pray leave me your commands fully, and stop the packet, that I may take her to go home in. For any private commissions that I can execute for you or Colonel Stuart, Morland, and Bowrie, command me, and I shall do my best.

"I beg my compliments to them and Lord Strangford."

TO LORD ROSSLYN.

"Lisbon, Oct. 11, 1806.

"My dear Lord,—I rejoice to think how completely the plan of intelligence is likely to succeed. Pimentel, I believe, will prove a very excellent subject. My people are all in Bayonne, or very near it, by this time. I have a letter from the last of them, dated 7th October, in Spain.

"The accounts of Spanish preparations induced me to make two persons take the route of Astorga and Pampeluna. I daily expect their reports.

"The correspondence through various channels is likely to be regular and full. I every post receive notices of this kind; but as they are hitherto all of a negative kind, or, at the utmost, only allude to rumors from other quarters, chiefly Madrid, I need not trouble you with them. Mr. Hunter — whose letters are very meagre, and who plainly shows by his own statements that he might have learned more — writes repeatedly that an expedition against Portugal is in preparation at Madrid. He has given us the names of the generals, of whom the P. del Infantado is one. But in another letter he says that the king said lately to his generals, 'We must all get ready to march either to Portugal or the Pyrenees.' He admits that no Spanish troops are moving—that Bayonne is deserted by the soldiers moving northward—and that Perpignan has not a man in it.

"Our friend at Badajos writes (date 3d) that the rumors of a war with Portugal continue, and that a confidential friend of his at Madrid gives him notice of Massena's defeat in Calabria.

"I have taken the proper steps for increasing our Spanish intelligence by means of correspondence. I think matters are so arranged on all hands that we are secure at every point; and our pickets, as it were, being all set, we may rest on our arms in full safety. I must, however, mention a circumstance which I rather think has escaped you. You talk of my proceeding to put Lord Strangford in possession of all our sources of intelligence. This I shall, of course, do the moment before I am to leave Lisbon; but it would answer no purpose, I apprehend, to do it now. You must be sensible in how delicate a situation I stand respecting some of our emissaries, and still more delicate is my connection with *certain Portuguese officers of high rank*. To divulge the part taken by them in our concerns, without the most obvious necessity, would be very unpleasant to me; and, to be plain with you, I would rather do it to another than to Lord S., who is somewhat too flighty and uncertain in his movements to gain my confidence.

"Whensoever I leave Lisbon, you may rest assured he shall be put in possession of every thing which may enable him to keep the channels open; and I presume this is enough. However, tell me if you think otherwise.

"A similar remark applies to what Morland says of 'vouchers for secret-service money.' Why, it is, nine times in ten, impossible to get any; at least, to get receipts from persons who receive pay as spies—or bribes, or even douceurs, of any sort—is next to impossible. Does Morland believe, for example, that the officer alluded to in my letter from Oporto would give us receipt for the money he might get to fit him out for going to Bayonne? Where this can be done, you may believe it shall; but I can give but very slender hopes of vouchers being fully or in a considerable degree proportioned to the sums expended. Perhaps he does not allude to receipts, but to some other means of proving our expenses: if so, I beg to be informed of it with as little delay as possible. Of course you will permit me to keep every thing on my own private credit until we settle what those vouchers are; for I could just as soon obtain a receipt from every spy I bribed, as I could think of letting the expenditure I take credit for be transferred from my account while there existed a doubt as to the way of proving it. I shall only add, that the expenses alluded to are very small in comparison of what I find Lord Strangford gives his people. What made him give thirty-five doubloons to a man for going to Badajos, and remaining out altogether nine days? When I made many words about this extravagant payment (which the office has allowed), he said his man had the Order of Christ: very likely; but what is the use of employing the worthy persons who bear that Order in such service? I have estimated the average expense of our men who would have been sent upon that service, and I find that they would have received just the sixth part of the above sum. The very best servant we have has four testoons a day for his maintenance. It is true, he is quite unmatched in his economy, and luckily had the sense to agree that his reward should be proportioned to his services and to his frugality jointly.

"During my absence from you I have procured a good deal of valuable matter respecting the Spanish privateering on our trade in the North. This I should like to have sent to Lord St. Vincent, as it may lead to some good consequences. I shall send it, therefore, to you by next opportunity, and trust to you for letting it come to Lord St. V., or whomsoever else you judge to be more proper.

"My general information respecting the state of Portugal has, of course, been greatly augmented. It all confirms the opinions already delivered by you, and also by myself. But it confirms likewise an opinion which I have long held, that, by a little care and judicious interference on our part, the interval of present quiet may be turned to excellent account in improving the resources of the country. Of this more fully hereafter.

"I may almost save myself and you the trouble of observing how dull Lisbon is since your departure. To me, who know nobody here, I assure you it is a *triste séjour*. My only hope is that my instructions may soon arrive. Indeed, I must rely upon you, my dear lord, for standing my friend, in case the idea of a Spanish communication should go off or be long delayed, that I may not be detained here in uselessness and idleness. I hope you will keep your eye on this point, so interesting to me in every respect. Should nothing be required here, I may, perhaps, be employed better elsewhere, as, in the North.

"The frigate will wait no longer; so with best wishes to Stuart, Morland, Bouverie, believe me ever, with the greatest esteem, most faithfully yours, H. BROUGHAM.

"P.S.—On looking over the above, I observe you might suspect, from the accidental mention of Strangford's name, that we were not likely to draw well together during my stay. This I add to prevent any such idea, for nothing could be more incorrect: we are as cordial as possible.

"I have received the copying-machine, saddle, etc., which you were so good as to leave, and thank you much for them. The guineas which you left are not to be found; nor will any body plead guilty to having received them."

TO THE VISCOUNT HOWICK.

"Lisbon, 11th Oct, 1806.

"MY LORD,—Upon my return from Oporto, on the night

of the 8th, I received the secret letter which your lordship did me the honor of addressing to me on the 3d, and by which I learn that I am to remain here until further orders may arrive from England.

"According to the instructions contained in that letter, I have let it to be understood that my stay here is connected with the business of the extraordinary mission lately at this Court. I had a good deal of conversation after my return with M. d'Aranjo, upon whom I waited, both to thank him for the personal civilities I had received from his family in the Northern provinces, and to inform him that I had discovered the robbery of my courier to be, contrary to every appearance, a tale invented by the man to screen himself from punishment for having lost his bag of letters in a scuffle. They have since been recovered, unopened. In justification of Messrs. Mayne & Browne, who had employed this person in forwarding your lordship's letter to me, I must remark that he had been well known as a courier at Oporto, and on the road for above twenty years, and bore the best character.

"In the course of this conversation with M. d'Aranjo, he alluded to the sensation produced at Madrid by Sir H. Popham's expedition. Upon my saying that this must doubtless have created a great alarm there, he observed, rather significantly, 'Cependant il faut que l'Angleterre en tire quelque parti;' and added, 'Il vaudra mieux que des nouvelles colonies dontelle n'a pas besoin.' This remark, I presume, bears a reference to what passed in the early stages of the negotiation relative to Spain. It appears to me, however, that the greatest care should be taken to prevent M. d'Aranjo from learning what are the designs of his majesty's ministers upon this very delicate and important subject; and, at any rate, that M. de Souza should receive no hints which may lead to a knowledge of the drift of those plans until they are fully matured. Indeed, I must be allowed to add that M. d'Aranjo's attachment to England is too slender, and his entire freedom from a contrary bias too problematical, to justify any confidential intercourse with his party upon such matters.

"Before leaving this subject, allow me to express my high sense of the honor conferred on me by the king's servants in thinking of me for the conduct of the business in contemplation. It would be improper to make promises at present, but I shall desire to be tried only by the event; and, without any reference to circumstances, shall be satisfied to have my services judged entirely by the actual success which may attend them. In the mean time, I shall spare no pains to fit myself for the duty in question, especially by the collection of such information as may bear upon the discussions likely to arise. I have the honor to be, my lord, your most obedient and humble servant, HENRY BROUGHAM."

TO LORD ROSSLYN.

"Lisbon, Oct. 13, 1806.

"MY DEAR LORD,—The frigate Mercury carried both a private and public letter from me. In case you may not have received them, I here shortly run over the contents of the former.

"My regret at not having seen you before your departure; my inability to comprehend what Morland means by sending home the vouchers of money given to spies, etc., as not one in ten of those gentry ever gives a receipt; my wish to be informed what other vouchers I can send, and how I shall procure them. I received saddle, etc., copying-machine, not a single article of stationery, nor any guineas, nor any thing else. Mounier and Mrs. Dove have made between them a clean board. I say this rather that you may tell me whom you gave the guineas to, than that you should blame them for the other depredations. Pray ask your servants if they took away my umbrella; if they did not, it has gone with the stationery.

"I also mentioned in my private letter that, until I knew what sort of vouchers might be required from you, I could not consent to transfer a single pound from my account to yours. Indeed, the whole expense is, I fancy, not likely to be great.

"I grumbled a little in the same letter at the dullness of Lisbon since you left it. I scarcely know it, and literally know nobody in it. From this circumstance, I devoutly hope my mission Eastward will soon commence. If it is very long delayed, I had better come home and go out again. I mean, better for the service, for God knows the two voyages would be *un peu fort*.

"So you were after the famous amethyst at Oporto? I was beforehand with you, however: have it lying beside me in a fine setting. I won't annoy you further by telling you what a trifle I paid for it. Hill says I got it for a quarter of its value. Can I be of service to you in catering for such things, here or elsewhere? Tell me freely.

"I give you a thousand thanks for your kind promise to write to me. It will be real charity. If you can give me accurate information as to the prospect of a dissolution of Parliament, I shall be much indebted to you. That point interests me very nearly; for, though I have some assurances that I shall be brought in at the election, yet if I am off the spot and have not warning of it, I know how little such promises avail.

"The hurry in which the packet sails has made this, as well as my public letter, a mere scrawl. I trust to your goodness to excuse it.

"Believe me, with real esteem, yours very faithfully,

"HENRY BROUGHAM."

TO LORD ROSSLYN.

"Lisbon.

"MY DEAR LORD,—Since writing the private letter of yesterday, I have added one public letter to my inclosures. My remarks on the consular business I beg your attention to; and my chief reason for stating them, when Strangford's department leads *him* more properly to the subject, is, that I know, from his great intimacy with Gambier, there is no chance of his doing it, nor indeed would it be proper in him. Nevertheless, I am persuaded the abuse is great, and indeed I look on the whole office of consul here as a mere job.

"I am sadly in want of boxes and copying-paper, and don't know that those which were coming to you are not stopped.

"I fear there is some *contretemps* at the Foreign Office about my letters, for I have not received one; therefore I suppose they were all stopped on the supposition of my coming home. May I beg you to let them be sent out speedily. Though I were to miss them, it would not signify: they can follow me.

"If you hear any thing about peace, I trust to your kindness to let me know it soon. I beg leave to repeat my offer of service to you in any thing you wish to have done here.

"Once more, believe me, with great esteem and respect, most faithfully yours, HENRY BROUGHAM."

TO LORD ROSSLYN.

"Lisbon, Nov. 9, 1806.

"MY DEAR LORD,—You will scarcely thank me for giving a hurried private letter, and I have not ten minutes to write it in before the packet goes. My chief reason for troubling you at present is to say that, in conformity with your desire, I have very carefully, and with no small labor and exertion of patience, kept perfectly well with Strangford. This was necessary for the public business; but I appeal to you, who know him, how difficult a thing it was. My temper has been tried perpetually by his infinite childishness in doing business, and indeed in doing every thing else; and really, however unpleasant to say so, there is a defect about him which I can still less pardon than his want of sense—I mean his *total want* of that first-rate quality which gives a man's words the right to be believed.

"I can scarcely express this more *delicately*. He has *on all subjects* the above disease, to a degree quite unexampled.

"However, let that pass. I have done my part of the business, and, I am sure, have humored him in every thing, to his merest caprices, and to his very heart's content. I only lament that the consequences of his character here are a total want of respect, either from common society or from those he has to do business with. I don't wish to judge harshly, but I can scarcely wonder at this, from what I know and see of him. Certainly he is not the man to change a ministry here. Pray discourage him from writing *loose* letters to you, for his silliness makes him brag of it everywhere, and so, I suppose, do his blackguard companions, to the great annoyance of one who has so real a respect and friendship for you as I have.

"Referring you to my public letters, pray allow me now to add that I have heard nothing at all from Permentile, which alarms me not a little for his safety. I feel he will go the way with Strangford's other agent, for it is now above seven weeks since he was sent. All the other agents and correspondents are doing their duty as well as possible; but I rather fear the effects of an old spy being lately condemned at Barcelona.

"Have you no bowels of compassion for me in this place? I am beginning my sixth week, and Burghersh is still here.

"The packets are strangely irregular. We have vessels from Falmouth and Cork in very short passages, and no packet since the one that sailed the 18th, though three, if not four, must have been due the week before last. They should always keep a look-out after our agent there, and the captains. I have the clearest proofs that the man who arrived with last dispatches lost nearly a fortnight by waiting three whole days after his time in order to get his smuggling goods, and then the wind changed. I think it rather hard that ministers at home, and we poor people here, should fag hard to get things ready, and then such delays should be occasioned by a rascally captain of a packet. The agent at Falmouth will positively never interfere until Government gives him a hint. If such abuses can't be prevented, the *dispatches of importance* must be sent by cutter. Indeed, the swarm of large Spanish privateers lately gone to sea renders this advisable at any rate. Will you do two *empenhas* for me? One is to give me a few lines of introduction to some of your Portuguese or foreign friends here, for I know nobody, not even the nuncio, and Strangford never has introduced either Burghersh or myself to any of them, notwithstanding his intimacy with both of us. Of course, I only give you this empenho in the unfortunate event of my remaining here.

"The other is, to get my servant John's wife put on the list of Corsican bounties. She is a Corsican subject, who came with the army from thence. He has served nine years in our army and in Egypt, where he lost his eye and had to leave the service. He has a son still in it, and two other young children, both born in Corsica. He has, I think, a very good right to this empenho; I believe he has it by the regulations—certainly by the practice; for there are people here who, I know, have such bounties merely by favor, and from *having been* in Corsica, though their wives and children never were, or near it. He has been extremely useful, both here and in the North—more so than I can easily describe."

While I was at Lisbon I received the following letter from London, from my excellent friend Whishaw. The unsolicited kindness of the concluding paragraph I can never forget.*

"Lincoln's Inn, September 19, 1806.

"MY DEAR BROUGHAM,—I am extremely obliged to you for your letter, and much pleased with the intelligence so far as it relates to yourself. It is highly satisfactory to know that you go on so well with Lord Rosslyn, and that he agrees with you in your general views. This being the case, I can have no doubt that the mission, whatever may be its final result, will terminate with honor and advantage to yourself. Not having seen Lord Holland or Allen, and knowing nothing of the plans which are suggested by your dispatches, I can only wish well to your diplomatic exertions, and sincerely hope that your achievements may be successful and short. Since I last wrote, the event which I then anticipated has taken place—poor Fox is no more. His death was perfectly resigned, tranquil, and happy. He had been in expectation of the event from Tuesday. He died on the evening of Saturday, and retained his senses, though not his speech, to the very last. He was only able to look in Lord Fitzwilliam's face, and grasp him by the hand. Lord F. was so much affected when he heard of his death that he fell down in a nervous fit, from which he was recovered with some difficulty. Windham is in a state of extreme dejection. They are in great trouble and consternation at Holland House; and Lord Holland, as you may readily suppose, is deeply afflicted.

"It was proposed by Lord Grenville that Fox's funeral should be at the public expense, and with the same honors as

* John Whishaw, now little known, is often respectfully referred to in the correspondence of the day. He was connected with Romilly, and appointed his executor. He took a keen interest in the abolition of the slave-trade, and was an authority on currency. In 1790 he gained the prize for a Latin essay on a theme by the Vice-chancellor of Cambridge, "Whether the French Revolution was likely to prove advantageous or injurious to this country," taking the side of "advantageous."—Mem. of Romilly, i., 404.

that of Pitt, and he undertook to obtain the king's consent to the measure. This offer was very properly declined by Fox's friends. But the ceremony is to take place with all circumstances of solemnity and public attendance, at the expense of Lord Fitzwilliam and the Duke of Devonshire. The procession is to be from the Duke of Bedford's, in Stable Yard, to Westminster Abbey.

"There has been great mystery as to the appointment of a successor to Fox. Having no authentic information, I can only give you the floating rumors. At present Lord Howick, under all the circumstances, is the most likely man. Our friends naturally wished for Lord Holland, and for some time had confident hopes. I do not believe that these hopes now continue. The admiralty, which will be vacated by Lord Howick, may perhaps be offered to him; but his indolence and want of habits of business would make this office very irksome to him. Report yesterday gave the latter appointment to Lord Buckingham, who is an *amateur* of naval details, and came up post-haste upon the news of Fox's death. I am far from thinking this probable, but the report is not pleasant; and the delay in the appointment seems clearly to show that the parties do not entirely agree. The present crisis is certainly very important to the fragments of a popular party which still remain in this country. If Lord Holland or Lord Lauderdale is not admitted into the cabinet upon the present vacancy, I shall consider it as the annihilation of their party in the administration, and the forerunner of a final rupture; but these are surmises, which I hope will be falsified by the dispatches which will convey this letter.

"It seems to be quite settled that Lord Howick is to be the leader of the House of Commons, and that this will oblige him to quit the admiralty, the constant engagements of which are wholly inconsistent with regular attention to parliamentary business. All these arrangements are very mortifying to Sheridan; and he is at no pains to conceal his discontent, which is now aggravated by being refused the support of Government for Westminster. You will see his speech on this occasion in the newspapers.

"I can not say any thing on the subject of the negotiation; but I hope that our late successes have not altered our tone, or made us more impracticable. Lauderdale's stay is a favorable circumstance, and I conclude that we have still some chance.

"Sydney Smith has at length got the promise of a living of £400 a year in Yorkshire. Lady Holland wrote to him in such terms that he concluded there was an actual vacancy, and he came up in great haste to get the presentation passed through the proper offices; and now he finds out that the incumbent is still living, though not likely to continue long. This is no small disappointment to the eager expectant, who came up in the mail-coach from a remote country, in the hopes of immediate possession. The living is the Rectory of Foston, between York and Malton, and about four miles from Castle Howard. The chancellor and Sheridan have been playing strange pranks in their water-parties, very much to the annoyance of the *feebles* and admirers of ministerial decorum. They have had a project of marrying Petty to Miss Drummond, Lady Scott's daughter, but it has entirely failed.

"Erskine has declared his intention of making Jekyll and Edward Morris masters in Chancery.* These appointments will be very unpopular, and do him a great deal of harm in his court. Upon the whole, he seems to be losing ground very fast.

"I told you the particulars of the intended conflict and proposed renewal of hostilities between Jeffrey and Moore; but every thing has been settled between them by the negotiation of Horner and Rogers. And Jeffrey is gone off in peace to superintend his October Review.

"I have now told you all the gossip, and have only to add that I beg you will employ me during your absence in any manner in which I can be of use to you. There is one subject, in particular, which you will allow me to mention, and which I ought to have mentioned before: your sudden journey and voyage may have involved you in some unexpected expenses; and it may happen that you have pecuniary demands, for which you may be not altogether prepared. If

* Jekyll was not made a master in Chancery till June, 1815, when Lord Eldon, much against his will, was *forced* by the regent to appoint him. Lord Eldon considered Jekyll most unfit for the office.—See full account of this in Twiss's Life of Eldon, ii., 266.

this should be the case, I have money at my banker's, and can without any inconvenience furnish you with any reasonable sum for which you may have a temporary occasion. Now I trust that you will at once accept this offer, if it will be of the least service to you. If it will not, excuse me for mentioning the subject.

"Yours ever most truly, JOHN WHISHAW."

CHAPTER VII.

POLITICS OF THE DAY.

Home Politics.—Whitbread's Motion on the State of the Nation.—Negro Emancipation and the local Press of the Sugar Colonies.—Continental Politics in 1807.—Correspondence with Lord Howick.—Continuation on his becoming Earl Grey.—Foreign Politics again.—Personal Prospects.—Consideration of the Bar as a Profession.—Selection of the Northern Circuit.—Practice and Politics.—Correspondence about Spain, Portugal, and the First Peninsular War.—Court Politics.—The Queen and the Prince of Wales.—Resumption of Correspondence on the Peninsular War.

TO THE EARL OF ROSSLYN.

"Albany, Piccadilly, Dec. 12, 1806.

"My dear Lord,—A slight illness, and some bother at the offices since my return, have prevented me from writing to ask you how you do, and to tell you I am at last come back. I wish to God my notification had been sent a week sooner, as it would have brought me home on the 1st of November, instead of December 9, and have prevented all the evils that have resulted to all my plans from so ill-timed an absence. But Secretaries of State and such great folks don't much think of other people in the lower departments of Government; and still less do they trouble themselves with thinking of absentees *hors de vue*, etc. I sincerely hope *your expedition* has not had such bad consequences to you. I need scarcely tell you that I am charged with most especial compliments from all your friends in Lisbon—at least from such of them as I know. Had I chosen to be acquainted with Kantrow, I presume he would have sent home by me flattery enough to sicken a court.

"I had intended to give you a longer letter of news and remarks on what I perceive, or think I perceive, as to the state of parties among our friends, because I suppose, of course, you will like to hear this from a near observer. But, in truth, I am so much fatigued with my illness and morning's work together, that I must give over for the present.

"Pray, how should I do as to money expended by me in Portugal? I take it for granted they mean to let all my own expenses fall on my own shoulders; and perhaps most of the secret-service money. But I honored Warre's bills and others to a considerable amount for ordinary consular services, etc., to save them trouble and keep them in good-humor; and I don't relish the joke of doing that without repayment.* It is quite inconvenient enough to *advance* the money.

"Ever most faithfully yours, HENRY BROUGHAM."

The following relating to the slave-trade I wrote to Lord Howick:

TO THE VISCOUNT HOWICK.

"February 23, 1807.

"MY DEAR LORD,—The Jamaica *newspapers* are nowhere to be found; but the fact stands thus on the positive recollection of those who have read them within *a few months:*

"1. The debates in Parliament on the abolition, from 1792 to 1806 inclusive, were published regularly in 'The Jamaica Gazette' by the Assembly's printer. Lord Stanhope's inflammatory speech in 1804 was given at length.

"This fact Mr. Wilberforce is ready to say on his legs that he knows, but that he has lost the Jamaica newspaper in which those debates were published.

"2. A memorial was prepared by a committee of Assembly, and inserted in the same Gazette in 1802; but perhaps it may have been 1801. The object of it was to show the danger of negro insurrection; and this it made out by a detailed statement of the means by which, and the ways in which, the slaves might revolt. Mr. Wilberforce recollects perfectly having read such an argument in the Jamaica newspaper, but is not prepared to say on his legs that it was in a memorial. Other persons, of West Indian connections, assert distinctly

* The result was, that I was left considerably out of pocket by this mission. My personal services were, I dare say, worth nothing; but it was a little hard, not only to do the work, but to pay for the secret-service of this LIBERAL Government.

that it was so. Upon the whole, I should think there is no danger whatever in stating the fact as above.

"3. Mr. Stephen distinctly states that his recollection of the general practice of publishing in the West India newspapers (St. Kitts, where he resides) matters respecting the slave-trade, and even to the best of his remembrance the revolutionary transactions in the *French islands*, induced him to suggest a search in the Jamaica coffee-house for such papers as are above mentioned, in consequence of which they were found there, in two different years, and passed through him to Mr. Wilberforce, who has mislaid them. To this he *could make oath*. I am, in great haste, your lordship's most obedient servant, H. BROUGHAM."

After the dissolution in 1807, but before the meeting of Parliament, the following correspondence relating to the expedition to Egypt, the war in Spain, the proceedings of our Government relating thereto, and other matters connected therewith, took place:

FROM LORD HOWICK.

"Stratton Street, June 16, 1807.

"MY DEAR BROUGHAM,—I received your letter and the accompanying papers yesterday evening at Wimbledon, and am lost in admiration of your activity. Nothing can be better calculated for the effect intended to be produced than what you say on Sir H. Mildmay and the Egyptian expedition. On the latter nothing further occurs to me, in addition to the general statement you have received from me of the motives and object of the expedition, except, perhaps, that the accusation of acting hostilely at the same time that we were professing to negotiate for peace comes rather oddly from those who blame us for not having, in the first instance, seized the castles of the Dardanelles. Sir Robert Wilson's book, which I have not by me, will, I think, furnish you with some useful information with respect to the position of Alexandria, particularly as to the length of time it was held by the French, not only after they were cut off by our army from all communication with the country by land, but were closely blockaded by our fleet by sea.* The accounts are so imperfect, that it is impossible to judge either of the necessity of occupying Rosetta or of the probabilities of success, if the attack had been well conducted. But this seems clear—that if Rosetta is of the consequence that it is stated to be, this might have been ascertained from Major Bisset, and from others, the first day of the arrival of our troops; and, as it is the first business of a general to consider and to occupy those points which are material to the safety of his troops, not a moment should have been lost in detaching for that purpose before the Turks could have had an opportunity of making any preparations for defense. If, on the other hand, the enterprise appeared too hazardous, he ought to have strengthened his position at Alexandria, waiting till he could receive further directions, and, if necessary, make reinforcements. Surely, with the sea open to them, Alexandria might have been maintained and supplied long enough for this purpose at least; and afterwards evacuated—if ministers, disapproving of our plan, should have given orders to that effect—without loss.

"I see they have got my circular letter in the 'Courier,' and make a foolish attack upon our determination to oppose, right or wrong, without knowing what is to be in the king's speech. There are subjects which *must* be in the king's speech. There are also subjects of so much importance that, if omitted in the king's speech, the House of Commons ought not to pass them over for a single hour without animadversion. The dissolution of Parliament comes within both these descriptions. It is impossible that it should not be adverted to in the king's speech; or if ministers, ashamed of what they have done, and afraid of the discussion, should wish to evade it by a total silence on this interesting subject, the case is so strong, and the circumstances connected with it so extraordinary, that no man jealous either of the real prerogatives of the crown or of the liberties of the people could avoid, on the first opportunity, proposing a representation upon this point to the king. I am yours very sincerely, HOWICK."

* "History of the British Expedition to Egypt, to which is subjoined a Sketch of the present state of that country, and its means of defense." By Sir Robert Thomas Wilson. 1802.

The following is also from Lord Howick (undated):

"It is very difficult to make a defense against attacks of this kind without saying more than perhaps ought to be said. It would be better, therefore, in the first instance at least, to confine any paragraphs that may be inserted upon the unfortunate failure at Rosetta to such general topics as will not seem to imply an intimate knowledge of all the circumstances of the case. The most obvious of these are the unfairness of judging merely from success, and the particular unfairness to the late ministers and to the officers employed, of forcing the former to defend themselves at the expense of the latter, when they have not had an opportunity—being deprived, by their removal from office, of a sight of the dispatches—of knowing the circumstances which have induced them to deviate from their orders. The truth is, that the attack of Rosetta was entirely the act of the officer who commanded; it formed no part of our plan, nor can I conceive on what ground it was undertaken. In adverting to this generally, it may not be amiss to take notice of the danger of officers disregarding their instructions, and the encouragement which has been given to this practice in the cases of Sir Henry Popham and Sir David Baird. I write this in great haste; but if you can call on me to-morrow about half-past eleven, I shall be glad to talk with you on the subject. I am going out of town between twelve and one.

"Ever yours, H."

TO THE VISCOUNT HOWICK.

"Albany, Sept. 13, 1807.

"* * * I have just seen a gentleman from the city. They are in very great dismay about the Buenos Ayres speculation, and talk of three millions and a half worth of goods on hand in the Plate.

"Considerable anxiety is entertained for the expedition to the Baltic. People naturally enough dread a change of weather in case the operations are protracted. This would be very unpleasant even if the King of Sweden gives us shelter, in spite of Russia. But at all events, though we completely succeed (which is perhaps, upon the whole, most probable), we are rather in a dilemma, for Russia will be more hostile, and will probably allow Bonaparte to do just as he pleases. We shall risk much by remaining in Zealand. We shall get very little trade by it, and he will have not, perhaps, twelve or fourteen bad ships, but a number of seamen, whom he wants a great deal more, and whom nothing but our own violence could have made very hostile to us. If, on the other hand, we give up the island, the Baltic is closed against us, which, indeed, signifies little, as it would be effectually closed at any rate. But we shall have done enough to make the Danes and Russians ready for any efforts against us. The love of this Baltic plan has sensibly subsided, and people are more desponding than ever upon the sum of affairs. The Yorkshire men are in great anxiety about the American dispute, which they say would ruin them.

"Munroe and Pinckney, however, greatly commend Canning and Perceval for their candid and temperate behavior towards them. I am afraid, however, that the West Indian and shipping interests will have great weight with Perceval at least, and the greater part of his colleagues.

"The king has been excessively anxious of late about the expedition, and all the people about Court have been as nervous as possible.

"I suspect something is in agitation with Portugal. Souza has been frequently in town, and full of something, but exceedingly afraid of being talked to.* He received a courier the other day, who told an Oporto merchant of my acquaintance, now in town, that demands had been renewed of the men and ships stipulated in the treaty of Badajos, but that the Portugal Government expected once more to buy them off. The English connected with Portugal seem to believe that their last danger is now come, and that they must bethink themselves of a change in good earnest. If left to the Portuguese and French (they think), the business may be spun out for a few months, but they have a great fear of something sudden from our interference. The ministers, three weeks ago, gave the Portugal committee the same per-

* José Maria, Marquis of Souza-Botelho, Portuguese statesman and man of letters, born June, 1758; died 1825.

mission as in 1801—viz., to bond, and to use any ships in bringing over their goods from that country. This intelligence they keep as secret as possible.

"I leave town to-day for Yorkshire, and shall perhaps go as far as Edinburgh, in which case I will avail myself with great pleasure of your kind invitation.

"If Lord Lauderdale or Lord Ponsonby are now with you, I beg my compliments to them, and desire my respects to Lady Howick, being, with great respect and esteem, faithfully yours, H. BROUGHAM.

"The people about the offices give out that they do not expect the Copenhagen business to be over in less than three weeks. Lord Sidmouth says 'he may, in less than three weeks, be ashamed of being an Englishman,' alluding to violent measures against the town."

TO THE VISCOUNT HOWICK.

"George Street, Edinburgh, Oct. 2, 1807—Friday.

"MY DEAR LORD,—On my arrival here I found Jeffrey very anxious to insert in his next Review proper discussions of the American and other neutral questions. As it is published about the end of this month, I think it will produce a very salutary effect if we can manage to deposit there all the right views upon the important and little understood subjects.* By this means we shall be able, I think, to furnish proper arguments and information to friends in different situations, and various parts of the country, and to give the tone to the press (in so far as it is favorably disposed), better and more conveniently than in any other manner. I have, therefore, promised to supply Jeffrey (whose own opinions on these subjects are perfectly liberal and enlightened) either with some articles, or, at any rate, with materials for these; and I should be glad to have any suggestions that may occur to you upon these subjects, in addition to those which you have already mentioned in the course of conversation. I wish you would also take the trouble of mentioning this to Lord Lauderdale, in case any hints should occur to him, as it might

* See the first article of the "Edinburgh Review" for October, 1807, a review of three pamphlets on America and neutrality.

rather seem *odd* if I were to write to him upon a thing connected with the 'Edinburgh Review.'

"I perceive a great change in the language and behavior of the people here since my last visit (in 1805). The Melvilles have none of the confidence and haughtiness which they formerly had, and, though very happy with the present flourishing state of things, manifestly *look up to* their adversaries with fear and doubt. With my best respects to Lady Howick, I remain, with much esteem and respect, most faithfully yours, HENRY BROUGHAM.

"The Hollands are expected here in six or seven days, and talk of remaining about a week on their way to Dunbar."

TO THE VISCOUNT HOWICK.

"George Street, Edinburgh, November 7, 1807.

"MY DEAR LORD HOWICK,—Since I was favored with your last letter, I have heard several times from London respecting the consequences of the Copenhagen business. It seems to be generally admitted that the public were pleased with the whole affair, and that the ministers have, upon the whole, gained considerably by it. Nevertheless, I find the abuse of it, which the opposition papers have very properly indulged in, and of which the 'Morning Chronicle' has set the example ever since it received the hint, is producing daily some impression. One advantage, at least, is gained by this means, that ministers are compelled to defend their conduct instead of raising a great exultation about the success of it. I strongly suspect they will be still worse off in Portugal, for the emigration of the prince to Brazil is a step which I never will suspect him of till I see him there. The most notable point, however, is the concession to America. This is all very well in itself, but comes with a sad grace from them, and must injure them incalculably with the country. I learn from my brother James, who has been in London for a few days, that the consternation of the class of people who are always with ministry, but especially with the present set, is great beyond description, and that the ridicule which this proclamation excites is very amusing. You will remark that the point conceded does not leave the other rights claimed in a situation at all more comfortable or easy than before. I drew up a statement of the whole American question for Jeffrey's review; and having procured a copy, I shall inclose it to Lord Lauderdale, and request him to forward it to you when he has read it. He was so good as to write me a letter on some points, at your desire; and I also had the benefit of consulting with Lord Holland and Allen respecting the negotiation with America. I should be very glad to have your opinion respecting the general principle which I have ventured to propose for satisfying the Americans without giving up our search of merchantmen—viz., redress in our *common law courts*, and not our Admiralty.

"Wilberforce, having promised to let me know as soon as he heard any thing certain about the meeting of Parliament, has written me two letters, stating that one of the ministers (I presume Perceval) told him they hoped there would be no occasion to meet before Christmas: and Lord Melville says here that it will not meet till the end of January. Though I know you will not dislike this, I am sure you must admit it to be a most reprehensible thing during such a state of affairs.

"I have received several letters from a friend of mine of the Orange party in Holland. The communication is so much interrupted that he can not send me a *mémoire* which he has just had the boldness to publish on the abolition of the Dutch slave-trade. Their anxiety for peace knows no bounds.

"Lord and Lady Ossulston were here for a day; and I find he has resolved, at all events, not to come in competition with Sir Charles Monk, unless he should find the sense of the county decidedly with him. Indeed, he says he does not care about it. I remain most faithfully yours,

"H. BROUGHAM.

"P.S.—I have to beg pardon for having misled you as to Lord Grenville being returned from Cornwall. I understood this from the Kings, but I now find that it was in Devonshire, on his way down, that they had seen him. He had not returned a fortnight ago."

TO THE EARL OF ROSSLYN.

"Edinburgh, Nov. 8, 1807.

"MY DEAR LORD ROSSLYN,—I have just received a letter from Mr. Warre, our consul at Oporto, and I inclose it, not only because it contains some late intelligence from that quarter, but because he seems to wish that the contents of it should reach the Foreign Office, which I think might be best effected by your desiring Vincent to look after it. I should have sent it direct to Hammond without troubling you, but I have understood there is some dryness between him and Warre. The case of the people at Oporto, and of poor Mr. Warre especially, is most pitiable. What he says of neglecting his own concerns, in looking after the factory under his care, I verily believe to be strictly true. He is, of all the mercantile men I ever saw, by far the least sordid; and I saw with my own eyes how constantly he sacrificed his private interest to his situation, which was indeed his hobby; and you will observe that, after all, he was only a vice-consul, receiving nothing like a repayment of the necessary expenses of his office; but he loved to play the old Castilian, and considered himself as the father of the factory. His zeal in the service last year was most exemplary; and I am certain that the best (indeed, for any thing I could see, the only good) information they have at Lisbon comes through him. You will remark that his remaining at his post for further orders is very laudable, for the risk is great. From Lisbon you can escape at a moment's warning, but the bar at Oporto is frequently impassable for six weeks at a time, and may probably have become so the day after the convoy sailed, in which case he must find his way to Lisbon as soon as the French come near; and will most likely be stopped for want of a vessel to bring him off, when things get so far on. As to the Brazil scheme, I still believe it never will be done as *we desire it* without our interference. They may send a part of the family over, but it will be to keep us out of the concern. The ministers are stark mad if they do not make Sir Sidney call in his way out; but Lord St. Vincent would have been the man for that business. H. BROUGHAM."

TO THE EARL OF ROSSLYN.

"Holland House, December 1, 1807.

"MY DEAR LORD,—Having come here for a couple of days, I shall have time to give you the political gossip which I promised some time ago.

In general, things have been pretty dull and uniform since my return. Lord Howick's appearances in the House of Lords have exceeded considerably the highest expectations that had been formed of them; but his speeches of last night for the negotiation, though certainly able, and perhaps superior in oratory to any of his former ones, are not very much approved of by those who like prudent and calm avowals of principles in leaders of parties. It must, I fear, be admitted that he is a little *too* warlike; and in general I fancy he is more Grenvillian, both in opinions and indeed in cast of character, than the rest of the remains of the Foxes. In his office he is, I should conceive, an excellent man of business. And he has appointed Stratton to the envoyship at Stockholm, though he was only known to him by his merit and services, having no friends nor influence.

"But the talk of the day is Whitbread's opposition, which I assure you is pretty fierce, and was even personal to Grey.* It seems to be generally admitted that he acted from principle, though I hear some people hint that he would in no wise dislike having his hands tied up by a high office—and this, I must say, I do not at all believe; and though I can not but think he liked the *éclat* of the thing after he had resolved to speak in this way, yet I am sure he acted a most conscientious part in forming his resolution.

"His praise of Yarmouth (whom it is really impossible not to blame, and whose appointment all our friends, I am sure, regret) was very like a little common factious opposition. Still more so was his putting the motion in Grey's former words—this is considered, I think, as rather spiteful. And in several points I conceive even those who agree with him in the main must admit that he argued his cause too high. By-the-way, he had no want of men to second him. The sensation excited is very considerable. I am quite clear the ministry will suffer by it—but most of all the Fox part of it; and this seems admitted.

"All is hitherto entire cordiality between the two parties in the cabinet. Nevertheless, no one can deny that there

* See the debate on Mr. Whitbread's motion, "That a committee be appointed to inquire into the state of the nation," July 6, 1807.—Cobbett's Debates, ix. 704. As strangers were excluded, the report is only an outline.

M 2

is a sort of hankering after Lord Grenville on the part of Hawkesbury, etc., which will look suspicious if it lasts much longer. It must be observed that the opposition (I mean the regular opposition) do not stand very well united. It is evident that they take different grounds; and I *know* that there are violent dissensions, in which I shall not much wonder to see Hawkesbury and Castlereagh wheel off.

"Most of the Foxites talk calmly and rationally on the state of affairs; build a *little* on the chances of Bonaparte being defeated by the Russians—a little more on his failing to beat them, if he advances far—and a good deal on our own naval or colonial experiments.

"They are in the main rational, also, on the subject of peace, though certainly not sufficiently clear and steady in their views of that question. I don't think they have a very right view either of the state of our connections with Russia or of the questions relative to Sicily, expecting a good deal too much from the former, and not seeing all the evils of our attempts in favor of the latter. Buenos Ayres is *not quite* given up; but at any rate they think it must have been retaken by our expedition.

"The merchants are a good deal laughed at for having been taken in by the scheme to such an extent, and Popham is given up by almost every body.

"The king's health is pretty good; but on *Irish* affairs he is by no means more sound than formerly. This part of the subject is very ticklish, and has *of late given very great uneasiness;* but nothing is to be done in the way of emancipation, though I much fear a petition will be presented, and, of course, opposed by Lord G. and the Foxites, which would be rather unpleasant. I believe they say within these two days that things are looking better in Ireland than before. All this is quite *extraneous.*

"The prince has been *really ill,* and is still in a very unpleasant way, though somewhat better. He is reduced to water or iced punch *and turtle,* and no wine nor animal food.

"This I know for certain. I have been down at Brocket Hall during the holidays, and the Melbournes (who, by-the-way, expected him there as an invalid) say he is exceedingly touchy about his health, so that he will neither take medicines nor allow any body to say he is ill. The story of his being so much in love with Lady Hertford is quite true, but certainly is not the sole cause of his lowness. She has treated him pretty cavalierly. Yarmouth's row about Hanover was all addressed to the prince, who has the family twist very strong.

"The elections are still much talked of. Sheridan says he is secure, and I rather suppose Paul may give in before many days elapse. But Windham, I *fear*, will be thrown out, as well as Coke, for treating, and so will their antagonists.

"They have all bungled it sadly, and there was a compromise not to petition, which was rendered ineffectual by a couple of rich old maids taking part, and raising a petition against them. For the mean time, ministers are to secure Windham a borough, and I suppose Coke also. Indeed all the loose seats are picked up, God knows how, before one hears of there being a vacancy.

"The chancellor is going on, I hear, as indifferently as possible in his court, and the bar are greatly displeased.

"The ministry are resolved to abolish the slave-trade in good earnest, and I hope will refuse to hear any evidence. I fancy this will be the great measure of the session, which, however much one must approve of it, is certainly not *all* that is wanting. Wellesley will certainly be screened. I fancy a whitewashing motion will be made; and then I should think his admission into place is almost certain.

"Every thing in this house goes on as usual, only little Souza is here almost every evening. They are coming to town next week.

"I shall not fail to write such intelligence as may interest you from time to time; and in the mean time I remain ever faithfully yours, H. BROUGHAM."

TO EARL GREY.*

"Albany, December 31, 1807.

"MY DEAR LORD GREY,—As there are various stories in

* Lord Howick became Earl Grey on the death of his father—14th November, 1807.

circulation among the newspapers about late events, I trouble you with a few lines to mention what I conceive to be the truth of the matter.

"Respecting the Lisbon business, Strangford complains bitterly that they have garbled his dispatch; but while he says this to me, and one or two others, who are likely to know the truth, as an excuse for the bragging which appears in his letter, he tells people whom he thinks he can take in, that, if the whole dispatch had been published, it would have appeared how much more concern he had in the transaction. I doubt not, indeed, that the original contained a great deal more bragging; but, unluckily, enough is published to deprive both Strangford and the ministers of every atom of credit which they may wish to take for the event. For the rest, the articles in the 'Morning Chronicle,' with another which will appear to-morrow, meet the opinions of all our friends, excepting the conjectures as to Bonaparte not wishing to detain the Court. This many people think a refinement; among whom are the Holland House folks. But I may add that some persons lately returned from Paris rather confirm it, by reporting that the wish there was that the Court might escape. I should be very glad to know your opinion upon this part of the subject.

"Every one is agreed that the choice of a minister to Brazil is of infinite moment, and could not have been worse made. It is conceived that Strangford has been appointed in order to give *éclat* to the management of the affair on our part, and to make the country think that we did the business. This, indeed, is quite of a piece with Gambier's peerage.* Ministers reverse the old rule, and reward men, not because they have performed important or difficult services, but in order to give their services an air of importance and difficulty.

"You will perceive contradictory statements as to Oudinot's marching towards Astrakhan; but I know it for a fact that the directors believe he is. The deputy-chairman said so at Hertford College last week to Malthus, from whom I heard it. It is supposed Oudinot will settle matters in Persia

---

* Admiral Gambier had just been raised to the peerage for his services in the bombardment of Copenhagen and the removal of the Danish fleet.

for an attack upon India after some interval; and the probability is they will enter the peninsula by the Punjaub, for obvious reasons. Such a movement will raise the Mahrattas and the Southern powers almost as certainly as if it were begun nearer the Carnatic, or Bombay, against which there are insuperable objections. If we lose India, there will be infinite clamor; but we shall be more frightened than hurt—thanks to the Company's monopoly, which has so much stunted our commerce with that country.

"The colonies, especially Jamaica, are all in an uproar; and to play such difficult cards the Duke of Manchester is sent with all his wisdom. Really, appointments like this are too bad, and, one should think, not beyond Parliament's interference. Gambier's peerage I should conceive clearly within it.

"I trust you will command me freely if you have any commissions which I can execute for you before your arrival in town. And I remain ever most faithfully yours,

"H. BROUGHAM."

FROM EARL GREY.

"Howick, January 3, 1808.

"DEAR BROUGHAM,—* * * My hopes are a good deal revived about Spain. We have now, I think, evidence enough that there is no want of spirit among the people. There has been nowhere any submission; the loss of the French has, I have no doubt, been much greater than they allow, while that of the Spanish armies is not stated, even by them, to have been very considerable, and the strongest part of the Peninsula yet remains to be conquered. But what cheers me most is the march of Moore upon Valladolid; it is a clear proof that he did not think things desperate. It is a bold and a decisive measure, not unlike what I think Bonaparte would have done in similar circumstances. It places the two armies in a situation more anxious and critical than any that I remember, as a battle seems inevitable, and under circumstances in which there appears literally to be 'nulla salus victis.' I only hope Moore, now that he has taken this step, will not hesitate, but push on, and attempt to strike some important blow before Bonaparte can turn upon him.

"You know I approved of the declaration, not of the style or the Canningisms in it, but of the thing done in rejecting an overture which could not, under the existing circumstances, be listened to, more than I have reason to believe many of my friends did. But in the answer to Pinckney, I think Canning has outdone himself. I am sorry it has not been more attacked and exposed in our papers.

"So 'all the ladies and gentlemen danced well,' as Jack Lee said of the figurantes at the opera. This conclusion of the military inquiry must, I think, give general dissatisfaction, and furnishes the strongest ground for some parliamentary proceeding. I do not understand how Lord Moira, etc., reconcile their condemnation of the armistice and convention with their unqualified approbation of all the generals.

"The Hollands, I find, are not coming home. Pray write whenever you have any news, and have nothing better to do.

"Ever yours, GREY."

TO EARL GREY.

"Albany, London, April 21, 1808.

"MY DEAR LORD GREY,—The Liverpool and Manchester delegates are gone at last, all tolerably well satisfied, except old Rathbone, who neither got his speeches out in the Lords nor Commons. The London merchants, however, kept him quiet, and the whole petitioners in a body met and passed a very handsome vote of thanks to me. The Londoners also invited me to practise in the Cock-pit, where they have the whole business in their hands, and have adopted me as Stephen's successor. I have ordered a copy of the report of my speech to be sent to you in an office cover. It is tolerably accurate—the four first and twenty last pages, I am sure, nearly verbatim. Stephen is more outrageous than ever. He has completely quarrelled with me, first, for saying what I did say, and next, for not preventing its being published. He says it is an incendiary and pernicious speech, and can only do mischief. But the real truth is that he does not like being attacked, and he finds Perceval is the only man who defends him. His witnesses all failed, and did more good to us than to the ministry, which exasperates them the more; and George Rose goes about saying he blames him greatly for not stopping me at every other sentence. They bitterly repent having allowed our petitions to be gone into. Burdett gave Stephen an unmerciful thrashing the other day, and is more wonderfully improved, I understand, in speaking than could have been thought possible. Paull had only lost £300, but he was quite ruined.

"Ever most faithfully yours, H. BROUGHAM."

TO EARL GREY.

"Middle Temple Hall, May 31, 1808.

"MY DEAR LORD GREY,—I ought long ago to have thanked you for your kind and friendly letter, respecting both the speech on the Orders in Council and my plans in general. I am extremely obliged to you, indeed, for the interest you take in these matters, so trifling to every body but myself. Notwithstanding this, however, I shall so far presume on your patience as to mention what I feel upon the subject.

"From accidental circumstances, I find myself placed in a situation which enables me to command a considerable degree of success in the profession of the law, and however odious that profession is (as God knows there are few things so hateful), I am quite clear that it would be utter folly in me to neglect so certain a prospect. I have, of course, been continuing my study of law, and pleading as diligently as possible—indeed, it naturally becomes easier and less disagreeable every day, and in a year or so more, I doubt not, I shall know more about it than is requisite. But I have resolved, in the mean time, to risk an experiment, which, I fancy, you will think not very prudent, and which, I own, is not quite safe. By means of a special motion at Lincoln's Inn, I may manage to be called to the bar early in July, and thus to go the next Northern Circuit—which I prefer to any other, as being the largest field, and in every respect the first thing in that way. I shall do this at the present moment, because, from my recent intercourse with *Liverpool* and Manchester folks, the *iron* in that quarter is hot, and should be struck before it cools. I set out with too slender a provision of law, no doubt, and may very possibly never see a jury until I have to address it, my stock of practice being so slender that I never yet saw a *nisi-prius* trial. But the points of law are few on a circuit, and by good-fortune none of any difficulty may fall on me, and, as there are no great wizards go the Northern Circuit, I may push through the thing with a little presence of mind and quickness. Besides, nothing was ever done without risk, and nothing great without much danger. Therefore I have taken my determination, and shall be ready to set out for York when the Circuit commences.

"In short, being so fairly in for it, I must make the best of an indifferent bargain, and addict myself to whatever will carry me upward at the bar. There are many openings—no formidable obstacles; and one may hope in time to make the profession a little more like what it used to be of old, when mercenary views were out of the question, and it was certainly the finest of all civil pursuits.

"The worst of all this is, that it forces me to give up every thing political, and in prudence should keep me clear of all party views and connections, for these, I daily see, are almost fatal to professional men. Now here lies my great and only difficulty. I could cease to think of a seat in Parliament, or, should I ever obtain one, I could manage to keep such an occupation very subordinate—that is easy enough; but to take no side in questions where my opinions happen to be all pretty strong, where I can not help feeling interested both in the actors and in the subject, would be next to impossible, cost what it may. So that I am in this dilemma, that one party stands plump in my way on every occasion, because I am politically attached to the other, while that other must of course in every case look to the interests of such lawyers as are directly engaged with them in politics; in short, do what I can, I am likely to be too much a politician for one set of men, and too much a lawyer for the other. This is a real dilemma; for I need only hint at Scarlett's case to show what power the chancellor, for the time being, has over a man's professional advancement—I mean by withholding a silk gown. So strongly does he feel this, that it is quite contrary to his advice that I think of the bar at all. I have troubled you much too long with my plans and difficulties to force on the one and to conquer the other. I believe the step above described to be the only means, and as such I embrace it without any great fear as to the result. When I shall once be fairly started, I must trust to the chapter of accidents for getting out of the other dilemmas.

"Ever yours, HENRY BROUGHAM."

TO EARL GREY.

"Middle Temple, June 4, 1808.

"MY DEAR LORD,—I trouble you with a few lines to say how Fox's book is flourishing. The cry is loud and universal in its favor.* All classes—political, fashionable, and literary—talk of nothing else, and talk in the same strain. Even Lord Aberdeen—whom I chanced to meet in company the other day—was in raptures, though a prodigious lover of kings and priests, and a pupil of Pitt and Melville—indeed, one of Pitt's *favorites*. And Lord Camden says he read it at a sitting with infinite avidity, and admires every line separately. You will say this is a proof of his stupidity, for, if he understood it all, he must necessarily be shocked at some parts of it.

"I expect it will still raise a cry, especially in the pulpit, and that you will soon see letters to Lord Holland, and perhaps yourself, by J. Bowles & Co., and hear of sermons by Rennel and all manner of holy animals.† But still the cause of liberty and liberality of opinion is prodigiously refreshed by it, and all its inferior supporters countenanced and encouraged. As a *party* event, too, you are great gainers. It is a rare set-off to such meetings as Pitt's birthday dinner, where, by-the-way, the chancellor covered himself with ridicule. Faithfully yours,

"HENRY BROUGHAM."

I wrote the following letter to Lord Grey, partly to give him some news about Spain, but chiefly to convey to him the

---

* "A History of the early part of the Reign of King James the Second. With an Introductory Chapter."

† John Bowles, barrister-at-law, the author of a multitude of pamphlets, chiefly directed against the Whig party, and some of them especially directed against Fox. Thomas Rennel, dean of Winchester, author of "Principles of French Republicanism founded on Violence and Blood-guiltiness," and other pamphlets of a like tenor. The chief attack on Fox's book was by the Right Honorable George Rose.

disappointment and disgust I was then suffering under from the spiteful proceedings of the Government in stopping my call to the bar. It is difficult to find a reason, much less an excuse, for a proceeding which I may call unparalleled. It might be that the Government had a foretaste of the fate of their Orders in Council; but it indicated pretty plainly to *me* what I was to look to in the future, and the kind of injustice I might expect to meet with in my professional career.

TO EARL GREY.

"Middle Temple Hall, July 2, 1808.

"MY DEAR LORD GREY,—I expected to learn some news about Spain which might be worth communicating. There is, however, nothing authentic arrived. Portuguese people have no letters, but believe that Oporto is freed from the French, and that Junot is intrenching himself somewhere about Lisbon. There is a tendency in Spain, no doubt, to rise; but one can not safely trust the flattering prospects held out until it appears that the insurgents have actually begun operations, and proved their constancy as well as their courage; for it is obvious that the former is more material in a contest which, if it is to do any thing at all, must be of no short duration, and quite unfavorable to the insurgents at the outset. As to the wild story which every man of every party was believing all yesterday, and I think even to-day, that the insurgents have defeated the French in a pitched battle and killed twelve thousand of them, I leave you to say what sort of evidence would be necessary to convince you of such a thing, when you recollect the campaigns of 1795 and 1796, 1805 and 1806, with the best regulars and leaders in Europe. Meanwhile, all is hope and castle-building here, literally 'bâtir des châteaux en Espagne.' People are busy fortifying the Pyrenees against *new invasions* of the enemy; contriving terms of peace which he may not be able to accept, and which will lead to a campaign in France; raising a fifth coalition in Germany, and bringing back the Bourbons. The first act of the peace, the defeat in Spain, is of course never doubted. I verily believe at this moment there are scarcely ten men in London who would give Bonaparte £100 a year of half-pay to retire to Ajaccio, and live quietly as an invalid officer the rest of his life. So incurable a malady is hope, notwithstanding the largest quantities of bitter disappointment which may have been administered to strengthen us against it. Materoza is a fine boy of eighteen, very promising, and I dare say well born. The other I have not seen, but hear him well spoken of. Argaelius is with them, whom I knew when he lived here last year and the year before. He is a sensible and accomplished man, infinitely sanguine on the present occasion.

"To drop down to a very trifling subject, I have been defeated in my plan of being called to the bar this term. To my great surprise they sent down the attorney and solicitor general, who frightened the benchers, and, leaguing with Saint Allan Park (one of the greatest knaves in the profession), rejected my application by a majority of ONE vote. Every one admits that this is a vile political job, and scarcely ever before attempted. They luckily can not easily prevent me next term; but I am infinitely injured by the delay, besides the foretaste it gives me of what I have to expect in future when I shall stand in need of a silk gown.

"Believe me ever most sincerely yours,

"HENRY BROUGHAM."

TO EARL GREY.

"Temple, July 21, 1808.

"* * * It is a very strange thing that the ministers have contrived to pick out a staff for Spain and Portugal which contains not one man who ever served there, except Sir H. Dalrymple, who is a mere name. I am persuaded the Duke of York, after the first success, will follow with the Guards, and—bring all back again. It must be admitted, however, that things are looking very well in Spain, and great things may follow if they go on in the same way; but I am no believer in the *duration* and steadiness of popular feelings, and a great believer in regular armies and well-bred officers.

"I am heartily tired of London and special pleading, especially the former, every body being gone out of town, and nothing remaining but heat, dust, and dullness. I shall shake myself loose in a week or ten days at furthest, and steer northward. Pray let me know if you are likely to be at

Howick in about a fortnight or sixteen days, that I may shape my course so as to find you at home.

"Believe me yours very faithfully,

"HENRY BROUGHAM.

"I shall write to you to-morrow or next day, and send you the Portuguese communications which Warre promises me."

TO EARL GREY.

"July 22, 1808.

"DEAR LORD GREY,—I wrote you a few lines yesterday, and mentioned that Warre had promised me the details, papers, etc., about Oporto. I have now gone over them, and they are very curious indeed.

"The bishop is at the head of every thing, and the Church is all up in arms. The Chapter and all the convents have embodied themselves, and form a large corps of stout and zealous soldiers. Part of the town, all the churches, hospitals, and some of the forts, are guarded by monks, with cocked hats, muskets, and their cloaks cut short off. The press is in equal activity with the Church. I have run over no less than *seventeen* proclamations issued by the Supreme Junta of Oporto in one week. They are very violent, some of them not at all badly written, though inferior to the Spanish, and talking much more about religion and the Church. The ribbons worn by the people, three of which Warre received, are about Jesus Christ and the faith, 'por lo *fee* vencer o morir,' etc. The Spaniards say 'per la *patria* vencer,' etc. So far the former are likely to be more zealous and more rash than the Spaniards. They have too many priests meddling, and too much fanaticism afloat, to act very wisely; but if well supported in the other quarters, they will do much good in spite of it.

"They have got hold of a part of a guillotine, in possession of the French, which exasperates them much. They have marched the French, consul, merchants, soldiers, etc., on board of a ship and sent them to England; and Warre's correspondents all state the numbers in arms to be fifty thousand. They are very anxious for assistance of any and every kind from this country. So far Warre.

"The Hollands are still very sanguine about the whole affair, and I hear you continue to be so too. But they admit that if the Seville Junta goes on by itself and does not call a general Cortes, the Arragonese will not submit to them, and that the whole will be blown up. They think our Government have very bad notions on these points, and this is the only thing which makes them doubt of success.

"Yours, etc., H. BROUGHAM."

The conduct of our Government in regard to the war in Spain, when ministers took no warning by the disastrous events of the Portuguese campaign—their treatment of Sir John Moore, placing over him generals in many respects inferior to him—and other matters connected with these subjects, had been the occasion of much discussion and correspondence between Lord Grey and me. In some of the following letters he refers to many written by me to him, which, I regret to say, I have been unable to find. I kept no copies, and the originals are not among the great mass of my letters, which my dear and lamented friend Lady Grey sent to me after her husband's death, most kindly placing them at my disposal, and of which kindness it will be found that I have throughout this memoir largely availed myself. Indeed, the appointment of such officers as were selected to take the command must have been as offensive to Sir Arthur Wellesley as it was unjust to Sir John Moore; for it is undoubtedly the fact that after Vimiera, and Burrard's command succeeded by Dalrymple's, Sir Arthur wrote to Lord Castlereagh, distinctly stating *his earnest desire to quit the army*, and urging as his reason for this step that, after having been successful as a commander, he could never serve in a subordinate situation with satisfaction either to the officer placed over him or to himself.

The following letter from Lord Grey shows his opinion of the *vexata questio*, the convention of Cintra, and also what he thought of the conduct of ministers and their treatment of Sir John Moore:

FROM EARL GREY.

"Howick, Sept. 29, 1808.

"MY DEAR BROUGHAM,—I received your letter last night.

There can be but one sentiment with respect to the convention, and I believe there has never existed a case in which the public feeling was so generally and so strongly excited. It is, therefore, an opportunity of attack too favorable to be neglected. But that it will overset the Administration I am not sanguine enough to believe. Nothing can do so till there is a body of men capable of succeeding them; and while the Catholic question remains in its present state, where are they to be found?

"The leading features of the case are sufficiently obvious, and the circumstances which led to the delay of the expedition, and to its being sent piecemeal, as it was, are all, I think, adverted to by you.

"The folly of sending Sir John Moore to the Baltic, where it was impossible he could do any thing, and where, by his prudence alone, I believe, we were saved from a scrape which ministers had in a manner contrived for him, productive as it was of so heavy a loss both of time and means, is undoubtedly one of the points chiefly to be insisted on. With respect to the choice of a commander, I am in general inclined to be very tolerant, not only because the attack coming from us, I am aware of the obvious retort about Whitelock, but because I know the difficulties which the army list presents to ministers on this point. In the present case, however, I think there is a good deal to be said. It is not only that ministers erred in making a bad choice, but that the cause of it was an intrigue to give Wellesley a separate opportunity to distinguish himself. If they had thought him the fittest man to command in a service of such vital importance, they ought in a manly way to have given him the command at once. If not, another commander should have been selected, who should have been fully apprised of the views of Government, and sent from the beginning to conduct operations, the success of which depended so much on uniformity of measures, on local knowledge, and, above all, on the absence of all jealousies among the officers at the head of the army. Looking at the matter in this view, the conduct of ministers has been as unjust to an individual as it has been injurious to the public service. When Sir John Moore came home from Sweden, they could not withhold the most unqualified approbation of his conduct. But at the same time that they made this acknowledgment, you must remember how very little pains were taken to conceal their discontent and dislike of him. Nothing was omitted to give him disgust, and to make him relinquish his command. But not succeeding in this, and not being able to put Wellesley over him, they determined to reduce him to the level of Wellesley, by putting Sir Hew Dalrymple, who had never seen any service, over both, and in the mean time detached Wellesley, with his division, that he might find the opportunity of which he availed himself, before the arrival of any other officer of higher rank. It is not, therefore, only the fault of having made a bad choice that is imputable to ministers, but that they did so for the express purpose of keeping the command from Sir John Moore, whom the general voice of the whole army, supported by his former services, would have pointed out as the man best qualified for it.

"With respect to the details of the expedition, and its deficiency either in cavalry or in any other article of necessary appointment, I am entirely ignorant. But I can not imagine that the want of cavalry could have prevented their advancing. On these matters, however, you have one of the best sources of information at hand in Lord Rosslyn.

"With respect to Spain I can not agree with you. That a most tremendous battle still remains to be fought is certain. Bonaparte, whether it be from choice or necessity, seems disposed to stake every thing on the conquest of Spain, and the effort he will make is not to be looked at without great solicitude for the event. But I am not dismayed; and if I was sanguine some months ago, when you all seemed to pity me for my folly, I am much more so now, for I think the situation of Spain much improved. Bonaparte, you say, was surprised by the resistance. But were not the Spaniards surprised by the attack? and when you recollect that he had in the month of May an army of one hundred and five thousand men in possession of all the fortresses, and of a strong position in the heart of the kingdom—that the provinces were cut off from the means of communication with one another, were without leaders, without arms, and subject to every disadvantage which a people could suffer, and yet that they have driven that army, with a loss of at least fifty thousand men, to the frontier—why are we to despond, even if a great army should be ready to be poured in upon them under the command of Bonaparte in person? He has made, and no doubt will make, great preparations. But the Spaniards have had time also for preparation, and have secured other advantages which are incalculable in their effect. And in whatever way I consider this subject, it appears to me that their means of resistance and their chance of success are both infinitely greater, as opposed to any army which Bonaparte can now bring against them, than they were when he began openly to attempt to enslave them at the commencement of last May. With these opinions, therefore, I can not approve of the discouraging language which you have held in the 'Edinburgh Review,' and which you hold in your letter. Even if my own hopes were less sanguine, I would willingly deprecate you from using such language publicly. To assist the Spaniards is morally and politically one of the highest duties a nation ever had to perform. And to check those feelings whose operation is of so much importance to the success of our attempt may do great mischief, but can not by possibility produce any good. On the passage of which I complained I will say little, because I confess it is a subject which I feel painfully. To be accused of abandoning, when in power, the principles I had maintained in opposition, is a severe charge even from an enemy; but for a friend to entertain, and to think it necessary to promulgate, that opinion, must inflict a much deeper wound, the more especially as I had hoped that all who knew me, and most of the members of the late cabinet, must have been convinced that, though we might have mistaken the road, we were sincerely desirous of peace. To Fox, at least, that credit has been allowed; and it is not one of the hardships that we have to complain of least, that a separation is made between him and those who survive on the question. The truth is, that we never departed from his views; and at the time he wrote the dispatch of the 14th June, the last he ever wrote himself, he considered the negotiation as having failed. I have said more than I intended, so will not add one word more, but that I am ever yours,

"Grey."

To this I answered immediately, as follows.

"October 6, 1808.

"My dear Lord,—I find you mistake me a good deal about the review of Spain, more especially if you think I ever wrote a word which accused you of swerving from your opposition principles; most especially if you imagine that I ever could fancy a distinction between you and Fox on this matter. In truth, I always thought that the most scandalous piece of injustice that ever was dealt out to a party, for the mere dates must have convinced any man that Fox's death had no more influence on the negotiation than Pitt's, or any other person's. But I won't trouble you further on this unimportant matter.

"I write at present to mention my having learnt with much surprise that the Hollands are going to Spain in good earnest, a plan which I had all along viewed as mere talk. Now it strikes me that such a proceeding will not only hurt Lord Holland incalculably, but will seriously injure your party. As for their returning to Parliament, that no one can believe; and certainly a more important session has not been known as the next is likely to prove.

"I can fancy nothing more certain than Canning's, etc., gibing and referring to R. Adair's Peterburgh mission, every time there happens a difference between our Government and the Juntas. Nor will the country be slow to blame Lord Holland for whatever goes on wrong in our communication with the Spaniards. But leaving that out of view, I am persuaded, fond as the people of this country may at present be of Spain, that rambling over there under the present circumstances will infallibly alienate their confidence from Lord Holland, or rather, I should say, will prevent them from viewing him as the steady and English sort of man whom they require for a statesman. I think he will assuredly be damaged by it, and at the moment when he was rising into very great estimation.

"Perhaps you don't think with me, but if you do, I wish you would write to him and her, to dissuade, for I *know perfectly well* that no other person can attempt it with half the chance of succeeding. Believe me very faithfully yours,

"H. Brougham.

"P.S.—I am greatly indebted to you for your kind expressions, but suppose you misunderstood me. Any parliamentary plans would, I believe, do me much harm for some time to come, and though I should like to have a share in running down the present drivellers, yet the satisfaction of doing so, and the trifling service I could render the party, would scarcely be a fair inducement to make me interrupt my professional pursuits."

TO EARL GREY.

"Temple, November 25, 1808.

"MY DEAR LORD GREY,—I have come up quicker than I intended, from meeting a newspaper at Darlington with a notice that the Cock-pit met to-day, and I knew I had a point of importance to argue. I accordingly came day and night, and got here about eight this morning, when, on going to the court, I found the cause compromised.

"I have a letter from Lady Holland, dated 9th, desponding somewhat, and abusing Ward greatly. He did not sail with them, which, I fancy, was rather beginning unfavorably.

"At the Cock-pit I had much conversation with *St. Stephen*, and found his tone about politics greatly altered and quite lowered. He is melancholy about the convention, angry at the generals, and has not the smallest hopes of Spain. I presume he speaks Perceval's sentiments to a certain degree. He denies the meeting of Parliament till after Christmas or the birthday, positively. Wilberforce is going to Bath for a month, so he must have changed his opinion, if he ever had the one mentioned by Tierney.

"It is singular to see how changed the public sentiments about ministers are. Every one of all parties (and I have seen more Tories than whigs) admits that they are *damaged* to the greatest degree. I can not help regretting that none of our friends are on the spot.

"Canning is on bad terms with his colleagues, talks loudly against the convention, and indeed washes his hands of all concern with the expedition, which was concerted by Castlereagh and Perceval, with scarcely any consultation of military men. Perceval wrote the answer to the address (as I always thought). This you may rely upon, and that Canning disapproved of it.

"The king and Duke of York violent against every thing Spanish and Portuguese, generals, etc. The official people despond about Spain.

"Now for the last piece of news which I have just heard in Ridgway's shop, where a man came who had been one at the Duke of Portland's, and said that the duke had received intelligence of Blake's defeat after long fighting, but a very complete defeat. The report of the evening is either that he was taken prisoner or had fled to the mountains. I much fear the substance of this dismal rumor will prove true.

"Believe me ever yours most faithfully,

"HENRY BROUGHAM."

TO EARL GREY.

"Middle Temple Hall, Dec. 2, 1808.

"MY DEAR LORD GREY,—Knowing that any little thing one happens to hear in town is worthy of notice to the *unfortunate* persons who live in the country, I just put down what occurs, however unimportant in itself, when I have a moment of respite from John Doe and Richard Roe.

"Touching Spain, I am more sanguine to-day than I have ever been, which you will not be surprised at (though most people might), because it is founded on your own view very nearly. The Spaniards have been beaten, but certainly after such stiff fighting as I never had expected. If their spirit continues equal, or nearly equal, to this last exhibition of it, I shall have scarcely any fears. Government is still quite as desponding as formerly. In truth their fears are founded on their wishes.

"It is quite certain that there was a flirtation, if not an intrigue, with the Doctor; but Lord Ellenborough is represented by people who dined with him yesterday as exceedingly factious and violent.

"Having received a sort of complimentary message from Miranda, I went to see him—rather to prevent his coming to see me, than from any wish to make his acquaintance—but I found him very clever and entertaining, and frank about his own plans and secrets, in a degree that is only to be found among finished adventurers (at least so I have generally found them).* He is furious at the ministry, though he seems still to be connected with them; admits that he and Wellesley were on the eve of setting out for South America with an army, when the Spanish deputies arrived; curses the folly of this Government in changing their certain plans in New Spain for any such chances as Old Spain affords; and denies that an army is the right way of aiding the Spaniards. He mixes a good deal of truth with much narrow, Peruvian, and selfish error on the subject; but I was struck with one argument on the small numbers of the patriots. 'Cadiz has 100,000 inhabitants; it is said to be full of patriots; and all Andalusia is open: yet they have raised a battalion of galley-slaves from the hulks and prisons of that town!' His details of the French commissariat are curious and frightful. It is on the plan of the flying-artillery, and *organized* with infinite nicety and care. Miranda was, you know, second in command at Jemmappes, and says the system was formed in that campaign. I should like to know whether you had any communication with him when you were in office.

"Sydney Smith found in Yorkshire a sixteenth edition of Plymley, five cheap ones having been sold in the West Riding.†

"The last review—about Cevallos—has given infinite offense here; but in Edinburgh I learn that both friends and foes are offended.

"The Hollands are retrograde, as appears from letters. Ward, his uncle says, has arrived at Bath, but I have not heard from him.

"The faint attempts at defending the convention and the ministry, which their papers began, have died a natural death. They now turn their whole force against the 'Edinburgh Review,' which every one ministerial newspaper has now been attacking almost daily for above a week. They have set on new hands to this work, some people think Cooke—some Ward.

"Ferguson's story of the dispatch about Moore not being

* Don Francisco Miranda, a Spanish soldier and politician of great renown in his age.

† The celebrated "Letters from Peter Plymley to his Brother Abraham," anonymous, but well known to be the work of Smith.

received till after the 17th, turns out erroneous, as we suspected. The re-embarkation at Mondego is correct. He (Ferguson) says Wellesley could not produce his case in Burrard's absence, for it consists in throwing the whole blame on Burrard's refusal to allow their pursuit. Burrard is to put all on want of cavalry. The Duke of York will be with him, I presume, so here is a new scrape for Government. Charles Adam, who brought home L'Oison, says they talk of the business exactly as the *people* here do.

"Seeing nobody but dull lawyers, and conversing only about pleas and issues, I assure you writing a letter to you is a very great luxury, as it approaches to tolerable society. This must excuse the length and unimportance of the present letter; and the paper and ink, which make it nearly illegible, must be set down to the account of the coffee-house where it is written. Believe me, dear Lord Grey, ever your faithful friend, HENRY BROUGHAM."

TO EARL GREY.

"Temple, Dec. 14, 1808.

"DEAR LORD GREY,—I take it for granted the melancholy accounts given of affairs in Spain by Moore and Graham in their private letters must have reached you; but as they are very important in considering the whole question, I shall state their substance in case you should *not* have heard it. Moore, by letter to Abercromby, of date November 26, says the army had advanced well and comfortable in every respect, but that the people were quite indifferent and torpid, not well disposed to us. He adds that he hears everywhere of Spanish armies, but sees none, and that the inactivity of the Central Junta is quite fatal. Graham (with Castaños) writes to T. Grenville the same account, and that the Spanish armies are very small in number. I fear the truth is that the enthusiasm has partly evaporated; that the Junta have been too sanguine and supine, that they have not been half revolutionary enough, and that the moment is irrevocably gone when the people might have been made to save the country. Allen's last letter to Sydney Smith admits that the Junta has acted with shameful remissness, and that it childishly thought Joseph's flight was the end of the business.

"But our ministers are more to blame than even I had thought, for they squandered away the golden opportunity, which now appears to have been so short and so irretrievable.

"The ministry give all up for lost, and seem resolved to abandon the nonsensical plan of a stand in Portugal. A stand in Andalusia may still be attempted. William Harrison (of the Treasury) abuses them loudly, and declaims against them for blindfolding the country, and the country for liking to be blindfolded. He allows all our blunders in the execution as well as the plan, and cries out for a Spanish revolution as the only salvation of Europe. Such rebellious talk in the Treasury is ominous; in truth, we see at present an odd spectacle—the Government deserted by all, even its own followers and friends, who only rest its case on the unpopularity of their adversaries. I trust that the ensuing session will remove this only prop of the ministry. You have the game in your own hands, and I doubt not that both the constituent parts of the great body which you lead will agree in such a view of the subject as may enable your particular branch to regain some of its former popularity, a thing easy in itself, as well as highly important to both the party and the country.

"Wellesley is raising his head, and ministers too are going to crow over Burrard. They, and not he, nevertheless, are to blame, but this must really be speedily enforced in Parliament, otherwise it will be disbelieved by the country. They are to give him a court-martial. In great haste, ever yours truly, H. Brougham."

TO EARL GREY.

"December 15, 1808.

"Dear Lord Grey,—I snatch a moment, as usual during dinner, to say that I have just seen H. Bouverie, who tells me his regiment, which was countermanded yesterday, is re-ordered to-day; that this is said at the office to be owing to a telegraph from Plymouth, announcing from the authority of the Indefatigable, which was off the Spanish coast, that Baird, Moore, and Romana are joined; which ministers believe, and disbelieve the French bulletins at the same time.

"This seems rather improbable; but one thing is certain, every degree of confusion reigns at the offices. All are at cross-purposes, and complain that they have no head, and no arrangement to help them. The prevailing belief now is that Mulgrave and Castlereagh will go by the board; and I heard of preparations in Canning's office for *his* departure.

"I lament nothing so much as the want of a *statement* such as I once wrote to you about, and feel my conscience smite me for suffering even the law to prevent me from doing it myself. But there is no help for impossibilities. It will be better done by debates.

"In haste, yours, etc., H. BROUGHAM.

"P.S.—Bulletin from Admiral Young's secretary at Plymouth:

"News up to December 3d. Junta going to Toledo. No doubt of Hope and Romana joining Moore. Romana at Seco, having collected 20,000 of Blake's army."

TO EARL GREY.

"December 16, 1808.

"DEAR LORD GREY,—The post is just going; but as there are different rumors about the fatal news, and some deny it, I write this to assure you it is as bad as possible. A letter from Allen, December 1, eight P.M. (Corunna), says that advice had just arrived of Castaños's total defeat, and Moore and Baird's retreat, the former to Ciudad Rodrigo, the latter to Gallicia—'by directions from Castaños himself ! !' I copy this literally, with the two (! !). This is the whole letter, and, being to *Perry* (who showed it to me), I am confident Allen did not write it rashly.*

"Ronald Ferguson saw the people at the offices to-day, and Hope of the Admiralty yesterday. They believe in the whole of the worst parts of the news, and say that Government have it in Baird's dispatches. Hope says the shipping is ordered round to Vigo to take in Baird. Ferguson is giving over his brigade for lost, it being with General Hope at Madrid.

"In haste, yours ever, H. BROUGHAM."

* Perry, well known as the editor of the "Morning Chronicle."

TO EARL GREY.

"Woolbeding, January 4, 1809.

"My dear Lord Grey,—I rejoice greatly on account of the country that you are coming to town; but I must say if your health is one of the causes of it, as I understood from Petty, I had much rather have heard of your wintering at Howick. I am the more disappointed at this, if correct, because your friends had of late been flattering themselves with the prospects of your complaints being entirely removed.

"I have been here these three days, and return to-morrow to town; but having heard from London, and before I left it, some things which seem authentic, I shall set them down.

"The regency story is not, perhaps, true, but I really believe it had some foundation. It was talked of at Mansfield's (the chief-justice) the other day in a Tory company, among whom was the attorney-general, and no sort of contradiction was given to it by any body; only all agreed in lamenting that '*so excellent a woman as the queen is in private life*' should allow herself to be so much under the prince's influence. I suspect, therefore, that the project was entertained at Windsor, and went off on some objection about the Duke of York. I should add that Lord Robert Spencer's man, Kent (whom he gave an office to, and who is much about the public offices), says he heard it still talked of at the Treasury as a thing to be brought forward. I guess this to be untrue, however. A very odd thing happened the other day. A report of the king's death prevailed so much that black rose in price, and the tailors were all in confusion, buying and running about. It was spread all over this part of the country as certain; yet the Archbishop of Canterbury told Mansfield he never had seen the king better than on Christmas-day. It strikes me as possible that there may, nevertheless, have been some alarm, perhaps an unfounded one, among them; and this would account both for the talk of a regency among themselves, and for the strange report of a dissolution of Parliament which prevailed about the same time.

"I have a letter from Allen at Vigo, dated December 13. They are going to Lisbon by land, and expect to winter in Andalusia, not having heard of Madrid being taken. But I conclude you have received letters from themselves by the same conveyance.

"A few days ago the intention of the ministry was to defend Lisbon, and sixty pieces of cannon, with engineers, etc., were embarking, as Ferguson assured me. Whether the advance of Baird and Moore has changed their plan I know not, but the report among the Guards at Portsmouth is, that they are going under Spencer to Cadiz. This is a wiser plan certainly. Indeed, notwithstanding all the sanguine expectations of the London folks, I shall be greatly surprised if Moore ventures between Bonaparte and Soult, at least if the statements of their force are correct. I hear Lord Grenville is decidedly of opinion that the whole conduct of Government must be fully discussed, as he objects to every thing they have done; and Wickham is, if possible, more desponding about Spain than ever. But this you have of course heard directly from Dropmore.

"Believe me, etc., H. BROUGHAM."

TO EARL GREY.

"January 6, 1809.

"MY DEAR LORD GREY,—* * * The Hollands were at Oporto on the 26th of December, and give, I understand, a bad account of the Portuguese, which can surprise nobody. The ministers affect to speak with great admiration of Moore's retreat, but their supporters keep cavilling at him. Lord Melville is certainly to speak at first against Government, but I fancy his opposition will be a very qualified one. He has desired his friends to stay away, and I know several who have complied. Ferguson was to have gone to Corunna in the ship which was appointed to convey the expedition, but it is stopped, and both he and Harry Bouverie are now at Woolbeding. I presume the whole are to be sent round to Cadiz. Was there ever such wavering, childish behavior yet seen, even upon ordinary occasions, as the ministers have shown through the whole of this greatest of all affairs?

"Lord Moira is much praised for his view of the convention, but some wonder is expressed at his joining in the vote about zeal, etc. The extravagant praise of Lord Moira in the 'Courier,' and their constant attacks on ministry, are very curious. Huskisson says the 'Courier' is an unmanageable paper, and I suppose it looks merely or chiefly to its sale; so that its attacks are rather a symptom of public opinion than of any disunion among the ministers.

"Always yours, most faithfully, H. BROUGHAM."

TO EARL GREY.

"Saturday evening, 6 o'clock, Jan. 21, 1809.

"DEAR LORD GREY,—I have only a moment to say that the arrival of Charles Stewart (Castlereagh's brother) seems a proof that Moore's army is out of danger; though certainly the transports had not all arrived, but were coming into Corunna, and there is a report that the news brought by Stewart is bad. It seems to be certain that we have lost considerably in constant skirmishes, and that all our artillery is gone. One account says, all the troops, except one regiment, had embarked when Stewart came. This is not true. The utmost extent of the ministerial information is that the *cavalry* had embarked. Senseless stories are told by people in office, such as Brodrick, whom I heard mention, with much exultation, that the Duke del Infantado had retaken Madrid, and that Moore was occupying a position, and making a stand, a diversion, and I know not what, at Corunna—and without his artillery!!

"If he waited three days at Corunna for transports, Bonaparte must either have been in smaller force than is supposed, or must have gone to Vigo. The date of Moore's dispatches is January 11.

"The Hollands at Lisbon, on the 4th, only heard that day of Madrid being taken. H. BROUGHAM."

CHAPTER VIII.

HOME AND FOREIGN POLITICS, 1809.

The Peninsular War.—Sir John Moore, his Retreat and Death.—Victory at Corunna. — Inquiry into the Conduct of the Duke of York.—French and Austrian War on the Danube.—France and Spain.—Home Politics.—Attempt to form a Coalition Ministry.—Spencer Perceval and Earl Grey.—Canning.—Criticisms on the Conduct of the War in the Peninsula.—The Princess of Wales and Canning.—Canning, Castlereagh, and Lord Wellesley.—Estimate of Sir John Moore.

"January 23, 1809.

"DEAR LORD GREY,—You will naturally be anxious about this sad news.* R. Ward and Harrison say six hundred men were killed. Baird died of his shot. Baggage, etc., gone; though Lord Paget hopes the artillery may be in part saved. But it is admitted that the débris of the army must come home. Thirty-one hundred were embarking safely when he came away. Craufurd and four thousand gone to Vigo, but not heard of. Greenwood says we lost five thousand or six thousand altogether *on the retreat.* Brand† showed me a letter from Graham,‡ who was with him, dated 13th January. He states that the French refused battle when offered at Lugo; that the English army is unfit for any thing but fighting; harassed by all wants, and by disease from climate and fatigue, and dying in great numbers. Of course this is before the battles.

"Altogether, I imagine a more disastrous affair has seldom been known.

"Buonaniti has just received a letter from the Hollands, at Lisbon. They are to go from thence to Gibraltar. This is, to be sure, just the proper time for running about from port

* The retreat of Sir John Moore, his death, and the battle of Corunna. Sir David Baird lost an arm, but recovered.

† Afterwards Lord Dacre. ‡ Afterwards Lord Lynedoch.

to port, and seeking any thing rather than home. I suppose they are now prepared to believe every thing except the real presence; for their frequent disappointments seem never to undeceive them, or to lessen their faith.

"In haste, H. BROUGHAM."

TO THE EARL GREY.

"January 24, 1809.

"DEAR LORD GREY,—I understand the dispatches are come, but contain nothing more than Lord Paget brought. The loss of the army is great on the retreat, but its abominable conduct in plundering, murdering, etc., etc., is much worse. So much for Lord Cathcart and Copenhagen. This I learn from one who was with the army the whole way, and an officer of rank.

"The Spaniards, who disliked us at first, of course now detest us, in that part of Spain at least. The information of all our emissaries—Frere, Stuart, Dyer, etc., etc.—is described as having been *ridiculously* incorrect; and the want of information in our army from spies, etc., is quite unintelligible. My informant says all the bribes in our military chest could not get the Spaniards to give any intelligence. Our men plundered *our own* ammunition, provisions, etc. Lord Paget lost his whole property in this way. Three men were just going to be executed for these things and others, when the French attacked us, luckily for the culprits. The army was drawn up to witness the execution.

"Sir Arthur Wellesley says the loss at embarking was about one thousand; R. Ward, six hundred. I believe the former is nearer the truth.

"The four thousand under Craufurd were heard from at St. Jago; and it was supposed they could get safe off, there being no tidings of any French thereabout. Junot commanded the attack. He sent back three women prisoners before the battle, with compliments from 'Junot and the army of Portugal.' The Hollands are going by land to Seville. I really wish they may not get into a scrape, though they do deserve a good fright.

"Poor Vincent! What a sudden and melancholy fate! They are of course all in great distress. It was the first thing Lady Rosslyn heard on her arrival; and you may believe she was dreadfully affected, though she exerts herself with great fortitude. I seriously think Lord Lauderdale should not put his name to the East India pamphlet.* Do advise him not to do so, if it strikes you in the same way. Every body objects to his writing it at all, but perhaps that is going too far, though there is something in it. As to the want of a name, we can easily puff it into proper notice and supply such a defect. It might, and indeed must, soon be known; but in the mean time its whole effect will have been produced without the impediment arising from the feelings in question. Pray do not expose yourself to cold in this most dreadful weather. I saw an instance the other day of the effects. H. B."

Lord Grey had, throughout this period of the war in Spain, been strongly impressed with what he considered the gross mismanagement of our affairs, and the incapacity of ministers. He was persuaded that Spain would never have ventured to disturb the French army behind the Ebro, well knowing that reinforcements were surely at hand, and that while the Spaniards were suffering under a most feeble government, our ministers were sending a British army into the heart of the Peninsula to march to certain destruction. The case against our rulers was no exaggeration of political opponents or of party feeling; it was clearly proved by the very papers laid before Parliament by ministers themselves. Their defense was by no attempt at justification, but by blaming or criticising the measures of the very officers they had themselves selected for command; and all this time while they had at their disposal a force amply sufficient to have rescued Spain, if the proper use had only been made of it at the proper time.

Lord Grey, in April, 1809, brought the whole subject before Parliament, with that great ability which he of all men best knew how to apply, to make intelligible details of the

* Perhaps the pamphlet, or rather book, by Lord Lauderdale, called "The Government of India under the Superintendence of the Board of Control." Edinburgh, 1809.

most complicated description; but in spite of the dignified eloquence, the admirable temper he displayed, so peculiarly appropriate in dealing with so delicate a subject, our legislators decided against him.

The object of Lord Grey's motion was to represent to the Crown the disgrace which the proceedings of the Government had brought upon England, and the injury which the British nation had suffered from the rashness and mismanagement of ministers, culminating in the loss of more than seven thousand of our bravest troops, together with their gallant commander—all sacrificed in an enterprise conceived without plan, combination, or foresight, without a single possible advantage, and as ill-timed as misdirected.

The wisdom of Parliament decided otherwise, and after a debate, in which Lord Grey was fairly supported by Lord Moira, and feebly by Lord Erskine, his motion was defeated by a considerable majority, and it was solemnly decided that the projectors and conductors of the campaign deserved the confidence of the country, and were the most fitting men to be intrusted with the conduct of its affairs.

Connected with these disastrous times there was no subject which more deeply interested and affected both Lord Grey and myself than the conduct of the Government in regard to Sir John Moore. His judgment and skill were only surpassed by his unconquerable valor; nothing was more remarkable than the matchless self-denial which on all occasions rendered his own interests subservient to his country's good, and concentrated all his faculties in her service, making him a bright example to the most famous warriors of after-times, when the wretched intrigues that sought to keep him in the background, or to crush him, had passed away, but had not been forgotten, when in future times it would be remembered that the hero of Corunna had fought no vain battles, had lost no trophies, no captives, had abandoned no hospitals to the enemy, had yielded no post of danger to feeble allies. Yet this was the man who, endowed with all the qualities that constitute the most fitting leader of armies, having successfully held the chief command in Sicily and in Sweden, was placed under officers one of whom had never served in the field as a general.

TO EARL GREY.

"Temple, June 19, 1809.

"MY DEAR LORD GREY,—I write rather to ask how you and Lady Grey are than from having much to communicate. Is it true that you are going to Scotland? and shall you be there, or in Northumberland, when our Circuit passes through your part of the country? Also, will you allow me to give Malthus (population) a few lines of introduction to you when he passes by Howick, in the course of July, on his way to Scotland? He writes the *serious* articles on Ireland in the 'Edinburgh Review.'

"Of the Hollands you have probably heard lately. By a letter from Lord John Russell to the duke, it appears that they refused to come home in the Ocean, because she sailed with convoy, and are waiting for the ship which carries Lord Wellesley out. She has not yet sailed; nor has Wellesley, I believe, left town; so that if the Hollands are home in a month or six weeks, it is as much as can be expected.

"One is disposed to doubt this story of the King of Prussia coming forward; he is a weak, undecided character, and he must be certain that, if he fails, he will lose not only the kind of crown he now has, but his very livelihood. —— thinks it is not to be expected, and he is rather good authority: he saw Count Munster on Saturday, who knew nothing about the reports in circulation (which is pretty decisive as to them); and as for Ompteda coming over (the ground with many for believing those reports), the reason of it is his brother having lately gone mad, who is in the German Legion, and Ompteda comes to look after his affairs.

"What do you think of the late victory? for victory it certainly was, and a pretty considerable one. If it had been decisive, however, what possibility was there of Bonaparte keeping his *tête du pont*, and being enabled to rebuild his bridges?* The Austrian bulletin is universally admitted to be a fabrication. Stahremberg (who has never been much elated with the news) denied it from the first; and Lord Liverpool

* In reference to the war on the Danube, and the capture of Vienna by the French in May, 1809.

told Scarlett the other day that they knew it to be a *French* fabrication. This seems to be rather a refinement.

"If the victory has not been so decisive as of itself to turn the fortune of the campaign, it should seem that upon a series of subsequent operations Bonaparte is much more likely to get the better in the majority of instances. But it is no small thing, and I am sure quite unexpected, to have seen any doubt arise upon the subject.

"What a pity it is that we had not a large army in the Adriatic at the time, or even now! The talk of sending one somewhere continues; and I know that General Leith has received orders to go to Chatham (I think) and report himself to General Hope. Some weeks ago its destination was certainly the north of Germany. I suppose now they are waiting for the event of the approaching battle.

"The *cries* of the winter are wearing fast away, and I dare say the kind of apathy which always succeeds is already begun. I am confident Wardle is discovered to be no wizard, and that Cobbett is seriously damaged.* His court-martial business is much against him, and would probably have been much more if Sir George Yonge had behaved with tolerable fairness and prudence.

"You promised to put down any thing that suggested itself as hints for some new Plymleys. I think Sydney Smith will still fulfill his promise to me on that score, though his soreness upon the attacks lately made in the 'Quarterly Review' may rather indispose him at present. I forgot to mention that General Murray is coming (if not come) home from Portugal. His wife says it is because nothing will be done in Portugal for some time; but others ascribe it to pique against Wellesley. However, if active operations were likely soon to take place, he could scarcely come away for such a reason. Believe me ever with the greatest esteem, most faithfully yours, H. BROUGHAM."

"Howick, June 24th, 1809.

"MY DEAR BROUGHAM,—I am much obliged to you for

* Colonel Wardle, now less known than Cobbett, was celebrated as the promoter of the inquiry into the conduct of the Duke of York.

your letter of Monday last. We certainly shall be at home at the time the Circuit passes this country. I have no thoughts of going into Scotland, and I hope you will give us as much of your time as you can in your way to the North. I shall be exceedingly glad to see Malthus.

"From what you say of the Hollands, nothing can be more uncertain than their return. Probably the ship that carries out Lord Wellesley will afterwards join Lord Collingwood. As I think the state of the Austrian war, whatever its ultimate result may be, likely for some time to prevent the sending any sufficient reinforcements to the French army in Spain, and this may very probably occasion a second retreat behind the Ebro, I shall not be surprised to learn that her ladyship has determined to stay where she is till after her accouchement, which I suppose you know is approaching. I had a long letter from Holland in answer to my speech, or rather to misrepresentations of my speech, in the newspaper. It contained, in my opinion, a great deal of false reasoning, and in some instances rested on falsehoods: upon the whole, it was nearly in the same strain as the defense of the ministers, though he imputes considerable blame to them; and I think it very lucky that he did not come home in time to announce any of these sentiments in Parliament. * * *

"Ever yours most truly, GREY."

TO EARL GREY.

"June 30, 1809.

"DEAR LORD GREY,—Lord Rosslyn having promised to write to you yesterday, I did not, but I find he has been prevented by interruptions of various kinds, though he certainly will to-morrow. He is to have the advanced guard, but does not expect to be off for some weeks. He denies both the Duke of York and Burrard, but I am disposed to believe they are still making a push for the former, although Lord Chatham is certainly acting as if he were the man, and nobody can imagine how the report of Burrard arose. Indeed it is universally disbelieved. Brownrigg's going as quarter-master-general certainly looks very like the Duke of York; but is there any expedition so certain of succeeding as to make it even tolerably safe for the present ministers to send him?

To be sure, Lord Chatham is much worse, but his failure would not hurt them so irretrievably. Lord G. Leveson is in the cabinet, and this is perhaps a douceur to Canning for giving up his opposition to Lord Chatham or the Duke of York. I have it from undoubted authority that he prevented them last year.

"The destination of the force is as uncertain as when I wrote last. I still think it must be liable to alteration from the next news of the Austrian operations; but it is probably calculated, in the mean time, for some specific object; perhaps Flushing and Antwerp. There are two battering-trains. Such a thing is surely most absurd, unless all possibility of making a diversion in Germany is at an end.

"Peace between Austria and France is much talked of, and certainly Stahremberg has been expressing great apprehensions of this. One should infer from such an extraordinary step (if it really is taken) that the late victory was much less considerable than it appears to have been. Charles Stuart (who is at Buda) writes the account which he had from the Primate of Hungary, who was in the battle. This makes it 35,000. Twenty generals disabled, seven killed, etc.

"It is very unsafe to infer much from Bonaparte's present inactivity. He did nothing for months after Eylau and Baylen.

"Malthus leaves Hertford to-day, and I suppose will call at Howick in the course of a week or ten days.

"I shall write again to-morrow or Monday.

"Believe me, etc., H. BROUGHAM."

TO EARL GREY.

"July 4, 1809.

"DEAR LORD GREY,—There are letters from H. Bouverie, dated Abrantes, June 17. They are stopped for want of money, and must remain there a week or ten days. Victor had just sent his baggage, etc., through Truxillo, meaning to retreat by that way to Madrid. I guess Wellesley will be well enough pleased to let him do so. They complain of Cuesta's obstinacy, but say his army is more respectable than any that had appeared among the Spaniards. Mellish had been with dispatches to him, and gives this account. You recollect what a bad one he gave of Silviera's, which is some reason for crediting his praises of Cuesta's.

"An intercepted dispatch to Joseph Bonaparte gives Junot leave to return to France, after he shall have fortified the bridge which commands Saragossa, planned a fort at Tudela, and sent all the spare artillery to France. This, with many of the other symptoms, looks like retreating to the Ebro again until things are settled in Germany.

"We are full of Wardle and Mrs. Clarke. Best,* I hear, denies the statements in Wardle's letter to the people, and says he wrote him (Best) a note during the trial, leaving the calling Dodd, etc., entirely to his discretion. But this looks so like madness in Wardle that I shall not believe it to be Best's story until I inquire further about it.

"Johnson the smuggler is about this expedition as well as Popham.† This makes for Flushing, etc., Antwerp being its destination.

"Lord Percy has been making a fool of himself at Cambridge, standing against the Duke of Gloucester as chancellor.

"H. Brougham."

TO EARL GREY.

"July 10, 1809.

"Dear Lord Grey,—Nothing further is known of the Expedition except that every body seems agreed that its destination can not be very distant, or its object likely to take a long time.‡ The orders are for each man to take two shirts only (one upon his back included), no women, aid-de-camps a single horse; short allowance of hospital stores, some say one pair of shoes only, but this I have not from good authority. One is disposed still to conjecture Antwerp and Flushing, though many talk of Brest. Browning leaves town on the 14th, and Lord Rosslyn thinks it can't sail for three weeks, as

* Sergeant Best, afterwards created Lord Wynford, 5th June, 1829. He was then Chief-justice of the Common Pleas.

† Captain Johnson, known as a daring adventurer, an ally of Lord Cochrane, and deeply concerned in the affair of the false news about the fall of Napoleon, for which Lord Cochrane suffered.

‡ The Expedition to the Scheldt, sometimes called the Walcheren Expedition.

they are waiting for those transports from Lisbon, for which a convoy had not been appointed on June 5th. The Duke of York's family are talking loudly against Lord Chatham's appointment, and they really have some reason.

"The trial of Wright *vs.* Wardle has excited great attention. Wardle says he is quite thunder-struck with the perjuries of Mrs. Clarke, etc., for that there is not, from beginning to end, a word of truth in the story. He is also outrageous against Best for not calling Dodd, and otherwise mismanaging his case. *We of the bar* generally have a bad opinion of a man's cause when he begins to throw the blame on his counsel; but Wardle is to make some public manifesto immediately, and to prosecute Mrs. Clarke, etc., for perjury. This will rather be funny, I think, but it will do Wardle more harm than it can do the Duke of York real good.

"Believe me truly yours, H. Brougham."

TO EARL GREY.

"July 12, 1809.

"My dear Lord Grey,—I am much obliged to you for your kind letter, by which I rejoice to find that you disbelieve in the reports of peace at Vienna. I have done so from the beginning, though I assure you it is the prevailing opinion here. My notion is that at present it would be too good for the Austrians. It would indeed be their salvation; and Bonaparte knows full well that he never could expect to see Vienna again if he left Austria at a moment when the regular troops have beaten him in the field, and the people in every quarter are in a state of insurrection against him. He must fight again, I should think; and if he is beat, it will go hard with him, though perhaps it won't be much worse than making peace at present. Negotiation will be always open, unless he is much more completely defeated than I fear we have any chance of seeing him. If he beats the archduke, he will *then* give him peace, but not such a one as he must give at present.

"The Russian army, according to General Bentham (now one of the Navy Board), consists of above 70,000. They are, of course, ill supplied and commanded; but when things are so nearly balanced, they may turn the scale.

"This foolish expedition, I find, you view in the same light in which every rational being must see it. Flushing and Antwerp are certainly the objects (unless some unexpected good news should come from Germany). I don't suppose there is much risk of its failing; but the loss of men will be considerable by the military operations, and the climate at the mouth of the Scheldt, I understand, is peculiarly fatal at this season. This will, at any rate, prevent the army from doing good afterwards elsewhere.

"A letter of Mellish to Ferguson gives a very favorable account of Cuesta's army—24,000 foot and 8000 cavalry. He saw them manœuvre, fire, etc., and speaks highly of them; but Cuesta, he says, is an obstinate, infirm old man. How many of the regiments he saw one does not know, and I dare say they showed him the best.

"Believe me ever yours most faithfully,

"H. Brougham."

TO EARL GREY.

"Carlisle, August 7, 1809.

"My dear Lord Grey,—H. Bouverie writes from Placenzia, July 12, that the French are moving towards them, and that Wellesley has been at Cuesta's head-quarters concerting measures for attacking them. Victor's force he states at less than in his last letter, but I can not see whether he calls it 30,000 or 40,000. However, from his saying that the event of the battle will depend on the Spaniards, and therefore must be doubtful, I conclude he means 40,000, for he says our army will amount to 28,000 when joined by Craufurd's brigade and the horse-artillery, which they are waiting for. Our advanced-guard was ordered to move to meet Victor.

"C. Stuart is arrived in town, much crippled with rheumatism, etc.* He talks most violently against the ministers for the whole of their conduct in Spain, and says that the article on Spain in the last 'Edinburgh Review' is so true an account of the case respecting Spain, that the resemblance can only have arisen from chance. He and I have long lived on

* See above, p. 74.

very intimate terms, both abroad (having travelled together) and at home; but we never agreed on any subject of politics, or indeed on any other; so this confession comes from him very reluctantly, and he makes it with a bad grace; but he promises to give me a great deal of information, to convince me both as to the behavior of our Government and the impossibility of any body knowing the Spanish question except by pure haphazard.

"I thought these things might interest you. I send in two separate covers an article on 'Reform,' which Jeffrey has written, but in which, though very able, he has committed some very great mistakes, I think.

"Believe me, etc., H. BROUGHAM."

TO EARL GREY.

"Appleby, August 10, 1809.

"DEAR LORD GREY,—Lord Rosslyn writes to me as follows: 'Many circumstances have concurred to render the reduction of Flushing much more difficult than I expected, and infinitely more so than was calculated upon. Huntley (who was destined for a separate service to secure the Island of Cadsand) has hitherto been unable to effect a landing, and I believe he has shown great good sense and discretion in not attempting it. My division is the only one left on board. They speculate on the reduction of Flushing in ten days, and I am persuaded that nothing can or will be attempted till that is over.' He adds that he expects to be in England before the middle of September, and that he has seen nothing hitherto to alter any opinion or view he had before joining the expedition. You know he had a very poor opinion of it.

"Ward is unexpectedly arrived in London, and says the Hollands were about to embark in the Lively. This agrees with Miss Fox's account. She had a letter from Lisbon of the 16th of July, saying they were to embark in the Lively the Wednesday following. I suppose they are now in England, unless some change of mind has again happened.

"Whishaw writes from town that no sort of elation is expressed at the capture of Walcheren, which was so confidently expected that it scarcely attracts the least attention.

"I shall be glad to hear what you think of Moore's correspondence, after you have had time to read it.* It gives a melancholy picture of the prospect in Spain, and I much fear the south is not greatly better. I expect to hear particularly about this from Charles Stuart.

"Ever most faithfully and sincerely,

"HENRY BROUGHAM."

TO EARL GREY.

"Lancaster, August 11, 1809.

"DEAR LORD GREY,—The following I copy from a letter I have just received from Charles Stuart: 'The whole of our misfortunes in Spain may be ascribed to the loss of the two precious months during which the French were behind the Ebro, when our ministers were solely occupied in discussions respecting that blockhead Sir Hew Dalrymple. During those months no communications took place with Spain. I never received one line from Government, and those beasts the Junta neither sought nor received advice. In short, Spain was as thoroughly forgotten as if it were at the bottom of the sea. I had indeed been told we should not interfere in the formation of the Government—a determination originating in the desire of ministers to shelter themselves from future blame in case of misfortune, and tantamount to the abandonment of a child at three years old by its parents, with directions to provide for itself in whatever mode it may think most expedient.'

"After some remarks on the necessity of our interfering, of which he maintains the whole Spanish nation would have highly approved, the letter proceeds:

"'Wellesley's victory is a great thing as far as relates to the abstract proposition of one Englishman beating two Frenchmen, but with respect to the Spaniards serves only to prove them useless allies in their present state. It will do little for Spain, or even for the security of our army, if he is not able to advance to Madrid, and to direct the population

---

* Narrative of the Campaign in Spain by the Army commanded by Lieutenant-general Sir John Moore, with original letters. By James Moore, Esq. London: 1809.

Reviewed by Lord Brougham, "Edinburgh Review," October, 1809, Article 14.

of that capital. Indeed he must go there if only to obtain provisions, horses, etc., whether to retreat or go forward. He will find nothing at Talavera. Marching forward is preferable, because if he retreats he must abandon wounded, artillery, etc., for want of means of transport. If he goes to Madrid, however, he must first drive the enemy from Toledo, and stand another action on the Guadarama, where they will probably make a last effort to save the capital. Having gained Madrid, he may retreat on La Mancha, if attacked by a superior force.

"'With respect to Austria, I fear she merely gives us breathing-time. I think Bonaparte will leave the emperor Bohemia, Moravia, and part of Austria; Poland, Hungary, and the south are probably gone. The archduke's miserable indecision has ruined that country; the soldier is good, the emperor excellent, but has not the courage to check the evils arising from his brother's influence. I am not quite sure that peace has taken place, though it probably will be the result of the present negotiations. My only hope rests on Stadion's continuance in office, and until I see his dismissal I shall be sure they have not complied with Napoleon's demands.* The emperor certainly opposed the armistice, but could not prevent it; indeed he appears to have had very little to say in the events, and subsequent to the affair of Wagram.'

"I thought this letter might interest you.

"Most faithfully yours, HENRY BROUGHAM."

FROM JOHN WHISHAW.†

"Saturday, August 19, 1809.

"DEAR BROUGHAM,—I am much obliged to you for your letter, which I have just received, and which was very acceptable, as I have been for some days very desirous of knowing your address, supposing the Circuit to be ended.

"The Hollands arrived last Saturday in good health and spirits, all of them looking very well, indeed much better for their journey. I went to them early this week, and am now there again, staying for a few days. Their views of Spanish

---

* Johann Philip Karl Joseph Stadion, Austrian statesman; born 1763, died 1824.

† See above, p. 259.

affairs are extremely rational—*i. e*, considerably desponding. They properly consider the question as in a great measure disposed of by the event of the Austrian war; but they think it will be a conquest difficult to be retained, and inconvenient and embarrassing to the conquerors. Except in Biscay and among the merchants in some of the port-towns, there is, properly speaking, no *French party*. But there is in many places a great languor and indifference, and disposition to side with the strongest party. Still there remains in the great body of the nation an excellent spirit, which deserves to be animated and called out by better leaders. The Junta appears to be feebleness itself, too numerous for an effective or strong government, and too few for any purposes of popular representation; for indeed they are in other respects altogether unfit. They are divided into committees of finance, war, interior government, etc., subject in important points to the control of the whole body. Old Jovellanos is an excellent and amiable man, of enlarged views and the most patriotic dispositions; but he is quite unfit, both by his temper and habits, for political management and intrigue—even that portion of it without which no government can be conducted.* His influence, of course, is not very considerable; and though there are some others, particularly Garay, the secretary of the Junta, and Calvo, of good talents and dispositions, with more activity than Jovellanos, yet, upon the whole, the *feebles* and procrastinators may be said to prevail. So much for their civil affairs. With respect to military talents, the want of them is sufficiently apparent in the whole scheme of their campaign, and almost in every battle that has taken place. Of all their generals, Blake, one of the most unfortunate, is supposed to be their best. Cuesta is much beloved by the soldiery, brave, and regardless of personal danger; but he is near seventy, of a violent temper, and of no military talents. They are anxious at Seville to get rid of him, and to supply his place by Albuquerque, a young man of high rank and great spirit, but without any military character.

* Don Gaspard Melchior de Jovellanos (or properly Jové-Llanos), born 1744, died 1811, a statesman and author. He translated part of Milton's "Paradise Lost" into Spanish. His name frequently appears in the political and literary correspondence of the time, though it is now nearly forgotten.

"With respect to Portugal I have heard them say little, except that the Government is most contemptible, and things in the most wretched state. The Spanish colonies in America are exceedingly well-disposed to the new order of things in the mother country (Buenos Ayres only excepted), and have furnished large supplies.

"The Hollands are no believers in the original treason of Morla, and the deep plan for delivering up Madrid, so much talked of in the account of Moore's campaign. He is a great coward, and was probably frightened into submission, and *afterwards* went entirely over to the French cause.* Charmilly also was a mere adventurer, and highly improper to be trusted by Frere, but no spy or traitor. In these opinions they were confirmed yesterday by Charles Stuart, who dined at Holland House yesterday. We had also at dinner the new Secretary at War (Lord Palmerston), who was silent and reserved, as became a Cabinet minister and man of fashion.

"But it was still apparent, notwithstanding his discretion and reserve, that they have no great hopes from the Scheldt expedition. It is generally understood that this is more a concern of the king than the ministry, his Majesty having been gratified with the nomination of the staff in return for his acquiescence in the appointment of Sir A. Wellesley to the chief command in Spain.

"Ward is returned to London, but I have not seen him, nor do I think myself sufficiently acquainted with him to put myself in his way. I hear that his accounts of Spain are very unfavorable; and he reports of Jovellanos (whom he met dining at Frere's) that he is 'about the standard of a second-rate Scotch professor.' This judgment alone would be decisive against him at Holland House; but there seemed previously to be a complete rupture between the parties. They say that he was only four days at Seville, passed the rest of his time in travelling to Grenada and other places, but saw no people except inn-keepers and muleteers. I am sorry to hear that the 'Edinburgh Review' joins against the sinking cause

* Don Thomas Morla, born 1752, died 1820, a Spanish officer, with an adventurous personal career, which subjected him to many accusations. A brief and distinct account of his strange career, by M. Adrien de Lafage, will be found in the Nouvelle Biographie Générale.

of the Reformers, who unfortunately (poor people) are very harmless and inefficient, and very unlikely to do much good or harm of any kind.

"Yours most truly, J. WHISHAW.

"P.S.—If you will let me know where you are to be found, I may possibly, if I hear any thing, send you a few lines before I leave town, which will be about the latter end of next week."

Soon after his return from Spain, I received from Ward the following letter:

FROM JOHN WILLIAM WARD.*

"1 Chesterfield Street, Sept. 14, 1809.

"MY DEAR BROUGHAM,—I should not have been so slow in answering a letter you wrote to me immediately after my return if I had known your direction. You were then upon the Circuit, and until you got fairly out of those borean regions, and quite clear of the company of Alan Park, there was no telling in what direction to fire a shot with any certainty of hitting you.† If indeed, during the late gales, I had seen any old lady sitting upon a broomstick, and riding in the storm, I should have considered myself as having found the safest, quickest, and most regularly *official* messenger, the proper Corréo di Gabinéte of your satanic majesty. But failing of that mode of conveyance, I was obliged to wait till I heard that you had at last ceased to walk to and fro upon the face of the earth, and had found, for a time at least, a resting-place. Waiving, however, for the present all discussion as to who is the evil principle, or rather, as to what is the form he now inhabits, we shall agree upon this at least, that there

---

* Afterwards fourth Viscount Dudley and Ward, Secretary of State for Foreign Affairs in Canning's Government in 1827, when he was created Earl Dudley.

† James Alan Park, Justice of the Common Pleas, author of the well-known standard law-book on Marine Insurance. The following rhymes used to be sung when his health was drunk on grand nights, on the Northern Circuit:

James Alan Park
Came naked stark
From Scotland;
Now hath he cares,
And breeches wears,
In England.

never was a moment when he was more triumphant. His second campaign in Spain, in which one would have imagined that it exceeded even his powers to persuade any dozen of the descendants of Eve (formed by his influence into a Cabinet) to engage—his advance into the heart of the country—his vision of a victory with which he deceived Sir Arthur at Talavera—*his* retreat without provisions through Portugal—and, above all, *his* grand expedition to Walcheren under *his own* general, my Lord Chatham—have, without a single exception, fulfilled his views, and carried his glory to the highest pitch. As to poor old Oromades, 'Il dort comme un ivrogne;' and I don't see any reason to hope that he will ever again cut the least figure in life.

"I have returned from Spain not confirmed in my original opinion about it, for it needed no confirmation—it could not be stronger; but astonished beyond measure that a contrary notion could ever have been entertained by a reasonable man. Were any well-educated person to assure me that, upon mature consideration, he believed in the story of the seven sleepers, I should not be more puzzled. And, doubtless, of all people the 'Ιβηροφίλοι are the least able to assign a reason for the faith that is in them. Of late, indeed, they have a little lowered their tone; and I understand from the Spartan general that it is now the fashion to say that though they can not, indeed, contend in the field with the French, and though Bonaparte will in all probability get military possession of the country, yet it will take him six hundred thousand men (I use words purposely, because if I employed numerals you might suppose I had in a hurry put a cipher too much) to accomplish it in the first instance, and half that number to retain what he has got afterwards. Now, my own opinion, I confess, is, that in a very short time he will be as completely master of the Peninsula as he is of Holland.

"The people of property will soon find out that it is much better to enjoy it under a new dynasty, and protected by the powerful arm of France, than to go on with a hopeless struggle under the auspices of such blockheads as for the most part compose the Junta.

"The people of talents will go, like O'Farel, Morla, and Cabarrus, to the highest bidder, which is sure to be the Government of France.* As to the populace, it will follow the higher orders, from which it never for long together estranges itself. As to the religion, it is always in the power of the French to bag the lower, and, of course, most numerous class of the clergy, by the spoils of the fewer and richer. Church property is very unequally divided in Spain, and the poor ecclesiastics look with envy and hatred at the wealth of the great bishoprics and overgrown chapters. Joseph, too, will probably go through some grievances, and pay some public respect to saints' relics, etc., such as will convince the people that he is a mighty good Catholic as well as a victorious and beneficent sovereign. Hatred, then, to the French is all that will remain as a principle of insurrection. Now, after all that has been said, this can not be a very violent feeling in a nation which allowed itself to be bequeathed, with almost as little ceremony as an old woman would bequeath her china jar, to the great-grandson of the King of France, only a century ago, and has continued ever since in most loyal obedience to him and his descendants.

"Besides, the French are great masters in the art of conciliation, which we hardly ever try, and in which we never succeed. By wise laws and a vigorous administration of them, they will ameliorate perceptibly the condition of every class of society. People soon acquiesce in an order of things from which they derive actual benefit; and I should not be at all surprised if in a couple of years the submissions were complete, Fernando VII. forgot, and the Junta and the English (who will have been long since sent to the devil) looked back to with nothing but contempt and dislike.

"Dry† is in London. He came over in the same ship with Lady Westmoreland; so you may easily imagine what discussions they must have had upon metaphysics and theology. He is, as usual, in a state of rampant atheism, teeming with publications, and completely satisfied with the wisdom and energy of his own diplomatic conduct. Adieu; I have twenty more things to say, but it grows late.

"Yours always very truly, J. W. WARD.

* François de Cabarrus, properly a native of France, was born in Bayonne, but connected with Spain, where he set his mark as a financier—born 1752, died 1810.

† Sir William Drummond.

"P.S.—From all I can hear, I am really inclined to think that there will be a partial change, and that my poor friend Castlereagh will be made a victim."

TO EARL GREY.

"Brougham, Sept. 17, 1809.

"Dear Lord Grey,—Charles Stuart tells me he has been urging Canning to look after South America, and received for answer from Bagot that nothing whatever in that quarter was in contemplation. Stuart is quite furious against them all—for nothing more than the Scheldt expedition and Wellesley, not on account of the event, but even if it had succeeded. He believes that they were persuaded by the Duke of Brunswick's acts to send the army to Hanover; however, according to Lord Rosslyn's account, that or any other scheme is now out of the question, the army being quite unfit for service.

"Lady Rosslyn (who is here) desires her love to Lady Grey and you. She expects Lord Rosslyn to arrive in town immediately. His plan is to set off for Scotland as soon as he has been at Court. He is particularly anxious to see you, which will prevent him from coming round by this place. So he will probably be at Howick soon after you get this letter.

"Most faithfully yours, H. Brougham."

The following letter is from Mr. Perceval to Lord Grey:

"Windsor, September 23, 1809.

"My Lord,—The Duke of Portland having signified to his Majesty his intention of retiring from his Majesty's service, in consequence of the state of his Grace's health, his Majesty has authorized Lord Liverpool, in conjunction with myself, to communicate with your lordship and Lord Grenville, for the purpose of forming an extended and combined administration.

"I hope, therefore, that your lordship, in consequence of this communication, will come to town, in order that as little time as possible may be lost in forwarding this important object; and that you will have the goodness to inform me of your arrival.

"I am also to acquaint your lordship that I have received his Majesty's commands to make a communication to Lord Grenville of his Majesty's pleasure.

"I think it right to add, for your lordship's information, that Lord Castlereagh and Mr. Canning have intimated their intention to resign their offices. I have, etc.,

"(Signed) SPENCER PERCEVAL."

To this Lord Grey returned the following answer:

LORD GREY TO MR. PERCEVAL.

"Howick, September 25, 1809.

"SIR,—I have this evening had the honor of receiving your letter of the 23d, informing me that, in consequence of the Duke of Portland's intention of retiring from his Majesty's service, his Majesty had authorized you, in conjunction with Lord Liverpool, to communicate with Lord Grenville and myself, for the purpose of forming an extended and combined administration; and expressing a hope that, in consequence of this communication, I would go to London, that as little time as possible might be lost in forwarding this important object.

"Had his Majesty been pleased to signify that he had any commands for me personally, I should not have lost a moment in showing my duty and obedience by a prompt attendance on his royal pleasure.

"But when it is proposed to me to communicate with his Majesty's present ministers for the purpose of forming a combined administration with them, I feel I should be wanting both in duty to his Majesty and in fairness to them, if I did not frankly and at once declare that such a union is, with respect to me, under the present circumstances, impossible. This being the answer which I find myself under the necessity of giving, my appearance in London could be of no advantage, and might at a moment like the present be attended with much inconvenience.

"I have thought it better, therefore, to request that you will have the goodness to lay my duty at the feet of his Majesty, humbly entreating him not to attribute to any want of attachment to his royal person, or to a diminished zeal for his service, my declining a communication which, upon the terms proposed, could lead to no useful result, but might be of serious detriment to the country, if, in consequence of a less decisive answer from me, any further delay should take place in the formation of a settled government. I have, etc.,

"(Signed) GREY."

FROM EARL GREY.

"Howick, September 26, 1809.

"DEAR BROUGHAM,—I hope you will have attributed my long silence to the true cause, my not knowing where to direct to you.

"Being uncertain whether you may still be at Aberystwith when this arrives there, I shall only write two lines. But I can not help thanking you for your letters, and telling you that I last night received a message, as you will before have heard reported. But as it contained only a proposal to treat with the present ministers on the ground of forming a combined administration, I did not hesitate in sending back an immediate and decisive refusal. I will send you a copy of Perceval's letter to me and of my answer, when I can be assured of their reaching you, if you wish to see them. Till then, also, I will defer sending back Whishaw's and Ward's letters. I have not time for more at present.

"Ever yours, GREY."

TO EARL GREY.

"Aberystwith, October 3, 1809.

"MY DEAR LORD GREY,—I received your letter last night, and am greatly obliged to you for the information contained in it. Had I known what the nature of P.'s letter was, I never should have entertained a moment's doubt as to the answer it was to receive. I confess I exult not a little in your victory over these miserable intriguers, whose folly is nearly equal to their meanness, and who seem to be quite as incapable of managing their own affairs as of governing the country. The motive of their message it is very difficult to unravel, but (as it is utterly impossible that they could have any hopes of their wretched offer being listened to) I presume it may have been sent in compliance with the injunctions of the Court, whom they may have made to believe that it was a fair offer of a coalition. The answer will open their eyes on this point; and indeed it is not impossible that the courtiers may have joined in the offer without much hope of your accepting it, meaning to come down with other terms should you refuse. One thing is clear, with the country it can do them nothing but harm if they stop short in their advances, and try to go on themselves. It is (and must be universally considered so) a plain avowal of their weakness.

"And now (supposing there is no further advance made to you) the difficulties which led to the message are at least as great as before. I am no believer in Perceval and Eldon taking in Lord Melville; and the former, at least, must be averse to Wellesley, from his saint connections. But even if those feelings are overcome by the impending danger of leaving their offices, what do they gain? Lord Wellesley is useless in the House of Lords, or nearly so; and neither he nor Lord Melville brings them one atom of weight in the House of Commons. Their grand difficulty is the loss of Canning, which can only be supplied in one way—viz., by Canning repenting and agreeing in some patch-work with Melville or Wellesley. My conviction of his baseness is so entire that this would not surprise me, nor would it, I own, greatly spleen me. I dread infinitely his being joined with the opposition, and am the more alarmed, because I hear that Lady Holland is intriguing very busily to bring this about. When I recollect her bitter hatred of him, this amuses me greatly. She is much under Lord G. Leveson's influence, and I doubt that he and Frere will endeavor (if it's Canning's plan to join the Whigs, or to threaten such a junction) to make some offer come from Holland House. I wish you would keep yourself and the Hollands on their guard against any such danger. If any thing were wanting to expose Canning's utter shabbiness, his late conduct is sufficient. It is a fact that he was dirty enough to take Lord G. Leveson's seat in the cabinet as the *price* of holding his tongue about Castlereagh for three or four months. This seems ground for impeachment with respect to the public; but what shall we say of his duplicity, his vile falsity towards Castlereagh in this whole business?

"Believe me ever most faithfully, H. BROUGHAM."

FROM EARL GREY.

"Howick, October 10, 1809.

"MY DEAR BROUGHAM,—I received your letter last night, and now inclose, according to your desire, in this and another cover, copies of Perceval's letter, and of my answer and Lord Grenville's. You may keep them, as I have other copies.

"I agree entirely in all the opinions you express of one of the ex-ministers. Holland is not acquainted with them, and I hope will be on his guard against such intrigues as you describe.

"I have thought the line taken by the 'Morning Chronicle' in some instances rather impolitic. I can see no advantage to be derived from sparing one more than another, either of the ministers who stay in or of those who go out; and as to the grounds of the quarrel, I think it impossible for any man possessed of honorable feelings to deny that Castlereagh was greatly injured by the conduct of his colleague.

"I am inclined to believe that Perceval was foolish enough not to be aware of the certain rejection of his proposal, and that he made it in the hope and expectation that it might lead to negotiation at least, which, if unsuccessful, might furnish him with a successful appeal against us to the public. His courage in taking upon himself the government at such a time and under such circumstances, I confess, surprises me; but I am not one of those who think it must be destroyed at the meeting of Parliament, and who doubt whether it can last even till that time. It is not weaker than Addington's appeared to be; and there is neither a powerful and united party under a Fox in the opposition, nor the secret intriguers in correspondence with a Pitt in the ministry.

"I expect Sydney Smith here in a few days.

"Lady Grey desires to be most kindly remembered to you.

"I am, dear Brougham, ever yours most truly,

"GREY."

FROM EARL GREY.

"Howick, October 22, 1809.

"DEAR BROUGHAM,—I have to thank you for two letters since I last wrote.

"You already know how completely I agree with you with respect to the most conspicuous of the ex-ministers. If there is any disposition towards him in any of our friends (I rather think you have been mistaken with respect to Lady Holland), it can not be too soon or too strongly counteracted. The impossibility of our joining, without the greatest discredit on public grounds, a person so deeply responsible for the whole conduct with respect to America, and for the Spanish and Walcheren expeditions, not to advert to what he did both when we went out and at the commencement of the succeeding Administration, needs only to be stated to be universally felt and acknowledged.

* * * * * * *

"Why all this is suppressed in the 'Morning Chronicle,' and why, on the contrary, that paper seems rather to favor his cause, and is become the vehicle of his explanations, I can not conjecture. I am sure if it is intended to serve us, by gaining a new ally against the present ministers, it is, as I have already stated, as bad in policy as it is indefensible in principle.

"Indeed I think the leading articles in the 'Morning Chronicle,' though some of them, considering the view they took of the subject, have been well executed, have not in general taken the most advantageous ground. The impossibility, without a dereliction of all public principle, of joining those with whom not only we had not approached to any agreement, but with whom our differences were much increased by all that has happened since they became ministers, and who have now to render an account to the country for the series of crimes and follies which have disgraced and nearly ruined us, was, in my opinion, the ground on which our declining all communication was not only the most justifiable, but the plainest and the most easily understood and felt by the country. To all the other objections of our not being called upon personally by the king, etc., etc., there are answers more or less good, but to these there could be none. I have ventured to say this, because in one of your letters you gave a hint that in the interval of leisure from your professional business you might give some attention to these matters.

"I do not see that Perceval has yet made any progress in filling up the vacant offices. The appointment of * * * Till lately, that office, which is one of the most important, and requires great experience in the business to which it relates, was not made subject to party changes. But now we have a minister who is bold or unprincipled enough not only to put the Government in a state in which it can decide upon no one point, not even upon the retention or evacuation of Walcheren while our men are rotting there like sheep, but who ventures to commit the department on which our safety principally depends to the most incompetent hands. It really now looks as if Perceval would not be able to make out his arrangement; but ultimately, I am convinced, the Catholic question will furnish the king with the means of forming a government, which he may call his own. There are differences between any government that can now be formed on that footing and Addington's; but the latter was, in my opinion, dissolved ultimately, not so much by the power combined against it in Parliament, as by internal treachery and cowardice. GREY."

TO EARL GREY.

"October 28, 1809.

"MY DEAR LORD GREY,—I presume you take the 'Morning Chronicle;' but in case you don't, I may mention that there is a very excellent attack on Canning in to-day's paper, by whom I know not; but I *do* know that Perry has been undeceived about Lord Holland's unwillingness to have Canning attacked. Lord H. suspects *Sheridan* to have given the tone that has been so justly complained of.

"I have been writing for the 'Edinburgh Review' an article on Moore's Expedition; and if it is not a satisfactory exposition of the ministers and Frere, as well as of poor Moore's case, it is not owing to want of pains, for I have seldom felt more interested in any thing. I have been perpetually regretting that I had not any tolerable report of your speech, as, in fact, the subject is the very same. Had that speech been published, I should not have done much more than make great extracts from it. If you write soon to Lord Lauderdale, pray tell him how I am occupied, as an excuse for my not having written to him since I came to town. I am sure *with him* it will be a sufficient one. I have a letter from a friend of mine (Dr. Eyre) on the medical staff at Walcheren, dated October 19. He says the cold and dry weather for a short time made the sickness abate, but it returned with the fogs; and they sent home that day two thousand sick, including two physicians: he adds that the fever was too many for the seven physicians who remained, and that, without reinforcements, they must surrender the moment they are attacked. They expected six or seven thousand, chiefly Germans—an idea having gone abroad that *their* constitutions bear the climate better; but Eyre denies this, and affirms that a German regiment which they had suffered more than any other. The enemy's guns from S. Beveland had that morning fired on our vessels, and cleared the Sloe Passage of them.

"Perceval (as Erskine says of a higher personage) don't get on. Milnes, who was sent for, declined, saying his friends thought him too young, but in reality because he had a very well grounded fear of taking an office and being forced to speak. Castlereagh has been offered an English peerage, presidency of the Council and Board of Control, all together, and *refused.* There was a story yesterday that Rose was to be Chancellor of the Exchequer, and 'young Saunders' to go back to the Board of Control. It is extremely gratifying to your friends to perceive the universal satisfaction which your refusal has given, and the very great increase of popularity and influence arising from it. The *manner* of it has been especially approved of, and that in quarters and in parts of the country where you would least suspect it. I am confident if Lord Grenville had maturely weighed the thing he would have done the same, but one of you having done so, it was of less consequence.

"In haste, H. BROUGHAM."

TO EARL GREY.

"Temple, October 30, 1809.

"DEAR LORD GREY,—When I wrote the other day, I believe I forgot to mention what Stahremberg says about the treaty. It seems when Bonaparte first made his propositions, they were peremptorily rejected, the emperor saying he had 300,000 men in arms. Stahremberg thinks, had the terms been insisted on, he certainly would have fought, and almost as certainly would have been beaten. The terms were, the cession of Carniola, Carinthia, and Styria, Trieste (of course), and Fiume, a very little of Austria, and some circles of Bohemia (to Saxony). If he has got much better terms, as may be presumed, he is not badly off, every thing considered; for I own I was prepared to see him cut down at least as much as the foregoing terms amount to.

"There is no news, that I have heard at least. The opinion seems to gain ground of Wellesley taking office. I own I have a greater opinion of his cowardice, but after the name of the thing for a few weeks he would be no great accession to them.

"My compliments to Lady Grey, and congratulations on Lady Hannah's marriage;* and believe me ever most truly yours, H. BROUGHAM.

"P.S.—If any thing particular occurs to you as to the Spanish question and Moore, pray give me a note of it, as it won't be too late to insert it."

TO EARL GREY.

"Temple, Nov. 9, 1809.

"MY DEAR LORD GREY,—I have heard nothing new since I last wrote. I suppose the Hollands have told you that Canning is quite in despair at Lord Wellesley having abandoned him. The Duke of Portland also declared off—it is believed by some with the intention of rejoining the Cavendishes. Lord Wellesley said, in the usual East Indian style, that 'he could not subscribe to the notion of the First Lord of the Treasury being in the House of Commons, as that would be signing his own degradation,' or some trash of this sort. Canning seems now only to have Lord Granville Leveson, and Dog Dent, who is barking very loud.

"You have also heard, I suppose, that Perceval wrote to

* Hannah Althea, married first, in 1807, to Captain Bettesworth, killed in action off Bergen, May, 1808; and, secondly, in Oct., 1809, to Edward Ellice, afterwards Secretary to the Treasury in Lord Grey's Government, 1830.

the Duke of Northumberland, and offered Lord Percy a seat at the Treasury, which mollified the duke, though he declined it.

"Lord Grenville seems to have some chance at Oxford. The letters to-day are flattering. It is said Eldon can't succeed, and this is itself a victory.

A strange report of peace, and Lord Wellesley going to Paris, has been circulated for some days, and I hear it begins to be believed in the city. It seems impossible, but may arise from Bonaparte having made one of his usual offers at this stop in the war.

"Best moved for a rule for a new trial in Wardle's business to-day. It was with some difficulty granted, but this only brings the question of a new trial to a discussion, and I am satisfied it will then be refused. Some of his affidavits were material, but I should think Messrs. Dodd, Glennie, Sir Richard Phillips, etc., won't stand a cross-examination. In that case Wardle is better off without a new trial. The bar are now, I find, against him; and the judges, especially Bailey, shamefully and officiously so.

"Ever yours, H. BROUGHAM."

FROM EARL GREY.

"Howick, Nov. 11, 1809.

"MY DEAR BROUGHAM,—I have been longer than I ought to have been in acknowledging your last letters, for which my excuse must be that I have had, as I now have, little or nothing to say after having thanked you for them.

"I am delighted at your having undertaken the review of Moore's book, as, without a compliment, I know no person in every way so well qualified to do full justice to this discussion. Nothing occurred to me on this subject that I thought likely to be overlooked by you, or I would have written immediately. I take it for granted the infamous article in the 'Quarterly Review' will not escape you.

"Sydney Smith passed ten days here, and enlivened us extremely. I am only afraid that he found us extremely dull. He talks of writing something in the spring, and I hope he will not be too idle to keep his resolution.

"No previous speculation could have hit upon any thing

like the combination of the present ministry, yet I am not one of those who are so confident in the impossibility of its standing. As far as I can judge, the public feeling is not much attacked by it. It is true, people in conversation lament the present state of affairs, and speak of the ministers as entitled neither to respect nor confidence. But there it ends, and we gradually accustom ourselves to things when they have taken place, which at a distance we should have declared it impossible to submit to. The disasters of Spain and Walcheren are now talked of with the calmness of history; and if, at the meeting of Parliament, it shall be found that the business of the country has gone on under these men for three months in its usual course without any new calamity, I do not think you will see much disposition to take active measures for a change. Even if the state of the House of Commons should prove, as Castlereagh would say, unsatisfactory, I should not be at all surprised if the Court were to succeed, as I hear they already threaten, in appealing to the people—in which I see our friends the Catholics are doing all they can to assist them.

"I certainly shall be in town two or three weeks before the meeting of Parliament, which I reckon I shall be by leaving Howick the end of next month, or quite the beginning of January. In the mean time, pray let me hear what you pick up. Has Grenville any chance? Oxford must be much changed if he can surmount both the influence of the Court and the cry of No Popery. I am, dear Brougham, ever yours most truly, GREY."

TO EARL GREY.

"Temple, November 15, 1809.

"MY DEAR LORD GREY,—I received both your letters—indeed I am in the Albany almost every day. But I regret your having taken the trouble to write for the purpose of rectifying the mistake; and though I am delighted to hear from you, I should be very scrupulous about writing to you if I thought you stood on so much ceremony as to acknowledge the receipt of every letter or note. It is quite unnecessary.

"I have just heard that Lord Lansdowne died last night,

but I can not say whether it is so for certain. My authority is Taggart the apothecary.

"All our friends still talk of Lord Wellesley's coming into office as certain. I suspect it not to be quite certain. He may be scared by the view of things when he arrives, having hitherto had only Perceval's flattering account of it, and they may disagrée about the offices.

"I am sorry to hear you have the measles among you, though of a gentle kind. Believe me yours truly,

H. BROUGHAM.

"P.S.—I finished the review of Moore before term began, and am in daily expectation of the sheets, which I shall send you. The short notice of your speech, which you will find in it, is no sort of compliment, for I can appeal to many witnesses whether I did not admire it as much as possible at the time and in private.*

"Wardle has got (cunningly enough) a hold over the 'Morning Post.' He has commenced suits enough to ruin it, and keeps them hanging over its head.

"There are letters from Harry Bouverie of the 26th October. They speak slightingly at head-quarters of the Duke of Parque's affair."

TO EARL GREY.

"Nov. 16, 1809.

"DEAR LORD GREY,—The news of Lord Lansdowne's death, you see, is confirmed. He never expected to live longer than to about this time, since he was last attacked.

"His death makes the *ultimate* co-operation of Canning almost unavoidable. Indeed, take it how you will, that most disagreeable consummation is likely to happen. At first he must be attacked, no doubt, for the late campaign; but as soon as that is over he will vote and speak against the ministry, and that is *such* a step towards being with the opposition! Then a little delay, all the while acting together and

* Article on "The Conduct of the War" in the "Edinburgh Review" for October, 1809; reprinted in Contributions, 297. It is called the review on Moore because the first title at the head of the article is "A Narrative of the Campaign of the British Army in Spain commanded by His Excellency Lt. Gen. Sir John Moore, etc. By James Moore, Esq."

being civil. In short, nothing but your getting speedily into office can prevent a coalition of this odious sort. A year's opposition on the same benches would almost make it unavoidable.

"The shabby fellow has, I hear, laid the blame of the late business with Castlereagh on the poor Duke of Portland, now he is dead, and his sons say the statement is not fair. It must soon appear. I shall send it immediately under an office cover. Yours, in great haste,

"H. BROUGHAM."

TO EARL GREY.

"November 20, 1809.

"DEAR LORD GREY,—I inclose the article in this and two other covers. Do not take the trouble to return it. You will observe that it is very incorrectly printed, never having been looked over. It was sent me in case there should be any errata in the sums and dates. Not a word of news to-day, except that Lord Grenville's friends continue very sanguine. I had a singular confirmation of the account, which I must have mentioned some time ago, from Wellesley's army—viz., that the wounded and sick (1900 in number) were four days left to themselves before the French came up, Wellesley having, with a very unusual want of calculation and arrangement, supposed the French to be at hand. An officer just arrived, whom I examined on this point, broadly denied it altogether; and on asking him more particularly, he said they left Talavera on the 3d, and they received letters dated the 5th, which stated the French to be twelve leagues (forty miles) off. By inadvertency he had forgotten that this exactly proved my statement. Had not a dépôt of chocolate-cakes been found, the wounded must have starved, for the Spaniards left them to themselves.

"A friend of mine (physician to the forces) is just come from Walcheren. He says 7000 have been brought over sick, and 5000 sick remain. Fifteen hundred are *nominally* fit for duty, but half of them can barely crawl about; and on the jubilee they mustered without firelocks, from weakness.

"H. BROUGHAM."

FROM EARL GREY.

"Howick, Nov. 22, 1809.

"MY DEAR BROUGHAM,—I am exceedingly obliged to you for your letter, and for the sheets of the 'Edinburgh Review,' which I received by the last post.* I read them to Lady Grey last night, and I am sure it will not be less gratifying to you to receive her applause than mine. I think it a clear and excellent exposition of all the transactions of the campaign. If I were disposed to criticise severely, I should perhaps say that it was better as a political paper than as a critical review; but if this does not interfere with the general object of the publication, the objection is of no importance. There is on· point on which, as I believe you are aware, we are perhaps not quite agreed—I mean on the policy of beginning in Portugal. I still am inclined to think that *that* was the best operation, if it had been properly and rationally conducted. There is one other point, too, on which I could have wished you had been fuller, and that is on what is the strongest plea of the ministers—viz., that the diversion created by Moore saved Spain at the time, and afforded the means of all the subsequent resistance that has been made. Nothing, in my opinion, can be more false than this. It did, indeed, create a diversion, which drew off Bonaparte with his main force for three weeks or a month. But being then free from all uneasiness with respect to any British army, which for the purposes of the campaign was annihilated, he had *champs libre* for his further operations against the Spaniards; and he would have made short work if he had not been called off by Austria. This, in truth, was the real diversion. These are, however, minor objections, not worth the paper I have wasted on them, particularly when the whole is so good. By your compliment to me I feel much gratified, being confident that it is sincere, though I must attribute it more to your partiality than to any merit of my own.

"What you say of the situation of Canning is too true. The evil, however, is, I trust, at some distance; and, contrary to the usual maxims of prudence, I am in this case unwilling to look at it before it forces itself upon me.

---

* See p. 329, note.

"By-the-way, I must revert to the Spanish business to state a fact which I wish I had known before your review was finished. It is now ascertained that Lord Wellington's army was starving in the midst of plenty. The expression used to me from the most indisputable authority is, that there were provisions in the country, not only for an army of 30,000 men, but for the host that Sir Robert Wilson advanced near Madrid, where he found abundance of every thing, and the same when he retreated through a country which had been twice passed by British and French armies. The fact is, that small patrols of ten and twelve men—too small to attract notice, but sufficient to keep back the peasants—scoured the country, and the consequence was what you have seen with respect to our army. This, it is true, is not saying much for Lord Wellington; but I am quite convinced of the fact, and you probably will not find much difficulty in believing it, after what you have told me about the sick and wounded.

"I am very anxious to see Canning's amended statement. Lady Grey desires to be kindly remembered to you. I am, dear Brougham, ever yours most truly, GREY."

TO EARL GREY.

"Temple, November 29, 1809.

"MY DEAR LORD GREY,—I wrote you a few lines relative to Wardle's business. I find the impression very general against him, which, from my dislike of him and his whole gang, I do not at all lament. He seems to be a shuffling fellow as well as a great coxcomb, and his political conduct is of the very worst description, founded on trick and quackery, and ultimately doing good only to the ministry by weakening all effectual opposition.

"Talking of shuffling naturally brings to one's mind Canning. It is confidently said that his letter to Lord Wellesley, lying for him at the office, will prevent Lord Wellesley from joining the ministry. I don't quite think so, though I can not help fancying that Lord Wellesley's taking office is not quite so certain as the ministers suppose. He has not seen their whole case, for he has had it only from themselves, and must find them much weaker than they represent themselves. If this does not make him shy of joining them, it will at any rate, one should think, make him extravagant in his terms, and lead to more squabbling and bargaining.

"I dined yesterday at Kensington, and the princess produced Canning's statement, which was read aloud, and pretty fully discussed. She affirmed it was quite satisfactory, and vindicated Canning entirely; and asked me bluntly enough if I did not think so too; which obliged me to say I thought it quite the contrary, and that it left Canning altogether in the wrong. Drummond very gallantly came to my assistance, and Lord Henry Fitzgerald took the same side as far as he durst. The only other person there, Lady Charlotte Lindsay, was of the same opinion, and the princess had all the defense to herself. She abuses every one of the ministers, chiefly Eldon, Lord Liverpool, and Lord Camden, and is canvassing for Lord Grenville as hard as she can.

"Canning's statement is plain, and not either clearly or forcibly written. It is carefully castigated by some discreet person, who has kept out every thing like a *Canningism.* It praises the Duke of Portland in extravagant terms; among other epithets it calls him a *great patriot.* But this is general, and in the detail it throws much of the concealment on him. Canning positively denies that he ever wished Castlereagh to be turned out, and asserts that he only wished for a change in the War Department, or rather in one branch of it. He was put off from day to day by his colleagues, who proposed various expedients, to which he successively agreed—first, that part of the war correspondence should be transferred to the Foreign Department, and the Board of Control joined to what remained of Castlereagh's office; and that among other parts of what remained under Castlereagh, should be comprehended the Scheldt expedition. To all this Canning agreed, though he thought it might not prove 'satisfactory to the public feeling,' meaning, I suppose, the Board of Control part of it, after the recent business of the writership. Soon after this, upon pressing the execution of the above arrangement, they told him they had thought of another which would be better. He does not say what, but he agreed to it. On pressing this, he was again told that they had given it up, and recurred to the first plan, to which he again agreed; and so on they went, putting him off from time to time. One plan was that Lord Camden was to resign, and Castlereagh to have his place; and it *was proposed to Canning* that Lord Wellesley should have the War Department in that event, he (Lord Wellesley) having been detained in England by illness. Once the king ordered him to say nothing. In short, Canning must, at the very least, admit that he behaved with the utmost possible weakness; but even that would not do, for he can't account for his never having written to Castlereagh himself; nor can he explain the manifest inconsistency of making such a fuss, God knows why, about turning Castlereagh out of the management of some part of the war, and consenting to his conducting the most important part of it; for it is remarkable that he acquiesced in the plan which left the Scheldt business in Castlereagh's department, and asked for no other arrangement. This statement is not to be published. If I can get a copy I shall send it, but I scarcely expect it. They say they are resolved it shall not get into the newspapers; but I don't see how they can prevent this. In a few days you will probably see it in that shape.

"Give my best remembrances to Lady Grey, and Lady Rosslyn (if she is with you when you get this); and believe me ever yours most faithfully,

"H. Brougham."

"Mrs. Bouverie says they have had a man from Oatlands, and another from Windsor, lately at Woolbeding, and the fashion of *both* places is to talk of you in the most extravagant manner."

TO EARL GREY.

"Nov. 30, 1809.

"My dear Lord Grey,—As the statement was in all the newspapers, I did not send you one. I am extremely gratified, indeed, with what you say, and no less with what Lady Grey is good enough to think of the article about Sir John Moore, having the greatest possible respect for her judgment and taste, in common with all who know her. I entirely agree with you about the diversion; indeed it is quite manifest from the dates. The Hollands, though in general approving much of the article, object on this ground, that they consider the diversion to have saved Spain. *Nobody* agrees with them, and I have given notice that I am going down to battle it with them next Saturday. I have not seen any of them for many weeks, but received a letter to the above effect. I was so anxious to supply the omission pointed out by you (which is really a material one), that as soon as it struck me I wrote to Jeffrey, but it was too late.

"Lord Wellesley *does* take the Foreign Office. This Drummond has just had from Hamilton (the Under-Secretary) at the office. They were not sure, however, for Lord Harrowby was to have gone back had he refused. The king not coming to the levee yesterday looks *monstrously* like some *hitch* in the intrigue: and I guess Lord Wellesley will make terms about the distribution of offices, which some folks won't like—*e. g.*, his brother in the War Department.

"I was at the annual election of the Royal Society to-day, which generally brings together a very courtly set. The alteration of tone was very striking. Every one talked of the new ministry as mere shift, and it is hard to say whether Canning or his late colleagues were most blamed.

"Believe me yours truly, H. BROUGHAM."

TO EARL GREY.

"Temple, Dec. 4, 1809.

"MY DEAR LORD GREY,—I have just seen two letters from Lord Blantyre to Charles Stuart (his brother), whom I will desire to send them to you to-morrow. The army at Badajos is, I think, as badly off as that at Walcheren. They buried seven hundred in two weeks, and the sickness increased on them. Blantyre's regiment, which is not strong (42d), had two hundred and thirty sick and ten officers, and buried fourteen in a week. Their melancholy is great, and no one can figure the reason for their lingering there, as there are healthy positions in the neighborhood. Blantyre is far from being either factious or croaking, and is one of the most judicious and honest men I know. Indeed I have the greatest regard both for his opinions and himself, and trust his account implicitly from knowing him well.

"The article on Moore, I most sincerely rejoice to find, is doing some good. It is very popular, and is giving infinite offense to the Canning school; but Lord Harrowby stands up for it in a surprising manner, considering who are attached to it. The Hollands have expressed much satisfaction at its *fair* treatment of Frere. His case must be very deplorable when that article is thankfully received by his defenders. I take it for granted James Moore won't be satisfied, because scarcely any one in his situation would be so with any thing except unmixed praise; but I am convinced the ground taken in the statement alluded to is the best for his brother's defense. But I wish you could learn what Lauderdale thinks, and whether he is satisfied, for he is a warm defender of Moore. I should like to know his feeling about it.

"Ever yours truly, H. BROUGHAM."

FROM EARL GREY.

"Howick, Dec. 9, 1809.

"MY DEAR BROUGHAM,—* * * Waithman, I see, has been attacking me, and, as usual with those gentlemen, on a ground previously formed by their own misrepresentation.* I wish there had been some friend of mine at the meeting to have told them that I was quite as much at war with the patriots of this class in 1792 as I am now, and equally denounced by them; that this did not prevent me, nor would it now, if, through their aid, a dangerous attack was aimed at the liberty and safety of the people, from standing forward in defense of the law and constitution; and I should only expect in return for it what I received in that instance—great professions of gratitude at the time, and another denunciation on the first opportunity; and that in the very speech, and, I believe, the very sentence, to which Waithman alludes, as you probably may remember, I professed the same attachment to the cause of moderate and constitutional reform which I had always manifested, and censured only the fashionable cant, which appears to me equally irrational and unprincipled; that there is no difference in public men, and no advantage to be expected from any change of ministers.

"Lauderdale has never mentioned to me your article in the 'Edinburgh Review;' but I think it impossible that he should

* Waithman, the popular alderman. His name is frequent in the newspapers of the period, but has dropped from the biographical dictionaries.

not admire it, and, as a friend of Moore's, that he should not be, upon the whole, extremely gratified by what you say of him. I have, however, put the question to him directly, and will let you know his opinion. I agree with you in thinking that indiscriminate praise is seldom advantageous, as it is hardly ever just, and that poor Moore's reputation is much more effectually served by a fair and candid discussion of the whole question—not supporting the points on which his conduct may appear somewhat doubtful—than it could have been by unqualified panegyric. Admiring Moore as I do in the highest degree, and thinking that what has appeared has proved him to be not only one of the best officers this country ever produced, but as a man to have possessed the most amiable heart combined with a lofty mind and independent spirit, I do not feel at all disatisfied with the manner in which you treat the question of his advance from Salamanca. I should certainly have been disposed to give more weight to the motives which determined him to take that fatal measure as being such as it was almost impossible for human nature to resist; and perhaps the cause might have been a little more pointedly fixed to Frere's interference, by showing the very moment almost at which his resolution appears to have been changed; for on the morning of the 5th he wrote to Baird that he continued his intention of retreating; and afterwards, when in the course of the same day he sent his counter-orders, he expressly states in his letter to Baird that, notwithstanding his doubts of the resistance of the Spaniards, he feels himself the more bound to give it a trial, as he has just received a representation from Frere against the retreat. * * *

"I am, dear Brougham, ever yours most truly,

"GREY."

TO EARL GREY.

"December 14, 1809.

"MY DEAR LORD GREY,—I have just seen Drummond, who was with Lord Wellesley the night before last on diplomatic business, and he talked for an hour against the whole management of Spanish affairs, which, he added repeatedly, 'I shall state in *the* Parliament' (cursed coxcomb!) This, however, is a new proof that Canning and he are not one.

The Princess of Wales yesterday abused the Wellesleys much —another proof. They say only Perceval will be in Parliament at the opening; but that is saying only their whole strength will be there.

"I forgot to say t'other day, in answer to your last letter, how well I remembered the passage in your speech alluded to. I have repeated it a thousand times in answer to the mountain; but I think them excessively unfair and even tricky in their way of stating things, and one can't help recollecting that when you were in office they said nothing of this kind.

"Creevey talks very moderately and candidly about Wardle's affair. He seems to think the execrable speech of Alley may have had an effect against him, and that his character may be somewhat bettered by the argument on the writ of error in the former action. It certainly may; for bad as Wardle's case seems to be, I am convinced it was not so desperate as that first of asses made it; and no doubt the people at large will be staggered by the dilemma that either Wardle is in the right, or he is guilty of about a hundred gross and willful acts of perjury. However, he is irreparably injured. Last night at ten, Lord Grenville's friends at Oxford were very sanguine. This is the bulletin at Sir Watkin's. I bet on Lord Eldon, for the reasons mentioned in my last.

"Believe me yours faithfully, H. Brougham."

CHAPTER IX.

HOME POLITICS.

Congratulations on the Election of Lord Grenville as Chancellor of Oxford. —Influence of the "Catholic Claims."—Question of going into Parliament. —Conflicting Claims of Law and Politics.—Duke of Bedford's Offer of a Seat.—Accepts, and is returned for Camelford.—First Speech on Whitbread's Motion against Lord Chatham in reference to the Scheldt Expedition.—Flogging in the Army, and Case of the Hunts.—Jeffrey and the "Review."—Lord Erskine.—The Regency Question.—Ministerial Difficulties.—To serve under Lord Grey on a "Supposed Event."—John Archibald Murray.—The Peninsular War.—Seat for Camelford no longer available, and Question of contesting Worcester in the "Popular" Interest.—Prospects of Continental Politics.

HAVING just received from Oxford the result of the contest for the chancellorship, in which Lord Grenville defeated Lord Eldon and the Duke of Beaufort, I lost no time in communicating the joyful intelligence to Lord Grey.

TO EARL GREY.

"December 15, 1809.

"Lord Grenville, 406
Lord Eldon, 393
Duke of Beaufort, 238

"Grenville's, chiefly non-residents; Eldon, fellows who never leave Oxford, and have no influence.

"DEAR LORD GREY,—I give you joy; never was any victory more important or more ominous to the Court. It is better than a majority in Parliament, because it is more permanent and general; it gives 'No Popery' a death-blow; Toryism and *twaddle*, and illiberality of every kind, such a shake as it can scarcely recover; it will even make Oxford a more liberal place, and affect the minds of those who are educated there for years to come. Perhaps the Church *is* now in some danger; its influence, hitherto exerted always for the worst purposes, will now be diminished or turned to good account. This victory is felt, from what I can perceive, by both parties equally.

"I forgot to say that the Duke of Cumberland called three times on Courtenay (son of the bishop), who stood neuter, to persuade him to vote for Lord Eldon, but he did not.

"Believe me yours, etc., H. BROUGHAM."

TO EARL GREY.

"December 16, 1809.

"DEAR LORD GREY,—C. Stuart (Blantyre) is just arrived in my chambers from Oxford. The joy is unbounded; the hurrahs were quite indecent in the room. The Eldonites had the mob *rather* with them; and the Bishop of Oxford and others were insulted by 'No Popery' proceedings in the streets. So sure were the Eldonites of carrying it that they had their letters of congratulation written, and blanks left for the numbers. Mills, the messenger, was in waiting to carry the news to Windsor. Christ Church has 239 votes; of these actually voted 184; of which for Grenville 113, Eldon 38, Beaufort 28.

"You know how unpleasant such a symptom must be at Court. The new dean, after promising to be neuter, exerted himself against Lord Grenville. Stuart saw a letter from the Duke of Cumberland's aid-de-camp to a voter stating that 'he was ordered to say that the Duke would consider himself as laid under the greatest personal obligations by his voting for his most particular friend Lord Eldon; that he would be considerably obliged by his remaining neuter, if he could not possibly vote for Eldon; and that he would always be ready to show his gratitude in either case.' The man (Cook of Yorkshire) voted for Lord Grenville, and wrote a short and cool answer. This is one of many instances; it makes the triumph more complete. The Duke of Beaufort's friends rejoiced almost as much as if their candidate had won; and one of the Somersets told Stuart that, though they might not have voted for Lord Grenville, nothing on earth could have made them vote for Eldon.

"Yours ever, H. BROUGHAM."

TO EARL GREY.

"Woburn Abbey, January 2, 1810.

"DEAR LORD GREY,—I have this moment received your letter, and I hasten to assure you that I did not misunderstand the motive of your letter to Lord Ponsonby. I understood your opinions, as then expressed, to be confined to the question of taking office without having the power conceded to you — proposing measures for the settlement of the Catholic grievances—the more enlarged view you may take of the question is scarcely of less importance; and it is with extreme regret that I find myself obliged to differ with you as to the policy of bringing forward the Catholic claims *under present circumstances.* The fundamental principle on which the question itself rests is in no degree affected by the resolutions of the Prelacy, however much those resolutions may be condemned; and in conceding to the Catholic population of Ireland what we have always maintained they have a justly substantial right to demand, we do not preclude ourselves from guarding and protecting the Established Church by every possible security which its most zealous friends can require.

"I can not help thinking that if you refuse to bring before Parliament, and support with all your power, the petition of the Irish Catholics, you are throwing away one of the few remaining means you have left of saving the country in the very perilous crisis in which we are placed. If you irritate the Catholics of Ireland by refusing to bring forward their unanimous petition, they will not stop to inquire into the causes of that refusal; but the great body of the Catholics will look to France alone for that relief, which they will say is denied to them by every party in England. A refusal from Lord Grenville in particular would come under a very suspicious color, so immediately after his election to the Chancellorship of Oxford.

"I have written my opinion shortly, and in accordance with your desire. Ever truly yours, H. BROUGHAM."

Among all the friends whom I consulted on the, to me, difficult question, whether I should give up the profession of the law and take to politics, or attempt to combine the two, there was no one who took a greater interest in the subject, on whose judgment I more entirely relied, or whose opinion I valued more highly, than that of my esteemed friend Lord Rosslyn. Towards the end of 1809, I had an intimation that a seat might be offered for my acceptance by the Duke of Bedford. I stated this to Lord Rosslyn, with all the *pros* and *cons* that had occurred to me, and I received from him the following answer:

FROM THE EARL OF ROSSLYN.

"Edinburgh, January 7, 1810.

"MY DEAR BROUGHAM,—You impose upon me a very difficult task, for it is almost impossible to offer any advice or opinion without some preliminary explanations.

"You must first settle with yourself to what objects your inclination leads you, and how far your judgment will allow you to sacrifice solid advantage to the more brilliant allurements of power, and reputation, and distinction.

"I have no doubt that, if you continue to work in your profession only, you must make a great fortune, and come to the head of it, but, in so doing, you submit to great slavery, and you forego a great many of the greatest gratifications, to the enjoyment of which you are sufficiently alive. If you go into Parliament, and devote yourself to politics, which most probably you then will do, you have the most favorable opportunity opening to you from the present state of the House of Commons in general, and that of your own party in particular; and there is no office in the country to which you may not look in a short time without any presumption on your part, or any disposition to compliment on mine; but, in pursuing that line, you will probably be two-thirds of your life in opposition, and if your private fortune and expectations be equal to the expenses which now or hereafter you may wish to incur, you will, like Fox, be standing in the full enjoyment of high consideration and great fame.

"I have not overlooked the middle course to which alone your letter points, and to that I should less object if I thought you were sure of being able steadily to pursue it, and not to be seduced into abandoning the profession entirely by the persuasions of your friends, and the temptations which the present state of politics must hold out to your vanity and ambition.

"The business of the Cock-pit will remain, but that may depend upon the war. There are, however, causes enough to last through some years of peace—perhaps as many as we can reasonably hope to see in our time.

"The Circuit you will retain, and if you get to the head of it rapidly, which, if I am rightly informed, you may expect, the situation of solicitor-general opens to you easily, and with few competitors. It would be too long to enter into all the calculations and possibilities of legal promotion within a given time if your friends are in power; but it is obvious enough that, being once solicitor-general, all the rest is smooth and easy.

"With respect to the King's Bench, I know not how far Parliament will interfere—it did not with Dunning;* but I have generally observed that those who took great leads in Parliament have for the most part attached themselves to Chancery, and there certainly it did not much impede the business of Thurlow, or my uncle Chancellor Loughborough; but, on the other hand, the profits were less considerable than of those who worked hard in the King's Bench. You will go into Parliament with advantages that no modern lawyer has tried; with a fund of political and commercial information more than adequate to the possible demand upon it, and sufficient to weigh down all those with whom you may have to contend. Your occasional preparation for parliamentary business will therefore be easy, and occasion less distraction. You will certainly sacrifice something of profit. If you really adhere to the resolution of *continuing earnestly* to seek professional practice, and if you can keep to that steadily, I should have no difficulty in advising you to accept the offer. If, however, you feel uncertain of your

* John Dunning, a celebrated lawyer, born at Ashburton, Oct. 18, 1731; solicitor-general, 1767; member for Calne, 1768; April 8, 1782, created Baron Ashburton, and Chancellor of the Duchy of Lancaster, by Lord Shelburne; died August 18, 1783. He had married Elizabeth, sister of Sir Francis Baring, Bart., whose son Alexander, in consequence of this connection, took the title of Ashburton in April, 1835, Dunning's peerage being then extinct.

own powers of resistance, or likely to yield to the innumerable solicitations and temptations with which you will be assailed, I should think that every prudential consideration ought to deter you.

"In deciding this question, it does not appear to me that you determine for future offers as well as this.

"There can be no doubt, even if you refuse, that you may and will have other offers; but I am clear that if you refuse this, you ought not to accept for a long time any other; because, except your situation was materially changed, and you came into Parliament as solicitor-general, you never can take any seat under circumstances so favorable.

"You will now come in without any decided leader to the party, in a state of the House of Commons the most favorable to the display and the success of talents, with no very powerful opponent to bear you down; and with the opportunity (from the eagerness expressed by all your principal friends to have you there, perhaps more for their own purposes than considering your advantage) of seeming to sacrifice your own interest to the general cause of the party.

"It is always a great advantage, especially in your situation, to begin in opposition. If I did not begin to see a possibility of our friends getting into office, I should not hesitate to urge you to accept. For the interruption to your profession in your present state of practice, while you continue in opposition, I should not much fear, setting always against it the good to be derived from success and celebrity, which I rate very highly.

"To conclude, I would advise you to accept, forming and declaring your resolution to adhere to your profession, and your intention to attend as constantly as your legal avocations would permit, but not beyond that point.

"You have what I advise; but probably you will have decided before you receive this. I have only to add, that when you become Secretary of State, it will be prudent to *seal* your dispatches. Your letter came to me open, and certainly unmarked by wax or wafer. Yours truly, R.

"H. BROUGHAM, Esq., Albany, London."

The following is an extract from a letter, dated January

2, 1810, from the Duke of Bedford to Lord Grey: "I write in very great haste, for they are waiting for me to go out shooting. The subject is one on which I am so very anxious that I could not delay writing for a single day. I expected Lord Ponsonby here to shoot, but he remained in town to see you. If you are disposed to come and look at us when you have secured a house, seen Lord Grenville, and found a leisure day or two on your hands, you will find us here till towards the meeting of Parliament; and, of course, delighted to see you.

"Ever yours very faithfully, BEDFORD.

"I hope soon to be able to offer the vacant seat at Camelford to Mr. Brougham; but do not mention it at present."

Having written to the Duke of Bedford, and with every expression of gratitude accepted his offer of a seat, I received from him the following very handsome letter:

FROM THE DUKE OF BEDFORD.

"Woburn Abbey, January 12, 1810.

"MY DEAR SIR,—It affords me much pleasure to learn from Lord Holland that you accept the proposal I made to you through him.

"The entire confidence I have in your attachment to those political principles which have uniformly guided my own conduct through life, and the advantages I anticipate to the party with which I act, as well as to the country, from the exercise of great and acknowledged talents in a just cause, in the crisis of unexampled difficulty and danger in which we are placed, combine to make this arrangement peculiarly gratifying to me.

"The writ will be moved on the first day of the session, and perhaps it may be necessary to give you the trouble of a journey to Camelford.

"In the mean time I must beg of you not to mention the circumstance to any but your own confidential friends, as from the particular state of the borough of Camelford some inconvenience might arise from the name of the candidate being prematurely known. Believe me to be, with very sincere regard, yours, BEDFORD."

P 2

On the 2d of March, 1810, Whitbread brought forward the motion of which he had given notice, of a vote of censure on the Government, but especially upon Lord Chatham, who had been commander-in-chief of the expedition to the Scheldt, for having, without any communication with his colleagues in the cabinet, or any intimation to his brother officer, Sir Richard Strachan, who commanded the naval force, laid before the king a narrative of that expedition, carrying it as far back as January, 1810.

Lord Chatham had requested the king to keep this communication a secret; and in pursuance of this request the narrative remained in the king's possession, secret and concealed from the ministers.

This proceeding of Lord Chatham was properly characterized by Whitbread as a most unconstitutional abuse of the privilege of access to his sovereign, and as being in its tendency most pernicious to his Majesty's service, and to the general service of the State.

The debate was adjourned from the 2d to the 5th of March, and on the latter day I made my maiden speech in support of Whitbread's motion.

I had no reason to be dissatisfied with my speech, which was favorably received, as indeed first attempts usually are; and I was afterwards told that my arguments had assisted to produce the defeat of ministers, who found themselves compelled to agree to Whitbread's motion.*

The following letter was written most kindly by Horner to my mother:

"House of Lords, March 6, 1810.

"My dear Mrs. Brougham,—You will naturally be very anxious to have some account of Henry's speech last night, which I had the pleasure of hearing. The manner in which he spoke was in every respect most parliamentary, and gave all his friends the most complete assurance of the success he will have in the House. His language and delivery were perfectly suited to the style which the House requires, and he showed himself to be in complete possession of it. It was

* The speech will be found in Cobbett (XVI., 7, * *), where it occupies four columns.

well judged to begin with a speech which was *extempore*, and to give this proof of what he can do, before the great opportunity of which I trust he will avail himself upon the Walcheren inquiry.

"I have stolen a few moments from my clients here to send you this little account, which I think you would expect from me.

"Believe me, dear Mrs. Brougham, ever most sincerely yours, FRA. HORNER."

During this my first session in Parliament, I took part in several other important questions, and chiefly on the abuse of flogging in the army and navy; but no motion was made upon the subject. A strong opinion had been expressed, both by myself and others, that some restraint should be placed upon the sentences of courts-martial, and the subject had much occupied both Parliament and the public.

In the year before, the attorney-general thought fit to prosecute several persons, and the correctness of several newspapers which had somewhat violently taken up this matter, and Mr. Cobbett had been sentenced to a heavy fine and two years' imprisonment. It was generally understood that the subject was next to forbidden in consequence of these prosecutions, and especially of Cobbett's severe punishment. Consequently, when the case of the Hunts came on for trial in 1811, there was no expectation of an acquittal; and I, acting as his counsel, had little or no hopes of saving him, although his publication was free from the violence of Cobbett. I, of course, exerted myself to the uttermost, and all the more for the strong expression of opinion which I had delivered in Parliament. My gratification was extreme when I found how my defense was received by all who heard me, and I began at the trial to entertain some hopes. The jury retired and were locked up for two hours. Having left the court, I heard, on leaving the Temple, of our success; and though far enough from ascribing it to my exertions, I considered it as of vital importance to my professional station, and had some hopes that a like success might attend the other case which was to come on at Lincoln, where I went on a special retainer. The disappointment was great at our failure there; for the author himself having been acquitted, there seemed little doubt that the printer might have the same success.*

FROM MR. JEFFREY.

"Edinburgh, March 19, 1810.

"MY DEAR BROUGHAM,—I have been annoyed for this last fortnight with my old nervous malady, which puts me in dread of apoplexy or palsy, and at all events really unfits me altogether for any sort of mental exertion. I am a little better now, chiefly, however, by force of spending my whole time in idle exercise of the body, and consequently you have my excuse for not writing, and the reason of my having nothing satisfactory to write about, both at once before you. As to my arrangements for next number, I am sorry to say that they are in very little forwardness. For my own share, I think of making an article on my 'American friend's' view of the genius 'and Resources of the French Government,' etc. —rather, however, on the title than the book, the greater part of which is filled with insignificant details of finance. I have not yet meditated the general subject, but it is easy to see that it is larger, and lets into many important speculations in foreign politics. If you think any thing is to be made of this, give me some hints and caution. I shall also do some poetry, I think, and any light thing that comes in my way. I have got very little positive promise of contributors, but am in treaty for several. Can't you suggest some theme for Playfair, or a job for Mill? or any thing safe and popular for Smith? I have not been able to find out the haunts of this vagabond priest; but I hope he is not forgetful of me; since the new arrangement don't pay, I find him much more tractable than formerly. I shall write you again, as soon as I am in a better state of preparation. In the mean time, what I am most anxious about is your own contribution, on which I depend more completely, perhaps, than at any former period. Do you take the Catholics? at all events, I hope the responsibility and something else political

* See the "Case of John Hunt and John Leigh Hunt," 22d January, 1811. —Speeches of Lord Brougham, i., 13.

—at such a moment as this it is really throwing away your great powers to employ them on any thing else. Do let me know about this as soon as possible. The *quid*, the *quando*, and the *quantum*.

"I believe I asked you before whether you knew any dull Whig who could read Gifford's Life of Pitt, and note the lies and blunders. It is so base and silly a book, that I think we should take some notice of it.

"You *must* go back to the Walcheren debate. I am myself more and more convinced that it will be by far the most important and most critical debate, not for the members only, but for the country, that has taken place in our time; and every effort should be made, and every nerve strained, to bring it to a right issue. If the resolutions are lost by forty or fifty, I look upon Parliament as irretrievably lost in public estimation, and all hope of any thing but a Court Government gone, for this reign at any rate, and probably forever.

"Your speeches are sadly reported in the papers I see, but I hear what I expected of them from better authority. You have begun with perfect prudence and good judgment, and I know will go on with glory.

"As for his highness of Gloucester, what shall I say? Present to him my humble duty and acknowledgments for the honor of his favorable opinion, and say that I consider it is by far the best omen for the country which late times have shown, that such persons as he should approve of such sentiments as we have been called on to make public. You must take the turning of this on yourself. I take it for granted you do not want an ostensible or separate note.

"I am not coming to town this spring; both your reasons and my own engagements forbid it. If I hear that Smith is come home, and my head continues unserviceable, I have thoughts of going for ten days to York; but, except this, I shall be at my post certainly.

"Murray sets off for London, I believe, in a day or two.

"There is nothing new here, at least I can not tell you any thing of it, for writing even so much has made me so giddy that I scarcely see the letters.

"Ever very truly yours, F. JEFFREY."

FROM LORD ERSKINE.

"Upper Grosvenor Street, April 14, 1810.

"DEAR BROUGHAM,—I dare not make any observations to a person of Mr. Jeffrey's most excellent taste and judgment. I have no doubt his candor will lead him to compare them with the *ordinary* pleadings at the bar *in former times*, and he will see the usefulness of maintaining the rank and character of a profession so inseparably connected with the safety of the Government and the liberties of the people. I am sure that this result will be exemplified in *your* future life; you have given ample proof and earnest already.

"It must be remembered in what utter contempt the press was fallen, and to what dangers it was exposed, when I came to the bar in 1778; and I flatter myself that the speeches collected by Ridgway in their chronological order will show its ascending progress, both in the preparation for the Libel bill and after it passed. The short interval was most favorable for exertion; because I have often thought that if the alarms of the French Revolution had come upon us before the press was established, it would have been beat down forever.

Many attempts were made by the Crown to crush me and to shake my business, but every conspiracy of that kind came in aid of it; and it has, I hope, operated, and will operate, as a useful example in the impression that time-serving and subserviency to judges is not the road to the Woolsack. In looking them over, I have this satisfaction—I do not see that from the zeal of the moment I have distorted the law, the application of which should be just and universal—by which I mean the law as I understood and still understand it. Whatever faults, however, may appear in them, they were delivered in the course of duty, and are not moved by me; the publication is not mine.

"With many thanks for the kind interest you have taken in them, I ever am most faithfully yours, ERSKINE."

TO EARL GREY.

"Brougham, October 23, 1810.

"MY DEAR LORD GREY,—I am ignorant of what is going on. I ought to except, however, the *bulletins* which Ward sends to Lord Lonsdale, and of which I saw his last yesterday. It is in the highest spirits; represents Massena as doing exactly what was to be wished, and Lord Wellington as having, from the beginning of his retreat, resolved on fighting at Torres Vedras. Ward adds that the battle is to be a grand and decisive one, and that the accounts from Wellington and his staff are such as to make every one very sanguine. They have no fears of the Portuguese. Massena has advanced without horses or guns (! !); he has a barren country in his rear as far as Coimbra, and Trant is there in force. The people at Lisbon, even Cochrane Johnston, quite confident. Such is the statement of this renowned witness, whom Lord Lonsdale seemed to believe implicitly, forgetting, I presume, Austerlitz, or supposing that a battle not yet fought is more easy to describe correctly than one already lost.

"As for Trant's affair, it seems either an exaggeration, or that he took what Massena meant to get rid of. The latter seems playing a pretty brisk game, and I own myself a little staggered by his movement. It argues a great confidence of succeeding. As for the affair of Buzaco, which we call a victory, it seems only that the French, instead of surrounding and destroying our army, drove it back seventy miles, which was the next best thing for them to do, and that for this success they paid very dear.

"A friend of mine just returned from Madras (a colonel in the king's service), who has been here, tells me very unpleasant things of the business in that quarter. Lord Minto's conduct seems to have been uniformly foolish, and to have dissatisfied all parties. Even Barlow has more adherents and approvers.* It would be a very pleasant thing to me if I could take Howick in my way to town next week; but the distance and the dreadful weather, with a bad deafness, make it impossible, so I must forego it.

"Believe me truly yours, H. BROUGHAM."

* Sir George Barlow, whose administration in India was an exciting topic in its day. On the death of the governor-general, Lord Cornwallis, in 1805, Barlow, in terms of a provision for such an event, was appointed to the office provisionally, and next year he received a formal commission as governor-general. The mutiny of Vellore, and other unpropitious events, occurred during his administration.

On my return to London for Michaelmas term, I wrote as follows to Lord Grey:

TO EARL GREY.

"Temple, Nov. 4, 1810.

"My dear Lord Grey,—I have little to say about any thing at present, for nobody talks of any subject but one, and on that one the falsities and idle rumors are so numerous that the safest rule an unconcerned spectator can lay down for himself is, to believe nothing at all. The idea of the king having had an apoplectic attack seems pretty generally current; and if so, Haslam, I understand, says his other complaint is incurable.

"But one reason for my, at least, doubting the whole story is, that at Michael Taylor's (where I passed a day on my way to town) they had heard nothing of it. Another story, not inconsistent with the former, is, that the malady arises from a running having stopped. But as I said before, one's faith should be in abeyance for some weeks. It is, however, *no* matter of doubt that, were you to come into office in any way at this time, you would succeed to a pretty inheritance of blunders and misfortunes. Among other parts of your succession would be the fine position of Torres Vedras; the vigorous government of Sir G. Barlow; the post of Lord Minto intrenched behind ninety-six paragraphs; the Scheldt, etc., etc. However, I need not say any thing to *you* to lessen the inclination for office, as I am confident your bitterest enemy never seriously accused you of it. Yours faithfully,

Henry Brougham."

Towards the close of this year, that very interesting and most difficult question of the regency occupied the attention of ministers and of both Houses of Parliament.

The mental malady of the king—produced, as was generally believed, by anxiety caused by the alarming illness of his favorite daughter, the Princess Amelia, and by grief at its fatal termination—became so serious, that early in November ministers were compelled to announce that Parliament could not be prorogued, the king being unable to sign the commission for that purpose, and Lord Eldon having (most properly) refused to affix the great seal to the commission in the absence of the sign-manual. The continued illness of the king rendered further prorogations necessary, from time to time, until the middle of December, when Perceval in the Commons announced the determination of Government to follow the precedent of 1788. He accordingly gave notice that on the 20th December he should propose the adoption of the three resolutions of 1788, Ponsonby expressing his concurrence in the two first, but that he should offer the most strenuous opposition to the third. It was undeniably the duty of Parliament to find some remedy for the difficulty caused by the incapacity of the third branch of the Legislature to exercise its functions; and it was proposed to do this by following the third resolution of 1788, giving, under the sanction of Parliament, the royal assent to a bill to be passed by the two Houses, there being no possibility of obtaining the assent of the Crown, either personally or by commission. This meant that the two Houses assumed to themselves the absolute power to legislate—an assumption the more monstrous because it pretended to be the act of *all* the branches of the Legislature. If this could be done, the two Houses might make war or peace, alter the coinage, create peers, and perform any act which the principles of our constitution vest in the sovereign alone. The difficulties were great, but unquestionably the least unconstitutional mode of proceeding was by an address involving any conditions or restrictions, which acceptance would render valid and binding on the party addressed. Lord Grey had been present in the Lords and took part in the debate of the 15th November; but family matters obliged him to return to Howick, where he remained during the rest of the session; accordingly, he asked me to keep him informed of the proceedings in both Houses, and hence the following letters:

TO EARL GREY.

"Monday, Dec. 17, 1810—half-past five.

"DEAR LORD GREY,—The House is just over. Perceval is to move the three resolutions of 1788 on Thursday. Ponsonby gave notice in a very proper manner of opposing the third. Sheridan spoke much in praise of the prince's letter, and forgot the matter of it, conceiving it to be on the general point; which gave Perceval an opportunity of sneering at and throwing him on his back.

The absence of the Grenvilles from the House (though I suppose accidental) is much remarked.

"Perceval is to state whether any, and (if any) what, restrictions are to be proposed, before he moves the resolutions.

"Adam called on him to say so now, and he refused.

"The examinations were not read. H. BROUGHAM.

"The post is just going."

TO EARL GREY.

"December 18, 1810.

"MY DEAR LORD GREY,—I should apologize for the horrid scrawl I sent you yesterday. It was written within a minute of the post going. I mentioned that the ministerial folks were remarking the absence of the Grenvilles. I have since learnt that Lord Temple is laid up with the gout.

"No one can tell what Perceval means to propose; probably he himself can tell as little as any body. There is, in all likelihood, a difference between the Wellesleys and him, and we shall then have a compromise—that is to say, very few restrictions, just enough to *save the principle*, as it were. If our friends manage wisely, they will enter their protest in the form of a single debate in each House, and then do nothing to protract the discussion. The prince's continued neutrality, however, is mischievous, and will affect the divisions. Sheridan said, pretty expressly (though in a parenthesis), that he only spoke for himself. It seems odd, however, that he should have spoken at all, if he did not expect the prince to stir; for in the former debate he said nothing.

"I have been confined for ten days with a bad cough, which has prevented me from hearing any thing or seeing any body, so that I only can speak to what I observed last night.

"Canning's friends seem a little puzzled, and the general impression of the committee who examined the physicians is said to be much less sanguine than before the examination. I take it for granted somebody has sent you their report, but I shall send it by this post if I can; if not, by to-morrow's.

"Believe me ever yours truly, H. BROUGHAM."

TO EARL GREY.

"House of Lords, Wednesday, six o'clock,
December 19, 1810.

"DEAR LORD GREY,—The Lords are nearly concluding their conversation. Lord Liverpool has told nothing more than Perceval did; Wellesley is there, but has not spoken. Lord Spencer stated his opinion very strongly, and Lord Grenville also spoke, and very well—first abusing the delay, and then on the question of right, and the *course of proceeding*, and on that *alone*, repeating his doctrine of 1788, with some very bad reasons, one of which Lord Lauderdale refuted, or, rather, promised to refute, and showed how he should do it.

"Lord Holland is up. H. B."

TO EARL GREY.

"December 28, 1810.

"DEAR LORD GREY,—I have just received your letter, having been out of town for a few days. They say this last paroxysm has been touch and go; indeed he must die before many months are over; and the next fit may very possibly carry him off. All the doctors (including *the* doctor*) have made but a poor figure, and there ought to be no delicacy in saying so, in either House.

"I am going to the House of Lords; and if there is any thing worth noting before the post goes I shall add a P.S. In the mean time, I wish to God Lady Grey's confinement were well over, both on her own account and yours, and that you were safe in Portman Square.

"Believe me, etc., H. BROUGHAM.

"P.S.—House of Lords, six o'clock.—Lord Carlisle began the night by an attack on the physicians and ministers, for the discrepancy of the report with the bulletins and statements, and suggesting a re-examination, but made no motion. Lord Liverpool is up; he began with stating hopes, etc., of recovery, and is going on exactly as if there had been no paroxysm two days ago. But they all look d——d miserable, the

---

* Lord Sidmouth.

chancellor in particular. Lady Holland is in the place at the bar. Lord Castlereagh is to rat, having luckily voted in the Irish House of Commons with the majority."

TO EARL GREY.

"December 29, 1810.

"DEAR LORD GREY,—The debate and division last night, I should think, will decide the restriction question, unless the bulletins are much more favorable than can be expected. There were *seven*, including Lord Grenville, who voted with the ministers; with him were Lords Carysfort, Carrington, Stafford, Buckley, and two others. Boringdon and Roden also were with the ministers, and are to vote against the restrictions. This makes a difference of eighteen. Lord Grosvenor also will vote against the restrictions, though he was not there last night. This leaves them *seven* of majority, of which I wish them much joy, as I do of Lord Grenville's vote when accompanied with his speech, by far the most violent he ever made against them. He never called them *ministers*, or even 'noble lords,' but '*those people*,' '*those men*,' and 'those persons.' And, among other things, accused them in plain words of 'forgery.'

"They were very much cast down, upon the whole, and the symptoms of ratting are manifest. Lord Alvanley voted with opposition. He said at White's that he had told the Duke of York, 'If you rat, I'll rat too.' The duke holds his proxy. There is to be a city meeting; and our friends are very confident of carrying instructions and resolutions, which have been prepared and sent to them.

"However, I look to Windsor for the results—in fact speeches and meetings are of no moment now—the bulletins must decide it.

"There must be some mistake in Ward's account of Castlereagh's having voted in 1789, for he was not in Parliament. However, it is said, he still means to rat. Lord Holland made an excellent speech last night, as I hear from all quarters.

"I only heard the few words which he spoke to explain why you were absent, which he did very properly. Any body who could even *think* of asking you to come up must be mad, or worse. I shall be very anxious till I hear that all is well.

"The bulletin to-day is somewhat better, but they say the difference is quite insignificant; and the Duke of Clarence says he is as ill as ever. They have fears of apoplexy, the determination of blood towards the head having been violently felt in the jugular, etc. If this is true, the first nausea or retching may carry him off.

"Young Fitzgerald (of the Irish treasury) has resigned; and he and Peel and Lord Desart are going a tour to America to await better times. So now you have all my news.

"Believe me ever very truly yours, H. B."

TO EARL GREY.

"December 30, 1810.

"My dear Lord Grey,—You will see by the newspapers what to-day's bulletin is. Private accounts, which I understand may be depended upon, say that the '*good night*' means four hours' sleep at first and the rest very disturbed; his being no better evidently means worse, both from the known language of the bulletins—and even if he were really no worse, that would be worse every succeeding day. I fear we shall still be beat in the Commons, at least if a material change don't take place. The princes are using their influence. One man whom I know well told me t'other day he was to vote with Perceval on Monday, as he had done on the last occasion. He is under the Duke of Cumberland's influence: and notice of this being conveyed to the duke, my friend's vote is *now* to be with us. He was assured (I presume to induce him, or save his honor) that the prince had declared to the rest his resolution of having the same ministers when the king recovers that the king now has. I wish he would, but it is, I fear, quite impossible.

"Burghersh tells all manner of things about the armies, as that Lord Wellington can annihilate Massena whenever he pleases, only it will cost 7000 to 10,000 men, so he is to wait till he learns that reinforcements are coming, and then he will fall upon him.

"A good thing happened at the Lords' debate. Lord Wellesley took the King of Sweden there on purpose *to hear him speak* (at least to *see* him speak). So he was seated on the single chair to the right of the throne, and an alley was made through the crowd that he might have a view of Wellesley; but, as usual, he could not contrive it, and sat silent. I suppose you have heard the Duke of Sussex's introduction to the king: 'Comment vous portez-vous, M. le Comte, ou, si vous voulez, votre Majesté.'

"In case any thing very material occurs to-morrow (Sunday) morning, I shall send a letter in such a way that you may get it on Tuesday evening, if you send to Alnwick.

"Yours, etc., H. BROUGHAM.

"Lord Stafford did *not* vote with Lord Grenville, which alters the calculation by two."

TO EARL GREY.

"Thursday, six o'clock, Jan. 3, 1811.

"DEAR LORD GREY,—I am just come from the House of Commons. Perceval stated that Lord Grenville had refused to issue the money required (under the last Appropriation Act) by warrant of the Treasury; that the crown lawyers had given their opinions that, taking the practice and the act together, the warrant was *illegal;* but that money being wanted, and the clerk of the privy seal (Larpent) refusing to join Lord Westmorland in the risk of being hanged, Perceval found it necessary to do it by warrant, which being disobeyed by Lord Grenville, he was forced to apply to Parliament; so moved for the warrant and correspondence (including the opinions), and is, at Tierney's desire, to make Larpent write a note, for the sake of bringing *his* refusal before the House. The papers will be printed to-night, and the question is to be discussed to-morrow. Fine fruits of their delays, and still more of the *glorious precedent* of 1788, which seems, in every view, full of absurdity.

"In the Lords the same proceedings nearly took place.

"The king is supposed worse, and all the underlings in office seem very desponding.

"I trust Lady Grey continues well; and am, in great haste, etc., H. B.

"Romilly almost *destroyed* Canning last night—nothing was ever better done; and but for an unlucky misunderstanding afterwards—which, I hope, will do no harm—it would have been quite complete. Nothing has happened more agreeable during the whole discussion. Don't believe a word of what the newspapers say of Sheridan's speech. It was a complete failure. He is quite done, and has nothing left but his mischief.

"The Master of the Rolls* was very powerful indeed."

TO EARL GREY.

"Jan. 27, 1811.

"DEAR LORD GREY,—I am quite ashamed of my delay in returning an answer to your very friendly communication. In truth, I was apprehensive that I should have found myself *compelled* to say no; and the temptations which you had held out to me were so strong that I could not make up my mind all at once to resist them. Some circumstances which afterwards occurred, and which you are apprised of, delayed this answer still further; and I knew that while Ward continued undetermined, my delay could make no difference. He has now given you his answer; and if you continue to think that I can be of any use in the event to which you alluded, I am at your orders. I will thank you, however, not to mention this, unless where it may be necessary, as the thing being known might injure me professionally, in case circumstances should render any further arrangements unnecessary, which seems at present not very unlikely.

"I need scarcely repeat my thanks to you for giving me the opportunity of '*serving under you*' in the supposed event. Indeed this forms by far the greater part of the allurement. The office in question, I am quite sensible, is infinitely above my pretensions, which are small enough in every sense of the word; but I should value it almost wholly from its connection with *your* department.

"Believe me, with the greatest esteem, most faithfully yours,

"HENRY BROUGHAM.

"I need scarcely add that, should any thing occur rendering it desirable for you to prefer somebody else, I must insist on your being on no ceremony with me; indeed I had just as lief contribute my mite to your department without the name and appointment."

---

* Sir William Grant.

FROM J. A. MURRAY, ESQ.

"Edinburgh, Feb. 26, 1811.

"MY DEAR BROUGHAM,—The exultation of your friends is great; and the humiliation of your enemies—if you have left any behind you here—must be in proportion.

"The accounts of your speech, and the verdict—which, like a victory, is the substantial proof of a good general—have given us more delight than any thing that has of late happened in these bad times.

"I was almost the only person who had any tidings of it yesterday. Horner had written me five lines before he went into the House of Lords, in which he said that Westminster Hall still rang with the eloquent speech which you had made, and that even Park, Garrow, and Dampier (though not very partial) mentioned it with great praise.

"When he concluded his letter, the jury was still deliberating. Charles Stuart added an appendix, and told me of the verdict. I think it a great victory for the public, for the prosecution of libels is carried too far, and it is a great object that it should be checked.

"You are the first person since Erskine who has done so, and you have now a much higher situation than any ministry could give you. Public affairs seem to be in a most desperate state, and the immediate recovery of the king seems to be the best thing that can happen.

"I will not take up your time with Edinburgh gossip, when you must have a great variety of business.

"Ever yours truly, JOHN A. MURRAY."

TO EARL GREY.

"March 10, 1811.

"MY DEAR LORD GREY,—I have not broken in upon you with letters while you were in such anxiety as I heard you were suffering for some time past. But I am extremely happy to learn that your alarm is over, and I think you may not be the worse for a little interruption on indifferent subjects.

"You observed, of course, the division on Wardle's motion,* which has completely done his business. The news-

* See above, p. 327.

papers, however, did not tell that Burdett treated him with the most marked coldness and distance, and hit him some pretty hard knocks in the course of his speech. It is also material to mention that among those who voted against him were Folkestone, Hanbury Tracy, Creevey, and Brand. I was not present, having purposely gone away before it began, as it had a connection with a trial for a libel in which I was counsel.

"I have seen a man (Gell) who returned yesterday morning from Lisbon. He has been in Spain and Portugal for some months, and reports that the French, since their reinforcements of 20,000, amount to 70,000 or 75,000, and that they don't apprehend in the army any further reinforcement for the present. He adds, however, that nobody but Lord Wellington knows any thing for certain, and that he keeps all he knows to himself. They are not alarmed either in the army or at Lisbon. At Lisbon, bread, etc., is only double its price in ordinary times, and they don't complain. They are supplied from Barbary. There was a story of Badajos being relieved, but he did not believe it. The French are *not* in want of food. They have a large space open to them; but beyond that are hemmed in so that they can not send a courier with any reasonable prospect of his reaching his destination. This man is a strong partisan of Wellington.

"The impression made on my mind by Perceval's manner last night was that he would be very well pleased to have a report of the committee, or a vote of the House, to *prevent* him from giving the merchants the money they want. It was clear that they did not venture to let Pole speak when Ward put the question.

"I shall go to the Circuit about the end of next week. In case you are coming up, and pass near York, pray let me know the time, that I may have the chance of seeing you. I am first going special to Lincoln, but shall be at York after Tuesday.

"I trust Lady Grey is not the worse for the anxiety you have all been suffering, and which I have felt on all your accounts very sincerely.

"Believe me most faithfully yours, H. Brougham.

"I dined the other day with the little princess at Kensington. She asked three or four times for you, and expressed the greatest desire to meet you again.

"She also spoke with great delight of Whitbread's last speech."

TO EARL GREY.

"July 23, 1811.

"Dear Lord Grey,—Finding you are at Southill, I fire this after you in the hopes that it may reach you before you set out. What I wish to apprise you of is a few particulars touching the late debates in the House of Commons, which the newspapers could not tell.

"All the prince's friends voted against us regularly on every question. Except on the regency, they have never attended so zealously.

"Sheridan both voted and spoke. After saying he should only vote for sending it to a committee, Tierney gave him a severe licking, which Sheridan did not like, and complains bitterly of. Jekyll voted with us once, which was very handsome. Adam never appeared the whole week, but has, I understand, a very strong opinion *with us.* William Lamb was always there some part of the debate, but never at the division. He durst not vote either one way or another. Pierce, governor of the bank, was under the gallery, and the Duke of Cumberland sat by him, flirting for two hours one night. In short, the whole Carlton House interest has been most actively exerted—with what views I think it not very difficult to guess.

"The king is certainly a *little* better; the private accounts say so; but the danger is not over. The physicians differed from each other so much on Saturday, when examined by the Lords' Council, that nobody can tell what their opinions are: no two spoke the same language. They have to-day had a Council at Carlton House, and resolved to prorogue; and one motive is, that something about the bank bill may be said in the speech. Perceval's wife told a person whom I know that the prince, in putting off the dinner at Perceval's, added, 'Be the event what it might' (of the king's illness), 'he should dine with him.' This story of Seville turns out a humbug, and Wilson says, 'The ministers are prepared for

Lord Wellington's retreating.' He denies that Soult is gone to the southward. Yours ever, H. BROUGHAM."

TO EARL GREY.

"Lancaster, September 6, 1811.

"MY DEAR LORD GREY,—What I chiefly trouble you for at present is in order to lay before you for your consideration and advice an offer which has just been made to me of (I use the words) 'coming in upon the popular interest, in the most independent manner and at a small expense, for the city of Worcester,' in the event of a dissolution. '*Coming in*,' of course, means having a chance of being returned, and a certainty of undergoing a most troublesome and laborious contest. 'A small expense' is afterwards explained to mean 'about £1500,' which I take for granted may be extended in fair interpretation to a good deal more.

"Now, certainly, I feel the propriety of making this attempt, if it should be at all consistent with prudence in a pecuniary point of view; but I have no thousands to throw away. On the contrary, I have been buying land. Nevertheless, I should be disposed to go a certain length, because it would undoubtedly be extremely desirable for the party both to extend somewhat its popular interest, and at all events to secure *another seat*. At the same time I feel that I might by such a movement risk the termination of my connection with the Duke of Bedford, in the course of which I am sure I have never experienced for a single moment any more restraint on my conduct than if I had been member for Westminster—indeed a great deal less. (This is one of the circumstances which I have stated in my answer to the above offer, because the mention of 'independent manner' seemed to call for such an explanation.)

"When I say it might risk such a termination, I, of course, mean that my present seat might be filled up, and new connections formed, which could not easily be broken to make way for me in the event of my afterwards being thrown out; so that I should be anxious for some explanation on this head before embarking in such a scheme. These, however, are matters which a party can not avoid looking into; and it is neither their duty nor their interest, as I think, to neglect such opportunities.

"Having stated the case to you, I shall now mention what I have said in return. A former letter having miscarried, I was forced to answer those which came last without delay; but for that reason I declined giving a definitive answer. I explained the matter of 'independence' as above stated. I also plainly told them that a very moderate expense was all I either could or would encounter; and I added, with respect to principles, that I am a very sincere and warm lover of liberty, and entertain the utmost hatred of every kind of oppression; and that I am generally friendly to reform, differing, however, with such reformers as will only listen to wholesale plans; and preferring, chiefly on the score of practicability, a more *gradual* change. Of course I have had no answer; but when one arrives, I take it for granted I must make up my mind; and therefore I beg you to give me your early assistance and advice. If you write on or before Tuesday, address to 'Lancaster;' if later, to 'Brougham.' If you think that I ought, in the first instance, to write to the Duke of Bedford, perhaps it would be better that you should do so, as if I had communicated through you, my connection with him having been through you. But of this you are the best judge. Excuse the trouble of this, and believe me ever most sincerely, H. BROUGHAM."

TO EARL GREY.

"Brougham, Sunday, Oct. 13, 1811.

"MY DEAR LORD GREY,—I have just received your letter, and rejoice greatly at its being written by yourself, as the accounts I had received made me apprehensive you had been a good deal pulled down by your attack. I had great hopes, however, that there was some imprudence in the case (which I find realized), and particularly counted upon oysters and stale beer—two things against which I warn you, from experience—having been almost killed by the former and bottled porter at Venice some years ago, after a bad voyage from Ancona, which had disturbed my stomach.

"Conceiving you were still too unwell to be troubled, I did not write to inform you of the *fatal* communication having come from the Duke of Bedford; but I begged Lord Rosslyn to let you know, as he seemed to expect you in Scotland.

I was not at liberty to tell the *reason* of the change; but as you have learned it from another quarter, I may now say that the duke assigns no other cause than the sale of Camelford, which he has nearly completed. I believe him most implicitly, and it gives me the greatest satisfaction; for it refutes all the other reports which I had heard, and never credited, nor, indeed, thought of. It also makes me disbelieve what I had recently learnt, and what this very post has brought me a repetition of from another quarter—that a year ago he had resolved upon a change. I am sure had he taken any such resolution he would have communicated it to me long since—for instance, at the time (February) that I wrote to him desiring his approbation previously to taking office under you. Nay, even if he should have formed the resolution, and concealed it, I will have recourse to any supposition rather than entertain the slightest doubts of his intentions; and will at the utmost only set it down to the account of his shyness, being as thoroughly convinced of his perfect fairness and liberality as I can be of any man's. I am sorry for the sale of Camelford on his account as well as my own. It proves his difficulties to be more considerable than I had imagined. I am sure, however, that no difficulties can induce him to part with it to a Tory.

"You may easily believe that as soon as I received the duke's letter I set about making inquiries, both as to Worcester and seats of a different description. Ward informs me that Bromley having started on the same interest on which it was proposed to me to stand, that is out of the question; but he is to make further inquiries. He seems to think he is to be out of Parliament himself, by virtue of Curwen's wise bill; for though he is willing to give £5000, he can get nobody to take it. This, I own, amazes me, nor can I quite credit it, if he has made a fair trial. Of course he wishes this to be concealed. Thank God, I always entertained a due horror of that most foolish if not pernicious act, though I own I rather expected to see it negatory than mischievous—rather evaded, than used to give the Treasury a monopoly.

"Ward says that Frederick Lamb thinks Lord Wellesley is rising fast with the prince, and I can answer for George

Lamb (who has just been here) having the worst opinion of his friend. Michael Taylor is in doleful plight; he must either give up Parliament or his party, unless the prince acts right. What he is to do I presume not even himself knows, certainly not the ministers. The Lowthers, who hear regularly from them, are quite at sea about it. One can scarcely believe in his going altogether wrong, till it happens. The ministers believe in a skirmish in Spain, but that the Liverpool story is false.

"Your illness prevented me from calling your attention to that abominable book of Trotter's, of whom I always had the very worst opinion, though he has now contrived to exceed it. Of course he must be chastised in the 'Edinburgh Review,' and I expect Jeffrey here to-morrow or next day, which will enable me to concert the matter advantageously. But merely chastising him is not enough, for it is proper his facts should be controverted; and as I know some of them to be utterly false, it seems fit that these should be singled out as specimens to throw a discredit on the whole.*

"It strikes me that you and Lord Holland should read the book and mark what occurs to you, which being communicated to me may be made the proper use of. It is too delicate to trust even Jeffrey with, so I intend to give him general reasons for begging he will leave it wholly in my hands. And I know he will, as a matter of course. When I first saw the extracts I was on the point of taking post and going over to confer with you, and indeed I doubt if any thing but your illness would have stopped me: but I am grown somewhat cooler now, notwithstanding the 'Courier' of t'other day, which I send in case you may not get that newspaper. It will show how much the thing merits a speedy notice.

"This is already too long a letter for an invalid, so I only beg my best remembrances to Lady Grey; and believe me ever yours truly, H. Brougham.

"I have not said any thing to Lord Holland, nor heard from him on the subject of Trotter. I was afraid of Lady Holland intermeddling and doing mischief."

---

* A "Letter to Lord Viscount Southwell," by J. B. Trotter, late private secretary to the Right Honorable Charles James Fox.—See "Edinburgh Review" for April, 1809, p. 60.

TO EARL GREY.

"Brougham, October 14, 1811.

"My dear Lord Grey,—Having written fully yesterday, I have only to acknowledge the receipt of yours to-day, and to thank you heartily for the kind interest you take in the concern in question. If *I could* point out any way in which you (or indeed any body) were likely to remedy the evil, I should do so without scruple, but the case if not hopeless is pretty nearly so, to all present appearances.

"This day's newspapers contain an account of Camelford having been sold, and that the purchaser is a *Mr. Carpenter, of Mount Tavy*. I suppose it was necessary to conceal matters; if not, I certainly have not had very long notice, for it was in common circulation before I heard of it. This, of course, I did not know when I told Lord Rosslyn that I was at liberty to mention the reason to him.

"In one particular you can greatly oblige me, by giving me your free and candid opinion whether it is incumbent on me, in point of delicacy towards the Duke of Bedford (to whom I lie under great obligations), to offer to go out at once, and leave unfettered the bargain, which he does not by his letter appear to have finally concluded. This step would certainly make some difference in it, and I certainly should not be the less disposed to take it, from the circumstance of his never having hinted at such a thing. It might be a convenience to him, and would (as far as I at present can perceive) do very little harm to me, or rather the contrary, as a single session is not worth speaking of, and would indeed render my return to parliamentary practice still more difficult than the two sessions already elapsed have at any rate made it. I should thank you to turn this matter in your mind, and let me know what occurs to you.

"Ever most truly yours, H. Brougham."

TO EARL GREY.

"Temple, Dec. 3, 1811.

"Dear Lord Grey,—I have seen scarcely any body, except Alexander Baring, who was here yesterday. He gives a curious account of some things, which, I have no doubt, will interest you. He is a very accurate man, and has better foreign correspondence than any body, and has lately seen Russell, the new American Chargé d'Affaires, who has come from Paris.

"First, then, Baring holds it to be next to certain that in spring there will be a rupture between France and Russia, and that Sweden is *not with* France. He says he knows that Bernadotte, not long since, said, 'Moi, j'aime la France jusqu'au Rhin.' But this is only a sample of his evidence. He is quite convinced of these things. Next, he has seen returns of all the French forces, and it results from thence that there are only 85,000 men of the French army, exclusive of the German allies (of whom one-tenth in the hospitals), to the east of the Rhine. This includes Germany, Poland, etc.; but is exclusive of 20,000 at the camp near Utrecht. These, however, can't be considered as disposable; and it is exclusive (of course) of 20,000 more at Boulogne. These are, I apprehend, more disposable. To proceed, Murat and Bonaparte are on bad terms, and the latter recently sent Murat notice that he must make preparations to receive General Perignon as commander-in-chief in the kingdom of Naples. He sent him with 10,000 French troops—picked corps. Murat's answer was, 'He should receive them at the frontier with 20,000 Neapolitans.' However, he has thought better of it, and let them and Perignon in.

"Next, Bonaparte lately demanded of the Emperor of Austria a passage for a corps from Dalmatia to Poland through the Austrian state, and the emperor in a very civil but firm letter, written with his own hand, explained that he could not, and gave his neutrality as the reason. Bonaparte received this letter when in private with the empress and Segur (a confidential officer of his household), and, turning round, said to his wife, 'Votre père est un f—— bête!' This was told by Segur to Russell; and Baring don't wish it to be mentioned.

"The above circumstances I should not have detailed but for the more than common authority of Alexander Baring. Such things are so easily fabricated that they are of no kind of value in general; but in this case, I imagine, there must be some foundation for them, and think it right to put you in possession of them, as I am sure that Baring, though he mentioned them in confidence, would wish it. He is to show me Russell soon. Ever truly yours, H. BROUGHAM."

APPENDIX OF NOTES.

I. (P. 17.)

David Stuart Erskine, Earl of Buchan, was one of three remarkable brothers, the others being Thomas, the Lord Chancellor, and Henry, or Harry, as he was usually called. Lord Buchan was born in 1742, and died in 1829. His career was eccentric rather than great. He was renowned for extreme egotism, and the relics of this propensity exist in a multitude of portraits of him, presented by himself to the universities and other public institutions in Scotland.

His two brothers figure at some length in the foregoing pages. Lord Chancellor Erskine naturally has a place among them from his eminent position. The notices of Henry Erskine are most valuable, as contributing to rescue from obscurity one whose abilities were far greater than his fame. Many thought him a man of higher powers than his great brother, but he worked in a more limited sphere, which gave him but a small place in the history of the time, and his abilities did not take the direction of literature, so as to leave a memorial by which posterity might estimate them.

II. (P. 17.)

In the days of Principal Robertson, descent from a Highland family was not so attractive and interesting as it would be deemed in the present day. Little is said of his Highland connection either by himself or his biographers, but it seems clear that his family were cadets of the house of Struan or Strewan, in Perthshire. This family was the chief of the Robertsons, or the Clandonachie, as they are called in Highland history. The believers in traditional Highland genealogy have the choice of admitting that they obtained the title of Donachie as descendants of the "gracious Duncan" slain by Macbeth; or of accepting from the historian of the "martial achievements of the Robertsons of Strowan" this account of the great progenitor, from whom the family took their Celtic patronymic: "Duncan, second son of Angus, Lord of the Isles, in the Gaelic language was called Donoch Ravir Macinnes na Coalich—that is, Duncan, the fat or corpulent son of Angus of Cowel, and his posterity were called Clandonachy." They had their share in the wild history of the Celtic tribes in Scotland, and produced one remarkable chief in comparatively modern times—Alexander, known as the poet-chief. When a youth of eighteen or so, he fought under Dundee at Killiecrankie. He appeared again in "the fifteen," bringing 500 followers to Mar's army. He was taken prisoner at the battle of Sheriffmuir, but he escaped, and joined the Jacobite refugees in France. When a third opportunity opened in "the forty-five," he was approaching eighty years of age, and not well fitted for field-duty, but he appeared on the scene, and his correspondence shows much zeal and activity in the cause.

There is an octavo volume with the title "Poems on various subjects and occasions, by the Honorable Alexander Robertson of Struan, Esq. Mostly taken from his own original manuscripts. Edinburgh: Printed for Charles Alexander, and sold at his House in Geddes Close, where subscribers may call for their copies." It is understood to have appeared about the year 1750, but the absence of date, and the other peculiarities of the title, may have been caused by the risk to those concerned in the publication of a work full of Jacobitism left by one of the chiefs of the insurrection. It was noticed for other defects besides its politics—a lubricity of a broad frank character, beyond the license of the age. The chieftain poet belonged to a set of scholars who worshipped the classical models. Whatever followed these was deemed legitimate literature; and as he addressed himself to Chloris, Strephon, and Lydia, he treated them as they had been accustomed to be treated by his masters. These effusions at the same time mix oddly with others more congenial to Scotland and the period—"The hundred and nineteenth psalm paraphrased, addressed to my worthy friend Duncan Toshach of Monyvard," and "An ode to the Trinity in the time of temptation." There is a later edition of these poems stripped of their offensive classicalities. It, also, is undated, with the title "The History and Martial Achievements of the Robertsons of Strowan—as it is selected from the works of the best historians that have written of the origin and valiant achievements of this honorable family and their descendants—and the Poems on various subjects and occasions by the Honorable Alexander Robertson of Strowan, Esq."

Many of the letters of the poet-chief of the Clandonachie relate to the secrets of the insurrection of 1745. Even when they bear on matters evidently of danger and difficulty, they have the easy recklessness of a wayward genius. Take as a specimen the following, addressed to the titular Duke of Atholl, better known as Tullibardine: "MY LORD DUKE,—I need not prompt a man to be honest who makes nice conscience of wronging the king. Few people scruple in that part. I have been cursedly used by your Grace's relations, though I am sure they were not properly related to your Grace. My ever-honored duke—you take me. If you don't, I refer you to Neil MacGlashan for half a pair of spectacles—for he can tell what he sees as well or better than, my lord, your ever faithful humble servant, Alr. Robertson of Strewan. Oct. 18, 1745. God direct you and your good-natured frailty." This brief document sprawls over three large pages, because it is written in characters varying from one to three inches long. In an another letter he says, "It seems a difficult point for me to put both orders in execution, unless, as the man said, I can be in two places at once, like a bird." So this Irish idea of unity in time and place is older than the age of Sir Boyle Roche, who has generally the merit of its invention. Many letters by the poet-chief are in a collection of manuscripts in the Advocates' Library, called "The Struan Papers." Others are in "Jacobite correspondence of the Atholl Family during the Rebellion, 1745–1746," printed for the Abbotsford Club.

III. (P. 22.)

Gilbert Stuart had a literary fame in his own day, but he is more known in the present for that ferocity of personal rancor and wild dissipation which gives him a conspicuous place in Isaac Disraeli's "Calamities of Authors." He obtained his reputation solely by a trick of style. He was accomplished in the balancing system of the period, learning both from Johnson and Gibbon, without lapsing into the absolute mannerism of either of them. Now that this style has become unpopular, there is nothing to induce people to read his many historical works. They were written chiefly to rival and supplant the standard works of the day, and with the idea that he would accomplish this by the mere force of genius without research. Much of his hatred was expended on Dr. Robertson, but much more on Dr. Henry, the respectable author of the "History of Great Britain." David Hume had written a good-humored review on this book, though it professed to be a rival of his own history. His desire to get it inserted in a magazine over which Stuart exercised some influence brought out the following paroxysm of literary fury: "David Hume wants to review Henry, but that task is so precious that I will undertake it myself. Moses, were he to ask it as a favor, should not have it—yea, not even the man after God's own heart. I wish I could transport myself to London to review him for the monthly; a fire there and in the critical would perfectly annihilate him. Could you do nothing in the latter? To the former, I suppose, David Hume has transcribed the criticism he intended for us. It is precious, and would divert you; I keep a proof of it in my cabinet for the amusement of friends. This great philosopher begins to dote. To-morrow morning Henry sets off for London with immense hopes of selling his History. I wish sincerely that I could enter Holborn the same hour with him—he should have a repeated fire to combat with. I entreat that you may be so kind as to let him feel some of your thunder. I shall never forget the favor. If Whitaker is in London he could give a blow. Paterson will give him a knock. Strike by all means. The wretch will tremble, grow pale, and return with a consciousness of his debility. I have a thousand thanks to give you for your insertion of the paper in the 'London Chronicle,' and for the part you propose to act in regard to Henry. I could wish that you knew for certain his being in London before you strike the first blow. An inquiry at Cadell's will give this. When you have an enemy to attack, I shall in return give my best assistance, and aim at him a mortal blow, and rush forward to his overthrow, though the flames of hell should start up to oppose me."—*Calamities of Authors*, ii., 67.

IV. (P. 22.)

James Keay entered the Scotch bar as a member of the Faculty of Advocates in 1794; he died in 1837. He was in his latter years a leading counsel in full occupation among the orators of the period. He was noted for the precision of his pleading, and young lawyers were recommended to study his speeches, as models to be more safely followed than those of the more celebrated advocates of the period. He was a Tory or Conservative, but took no further share in politics than to give his vote and countenance to the candidate on his own side.

V. (P. 32.)

The "Translations and Paraphrases of several passages of Sacred Scripture" were first printed at Edinburgh in 1745. The introduction states that "these poems which are now printed and transmitted to Presbyteries by Act of Assembly are partly collected from the pious and ingenious Dr. Watts, and from other writers, with such alterations as appeared to fit them more for the present purpose, and partly furnished by ministers of the Church. The use for which they were intended required simplicity and plainness of composition and style. The committee who prepared them chiefly aimed at having the sense of Scripture expressed in easy verse; such as might be fitted to raise devotion, might be intelligible to all, and might rise above contempt from persons of better taste." Of the authorship we are told that "nineteen were by Dr. Watts; three by Blair, the author of 'The Grave;' three by William Robertson, minister of Greyfriars, and father of the historian; two by Dr. Doddridge; and one by Mr. Randal of Stirling."—Cunningham's *Church History of Scotland*, ii., 596. Any one desirous of seeing this primitive collection will find it extremely difficult to get access to a copy of it, and not easy, even among Scotch Presbyterians, to find any one aware of its existence. It may be hoped that the interesting incident in the text may draw attention to this obscure department of devotional literature. In the year 1781 the collection was recast, and appeared in the condition in which it is still used in the Presbyterian Churches, with the title, "Translations and Paraphrases in verse of several passages of Sacred Scripture, collected and prepared by a Committee of the General Assembly of the Church of Scotland, in order to be sung in Churches." The one heard by Lord Brougham was much altered from the original as composed by his ancestor; and on a comparison of its two shapes, it may be doubted whether the alteration tended to the Assembly original design of "simplicity and plainness of composition and style." The original stands thus:

"JOHN xiv. 1–5.

"Let not your hearts with anxious thoughts
Be troubled or dismayed;
But trust the Providence divine,
And trust my gracious aid.
I to my Father's house return;
There numerous mansions stand,
And glory manifold abounds
Through all the happy land.

If no such happy land there were,
The truth I'd have declared;
And not with vain delusive hopes,
Your easy minds ensnared.
Now in your name I go before,
To take possession there;
And, in the land of promised rest,
Your mansion to prepare.

But thence I shall return again,
And take you home with me;
Then shall we meet to part no more,
And still together be.
Thus whither I am bound you know,
And I have shown the road;
For I'm the true and living way,
That leads the soul to God."

VI. (P. 33.)

Principal Robertson's interest in the drama, and his inclination to countenance it anywhere out of that theatre which he had abjured, is curiously shown in an interesting letter, hitherto unpublished, by his close friend Dr. Carlyle of Inveresk. The letter comments on a paragraph in a newspaper now, of course, forgotten. In "The Edinburgh Daily Advertiser" there appeared the following account of laying the foundation of a new parish church at Inveresk:

"The Duke of Buccleuch (patron of the parish), Major-general Sir James St. Clair Erskine, the Rev. Dr. Carlyle, Charles Stewart, Esq., etc., etc., assisted lately in laying the first stone of the new church, Inveresk, East Lothian, Scotland. Sir James S. Erskine, as Grand Master, addressed the duke in a short but pertinent speech on the occasion. He was answered by his Grace, who also addressed the magistrates of Musselburgh. The meeting concluded, as all such meetings do, with good eating and drinking in the Town Hall. Dr. Carlyle, the respectable clergyman now mentioned, must be rapidly verging to his hundredth year. Above fifty years ago the Doctor's age had exceeded forty years, when he assisted as one of the *dramatis personæ* in the first rehearsal of the 'Tragedy of Douglas' at Inveresk, where the Doctor has since resided as clergyman. The rehearsal now noticed was memorable on account of the assemblage of certain eminent literary characters who gave their cheerful aid to the establishment of the fame of their friend Home, the ingenious author, still living, we believe. Among the others who composed this meeting as actors in the play were the following four celebrated characters: David Hume the historian, William Robertson, Dr. H. Blair, and Dr. Adam Ferguson."

This paragraph was sent by Caroline, Marchioness of Queensberry, and daughter of the Duke of Buccleuch, with an inquiry as to its accuracy. Dr. Carlyle's answer—the original of which is in the possession of the Earl of Home, who has kindly permitted it to be copied—is as follows:

"The paragraph in the 'Daily Advertiser,' of September 25, may be partly true, but there are mistakes in it that tend to mislead the publick mind, in a matter of importance, and should therefore be corrected.

"The first rehearsal of the 'Tragedy of Douglas' was not at Inveresk, but at the lodging of Mrs. Sarah Ward in the Canongate, and was designed to make her fully apprehend the author's meaning. The *dramatis personæ* were—

"Lord Randolph, Dr. Robertson; Lady Randolph, Dr. Ferguson;

"Glenalvon, David Hume; Anna, Dr. Blair;

"Old Norval, Dr. Carlyle;

"Douglas, John Home.

"The rehearsal was not completed. The audience were Patk. Lord Elibank, Lord Milton, Lord Kames, Alexr. Wedderburn, Esq.; Jas. Ferguson, Esq., junr. of Pitfour, and such-like; with Mr. Digges and Mrs. Ward.

"The company, all but Mrs. Ward, dined afterwards at the Griskin Club, which then met at a tavern in the Abbey."

"Mr. Digges" and "Mrs. Ward" were professional actors of celebrity in their day.

VII. (P. 39.)

John Clerk of Eldin, the elder, died at an advanced age in 1812. He was for some years a Baron of the Exchequer in Scotland. He had an early passion for the life of a sailor, but circumstances did not permit his indulging it, except in the study. His celebrated work on "Naval Tactics," concerning the theory of the breaking of the enemy's line, was first printed for distribution among his private friends. It was published in 1790, and a second edition appeared in 1804. There is a memoir of Clerk and a commentary on his system by Professor Playfair in the eighth volume of the "Transactions of the Royal Society of Edinburgh." His son John, who was for some time a judge of the Court of Session, had a reputation in his day of a different kind. He was a wit and punster, but he carried these accomplishments into the range of wild and sometimes indecorous buffoonery. There was something peculiarly national in his sallies, and they were always watched for and reported with avidity. Perhaps no man in his day in Scotland was more popular, except Scott. When he became a judge of the Court of Session in 1823, he took from the paternal estate the title of Lord Eldin, saying that the difference between him and the Chancellor was "all in my i." He died in 1832. Many characteristic notices of him will be found in "Peter's Letters," Lockhart's "Life of Scott," and Cockburn's "Life of Jeffrey."

VIII. (P. 57.)

In the long debate in the Commons in March, 1809, on the motion for taking into consideration the minutes of evidence in the inquiry as to the conduct of the Duke of York as commander-in-chief, Lord Folkestone addressed the House on the 10th, following Mr. Leach. This speech was remarkable as containing an indignant remonstrance against efforts to shield the duke, by crushing some of the humble witnesses who gave testimony against him. Canning, who is spoken of as praising the speech, was severely handled in it. It will be found in Hansard, xiii., 299.

IX. (Pp. 70, 71.)

In the roll of members of the Speculative Society there is entered:

"316. Henry Brougham. Admitted, November 21, 1797; extraordinary, December 2, 1800; honorary, April 19, 1803.

Essays: Political Remarks on the Union; The Balance of Power; Indirect Influence of the People; Influence of National Opinion on External Relations; An examination of certain Plans that are at present entertained of cultivating the Crown Lands in the Ceded Islands."

The third essay has been preserved. It is written in a bold, peculiar hand, in which one would at once recognize the germ of the peculiarities which distinguished it in later life, though it is naturally far more legible.

The subject afforded scope for the rhetorical powers the author had been cultivating, and the following conclusion will perhaps be sufficient to show that he had done so with success:

"Before concluding these few desultory observations, it may not be improper to take notice of a consequence which will perhaps occur to some as deducible from them. It may be said that if the measures directly taken by a government—the laws, for instance, which are passed—only derive force from submitting to the assimilating power of the constitution, it becomes a matter of little consequence strenuously to exert those rights of opposition which a popular form secures. Thus, it is acknowledged that laws, if too severe, are not put into execution—if too mild, their bounds are apt to be exceeded; and if they arm any one branch with power hostile to the spirit of the constitution, there is no fear of that power being exerted. But it should be remembered that the laws have an indirect influence themselves—that though arising from circumstances, they react in their turn—and that they may gradually lead to a state of things in which the controlling power of the whole body may be much impaired. It is no doubt true that while we retain that general diffusion of knowledge for which this age and these countries are so eminently distinguished, and, above all, while those impressions of freedom remain which have produced such mighty effects in the situation of modern Europe, we have no reason to dread the establishment of those despotic governments which debase our species in other climes. But it is no less true that there are degrees of freedom, and that a people may be cajoled out of its most valuable rights by sinking into a careless security whence it may not be roused till too late for its peace. In the mean time, so long as there remains that watchful jealousy of the prerogative which seems to be naturalized in Great Britain, and whose vast importance to her liberties may be estimated by the unremitting pains that have been taken to lull it asleep, we may rest assured that no Court intrigues, no ministerial influence, no majorities in parliamentary forces, not even standing armies themselves, shall prevail against our happy constitution. That constitution consists, not in *statutes*, for these may be repealed—nor in *charters*, for these may be revoked—nor in *forms*, for even these fences may be broken through—but it is installed in the hearts of those whose fathers shed their best blood for it. And along with that inheritance, they received the swords which had been drawn in its defense. And these swords were accompanied with the solemn injunction of the great American patriarch—an injunction which they still keep in mind, however they may on some occasions have neglected it—'Not to unsheathe them for the purpose of shedding blood, except it be for self-defense, or in defense of their country and its rights, and in the latter case to keep them unsheathed, and prefer falling with them in their hands to the relinquishment thereof.'"

X. (P. 73.)

A sketch of Lord Brougham by an eye-witness, at this period of his life, is found in a quarter where it would scarcely be looked for: "A visit to Germany and the Low Countries, by Sir Arthur Brook Faulkener." He says: "Brougham was then distinguished for the same gift of sarcasm which has since made him the terror of the Senate; yet was he one of the best-humored fellows breathing—full of fun and frolic." And coming to particulars, Sir Arthur tells the following story:

"A party of us had supped in the rooms of a Dr. Parry, the brother of the circumnavigator. After supper, as we were crossing the South Bridge, we chanced to be witness of a very disgraceful scene—a mob of idle scoundrels (most of them bakers) beating an unfortunate woman with a brutal ferocity. It was impossible to stand by and not make some attempt towards her deliverance. The tumult, in place of abating by our interference, grew frightful. All the watchmen within hail were about our ears in an instant, and, in return for our chivalry, lodged us all fast in the watch-house. The Chancellor possibly never found himself in a position less congenial to his taste and habits; but even here a mind so avaricious of knowledge was not to be unemployed. Among our associates in this vile prison, which was filled with the refuse of both sexes, an old soldier sat cowering over the embers of a fire that 'taught light to counterfeit a gloom.' He had campaigned it in the American war; and with this hero our embryo candidate for the Woolsack picked up an acquaintance, and continued during the whole space of our durance extracting all he could on the favorite theme of his martial exploits —the names of the several officers under whom he served, the amount of the forces opposed to each other in particular engagements, the scene of battles, position of the combatants, skill of the manœuvres, advantages, reverses; in short, every thing that was likely or not likely to come within the veteran's ken was asked and responded to. So passed our night, until it pleased Aurora to leave her saffron couch; when, by Brougham's interference, we were set at large by a sort of general jail delivery."—I. 246, 247.

XI. (P. 73.)

There is an amusing confirmation of this incident in the local literature of the day. The author of the condemned play made a frantic appeal to the world against the condemnation, with no better effect than to confirm the justice of the sentence and widen its publicity. In the collection of some of the curious in literature there may be found a small volume, with the title, "St. Kilda in Edinburgh, or News from Camperdown; a Comic Drama in Two Acts, with a Critical Preface. Edinburgh, 1798." The piece deserves all that is said against it in the text, and more. According to its clumsy plot, a lovely damsel from St. Kilda finds herself unprotected in Edinburgh, because her brother and lover are in Admiral Duncan's fleet. An old profligate begins his plots against her by starting a report that the Dutch have been victorious and are on their way to Edinburgh. Suddenly the brother and lover appear on the scene. They bring officially the news of the victory at Camperdown; they have both been promoted from before the mast to be commissioned officers; and they act the *deux ex machinâ* in putting every thing right.

Robert Heron, the author of the play, had a literary career of his own. The eclipse of his dramatic ambition might perhaps have been mentioned with more sympathy in the text had his sad history been known to the author. It was too obscurely wretched to come naturally in the way of a man with a great career; but it served to help Isaac Disraeli to a picture for his "Calamities of Authors." Heron had a ready pen, such as it was, and was prepared to undertake any task. It was his misfortune that when he found himself master, or likely to be in the course of time master, of a hundred pounds, he set up his carriage and troop of footmen, as one whose fortunes were in the ascendant. Among his multifarious literary achievements, one was a history of Scotland in six volumes. It is suggestive of the amount of research that might suffice for history-writing at that period, that a great part of this work was composed from such materials as the author could command in a debtor's prison.

XII. (P. 74.)

In the journey described in the narrative (p. 74 *et seq.*), the author had for his companion Charles Stuart, eldest son of Sir Charles Stuart, who was the fourth son of John, third Earl of Bute. Lord Brougham's travelling companion, not only on this excursion, but afterwards in the tour he took in Sweden and Norway, was perhaps the most intimate friend he ever had; a friendship in no way impaired by the wide difference of their political views.

XIII. (P. 85.)

This letter, apart from its other attractions, is a substantial addition to our scanty literature relating to St. Kilda. A century earlier—in 1698—we have "A Voyage to St. Kilda, the remotest of all the Hybrides or Western Isles of Scotland," by M. Martin, Gent. If we are to believe both accounts, the inhabitants had grievously degenerated in civilization since Mr. Martin's visit, as the summary of contents will suffice to show, announcing an account of "their genius for poetry, music, and dancing; their surprising dexterity in climbing the rocks and walls of houses; diversions, habit, good language, diseases and methods of cure, their extensive charity, their contempt of gold and silver as below the dignity of human nature, their religious ceremonies, notions of spirits and visions, etc., etc." For notices of more recent visits to St. Kilda, see "The Highlands and Western Isles of Scotland," by John Macculloch, 1824, vol. ii., p. 168; and "A Voyage Round the Coast of Scotland and the Isles," by James Wilson, 1847, vol. ii.

XIV. (P. 99.)

The accuracy of this sketch of social and political life will not be obvious to those whose knowledge of the country is limited to the Denmark of the present day. That the leaders of Danish society pay an extreme homage to Court decorations and etiquette is generally believed; but we are not accustomed in the present generation to think of their king as absolute and irresponsible; but so he was towards the conclusion of the eighteenth century. The term used by the author to estimate his capacity for personal government is strong, but it only concurs with the evidence we otherwise have of the intellectual condition of King Christian VII. The whole will be found in harmony with several letters from Denmark printed in "Memoirs and Correspondence of Sir Robert Murray Keith, K.B., Envoy Extraordinary and Minister plenipotentiary at the Courts of Dresden, Copenhagen, and Vienna, from 1769 to 1792," 2 vols. 8vo, 1849. Sir Robert was British ambassador to Denmark during the affair of Count Struensee; and his correspondence gives much light on this and on other matters referred to in the text as events of recent occurrence

XV. (P. 163.)

He "passed advocate" on 1st June, 1800. To "be called to the bar" is not the technical expression in Scotland. The reception into the profession was, and still is, of the old academic character. After certain private examinations by committees of the Faculty of Advocates, there is a public "disputatio," where the candidate for honors, as in the old universities, publicly defends certain theses or propositions before all comers. The theses opened to impugnment must be from the Pandects. His public impugnment and acceptance are thus entered in the Faculty Minutes: "1st June, 1800. Mr. Henry Peter Brougham, eldest son of Henry Brougham, Esq., of Brougham Hall, was publicly examined in Title 5, Lib. III., Digest. De Negotiis Gestis, and found sufficiently qualified."

XVI. (P. 170.)

Charles Hope, Lord Advocate in 1801, and Lord President of the Court of Session in 1804; died 1851. The speech on the powers and duties of the Lord Advocate will be found in Hansard's Debates for 22d June, 1804. It has been severely commented on as announcing dangerous and unconstitutional doctrine. The Lord Advocate of the day had written a vehement letter to the sheriff of a northern county, denouncing the conduct of an employer who had dismissed a man for deserting his service to become a volunteer.

It was a period of panic about invasion by the Boulogne armament, and the gravity of the Lord Advocate's letter lay in the steps which he directed the sheriff to take against the employer "on the landing of the first Frenchman." Hope, in his defense of his successor, cited the instances in which executive officers in extreme emergencies had taken extreme measures on their own responsibility.

XVII. (P. 176.)

Somewhere about the year 1856, Sydney Smith's daughter Saba, the wife of Sir Henry Holland, compiled a memoir of her father. This was not published, but she most kindly sent me a copy. I have already referred to Smith's not very accurate account of the origin of the "Edinburgh Review." I have no further desire to criticise or to find fault with Lady Holland's book; but I lately laid my hands on a letter I received from Sir David Brewster, which relates to a matter connected with Sir Isaac Newton, a name at all times quite as interesting to me as to Sir David.

Lady Holland, in the pedigree she gives of her father, makes the following statement: "My father's grandfather married a Miss Barton, whose mother was half-sister to Sir Isaac Newton (the only ancestor the Smiths ever had, but one not lightly to be passed over)," p. 8. From the pedigree thus set out, it appears that Sir Isaac Newton's mother married, as her second husband, Mr. Barnaby Smith, and their daughter married Dr. Barton, whose daughter Catherine married Mr. Ollier, Sydney Smith's maternal grandfather. Now, according to Sir David Brewster, this marriage with Mr. Ollier is a mistake; for the Catherine Barton in question married a Mr. Conduitt. Here is what Sir David Brewster says on this subject:

"Bridge of Allan, June 13, 1856.

"DEAR LORD BROUGHAM,—Nothing ever surprised me more than the *dream* of Sydney Smith, that he was descended from Catherine Barton, Newton's niece.

"Having accidentally got a sight of the first edition of his Life, I sent to Sir H. Holland two pedigrees of Newton's family, one fuller than the other; and in consequence of this the pedigree was suppressed in the next edition; but Lady Holland was still skeptical, and I put her in communication with

Mr. Cutts Barton, the descendant of a half-brother of Mrs. Conduitt; but though he gave her a choice of making out her connection with *several* Catherine Bartons, yet no connection whatever has been traced between the two families.

"Mrs. Catherine Barton's history from 1700 till the time of her death is so well known that Lady Holland will find it impossible to establish any connection with her, or indeed with any other member of Mr. Smith's family.

"I have not felt it a duty to subscribe to Newton's monument at Grantham on the ground that it should be a national tribute to his memory. I am, dear Lord Brougham, ever most truly yours, D. BREWSTER."

Miss Barton was a witty and very handsome woman, greatly admired by Lord Halifax, who left her at his death in 1715 a large legacy, and also an annuity of £200—leaving to her uncle, Sir Isaac Newton, £100, "as a mark of the great honor and esteem he had for so great a man." On the 24th of August, 1717, Miss Barton married Mr. Conduitt of Cranbury, in Hampshire, member of Parliament, and much valued by Newton. Their only child, Catherine, born in 1718, married, in 1740, Mr. Wallop, afterwards Lord Lymington. From one of her daughters the Portsmouth family are descended. There can, therefore, be no question that if Mr. Ollier did (as nobody denies) marry a Miss Barton, it was not Catherine, the niece of Sir Isaac Newton.

I am equally persuaded that Sydney Smith himself would never willfully have claimed this connection with Newton; he was far above any such pretensions, unless upon sure grounds. From all I ever knew of him he would not only have objected to, but would have laughed at, his nephew's foolish weakness in dropping the most respectable, and in their case distinguished, name of Smith, and assuming that of Vernon, merely because his father Bobus married a Miss Vernon of Hilton, but who no more represented the Vernons of Hilton than she represented the Plantagenets.

XVIII. (P. 183.)

Dr. John Thomson, born at Paisley, 1765; died at Edinburgh, 1846. He was called by his contemporaries "the most learned of physicians;" and the discursive character of his scientific acquirements rendered him valuable to the body of young men in Edinburgh, who, at the beginning of the century, were ambitious of adding physical science to their acquirements in law, politics, and general scholarship. In January, 1800, writing about the condition and prospects of "The Natural History Society," he says: "Various plans of relief were proposed, and I at last suggested the turning the Society into a chemical society, that should provide itself with an apparatus and occasionally make experiments. The proposal has since been talked of among the members, and is, I believe, universally approved of. In mentioning it to Horner, he proposed an alliance with the Academy of Physics. Brougham, in the mean time, came home, and has entered keenly into our views. * * * Perhaps I am too sanguine; but I conceive that if I can give to the infant society a good organization, it may become an institution which you will have pleasure in patronizing. We shall be able to draw into it all the young men of the place who have any turn for physical researches. It is proposed to meet in summer. Brougham is to write you in a day or two. He looks well, and his present appearance would give you much satisfaction. Horner and he are both particularly anxious that you should approve of the plan of a chemical society."—Letter addressed to John Allen, in biographical notice of Dr. Thomson prefixed to his "Life of Cullen," p. 16. Failing health compelled Dr. Thomson to retire from active life in 1835. It used to be his pride to tell how in that same year he was sought in the privacy of his cottage at Moreland by his friend of thirty years before, now Lord Chancellor, and visiting Edinburgh on the occasion of the Grey festival; and how they talked over their old chemical recreations as if they were still young students with the world before them.

The contemporaries of John Allen who knew him in his social eminence are fast diminishing, and his fame was not of a kind to be revived in a new generation. He was born in 1770, near Edinburgh. There the small mansion of Redford, his birthplace, the possession of his family, still exists: it happens to be close beside Colinton, where his friend James Abercrombie, Lord Dunfermline, spent his latter years. He studied medicine, and lectured on physiology and the other branches of science connected with the medical profession; but he did not settle down in practice. The theatre of his great reputation was Holland House, where he was the admitted chief among the wits and scholars who frequented the hospitable table there. Besides science, he wrote on constitutional history and Spanish politics. His small work called an "Inquiry into the Growth of the Royal Prerogative" (1830), is so important and conclusive as to have often elicited the remark that there is nowhere else so much light on the British Constitution within so small a space. Another brief work, a "Vindication of the Ancient Independence of Scotland" (1833), is a singularly clear explanation of the historical conditions in which the Plantagenet kings vested their claim for asserting a superiority over the crown of Scotland. His articles in the "Edinburgh Review" are said to have exceeded thirty in number. He died in 1843. Soon after his death there was a design among his personal friends to collect and publish his scattered works, but it unfortunately came to nothing.

Malcolm Laing, born in Orkney, 1762; died in 1818. He was for some time member of Parliament for Orkney. He was intimate with Fox, and a valued and influential member of the Whig party of the day. He wrote a "History of Scotland," beginning with the union of the crowns in 1603, and ending with the incorporating Union of 1707.

John Stoddard, born 1773; died 1856; knighted in 1826. From the Church, for which he had his earliest training, he turned to law, giving much of his time to civil or Roman law. He became thus available for service in the dependencies where that system prevailed. Early in the century he became King's Advocate at Malta, and in 1826 returned thither as Judge of the Vice-Admiralty Court. During the interval of nearly twenty years between these services he became a distinguished journalist, writing for several years the leading political articles in the "Times."

END OF THE FIRST VOLUME.

www.ingramcontent.com/pod-product-compliance
Lightning Source LLC
LaVergne TN
LVHW010137110826
845151LV00002B/370